Theatre

Editors
Martin Banham
James Gibbs
& Femi Osofisan

Reviews Editor
Jane Plastow
School of English, University of Leeds

Associate Editors

Eckhard Breitinger
Forststr. 3, 95488 Eckersdorf, Germany

John Conteh-Morgan
Dept of French & Italian, Ohio State University, 248 Cunz Hall, 1841 Millikin Rd, Columbus, Ohio 43210-1229, USA

Frances Harding
SOAS, Thornhaugh St, Russell Square, London WC1H OX9, UK

Masitha Hoeane
Moshoeshoe II High School, Box 35, Morija, Lesotho

David Kerr
Media Studies Dept, University of Botswana, PB 00703, Gaborone, Botswana

Amandina Lihamba
Dept of Fine & Performing Arts, PO Box 35051, University of Dar es Salaam, Tanzania

Olu Obafemi
Dept of English, PMB 1515, University of Ilorin, Ilorin, Nigeria

Ian Steadman
The Open University, Walton Hall, Milton Keynes, MK7 6AA

Titles already published in the series:
African Theatre in Development
African Theatre: Playwrights & Politics
African Theatre: Women
African Theatre: Southern Africa
African Theatre: Soyinka. Blackout, Blowout & Beyond
African Theatre: Youth

Future Volumes
African Theatre: Companies
African Theatre: The Diaspora

Format: Articles not exceeding 5,000 words should be submitted as Word files and always accompanied by a double-spaced hard copy. Please label all files and disks clearly. Typewritten submissions may be considered in exceptional circumstances if they follow the standard double-spaced format.

Style: Preferably use UK rather than US spellings. Underline or italicise titles of books or plays. Use single inverted commas except for quotes within quotes. Type notes at the end of the text on a separate sheet. Do not justify the right hand-margins.

References should follow the style of this volume (Surname date: page number) in text. All references should then be listed at the end of article in full:
Surname, name, date, *title of work* (place of publication: name of publisher)
Surname, name, date, 'title of article' in surname, initial (eds) *title of work* (place of publication: publisher).
or Surname, name, date, 'title of article', *Journal*, vol., no: page number.

Reviewers should provide full bibliographic details, including the extent, ISBN and price.

Copyright: Please ensure, where appropriate, that clearance has been obtained from copyright holders of material used. Illustrations may also be submitted if appropriate and if accompanied by full captions and with reproduction rights clearly indicated. It is the responsibility of the contributors to clear all permissions.

All submissions should be accompanied by a brief biographical profile. The editors cannot undertake to return material submitted and contributors are advised to keep a copy of all material sent in case of loss in transit.

Editorial address
8 Victoria Square, Bristol BS8 4ET, UK • james.gibbs@uwe.ac.uk

Books for Review & Review articles
Jane Plastow, Reviews Editor, *African Theatre*, School of English, University of Leeds, Leeds LS2 9JT, UK • j.e.plastow@leeds.ac.uk

African Theatre
Youth

Guest Editor
Michael Etherton

Reviews Editor
Jane Plastow

James Currey
OXFORD

African Academic Press
a Tsehai Publishers imprint
HOLLYWOOD, CA

First published in 2006 in the United Kingdom by
James Currey Ltd
73 Botley Road
Oxford OX2 0BS
www.jamescurrey.co.uk

and in North America by
African Academic Press
a Tsehai Publishers imprint
PO Box 1881
Hollywood, CA 90078
www.tsehaipublishers.com

© James Currey Ltd 2006

First published 2006
1 2 3 4 5 10 09 08 07 06
All rights reserved

No part of this book may be reproduced or utilized in any form or by any means, electronic or mechanical, including photocopying and recording, or by any information storage and retrieval system, without permission in writing from the publisher. The Association of American University Presses' Resolution on Permissions constitutes the only exception to this prohibition.

British Library Cataloguing in Publication Data
African theatre: youth
   1. Children's theatre - Africa
   I. Etherton, Michael, 1939- II. Banham, Martin
   792'.083'096

ISBN 10: 0-85255-590-3 (James Currey paper)
ISBN 13: 978-085255-590-3 (James Currey paper)

ISBN 10: 59907-011-1 (Tsehai Publishers paper)
ISBN 13: 978-1-59907-011-7 (Tsehai Publishers paper)

Typeset in 10/11 pt Monotype Bembo by Long House, Cumbria, UK
Printed and bound in Britain by Woolnough, Irthlingborough

Contents

Notes on Contributors vii
Introduction by Michael Etherton, Guest Editor x

Creating For & With Children in Ghana
Efua Sutherland: a retrospective
ESI SUTHERLAND-ADDY 1

Competitive Youth Theatre Festivals in Ghana
Stage Motion & Studrafest
AWO MANA ASIEDU with SARAH DORBGADZI 16

Three Malawian Student Performances
Playing pains
PIA THIELMANN 23

African Youth, Performance & the HIV/AIDS Epidemic
Theatre of Necessity
ESIABA IROBI 31

Young People's Drama & Social Action in Northern Nigeria
A case study of the Zaria 'For Tomorrow...' Project
OGAH STEVE ABAH with Faith, Mahmud & Nuhu 42

Promenade Theatre in a Sudanese Reformatory
Divining for stories: *The Cockerel & the King's Ear*
ALI CAMPBELL with JANE PLASTOW 61
& a team of Sudanese practitioners

Youth Theatre in the Displaced People's Camps of Khartoum
Kwoto
LUKE DIXON 78

Theatre with Street Children in Senegal
ROSA STOURAC McCREERY 86

West African Child Rights Theatre for Development
Stories as theatre, theatre as a strategy for change
MICHAEL ETHERTON 97

The Impact of Child Rights Theatre in Sierra Leone
Umo is talking
PAUL MOCLAIR with MIKE CHARLEY & children
in Daru 122

Sewit Children's Theatre in Eritrea
CHRISTINE MATZKE & JANE PLASTOW 138

Project Phakama: Stories of South Africa, London & Lesotho
Landscapes of the heart
YVONNE BANNING, CAROLINE CALBURN
& LUCY RICHARDSON 151

Approaching Theatre Work with Children in Zimbabwe
'Share what you have'
ROBERT MSHENGU KAVANAGH 166

On the Making of Journeys: Young People's Theatre in Zambia
Tansitha, Safe-T-Child & others
DAVE PAMMENTER 189

Hopeful Youth Drama in Kibera, Kenya
PHAN Y LY 202

Playscript
The Ghosts Return
Devised by students at the University of Botswana
Transcribed & with an introduction by David Kerr 218

Book Reviews
Sandra Richards on
    Richard Boon & Jane Plastow (eds)
    Theatre & Empowerment: Community Drama on the World Stage 252
Jane Plastow on
    Louise M. Bourgault
    Playing for Life: Performance in Africa in the Age of AIDS 256
Martin Banham on
    Effiok Bassey Uwatt (ed.)
    Playwriting and Directing in Nigeria: Interviews with Ola Rotimi
    Ola Rotimi (ed.), *Issues in African Theatre* 258
Christine Matzke on
    John Conteh-Morgan & Tejumola Olaniyan (eds)
    African Drama and Performance 259
Dennis Walder on
    Martin Banham (ed.), *A History of Theatre in Africa* 262
Michael Carklin on
    Dennis Walder, *Athol Fugard* 265

Index 269

Notes on Contributors

Oga Steve Abah is a Professor of Theatre for Development at Ahmadu Bello University, Zaria, Nigeria where he has taught since 1979. He is one of the leading theorists in Theatre for Development, an area in which he has researched since 1980. His current research has focused on what he calls the 'methodological conversation' between TFD, participatory learning and action (PLA), and traditional social science research.

Awo Mana Asiedu is a lecturer at The School of Performing Arts, University of Ghana, Legon. Her research interests include the reception of theatre, African dramatic literature and theatre practice in Southern and Eastern Africa.

Yvonne Banning is a senior lecturer in the Drama Department at the University of Cape Town. She is also an active trustee and facilitator in a number of professional and community-based theatre organizations.

Ali Campbell's field is the use of performance as a language of advocacy and activism. His career spans 25 years from membership of Professor Dogg's Troupe in the early eighties to 10 years as co-founder of BREAKOUT TIE, during which time he toured with participatory work devised by and for young people and met Augusto Boal, later making Boal's techniques accessible to children, disabled people and other marginal groups. He used these methodologies in AIDS educational work in Uganda in 1990 and continues to work in development theatre in Africa, India and Brazil.

Luke Dixon is a theatre director and teacher. He has lived and worked in South Africa and collaborated with other theatre makers in Sudan, Senegal and Malawi. Luke is Artistic Director of theatre nomad: www.theatrenomad.com

Sarah Dorgbadzi is a lecturer in Acting in the Theatre Arts Department of the School of Performing Arts, Legon and holds an MFA degree in Theatre Arts from the University of Ghana, Legon. For several years she worked with pupils of the Ghana International School in Accra, producing their annual school plays.

Notes on Contributors

Michael Etherton has worked for international NGOs in both Asia and Africa in Development since 1988. Before that he worked in universities and colleges in Africa and the UK. He is the author of *The Development of African Drama* (Hutchinson, 1982), *Contemporary Irish Drama* (Macmillan, 1988), and is currently co-editing *Research in Drama Education. Special issue on Impact Assessment*, Volume 11, No. 2 (Carfax Publishing: Taylor and Francis Group, forthcoming 2006).

David Kerr has been involved in theatre and media projects, particularly on social and human rights issues for over 30 years in Botswana, Malawi and Zambia. He is currently Head of Media Studies at the University of Botswana and is working on a manual on using theatre for communication about HIV/AIDS.

Esiaba Irobi is currently an Associate Professor of International Theatre at Ohio University, Athens, Ohio. He is the author of *Why I Don't Like Philip Larkin and Other Poems* (Nsibidi Africana Publishers, 2005) and *African Festival and Ritual Theatre: Resisting Globalization on the Continent and Diaspora since 1492* (Palgrave Macmillan, forthcoming 2007).

Phan Y Ly was a development worker in the UN and with international NGOs in Vietnam before becoming the first Vietnamese scholar to pursue graduate studies in Theatre and Media for Development in the UK. Ly is now consulting for Plan International Vietnam on the use of theatre to promote child participation. Ly is the founder and artistic director of SameStuff Theater, an independent contemporary theatre group in Vietnam. Her on-going projects include a Thai-Vietnamese theatre and multimedia collaboration performance tour in SouthEast Asia on 'Cyber sex', and a two-women show with a young American actor exploring how the post-war generation experience the history of the two countries.

Robert Mshengu Kavanagh is currently Executive Director of the arts education trust, CHIPAWO, Harare, Zimbabwe. He previously founded and chaired Theatre Arts Departments at Addis Ababa University, Ethiopia and the University of Zimbabwe. Publications include *South African People's Plays*; *Theatre and Cultural Struggle in South Africa*, and *Making People's Theatre*.

Rosa Stourac McCreery has studied and worked in many countries in Europe and Africa and is now based in the North East of England. She is a performer, theatre facilitator and one of the directors of Jambo Africa, an organization facilitating and promoting African arts and culture.

Christine Matzke currently teaches African literature and theatre at the Institute of Asian and African Studies, Humboldt University, Berlin. Her research interests and publications centre around theatre and cultural production in Eritrea and, more recently, postcolonial crime fiction. She is co-editor of the African studies series *Matatu* published by Rodopi.

Paul Moclair is currently responsible for the redesign of UNICEF Sudan's Theatre for Life project, establishing 450 grassroots, child rights advocacy theatre groups across the country. He has previously devised and implemented Theatre for Development projects with street children in Sierra Leone, and as part of Save the Children UK's HIV/AIDS programming in Kenya.

Dave Pammenter is the Programme Director for the BA in Community Drama and Media, and course tutor on the MA in Theatre and Media Development at the University of Winchester. He has facilitated workshops using participatory theatre processes for social transformation in many parts of the world. His most recent work has been in Greece in support of the Theatre in Education net, and in Kenya where he is working on setting up an East African Theatre for Development network.

Jane Plastow is Senior Lecturer in Theatre Studies at The Workshop Theatre, University of Leeds, and Director of the Leeds University Centre for African Studies. She has written extensively on African theatre and Theatre for Development, and works practically in both the UK and the Horn of Africa. She is currently developing a major primary schools-based project using theatre to empower children and communities in Eritrea.

Esi Sutherland-Addy is currently Senior Research Fellow, Institute of African Studies, University of Ghana, and head of the Language, Literature and Drama Section. Sutherland-Addy is co-editor of *Women Writing Africa: West Africa and the Sahel* (The Feminist Press, CUNY, 2006)

Pia Thielmann is a scholar of African, African American and Caribbean literatures, and was a senior lecturer in the Department of English at Chancellor College, University of Malawi.

The editors of *African Theatre* are sad to report the death of our friend and Associate Editor Hansel Ndumbe Eyoh on 7 September 2006. Hansel's Leeds doctorate (1979) was probably the first substantial analysis of Cameroonian theatre, and his 1986 publication, *Hammocks to Bridges*, a report on a workshop for integrated rural development, is an early and authoritative contribution to the theory and practice of Theatre for Development. This was followed by *Beyond the Theatre* in 1991. His plays, always with Cameroonian themes, were lively and socially and politically relevant, and he devoted much energy and skill to working with children and young people in theatre. Hansel made a major contribution to the cultural life of Cameroon, both as a university teacher and a public servant, and did much to promote the theatre of Africa on a world stage. With the Ancestors.

Introduction

MICHAEL ETHERTON

This volume of African Theatre tries to reflect the extraordinary range of drama, theatre and performance there is today in Africa, which is now engaging young Africans. Some of this creativity is by young people who are addressing adults with their performances. They are using theatre and performance to advocate for change in the adult world, a world that some of them have already joined, young though they are. Their kind of theatre in performance addresses their multiple disadvantages of poverty, exclusion, exploitation. It also addresses their youth.

Other performance work is by both young people and adults, working together, who combine their imaginations and performance skills to perform to, and engage with, other young people. This reflects a desire to build new constituencies among the youth, using theatre and performance.

A third strand is that of children's theatre, what in the West is referred to as Theatre in Education [TIE] and Drama in Education. Some of this is produced by adults, written for younger children to perform; or it is a process of devising by adults with younger children. Complementary to this, and perhaps indebted to it, is the amount of theatrical performance by students in the high schools, colleges and universities that presents the plays, old and new, in the African Theatre canon.

An example of this student theatre is in the article by Awo Asiedu on Studrafest, the Ghana Student Drama Festival. There are other competitive festivals in other African countries. Although some are still part of colonial and post-colonial theatre traditions and education systems, others offer new productions to a wide range of audiences in their countries. These student productions often break new ground in terms of staging and performance techniques, particular in the drama and theatre departments of the universities. Some of this work then extends into African drama on film and television.

Young Africans, therefore, see themselves advancing the mainstream of African theatre and performance traditions in their country – for example Zambian Theatre or Nigerian Theatre – but they also see themselves going beyond the mainstream. They are also beginning to challenge what constitutes 'African Theatre' in terms of purpose, devising, content and aesthetics. This collection of articles shows both the support for the mainstream and some attempts to forge a conscious alternative drama process.

The various accounts of youth theatre, drama processes and performances not only indicate this youthful creativity. They also, in content, indicate a number of specific concerns of young people in Africa today.

First, they indicate how young Eritreans, Batswana, Malians, Sudanese, endeavour to contribute through their performances to the political processes in their countries. Often, these political processes are going into, or coming out of civil wars; and conflict remains unresolved. Luke Dixon describes how South Sudanese youth use the travelling performances of the *'Kwoto'* dance to show solidarity with South Sudanese communities living in Khartoum. These performances celebrate and often extend South Sudan's dance traditions. Christine Matzke and Jane Plastow give a detailed analysis of the history of children's theatre in Eritrea showing how it became part of Eritrea's struggle for independence. Their article describes the role of young adults who involved children in this process.

Paul Moclair, writing on young people's child rights-based Theatre for Development [TfD] in Sierra Leone, meets some adolescents who were child soldiers in the civil war and finds out how they feel now about the TfD workshop they did in connection with their rights two years before. How did it help them solve their problems, or not, during the difficult process of demobilization, and rehabilitation? Moclair's article is as much about TfD as it is about civil war and subsequent political processes. His action research gives us some insights into the personal and independent views of these young people.

Pia Thielmann, describing the overtly political Malawian student theatre; similarly indicates how young people achieve powerful drama with very limited resources. Her article celebrates the resourcefulness of these students' theatre, which is very much a political act in itself. This reflects some of David Kerr's work; and it is his work with Batswana students in Botswana that has resulted in *The Ghosts Return*, which is the play-script included in this volume. Devised by the students, it gives an even more direct insight into their new drama as an extension of political engagement. The play explores post-colonial and neo-colonial pressures on young professionals working in the media.

If adult politics is a primary concern of young Africans, so too is their concern with the spread of HIV/AIDS. Esiaba Irobi explores the increasingly crucial relationship between the scourge of AIDS, young Africans and performance. His analysis introduces the concept of the Theatre of Necessity, and demonstrates the convergence of independent responses by young people across the continent to changing attitudes and solving problems. The detail of this activism is articulated in Dave Pammenter's powerful account of how young Zambian sex-workers use the methodologies of Freire, Boal, and a later Rights-based Theatre for Development, to realise their worth, gain confidence and communicate to audiences exactly what they think and feel about their exploited lives. Pammenter depicts the communicative power of this kind of theatre devising. He suggests that the aesthetic of the performance of these young people is inextricably tied up in its political significance.

AIDS, together with young people's sexuality, is also the over-riding issue in Abah's article about the TfD sexual health project with young people in Zaria and Jos, Nigeria. In this article there is the testimony of three of the young performers. AIDS and sex are the themes of a great deal of youth drama and performance the length and breadth of Africa. Ali Cambell used Promenade Theatre to engage young audiences in the workshop he and Jane Plastow conducted with young people and AIDS outreach workers in a reformatory in the Sudan. My own piece on Save the Children's work in West Africa shows how young people used TfD to advocate for their rights and full participation in civil society as a way of tackling the ever-present scourge of AIDS in their lives.

In all these accounts there is an absolute rejection of the prescriptive message-laden theatre on HIV/AIDS by development agencies, including INGOs (International NGOs) and the UN, urging the use of condoms and/or total sexual abstinence. These ubiquitous development-as-messages performances are seen by young Africans as both bad development and bad theatre. It does not touch the reality of their lives at all and fails to engage with the actual difficulties of they face. The complexities in the lives of poor young Africans, particularly, the awful choices and tough daily decisions they are forced to take, are much more effectively communicated in the dramas and performances of their own devising, using a range of methodologies that allow for effective audience interaction with the actors during the performances.

The third concern of young people is to find ways of using theatre techniques much more holistically. How can both the drama and the performance of it express their whole being, their individuality, their particular qualities of being youthful? This approach is reflected in the work that McCreery did in Senegal with a number of groups of street children; and she analyses how she tried to develop young people holistically through the drama workshops and improvised performances. Plastow and Campbell's article on the Promenade Theatre also explores how this holistic experience for the children was achieved.

There is also a desire by young people to merge the content of their work and their commitment to it with a style of personal presentation in everyday life, and a specific style in their music, their dance and movement. Robert Mshengu Kavanagh's article on CHIPAWO in Zimbabwe, and Yvonne Banning's descriptions of the work of Phakama in South Africa, both describe a youthful drama performance phenomenon that seems more of a children's cultural movement than a one-off project. These large-scale initiatives in both countries have generated powerful theatre, and are on-going and expanding. The work involves comprehensive training in theatre skills and in methodologies of devising performances. In the process, a new African drama aesthetic is further defined. CHIPAWO has developed professional training in theatre and performance skills with all age groups, including some brilliant work, described by Kavanagh here, with very young children.

The collection in this volume in fact opens with Esi Sutherland-Addy's account of Efua Sutherland's work in the 1970s and 1960s in developing creative performances with and for young children in Ghana. I recall being inspired by *Vulture! Vulture!* and *Tahinta* when I was teaching theatre in Nigeria in the late 1970s and 1980s. Her work was, and probably still is, a model of African children's theatre, in terms of understanding childhood in rural [West] Africa, post-independence, and also in terms of knowing what is significant in African cultural traditions, particularly in the use of chants, dances and games.

Children's games are significant in the creation of young people's theatre, drama and performance, and also increasingly in adult mainstream theatre. Games are an important element in how young people first tackle collaborative drama and in creative devising techniques. They are an integral part of the process; and they also become embedded in the performances. They are a vehicle for expressing difficult issues. Games – impro and theatre games specifically – are also a significant part of Child Rights TfD. Games for Moclair are the basis of his rights-based drama work in Sierra Leone with dislocated and orphaned children. Games, it seems, enable children to claim those key rights so often brushed aside: their right to association, their right to expression of their own ideas, their right to be consulted, and their right to play.

The last article is a piece by Phan Y Ly, a Vietnamese post-graduate student who engaged with a group of creative youths in the Kenya slum Kibera on a three-month project. Through her facilitation, the group worked together on the meaning of their lives through drama; and Ly used digital video to capture their journey together. Her article is perhaps emblematic of what others have observed: an expanding global consciousness of young people in Africa.

I hope this volume of *African Theatre* will surprise and delight readers with the depth, quality and excitement of the drama, theatre and performances presently being developed by African children and young people across the continent. Despite these qualities, the work is ephemeral. It is remembered by those who were, and continue to be, involved in it and by those who witnessed it; but it is not widely known. It is important that more records are kept of the work, both as process and product, using digital technology.

The collection of articles here is by no means conclusive. Indeed, there are a number of exciting projects I am aware of that are not included here. Perhaps the work suggested by these articles will prompt calls for a wider representation of the theatre and performance of young people that would include the new youthful drama in all the other African countries not recalled here.

Compiling this collection presented me with a number of problems. The first set of problems relate to oral and spontaneous improvisation. Much of the exciting new drama work is with young people who have limited literacy but enormous linguistic skills in oral communication. The quality and the idiom of the language young people spontaneously use in good theatre devising is difficult to capture in a written form, so these exciting performances are ephemeral. They are remembered by those present, but not recorded in ways that make the experience more widely accessible to others not there. If the product is difficult to capture, the process of devising is even more so, as Ali Campbell tellingly describes.

xiv *Introduction*

The second problem is that there are great difficulties in getting young people to author accounts of their own work, particularly for an essentially literary publication like *African Theatre*. I have relied, therefore, on adults to write about the young people and their achievements. Hopefully, the young people involved in the work have had a say in the authoring, or at least 'authorizing', the account prepared for academic publication. Abah's article, with sections authored by some of the young participants themselves, is an interesting model.

The third problem in compilation is that much more of the texture of the performances is visual than literary: audience reactions, discussions with the audiences, the settings for experimental performance, unconventional devising processes. Images of these processes authenticate the 'texts' described in this volume to an extraordinary degree. My sense is that the next collection of young Africans' creativity in performance could be on DVD, rather than in a book, with video and audio material determined by the young creative artists themselves. This is already starting to happen in other parts of the world. It requires young Africans to demand access to electronic video and audio media equipment, and to demand training as well in using these new tools creatively.

This volume of *African Theatre* has the regular Book Reviews section compiled by Jane Plastow. The section is not restricted to new books about young theatre and performances, but covers most of the significant new publications on African Theatre.

Creating For and With Children in Ghana
Efua Sutherland:
A retrospective

ESI SUTHERLAND-ADDY

Introduction

The world of the child has held a fascination for Efua Sutherland. This is evidenced consistently in her research and writing, dating from the early 1960s. For the picture book *Playtime in Africa*[1] with photographs by Bill Bell, Sutherland created a flowing poetic text composed in childlike cadences to accompany the photographs of children at play in a wide variety of circumstances in Ghana during the late 1950s and early 1960s. The intensity of her preoccupation with the insights to be gleaned by playwrights from children at play peaked within the period 1967 to 1980 when she created and produced experimental drama for children. The plays which are examined in this article, *Vulture, Vulture!*, *Tahinta*, *Children of the Man-Made Lake*, *Anansi and the Dwarf Brigade* and *Tweedledum and Tweedledee*, were all produced during this period with the first three being published. More significantly, these plays formed part of an integrated body of work aimed at creating with and for children comprising poetry and stories, action research projects, academic papers, course syllabuses and short courses.

Sutherland was convinced that one could not write drama for children if one did not understand the play life of children. Her germinal paper 'The Playwright's Opportunity in Drama for our Children', delivered at an Institute of African Studies seminar on writing and production of literature for children (5–10 April 1976), definitively encapsulates Sutherland's thoughts. This essay, more than any other, sets out succinctly the paradigm she had been developing since the 1950s. She first of all sets the broad social and ideological context for her commitment. Sutherland posits in this paper that drama is a process of composition and that writing may be one of several possible emanations of a piece of drama. She was confident that she had embarked on a process of discovery of '... African society's established ideas about the art of drama, in concepts, form and practice':

..... I belong to the breed of Africans who have to engage in this finding-out exercise, and thus I hope that the *prescription* [emphasis mine] will be interpreted in

1

the same vein as the proverb ... If the alligator surfaces from underwater to inform you that the crocodile has a lumpy mouth he is not to be refuted. (Sutherland 1976: 2)

To Sutherland, then, by time she was writing this essay, she had consolidated the findings from her research, her thoughts and her convictions sufficiently to posit a paradigm for composing drama for Ghanaian children. From her observation:

> ... play is the child's natural means of exploring the human and natural environment of his existence, of learning how to exist with and within them and for resolving the problems he encounters in the process. (Ibid: 3)

She cites children's ability to simulate and imitate life with great spontaneity and absorption. She considers these to be 'ideal dramatic processes at which they [*children*] are supremely masterful'. She encourages playwrights to regard children as composers of their own drama, asserting that playwrights should compose as if they were a 'participating partner or playmate...' (ibid: 4). Her reasons for recommending detailed observation of child play become apparent later on in the paper where she makes the following point:

> If he is privileged to observe the play in its entirety, that is from how it begins, to how it develops and ends, noting every aspect of its expression, he ends up, in essence, with a play script which he himself could never have created. (Ibid: 9)

She also goes on to portray the observation of children at play as an efficacious method for developing the skills in what she calls 'the delicate art of creating plays for children'.

In a bid to develop these ideas, Sutherland established the Children's Drama Development Programme: a five-year project funded by the VALCO Trust Fund.[2] The project was used to collect information about children at play both in formal and informal terms. The roles assigned to children in the traditional festivals and rituals were also studied.[3] In addition to this a children's theatre laboratory was established at the Ghana Drama Studio[4] which offered groups of children from selected schools the opportunity to explore theatre in a variety of dimensions while at the same time learning about African culture and picking up basic techniques for the stage. Playwrights were also identified and brought within the ambit of the project to counter the trend of writing plays in wooden and ponderous language for children, and to develop their skills in the composition of imaginative and lively plays. By the end of the period some ten plays had been developed and tested.[5] These plays were produced for public consumption but were never commercially published although copies exist as part of the report on the project.

The purpose of this paper is to examine the extent to which Efua Sutherland's own plays were influenced by her convictions about the synergy between creating drama for children and children's play. Specifically two key contentions held by her will guide our study of her dramatic works for children:

- First, that children's play provides an inexhaustible and profoundly rich resource for the creating of drama for children; and

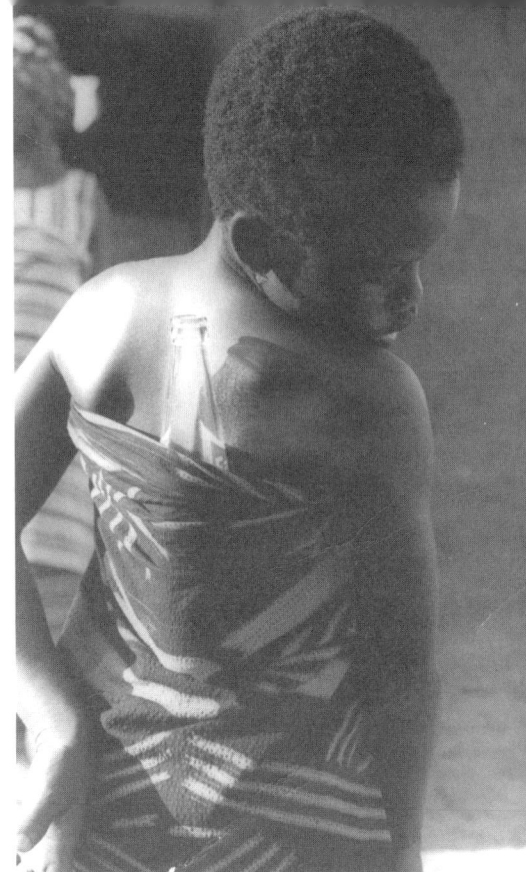

1. *Ghanaian child playing mother, from Sutherland research archive*
(© Estate of Efua. T. Sutherland)

2. *A traditional children's game from Northern Ghana, from Sutherland research archive*
(© Estate of Efua. T. Sutherland)

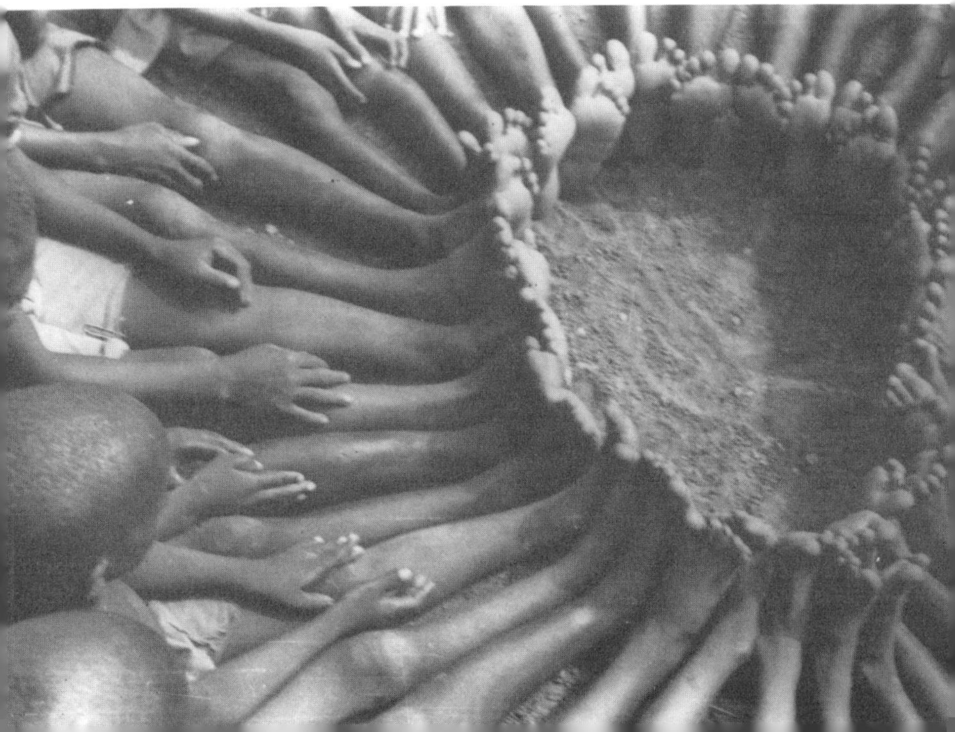

- Secondly that children should be given recognition for their masterful competence in creating drama.

To undertake this investigation we shall examine four of Sutherland's children's plays, paying close attention to structure, dialogue and language and characterization as possible indicators for assessing whether Sutherland was able to live up to the ideals she sought to prescribe to persons aspiring to write plays for African children. A synopsis of each is provided below for ease of reference:

Tahinta (1968/2000)[6]

A young boy goes fishing in the Birim, a river reputed to be full of fish and alluvial gold, and running through the fertile forests of the Eastern Region of Ghana. He leaves home very happy but almost despairs as his attempts at catching a fish nearly fail. Suddenly, he hears a splash in his fish trap: he has finally caught a lovely mud fish but just as he gets ready to leave the riverside, a ghost comes walking across the river and snatches his fish. Even his strong father who comes to help him cannot retrieve his precious catch. The boy threatens to tell his mother, but as his father explains 'A ghost is a ghost.' (Sutherland, 2000: 17)

Vulture! Vulture! (1968)

Vulture perches sadly in the sun. He is feeling lazy and hungry. His wife sends twice for him to come and eat appetizing dishes. He refuses both times, offering the meals to the children. However when he is finally told that there is a dead rat 20 days old waiting for him, he perks up and happily sets off to eat his favorite meal, making it clear that he is not about to share this with his children.

Children of the Man-Made Lake (2000)

The people of the ancient Apaaso Village situated on the bank of the river Afram in the Eastern Region of Ghana are told that the government is about to build a great dam across the great river Firaw (Volta) that will in turn cause their own river to flood. Apaaso is destined to disappear under the flood together with seven hundred other villages. The children in school are told that a lake will be formed which will be the biggest man-made lake in the world. A town meeting is held to receive the government officials. Every one in the village is confused and sad.

It is 1963. The flood does come, spreading closer and closer. The villagers must prepare to leave their old village for ever. The children of the village must help their parents to pack their valuables, dismantle their homes and take a terrifying trip across the lake to New Senchi, their new resettlement village.

After seven years the children from Apaaso have grown into young adults and have adjusted to their new life with numbered homes, tractors and factories. The beautiful essence of their traditional culture however lives on. There is excitement in the air, for one of them, Yaa Amponsah, has come of age and is to be out-doored. So is the new queen mother of the town. As they get ready for the festivities, these adolescents reflect on their journey from Apaaso and their awe-inspiring experiences since then. They do not understand everything that has happened but they know one thing: they will never be the same again.

Ananse and the Dwarf Brigade (c. 1968/2000)[7]

Ananse, the wily 'man-spider' abandons his family and goes far away to establish a farm just for himself. He gets to a strange clearing where the slightest noise activates a rumbling Voice. Greatly frightened, he answers the Voice's questions, explaining why he is there. The Voice commands the Dwarf Brigade to appear and help him. The Dwarf Brigade is a terrifying and highly organized but mischievous group of dwarfs. They help Ananse make his farm and he does nothing but dance and read newspapers. They seem to know something he does not know and even as they work hard they also laugh a lot.

When the crops are nearly ready for harvest, Ananse's wife Okonore and his son Ibrahim Ananse appear at the farm. They try to pluck some of the corn and activate the Voice who, on hearing their story, orders the Dwarf Brigade to come and help them to harvest. Shortly afterwards the farm is totally destroyed. Ananse arrives and is wild with disappointment and anger. As he hits his wife, the Dwarfs are commanded to help him do so. However, he makes the mistake of thumping his chest triumphantly and immediately the ubiquitous Voice commands them to turn on him. As he is pummeled, his only escape from further punishment is to turn into a spider and to slip through their hands into his web.

Structure

Formula games, play songs and choric stories are seen by Sutherland as prototype community drama. In her research notes, the writer also identifies insult games, games of self-assertion, games which imitate events, child-made dramas, all of which are resources upon which she calls for composing the plays under study.

In many story-telling traditions in Africa, the choric tale is often classified as a juvenile form. Indeed Hausa and Dagaare speaking societies, for example, consider it below the dignity of men to indulge in such forms. These tales are mostly or totally based on, or propelled by, a melodic chant or song. While songs feature as part of all the plays cited above, they are structurally based on different genres. 'Pete, Pete', [Akan for 'Vulture! Vulture!' pronounced 'pet eh, pet eh') from which *Vulture! Vulture!* is derived may be classified as a play song/formula game.[8] These songs accompany games played by groups of children with a leader. On the other hand, *Tahinta* is a choric story in which the entire story is recited with the narrator chanting the verses and the audience taking up the refrain. There are indeed at least two different versions of this story, one from the Akan Twi-speaking tradition and another from the Akan Fanti-speaking area. The version retold and expanded by Sutherland is the latter.

She sees these formal play songs and choric stories as providing the opportunity for creative rhythmic composition involving mime and physical exercise. This she denotes as motional activity which can be elaborated with verbalization and song.[9] In the case of *Vulture, Vulture!*, the author sticks very closely to the original text, exploring techniques of statement followed by expansion and parallelism associated with some types of oral poetry.[10] These are useful techniques that make it possible to substitute slightly modified statements within the same breath. For example, in response to a question raised by Vulture about the meal prepared by his wife, he is told that it is *fufu* and palm soup. In Sutherland's version, there is semantic parallelism in which a second verse is created substituting roast chicken for *fufu* and palm soup in Part Two of the play.

By the time we reach Part Three which is the climax of the play we are lulled by the regularity of the rhythm and may be unprepared for the ironic twist of the finale when Vulture finally gets what he wants. This is again achieved by a surprising semantic switch while the rhythm remains deceptively consistent.

Tahinta is structurally more of a departure from the traditional story because the author takes liberties with the structure by intensifying the role of the participating audience or chorus. She does so by creating space for them to engage in substantial dialogues which sometimes involve commentary on the action, beyond the lines of the refrain and also extending the refrain itself:

Tahinta
Kind River Birim!
Tahinta
Whatever happens,
Tahinta,
Let him catch his fish
Tahin Tahin Tahin Tahin
Tahinta (Sutherland 1968:19)

Sutherland's plays may also be based on the dramatic interpretation of the plot of an oral tale. In this case, the plot is more closely followed. In *Ananse and the Dwarf Brigade*, Ananse is the traditional greedy and selfish spider-man character who courts severe punishment in the end for his greed.

Structurally, the playwright builds into her theatrical pieces for children informal aspects of children's play such as 'imitation of life through mime'.

Action in *Ananse and the Dwarf Brigade* is quite physical and sometimes even tactile. It involves the imitation of detailed physical movements involved in farming such as slashing, stumping, raking, stacking and turning up the earth. The Dwarf Brigade executes marching drills both as a realistic imitation of the military and also as a depiction of movements of these forest beings as depicted in mythology. Their toes, for example are said to point backwards. This provides child actors with ample opportunity to let their imagination run free. Again, in the final scene when the dwarfs are instructed to help Ananse beat his chest, it is a field day for children who love tactile action. In productions of this play which we have observed, (for example, January 2001) the actor who played Ananse was pummeled by little fists and as he rushed to make his exit, the children literally tumbled upon him.

Humour here is slapstick and provides an opportunity for spontaneity and momentary indiscipline. This is also true when the dwarfs are required to laugh in the stage direction 'Loud laughter from the dwarfs', which appears frequently thoughout the script.

Children with agency

In all of Sutherland's plays, children do not only constitute the majority of characters but are imbued with strong personalities. They drive the plot, and often determine the denouement of the play.

In *Ananse and the Dwarf Brigade*, it is true that there is the Voice referred to as Nana (Grandfather or Royal one) who commands the dwarfs and brings them into the flow of the drama, but there is no question that they know what they are doing. They raise Ananse's hopes by creating a beautiful farm but they have no difficulties in demolishing it just before the fruits are ready for harvest with the destructive glee that children are so capable of. They themselves are liminal creatures, appearing to be of ancient origin and yet remaining forever children. The dwarfs are depicted as impish beings with power. They can be very rigid in their behaviour but are unpredictable. They disappear, and reappear, and are allowed to do things that would plausibly be frowned upon in disciplined family life, such as whistling.

Again, the dwarfs are only too happy to oblige Ananse by hitting his wife, Okonore, on her mouth and absolutely delighted to rain blows on Ananse who, unable to withstand the punishment, turns into a spider. These scenes depict role reversals where children who are often subject to corporal punishment in Ghanaian society are able to thrash a badly behaved adult. The free-for-all implied by this episode again provides children the opportunity for complete abandon to respond to their basic instincts, uncomplicated by binding social norms of behaviour and etiquette.

In *Children of the Man-Made Lake*, child characters are of another ilk. The children are endowed with wonderful insight. Beyond echoing the discourse of the adult world about the events surrounding the construction of the Akosombo Dam, they have their very own thoughts. The writer is able to evoke the sense of wonder and bewilderment which the experience necessarily implies. Characters like Kwasi Akroma who hides in a tree to think and Ansah Kofi, who makes the most startlingly sensitive statements in the midst of the apparent frivolity of conversation among friends, imbue the text with a disturbing, yet moving reflectiveness. For example:

> *Ansah Kofi*: Isn't it surprising? When we traveled here on the lake it was so frightening! And now people are traveling safely on it to the north and safely back again. And yet something puzzles me always. It is not like old Apaaso here at New Senchi. Why? Why? Kwesi Akroma?
> *Kwasi Akroma*: What do you mean Ansah Kofi?
> *Ansah Kofi*: I don't know. I often think about it but I don't know why. And when I think about it, it makes me unhappy. Strangely, I think about water when I think about it sometimes. Is Kwasi Akroma right? Is water a spirit? Are our mothers right?

Is water a god? Why don't you answer me? Why are all of you so silent? (Sutherland 2000: 114)

In this extract, despite the cheeriness in the air, apparently depicting a people reconciled with a new beginning and cognizant of its advantages for future development, the unresolved issues which carry on in the psyche of this displaced community resurface in this metaphor. The child finds it difficult to define what water should mean to him and by implication to his community.

Again, the Boy in *Tahinta* experiences a range of emotions making him a rounded character with integrity. He starts the day gaily and experiences the disappointment of failure as he tries again and again to catch a fish. He slides towards despondency only to be filled with anticipation as he hears a sudden splash. His exhilaration is palpable as he discovers that he has trapped a fish. This makes his terror all the more believable as the Ghost comes across the water to snatch his fish. Having called on his role model, his father, to retrieve his fish he is full of hope and confidence that he is fully defended. It is for this reason that he is crestfallen and somewhat indignant about his father's failure to overcome the Ghost. He thus threatens to apply the ultimate sanction: humiliation before his father's wife. Indeed the momentum of the entire play rides on the emotional experiences of the Boy.

The group as an essential character cluster related to children is featured in all four plays, capturing a variety of group dynamics for theatrical effect. For example, Sutherland explores the structural potential of this dynamic in the rhythm plays by keeping up the refrain throughout the play so that the protagonist is in constant and somewhat formalized communion with his 'playmates' as he would have been if he had been engaged in a formula game. In *Vulture! Vulture!* the chorus takes on the familiar mode of goading the protagonist and holding him in suspense. Vulture is plied with foods that he does not find palatable and one cannot help wondering if the little vultures' invitation is not made with tongue in cheek.

The Chorus in *Tahinta* is more empathetic to the Boy and echoes his moods, acting as his alter-ego. For example, Boy begins to comment excitedly on the fight between his father and Ghost. Excitement mounts to a crescendo as the chorus takes on a typically rousing cheering around a good fight:

Tahinta
They are fighting
Tahinta
Bim! Bam! Bim
Tahinta
They are struggling
Tahinta
This way! That way! This way!
Down! Kudum! (Sutherland 1968: 32)

Having produced this play several times, I have noted the glee with which the chorus often takes on this part, closing in on the main actors as they would on the playground and getting louder and louder.

3. *Efua T. Sutherland (left) directing a young actor* (© Estate of Efua T. Sutherland)

4. *Scene from the first production of* Tahinta, *featuring Amowi Sutherland as the Boy*
(© Estate of Efua T. Sutherland)

Children of the Man-Made Lake, on the other hand, is constructed around groups of children in different contexts. This play seems to have provided Sutherland with the latitude to elaborate on the potential of the group dynamic without the structural constraints imposed by formula games or the choric story. From scene to scene, child characters of different ages (and in some cases gender groupings), elaborate the plot and determine the mood and direction of the play. In Part One, for example, girls, on their way to fetch water, introduce us to the rites which symbolize the stability of the community of Apaaso, confident in the immutability of its traditions. Indeed towards the end of Part One, this confidence is expressed by the Women's Leader who says:

> The festival has begun. Sing mothers of Apaaso, now, about the land that is ours. Our land, through which flows our generous river, Afram (Sutherland 2000: 99)

The girls are discussing the terror which they felt during the rain storm of the previous night. Their parents are certain though, that the storm, as always, was a sign of a bumper harvest and the girls laugh as some of them describe how they had expressed their fright. However, there is some dramatic irony built into the scene, for perhaps this not a laughing matter, nor does the storm represent the predictable bounty their parents and ancestors have learnt to expect. The storm and the terror that is evoked in the girls could be seen as a premonition of an event, worse than the most horrid nightmare of the people of Apaaso. The device of foregrounding the children's experience of social reality is sustained throughout the play.

In Part Two, the school setting is used to convey authoritative information from teachers to children. The seemingly naïve questions of the children betray the scepticism and denial of their elders. As happens throughout this play though, the notion of 'children without a care in the world' comes through very forcefully. For example, in this scene, when they are subsequently told that there is an important meeting for which school must close after the first lesson their reaction is 'Yee! Holiday!' The atmosphere in the school is full of disruptive behaviour. For example, the naughty little Dentaa teases one of her class mates who reacts as follows:

> Dentaa says I didn't bath this morning. *Laughter from class.* I bathed! My mother won't let me come to school if I don't bath.

In tropical southern Ghana, the banter around bathing occurs very often as some children try to get round this daily ritual. The group dynamics here evoke the insult games found in many classrooms and playgrounds around the world in which an individual child may be at the mercy of a group. Here, these insult games are spontaneously created with a cruelty typical of power play among children.

In Part Three, the child characters are broken into their gender groupings to enable the play to cover the multi-focal nature of the hasty preparations finally being made in the face of the reality of the flood.

The girls, staying close to home, reflect on the cultured space and the once-built environment which is disintegrating in the face of the floods or being dismantled by the very hands that built it. They speak of the symbolic treasures which the women are trying to save. They also look forward with some trepidation to the impending journey. The boys on the other hand cover the uncultured space of the bush and the river bank, bringing back home news of the reaction of the flora and fauna to the flood.

The two groups merge as they turn to playing games even as the sacred ancestral stool is being moved, marking the abandonment of the cultured space which their people have known for so long. The poignancy of the moment is highlighted by the fact that the children are playing as if nothing of great import is happening.

In Part Four, the children of Apaaso have arrived in a new and somewhat unsettling environment. In this scene, sticking together is a matter of survival. Ansah Kofi at the end of this scene says: 'Kwafo, we will go in a group as you said.'

The writer brings the child characters together again in the final scene set seven years later. The group is built up as the scene progresses. There is talk of 'out-doorings' and possible marriages. It is a scene of children and a society in transition. This is a group in adolescence, straddling childhood and adulthood, the old and the new. Typical of persons in that age bracket, they share, if in a rather competitive and raucous manner, their discovery of new worlds and skills. They anticipate adult life as careers and marriage. They are truly friends, covering each other's backs and caring for each other. For example, they all worry because Asarebea who has gone to the port city of Tema has not returned and decide to go to the road side to meet her. Their discussion even turns philosophical and reflective.

And yet for all this adult behaviour, they are still children at heart. Kwesi Akroma still spends time in his favorite tree haunt. Again, when the children hear the sound of the bus belonging to the new wax cloth factory situated at the brand new industrial town of Akosombo built near the dam site, they chase after it with cries of 'Akosombo Textiles'.

Sutherland's child characters are therefore complex personalities. Whether depicted as a collective or as individuals, their experiences are not predictable. While they are children they are not depicted as adjuncts to adults but as self-sufficient beings, interacting with the society and with their environment on their own terms and in their own right. The protagonists of both *Children of the Man-Made Lake* and *Tahinta* are children. They are neither placed in the texts merely for reasons of verisimilitude nor representing adults. In terms of composition, she depicts them as existing in their own space and perceiving the world from their own point of view, negotiating their way based on their own resourcefulness.

Structurally then, Sutherland can be said to have demonstrated aspects of the creative partnership between adults and children that she recommends should exist between playwrights. In her case she seems to enter into the world of children and to present it such that they can display their creativity naturally and indeed engage in play as the core dynamic for action.

Language, style and play

Language is both a means and an end in Sutherland's work and when she writes for children it seems to take on an even more important diversity of roles. As she clearly states in 'The Playwright's Opportunity in Drama For Our Children', she finds that too many plays written for children lack '.... the freshness, flexibility and imaginativeness of dialogue which characterize children's authentic verbal expressions and exchanges in that venue' [of free spontaneous play] (p.10).

Furthermore, she advises playwrights to use audience-conscious language (p.15).

In her hand-written notes on 'The Training Aspects of a Children's Drama Workshop Programme' Sutherland has the following bullet points
- The Principle of Mother-Tongue Priority
- The Bilingualism Objective. (From Mother Tongue – English)

Sutherland was concerned about the school environment as both a space in which the speaking of indigenous languages was disparaged (the 'No Fante Spoken Here' syndrome); and one in which English was taught unimaginatively. For her, this led to a jeopardy of imposing incompetence on children and suppressing their creativity.

Sutherland elaborates these two principles in her work and appears to be seeking to make Ghanaian children confident about formally developing the multilingual skills which they use in their communal and play lives. First, Sutherland's approach recognizes that many Ghanaian children have at least two languages but only use these multi-lingual skills in informal settings such as the market or the playground. The playground offers the opportunity for code switching and for creating and composing in different languages including English.

Secondly, in all four of the plays under discussion, Sutherland appears to have engaged in much experimentation with the stylistics of multi-lingualism. In *Vulture! Vulture!* the simplest rhythm line from the original song is maintained throughout the play. Although an effort is made to create variety by means such as twists in the plot and a dynamic application of parallelism, there is no doubt that the text and prosody closely follow the original Akan language.

Furthermore, the diction which she applies to her texts is palpably childlike. The author deliberately validates the play-language of children. For example, dialogue in Sutherland's plays is often a convincing imitation of conversation among children. In Part One of *Children of the Man-Made Lake*, the girls discuss their reaction to the storm:

> **Kwabea** The storm last night made me so afraid. Asarebea, weren't you afraid? That thunder. It was so loud. I was scared.
> **Asarebea** Yee! Do you know what I did? I covered up my head with my cloth. And I shut my eyes tight; tight like this. And I put this finger and this finger in my ears.

(*Laughter from all the girls*)
Kwabea Oh, Asarebea, you are so funny.
Asarebea I didn't like it. What did you do, Daakowa?
Daakowa Me? (*Loud voice with laughter*) I moved close to my mother and held her tight.
Three Voices Hee! Daakowa! (*Loud laughter from all*)
Ason Listen to the wind. Didn't you hear that whistling. Hy – Hy – hy. Hwee Hwee! Everywhere. This morning there are leaves all over our courtyard. I'm glad it's Brother's turn to sweep.

Again the story that the children in class one tell in Part Two of the same play is extremely simple and has an infantile ring to the diction:

Ofosuaa There was a little bird. And he went and stood on elephant grass. And the elephant grass cut his food. And he flew away. Then he went and stood on a pepper plant. And the pepper plant hurt his wound, bad, bad, bad. And he cried and cried: 'Amako aka me kurom'.
Chorus Oya hyew! Hyew! Hyew!

The phenomenon of children boasting and exaggerating in their narrative culture is employed in *Children of the Man-Made Lake* to good effect. The hyperbolic description of the pylons carrying electricity from the hydro-electric plant at Akosombo towards the Port City of Tema is one such case. Ansah Kofi claims to have seen thousands of them.

In this play Sutherland uses juxtapositions to underline the almost unbearable trauma of the community, precisely by breaking into the pathos with apparent childlike banality. This is achieved in part through the manner in which children express themselves. For example, Ansah Kofi, a child in the same play, is impishly curious and dares to defy the taboo of observing the removal of the Royal Stool, the very soul of the people of Apaaso, from its sacred abode to be transported across the water, signifying the final abandonment of the ancestral land. This solemn moment is broken by Ansah Kofi saying off-handedly: 'But I went to see! Ah! Kwafo let's continue our game.' That one casual line juxtaposed against the description of these solemn events by the other children and their awe of it, far from being dismissive, highlights them.

At all times there is a childlike playfulness which averts the sense of the tragic but often amplifies the poignancy of the situation being presented. The communal sense of bewilderment is transferred into the children's world of play, making the inexorable advance of disaster more bearable. The children wonder and muse over their impending fate. There is solidarity among the children of Apaaso who are the most vulnerable victims of the evacuation of their people in the face of the powerful political force of the national government and the immense natural power of the dammed waters of the Volta River and its tributaries. Even though there are moments of nostalgia and some bewilderment, by the end of the play they take collective ownership of the future which is theirs to own. In her notes, Sutherland calls this 'play power'; defining it as follows:

This is the child's use of the means drama affords to overcome his bewilderment about a world that dishes out to him – conditions and challenges not of his making. [Undated notes]

A word on the denouement of the four plays

As we conclude our examination of the notion that a playwright might consider creating plays for and with children, we are struck by the denouement of all four of Sutherland's plays discussed above. In none of the plays does she as author take a moralistic position. Texts written for children in Ghana such as retellings of tales, are often highly didactic and moralistic. While the plays certainly have a number of embedded messages, these are quite complex. For example, the Dwarfs in *Ananse and the Dwarf Brigade*, who are agents of retribution, are mischievous imps, not holy angelic beings. The Ghost gets away with the Boy's fish in *Tahinta*, while Vulture in *Vulture! Vulture!* is off to eat a dead rat. At the end of *Children of the Man-Made Lake* the children are trying to sort out as best they can a deeply traumatic experience of displacement. In other words, these denouements contribute to the removal of the adult as an intrusive agent of dominant power, constraining the element of play and creativity. There is something for the children to think about and come back to.

Efua Sutherland's work as a dramatist has shown the elaborate processes of self-education that she engaged in, in order to prepare herself to write plays that would make it possible to recreate the world of the child on stage. Her four plays discussed above, demonstrate the choices she makes in terms of compositional structure, characterization, language and style to meet her own highly rigorous standard of writing plays for and with children.

NOTES

1 *Playtime in Africa* was illustrated with photographs of Ghanaian children at play taken by veteran photographer, Bill Bell (1924–2000).
2 VALCO is an aluminium smelting plant which was set up by Kaiser Engineering Company in the early 1960s. This enterprise established an independent trust fund which has established a reputation for supporting educational causes.
3 These studies have been documented in the form of field reports and a compendium of photographs. Reports include 'Child Rearing in Nzema' (1975) by Egya-Blay, and 'Lobi Gonja/Vagla/Safalba and Frafra Games' (1975) collected by Abubakr Von Salifu.
4 The Ghana Drama Studio was established by Sutherland in down-town Accra in 1958. The building was constructed with funding from the Sloan, Ford and Rockefeller Foundations and inaugurated in 1960. It served for many years as the hub and the cutting edge for drama in Ghana. It was demolished at the beginning of the 1990s to give way to the National Theatre. It was subsequently rebuilt on the Campus of the University of Ghana and was named The Efua Sutherland Drama Studio in 1999.
5 Among plays written are *The Perpetual Stone Mill* by Sebastian Kwamuar, *Ghana Motion* by R. A. Cantey and *Akpokplo* by Kofi Anyidoho, *Hwe No Yie* by Kwamena Ampah, *The New Born Child* and *The Maid Servant* by Koku Amuzu, *A Bench of Chances* by Kofi Hiheta and *Gates to Mother* by Joe Manu-Amponsah.

6 *Tahinta* has been published in two editions. The first was in a two-play volume of children's plays entitled *Vulture!Vulture! Two Rhythm Plays*. In its second iteration, the play was published posthumously with an accompanying audio tape featuring the children of the Mmofra Foundation Language Club. It was produced by her daughters Amowi Sutherland Phillips and Esi Sutherland-Addy to support the children's cultural foundation (Mmofra Foundation).
7 The date change to 2000 clarifies things as that is the first time the play was published in print. I cannot find the document to prove it at the moment but I know that there is a reel-to-reel audio edition of the play which was produced for PBS in the United States. That is the edition that I believe was produced in the late 1960s.
8 Abu Abarry discusses the structure of playsongs by Ghanaian children in his article 'The Role of Playsongs in the Moral, Social and Emotional Development of African Children', published in Anne V, Adams and Janis A. Mayes (eds) *Mapping Intersections: African Literature and Africa's Development* (Africa World Press, Trenton, NJ, 1998).
9 This terminology is taken from a set of bullet points discovered among Sutherland's papers on Children's Education of the Drama Composer.
10 Isidore Okpewho describes these techniques his book, *African Oral Literature* (1992: 78–83).

BIBLIOGRAPHY

Abary, A., 1998, 'The Role of Playsongs in the Moral Social and Emotional Development of African Children' in Anne V. Adams and Janis A. Mayes (eds) *Mapping Intersections: African Literature and Africa's Development* (Africa World Press: Trenton, NJ).
Anyidoho, K. and Gibbs, J. (eds), 2000, *Fontomfrom, Contemporary Ghanaian Literature, Theatre and Film, Matatu,* 21–22 (Rodopi: Amsterdam-Atlanta, 2000).
Okpewho, Isidore, 1992, *African Oral Literature* (Indiana University Press: Bloomington, IN).
Sutherland, E.T., *New Life in Kyerefaso* in *An African Treasury,* 1960, ed. Langston Hughes (Brown Publishing: New York).
—— *Tweedledum and Tweedledee,* (unpublished draft) April 1967 (Accra).
—— *Araba: The Village Story,* 1966–1967 (Film; See *L'Afrique Littéraire et Artistique 20,* 1971).
—— *Edufa,* 1967 (Longman: London).
—— *Foriwa,* 1967 (Longman: London).
—— *Ananse and The Dwarf Brigade* (unpublished) circa 1968 (Accra).
—— *Ananse Na Mbowatsia Asafo* (unpublished draft January 1968) (Accra).
—— *Pete! Pete!* (unpublished) circa 1967.
—— *Vulture! Vulture! Two Rhythm Plays* 1968 (Ghana Publishing Corporation: Accra).
—— 'The Playwright's Opportunity in Drama For Our Children', 1976 (unpublished for Seminar on Writing and Production of Literature for Children (Institute of African Studies, University of Ghana: Legon).
—— *The Marriage of Anansewa 1975* (London: Longman).
—— 'Children of the Man-Made Lake' in K. Anyidoho and J. Gibbs (eds) *Fontomfrom, Contemporary Ghanaian Literature, Theatre and Film* (Rodopi: Amsterdam-Atlanta), 2000.
—— *Tahinta, A Rhythm Play for Children* (with cassette by the Mmofra Foundation Language Club), 2000.
—— (with photographs by Willis Bells) *Playtime in Africa* 1960 (Brown, Knight and Truscott: London), 1960.
—— (with illustrations by Ralph Sutherland and CD read by Abena Busia) *A Voice in the Forest,* forthcoming (Afram Publications Ghana Ltd: Accra).

Competitive Youth Theatre Festivals in Ghana
Stage Motion & Studrafest

AWO MANA ASIEDU
with SARAH DORBGADZI

Much of the theatre activity among young people in Ghana takes place in the context of schools' drama clubs, church groups and children's clubs. These clubs are occasionally organized in competitive theatre festivals. In this article, I shall attempt a general overview of some of these activities, but the main focus will be on two annual, competitive theatre festivals dubbed Stage Motion, which takes place in Accra in February and Studrafest in Cape Coast each November.

There is a general feeling in Ghana that there is little theatre activity these days compared to some two to three decades ago when theatre appeared to be on the increase and had tangible support from government agencies. This sentiment surfaces in different contexts. Our research for this article has, however, pleasantly surprised us, making it clear that Ghanaian youth are very much engaged in theatre and feel they derive specific benefits from participating in it. It must be conceded, though, that many of the youth involved in these activities represent the privileged few and not necessarily the rank-and-file of children in Ghana. This is obvious when we consider that they are mostly children in second cycle schools, often situated in urban areas.

Within Accra, the capital city alone, we identified more than a dozen schools with active drama clubs. These include; Accra Girls' Secondary School, Accra Academy, Happy Kids Academy, Achimota Secondary School, West Africa Secondary School, Holy Trinity Cathedral School, St. Thomas Aquinas Secondary School, Labone Secondary, Presbyterian Boys' Secondary School and Ghana International School. This list is by no means exhaustive. We found that some of these schools took the drama club very seriously and some had special budgets and were actively supported by their PTAs.

The case of Ghana International School (GIS) is particularly worthy of note. This school, as the name suggests, is made up of international students, mostly children of ambassadors and other expatriates working in Ghana, and Ghanaian children mostly from affluent homes. For several years now, GIS has had as part of its annual calendar, two drama performances. Students have performed European as well as African plays, including Shakespeare's *Much Ado About Nothing,* Molière's *Tartuffe,* Ene Henshaw's *Dinner For Promotion,* Ola Rotimi's

Our Husband has Gone Mad Again and Sophocles' *Oedipus Rex*. The school has engaged Sarah Dorbgadzi on several occasions to help the children rehearse and prepare plays for production. Currently there is a permanent member of staff responsible for theatre activities. Sarah asked some of the students about what they saw as benefits of being a part of the drama club. Here are some of their comments:

'Drama makes me express my feelings through the characters.'
'It helps me overcome my shyness.'
'It makes me confident when I talk to a lot of people.'
'It is fun.'
'Through drama I have learnt to behave responsibly.'

The enthusiasm and commitment of the children to the club, makes rehearsing them for the productions very rewarding.

Sankofa and Stage Motion

Sankofa is an NGO founded by a theatre enthusiast and former student of the Theatre Arts Department of the University of Ghana, Daniel Clark. He had been a keen participant in his secondary school's drama club. By 1999, when he was nearing the end of his university training, he felt there was less interest in stage productions compared to when he was in secondary school. He decided to do something about it, and *Sankofa* was born. '*Sankofa*' is an Akan word, which literally means 'go back and take what has been discarded'.[1] His main aim therefore, is to encourage Ghanaian youth to 'go back for' stage plays. He believes inculcating an interest in them at this stage would ensure a future for theatre in Ghana. If they do not become leading players in theatre practice themselves, they would, at the very least, become interested patrons of the art.

Sankofa is made up of senior secondary school leavers who were once members of their schools' drama club. The group, by its nature is often in flux as new members each year replace old members, who move on in their pursuit of higher education. Currently, there are about nineteen young people committed to the group, who meet regularly with Clark in his house for discussions and training. They organize annual drama competitions for second cycle schools, dubbed Stage Motion. The fourth competition lasted two days, on the 19th and 20th February 2004 at the Centre for National Culture in Accra. There were fourteen participating schools from Accra and two from the Eastern region. The next competition, which was planned for 19th to 21st February 2005, involved nineteen schools from the Eastern, Volta and Greater Accra regions. Members of *Sankofa* are assigned to participating schools to help them prepare for the competition. Whenever necessary, Clark himself goes round to supervise the process. *Sankofa* members also go round to solicit sponsorship from various companies and individuals for the annual event.

The group has gained recognition by a number of agencies including the Ministry of Education. The Ministry lends its support by giving them letters of introduction to the schools and possible sponsors. This is an achievement Clark is proud of as it indicates that the Ministry recognizes their contribution to the schools' drama clubs as useful. They now receive several invitations from schools to help them organize their drama clubs. Prominent amongst their sponsors has been the Ghana Broadcasting Co-operation, which decided to telecast the best plays from February 2005. Others include Busy Internet, a communications agency, Asanka Locals and Papaye, which are both popular restaurants in Accra.

Sankofa insists on only African plays at Stage Motion. These may be published plays by African writers or devised plays by a group of students or written by one individual student. Clark believes this helps promote African plays and encourage creative writing in Ghana. Judges are drawn from among theatre practitioners in the country and they are given specific areas to look for in awarding marks. These include the quality of acting, speech and grammar, use of space, sound and lighting design, as well as set and costume design. The level of talent exhibited in these areas of performance by the young people is really amazing. St. John's Grammar School in Accra won the 2004 competition, with an original play written by one of the students. Other plays presented in 2004 included Asiedu Yirenkyi's *The Queue* and Joris Wartenberg's *Corpses Comedy*. The plays rehearsed towards the competition in 2005, included Femi Osofisan's *A Restless Run of Locusts* and *Mambo* by Joe de Graft.

Since 2000, when Stage Motion started, according to Clark there has been a consistent improvement in the quality of performances. Students have become very keen and there is a lot of healthy competition, with each school giving its utmost in order to win. These drama activities are also serving to build self-confidence in these young people and have contributed to their ability to express themselves and to speak good English. Clark also notes that many of his young people who go on to tertiary institutions are at the forefront of organizing entertainment activities for their peers especially stage productions. Others are actively involved in their church youth groups where they often organize drama performances. A few of them have also enrolled in Theatre Arts programmes at the University of Ghana, to get professionally trained. There is no doubt that *Sankofa* is making a contribution towards building, not only the human resource base, but also the interest in and patronage of theatre in Ghana.

Clark envisages that in the near future, Stage Motion will become a national affair, covering all ten regions in the country. Eventually, he hopes it will become international, involving other African countries.

Daniel Clark is currently employed by Shangri-La Hotel as Events and Entertainment Officer and he also uses that opportunity to encourage the production of theatre by children and youths. He has created a Shangri-La Kids Theatre Club for children between the ages of 8 and 15 years. These children meet fortnightly at the hotel to learn traditional dances, drama, songs and poetry. The group performs at special functions organized by the hotel and has an annual Christmas programme of drama, poetry, and music and dance every Boxing Day. He says his main aim for this club is to make Ghanaian children bold and confident, give them an opportunity to develop their talents and to create friendship and love among children from different schools and with diverse social and economic backgrounds.

The children generally really enjoy participating in these performances and feel that they are exciting. It makes them learn things they would never have learnt otherwise about themselves. An adult who accompanied some children to one of the performances observed that 'in educating children, there needs to be a way to develop their creativity. This kind of exercise also gives children from less privileged homes an exposure and is excellent for relaxation. It also gives the children confidence in public speaking.' The children pay a fee of twenty thousand *cedis*[2] each time they attend a meeting, which also entitles them to some refreshments from the hotel. Clark is currently seeking a total sponsorship for this programme to enable more children who cannot afford that sum to participate.

Studrafest

The central regional branch of the Centre for National Culture in 1995 instituted an annual drama festival for secondary schools in the region, dubbed Studrafest. In November 2004, I had the privilege of being one of the judges at their tenth anniversary edition of the festival. The experience was both exciting and revealing and overall, gave me hope for the future of theatre in Ghana.

The organizers of the festival took their inspiration from a paper presented by the late Efua Sutherland in 1980, which proposed the establishment of a drama festival in Cape Coast that would serve as a platform for talents to be exposed. (Studrafest 2000 programme notes).

In addition, they see the festivals as a way of keeping theatre alive in Ghana. In their estimation, at the time the festival started, theatre was on the decline in Ghana and there was a danger that it might die out completely. Their main aims therefore included the following: 'To initiate a new era to produce new playwrights to keep the theatre going'; 'to unearth talents among the students, thereby helping to guide the youth of today ... in a more useful direction.' The latter aim is seen as important because of the apparent disposition of Ghanaian youth towards foreign cultures. It is believed that these festivals would in some way draw them closer to Ghanaian culture.

Studrafest, at its inception included some teacher-training colleges, but it was soon realized that there were large differences between the output from the secondary school students and that of the older trainee teachers. The organizers then decided to limit the competition to secondary schools. The age range of participants in this festival is thus between 14 and 19 years. Initially, the students were encouraged to choose any published play, but from 1997, to help in unearthing talents in playwriting, original scripts were encouraged. For the purposes of the tenth anniversary celebrations, however, the students were given a choice from four plays. These were: *The Opportunity* by Arthur Maimane; *Joseph Haven't You Got Your Bicycle Yet?* by Jean Ngo Lirondo; *Ananse and the Gum Man,* by Joe de Graft; and *A Bird in Hand* by Saint Abdulai Alhassan. The last two are both Ghanaian playwrights while the first two are from South and East Africa.

The organizers, it appears, were not too comfortable with the sort of plays students were coming up with, as they always seemed to focus on boy-girl relationships and marriage situations. They wanted more diversity in themes and treatment of issues. As it turned out, eight out of the sixteen schools chose Saint Alhassan's play, which deals with issues concerning marriage and love relationships! Lirondo's play, a comedy about 'red tape' in the civil service of so many African countries, attracted only one school, Aggrey Memorial. They gave a delightful representation of the play with very effective staging and use of colours and came second in the competition. Joe de Graft's play was chosen by four schools, Wesley Girls', Adisadel, Presbyterian Boys' and Breman Asikuma Secondary. This play, perhaps more than the others, offered the students room for creativity. It is a storytelling drama with opportunities for use of music, dance and mime. Ananse, the trickster, feigns his own death in order to have the lion share of the harvest from his farm all to himself. Prior to his 'death' he makes his family promise not to bury him but let him lie on a mat in his farm, with all the items he would need to prepare a meal by his side. His unsuspecting family complies with his wishes. Each night, Ananse wakes up and harvests crops from the farm, has a good meal and lays back down again before daylight. Kweku Tsin brings his father's deeds to light by setting a trap for him with a gum man.

All four schools did a good job with this play, with some interesting stage arrangements, dance choreography, sound effects and costume. The first and third positions in the competition were taken by two of the schools who presented this play.

The remaining three schools, University Practice Secondary, Ghana Secondary Technical School and Boa Amponsem Secondary, presented *The Opportunity*. Arthur Maimane's play looks at what some families went through in the early days of independence in Africa. Solomon is offered an ambassadorial position in the UN, but he can only take the job if he divorces his illiterate wife of over thirty years and marries an educated woman. The play examines whether this is an opportunity worth taking. Solomon's highly educated daughter, certainly thinks not and breaks off her engagement with her fiancé, who appears to be in support of her father's action.

This play, the only one with a consistently serious tone, also offered some opportunities for good acting and character analysis. The student who played the illiterate wife in Boa Amposem's presentation was striking in her representation of the character and was adjudged the best female actor of the competition.

It is not clear what informed the choice of scripts by the organizers of the competition, but one may guess that they were interested only in African plays. Some weeks to the competition, training workshops are set up for all participating schools. Each year, the workshop focuses on specific areas of performance and experts in the field are invited to work with students and their teachers. In addition to this, some schools employ the services of people in the field to assist their students in their preparations towards the competition. Unfortunately, not all schools are able to benefit from such help and this shows up in their performances. It is hoped that more efforts will be put into organizing these workshops and help offered to all schools interested in participating in these competitions. This is where collaboration between the Centre for National Culture and *Sankofa* could be useful. Indeed, with the involvement of schools from the greater Accra Region in the Central region's competition this year, (and the organizers are looking to encourage more of such participation), such future collaboration may not be far off.

Sankofa's effectiveness is evident as one of the schools they assisted, Presbyterian Boys' Secondary, who were participating in the Central region's competition for the very first time took the first position with their excellent presentation of de Graft's play. The student who played the role of Kweku Ananse also took the best male actor award. This student, Jesse Ayertey, a science student, thoroughly enjoyed playing the role and believes he has gained a lot by participating in the drama club. It was his first time in such a big role and he feels it has helped him to discover a talent he did not realize he had. His creativity has been greatly enhanced and he looks forward to acting in other plays. Emmanuel Yawson, another student from the same school, who played the role of Okonnor, Ananse's wife, was also very excited about his role and their achievement as a club. He did not think they could win, as it was their first time participating in the competition. 'Wining was just awesome', he beamed. He said his peers had always teased him about his obvious feminine mannerisms. Acting the role of a woman on stage had, somehow, made him feel more comfortable with himself. He knew he was good at it and is happy with the outcome and does not mind all that teasing anymore.

The production had involved quite a few students and they had had the opportunity to use their talents and to express their creativity, they told me. Their set was designed and beautifully painted by drama club members who were Visual Arts students. They were appreciative of Daniel Clark and his group for their assistance. They noted that Clark paid attention to their suggestions and did not impose his own ideas on them, which for them was liberating and made them feel they had made a significant and creative contribution to their successful production. Both Ayertey and Yawson want to continue to perform, Ayertey more as a hobby, while Yawson, a literature student, feels he would like to get more training in acting and perhaps pursue a career in the performing arts. They are both certain that the experience has boosted their levels of self-confidence.

There is no doubt that school drama clubs play a significant role in the development of creativity and self-confidence of young people. Beyond these advantages, the activities of these drama clubs are laying a good foundation for the future of theatre in Ghana. Competitive theatre festivals, such as Studrafest and Stage Motion must be encouraged and their organizers need to work in closer co-operation towards a more co-ordinated competition, which would cover all ten regions of the country.

NOTES

1 The concept of Sankofa in the Akan philosophical worldview implies more than going back for something discarded. It also incorporates the idea of history informing present actions, i.e. learning from the past for present and future gain. This is a popular concept that is applied variously in political, religious and other contexts.
2 That is about US$2, the cost of four big loaves of bread in Ghana at present.

Three Malawian Student Performances
Playing pains

PIA THIELMANN

The objective of this essay is to introduce how the political, psychological and inter-ethnic conflicts that are pertinent to contemporary Malawi are presented on stage in a short time, with no money, simple props, a delapidated arena, poor lighting and electricity cuts. They are effectively staged through theatre skills of the student performers, with lots of enthusiasm and abundant creativity. I take three plays as examples, *The Monster Within*, *Murdering the Soul*, and *It's All About Dialogue*, performed by drama students at Chancellor College, University of Malawi. Through these projects the students acquired skills in playwriting, acting, directing, design, stage-management and drama theory, all under the guidance of their professor, David Kerr, in 2003 to 2004. This discussion is an appreciation of powerful 'edutainment' from the perspective of a non-practising outsider.

Historical background

During Hastings Kamuzu Banda's dictatorship since Nyasaland's independence in 1964, to the end of his 30-year rule in 1994, any artistic creativity, any public expression with the slightest hint of political and cultural dissent was severely censored. Playwrights and other writers who dared to follow their social consciousness lived dangerously and often became victims of the censorship board. This is why plays had disguised contents, for example through the application of local myths.

Mufunanji Magalasi points out that 'drama in Malawi cannot be overemphasized. Malawi is a developing country, as such drama is also used as one of the tools for communication in development. Apart from helping in education, plays are also used to communicate issues in Civic Education, Health, Agriculture, gender sensitivity, children's, women's, and human rights etc' (Magalasi 2001: v–vi). Recently, NGOs such as The Story Workshop have been '… using drama in communicating issues like Aids awareness and behavioural change, or the importance of education for girls in Malawi' (Magalasi 2001: vi).

Expressive form and content in the three plays

All three plays concern themselves with Malawian content through a combination of speech, dance, music and mime as integral parts of cultural expression. David Kerr quotes Atta Mensah (1971) maintaining that in African culture 'the arts come together in one context, highlighting one another and accentuating one effect after the other' (Kerr 1998: 25). Further, the financial situation of the University of Malawi makes it necessary for the students not only to be extremely creative, but also resourceful. In order to perform a play off-campus in a different town, it first has to be performed on campus a few times, so the low entry fee collected there can then be used to buy petrol to get the students to their intended performance destination. Now this sounds as if they always play on campus first and then off-campus. But that varies. Most plays are only performed on campus anyway.

The Monster Within

The class project *The Monster Within* is a history lesson through dance, mime and satire. This was also performed after the semester's end during a week-long DAAD (German Academic Exchange Service) Alumni Summer School/ Theatre Workshop in September 2003 at Chancellor College. A child's nightmare about a monster prompts her grandmother to tell the story of the nation whose monster, represented by a mask, is courageously tackled in the final scene. Devising and rehearsing this play was difficult. Because of numerous electricity cuts and the problems with the non-functional lighting system in the College's Great Hall, the students often rehearsed with kerosene lamps and candles brought by the instructor. They also came up with ingenious ideas for costumes that they themselves could provide. This is true for all plays.

In the play, a young girl wakes from her nightmare about a monster. The monster of colonialism is played by a person with a white plastic face-mask. Colonialism is further represented by an overseer-like person who terrorizes farmers. Resistance to colonialism is represented through fighters/dancers who rip off the white mask.

Banda is mocked in the way he dressed and talked. Banda, who was unmarried but had a so-called official hostess, Cecilia Kadzamira, is dressed in European clothes, with a hat. He speaks English and has a chiChewa translator. His speech and mannerisms are mocked. The camera man has no camera but mimes using one. Banda's use of women as his praise singers and his self-declared role of *nkhoswe* of the nation (literally the *nkhoswe* is a marriage negotiator and counsellor) is mocked by his hitting a singer's bottom with a fly whisk.

Banda's dictatorship is represented by the monster again, this time with a blood red mask. The sleeping girl wakes up from another nightmare and asks her grandmother whether Malawians tried to kill the monster. The grandmother's affirmative answer is play-acted on centre-stage. The scene of the fighters for democracy's secret activities is a particularly impressive example of creative miming without any props: a person comes into a room, switches on the light by pulling on an invisible string of a lamp played by an actor. The light goes on when the actor opens his eyes. The coat stand is another actor. The chair, table and computer used to write pamphlets are also people. Particularly effective is the idea of pulling out paper from under a person's t-shirt to indicate a printer. The person takes her coat from the coat stand and switches off the light before leaving. The 'lamp' closes his eyes.

The Banda speech scene is balanced by a Muluzi speech scene. The similarities of the scenes indicate that not as much had changed under Bakili Muluzi, the country's leader from 1994 to May 2004. There are still dancers, this time in yellow, the UDF colour, the president is accompanied by his wife, he speaks chiChewa. In this performance of the play he speaks more English for the benefit of the international conference audience than in the previous performance. He leaves by helicopter, represented by an umbrella twirled to indicate the rotor blades.

The monster puts its red mask on again, suggesting that the situation has not improved sufficiently, that there is still poverty, maltreatment and bloodshed. There is also stone-throwing as protest against the government. The scene resembles the opening scene. This time, the girl wants to kill the monster but is afraid. At another attempt, the girl gathers enough courage to de-mask the monster. The burning of the mask with invisible matches indicates that it is possible to end destruction if one finds the courage to act.

The technique of having the girl's bed, i.e. a big box at the side of the stage on which the girl sleeps, covered with two pieces of cloth for bedding and the minimal dialogue between granddaughter and grandmother, leave the stage free for the main action. No complicated, time-consuming and distracting set changes are necessary and this makes the play flow more smoothly. The girl and the grandmother provide the narrative skeleton.

Murdering the Soul

Another class project, *Murdering the Soul*, was first staged in 1999 at the University of Botswana. The play was devised by the Botswana students and then scripted by a committee which consisted of a selection of the class. It is based on real child-abuse cases. The Chancellor College students subsequently adapted it to the Malawian situation. Through flashbacks, mime, song and dramatic dialogue the play portrays problems of sexual abuse of children and the acquiescence of some of the adults in their environment. In parallel performance, the stories of two raped girls and their psychiatrist shed light on each other and lead the characters to confront their respective histories to preserve their sanity.

The central characters of the play are a middle-aged social worker, a young psychiatrist and two girls. Fatima is abused by her maths teacher, then by a paedophile tourist, before becoming a child prostitute. Esnat has been raped by her stepfather and consequently becomes dumb. The social worker, Mrs Ndaona Chimutu, realizes during her consultations with the psychiatrist, Dr Fernando, who hides himself behind professional jargon, that he is also a survivor of abuse which affects his ability to treat the girls.

His personal therapy becomes intertwined with that of the two girls. In an article about the play's production in Botswana, Kerr maintains that this play was therapeutic to some students. It is about reconciliation and conflict resolution. The process of making the play was revealing to others in so far as the students learned about the facts of child sexual abuse and the cultural, social and economic conditions that give rise to it (Kerr 2000: 135).

During the first part of the play, Fatima is shown as a school-girl who mimes skipping with a rope. The maths teacher punishes Fatima for alleged bad school performance by making her do degrading tasks at his home such as taking off his shoes, socks and tie. The sexual innuendoes of the 'punishment' indicate the subsequent rape. A concerned female teacher goes to the headmaster to report the incident, but the headmaster does not follow up on it, despite the evidence of bloody underpants that the teacher shows him. He threatens to put a note into the teacher's personnel file which would ruin her career.

Later, Fatima is shown performing a traditional dance, arousing the desire of a paedophile tourist. The tourist is easily recognizable by his white-painted face, rucksack and mimed camera. He offers money to the guide if he arranges for him to spend three days with the girl. The guide agrees to talk to the parents. The parents, especially the father, do not fully understand the situation and give in to the promise of the badly needed money.

The tourist takes the girl to his room. The room-service waitress is suspicious and reports that the tourist has a young girl in his hotel room. However, the manager does not act.

Later, the female teacher and a male teacher talk about Fatima who has run away and has been spotted as a prostitute. The story of how she ends up as a prostitute is shown on stage. She is found by other prostitutes who take her in and initiate her into prostitution. She changes from a shy to a tough girl. The scene in which the prostitutes initiate the young girl is done in a hilariously funny way in which the actresses have the opportunity to shock the audience and provide them with comic relief. It is also an opportunity to break social taboos by the way they are dressed and use their sexuality on stage.

The female teacher and her colleague decide to rescue the girl with the male teacher posing as a customer and the woman hiding in the back of the car.

The girl's trauma is expressed in the way she plays down the incidents with her abusive maths teacher and blames herself, taking on all responsibility during therapy by calling herself a bitch. In the Malawian context, the term bitch refers to a supposedly oversexed woman.

The other girl, Esnat, is punished by her stepfather for not serving his food fast enough and to his full satisfaction. The rape is indicated by a scream from behind the scenes.

The dumb girl who resists the male psychiatrist's attempt to help her and who behaves like a baby by sucking her thumb, had demonstrated to the social worker with dolls what her stepfather had done to her.

During the consultation sessions between Dr Fernando and Mrs Chimutu parts of the psychiatrist's story come out in flashbacks. He is Mozambican. He had to witness how the women, including his mother, were raped by RENAMO and later burned to death. He escaped to the woods, living on wild fruit only to be found by RENAMO soldiers who fed him but forced him to kill.

The link between the abuse of the two girls and the boy soldier is created when Dr Fernando wonders what horrors go on in the minds of the abused girls. Mrs Chimutu acknowledges that he had suffered a rape of the mind, comparable to the rapes the girls suffered. And during their nightmare, the girls kill their tormentors with knives. When Esnat wakes up with a knife in her hand she attacks Dr Fernando and hurts his shoulder. (The students made the knife out of an aloe leaf wrapped in aluminium foil.) Dr Fernando understands her aggression against men and does not accuse her of hurting him. Instead, he narrates the rest of his abuse which is also shown in mime: he escapes from RENAMO and is taken in by Catholic missionaries who bring him to Malawi. While Dr Fernando narrates his story, the missionaries leave him alone with Father Nolan. The rape by Father Nolan is indicated by the boy kneeling and the Father standing behind him, his hands on the boy's shoulders.

The children and Mrs Chimutu are the first ones ever to hear his story. When Esnat approaches him, Fatima is worried that she might hurt him, but instead, Esnat speaks for the first time and apologizes to Dr Fernando for having hurt him, a fellow victim. The reconciliatory hug and a song end the play.

It's All About Dialogue

This love story between a Chewa woman and a Tumbuka man demonstrates how cultural differences can be negotiated and resolved. The play is performed bilingually, in chiChewa and chiTumbuka.

This 15-minute play by Chancellor College students was devised on request by the US Embassy as part of Black History Month in February 2004. The students had about a week to come up with an idea and to realize it. There is no script and no visual record of the performance. Rather than choosing a portrayal of black-white tensions, the students chose a related topic that is probably now even more significant in Malawi. The tensions between the Chewa and the Tumbuka, the two major ethnic groups, played against each other by Banda, can be transferred to a broader situation of racial tension and to the necessity of re-examining the basis for these tensions.

Suzgo Kumwenda, a man from the Tumbuka North, and Lignet Chanza, a woman from the Chewa South, want to get married. When the young man's *nkhoswe* meets the Kumwenda family, he is ridiculed for his accent. The giggling and facial expressions make it obvious that he is considered strange. Not just language but also customs are barriers to the young couple's happiness. The Tumbukas want the wedding to follow the patriarchal *lobola* system in which the groom gives an appreciative gift of cattle to the bride's family. The Chewas want to follow the matrilineal *chikamwini* system, according to which the groom moves to the bride's village and builds a house there. The argument between the two families nearly leads to a physical fight. The young couple solve the problem by eloping to the city.

The woman's pregnancy forces both families to deal with the situation in a constructive way because the matter is embarrassing for both sides. The

1. (Left) Dr Fernando and Mrs Chimutu discuss their two 'charges', Fatima and Esnat. (From left: Thokozani Kapiri, Sibosizo Twea)

2. (Below) Fatima and her school mates miming skipping ropes. (From left: Chilungamo Bonga, Christine Nyambolo, Sophie Dambe, Lusizi Mhoni)

3. (Bottom left) Fatima as a traditional dancer, photographed by the paedophile tourist. (From left: Chilungamo Bonga, Linda Dembo, Lusizi Mhoni, Christine Nyambolo, Roderick Mhango)

4. (Top) The prostitutes who found the runaway Fatima prepare her for her new job. (From left: Christine Nyambalo, Chilungamo Bonga, Lusizi Mhoni, Sophie Dambe)

5. (Above) Rescue mission: the male teacher poses as John while the female teachers hides in the back seat of the car. (From left: Lusizi Mhoni, Lungireni Mwantisi, Basimenye Mwalwanda)

6. (Right) Father Nolan rapes the young Fernando. (Standing: Roderick Mhango; kneeling: Victor Mkandawire)
(All photos © Pia Thielmann)

Kumwendas visit the bride's family again and agree to pay damages to the Chewa village chief. During the following negotiations the families decide that the wedding will take place neither following the *lobola* nor the *chikamwini* system. The reconciliation is made obvious by the way negotiations take place in a calmer way than in their initial confrontation, and it is female members from both families who speak in support of the children. The play ends with the families singing wedding songs in both chiTumbuka and chiChewa (Kerr 2004). The message of the play becomes clear: feelings of superiority are sustained by a lack of knowledge and tolerance. Listening to the other side's arguments, thus getting to know them and their culture, leads to a situation in which differences may be accepted and problems solved.

Conclusion

One could argue that these particular students are exceptionally talented and devoted. The students are undoubtedly talented. But, in addition, there is a great need to speak out; and this is combined with the ability of a self-confident generation to do so – less constrained by notions of prescribed political and sexual behaviour than earlier generations, and this makes the students not only freer in expressing a character, but also in giving room to sometimes outrageously hilarious creative drama. The young people push their theatrical talents to the limit and play with the audience. They provoke the audience to respond and thus participate in the shaping of the performance event. They have, in fact, adapted Jerzy Grotowsky's (1991 [1968]) concept of 'Poor Theatre' to the Malawian condition by transforming the material constraints into an aesthetic concept of an actor-centred theatre.

BIBLIOGRAPHY

Grotowski, Jerzy, 1991 [1968], *Towards A Poor Theatre*. (London: Methuen Drama).
Kerr, David, 1998, *Dance, Media Entertainment & Popular Theatre in South East Africa* (Bayreuth: Bayreuth African Studies).
Kerr, David, 2000, 'Sexual Abuse and Gender Conflict: The Experience of a Play Creation Process at The University of Botswana,' *Journal of Dramatic Theory and Criticism*, vol. xv, no. 1: 121–35.
Kerr, David, 2004, *Zonse Nkukambirana/Vyonse Nkhudumbirana (It's all about Dialogue)*, Unpublished programme notes for non-chiChewa and non-chiTumbuka-speaking audience members, (Zomba).
Magalasi, Mufunanji, 2001, *Beyond the Barricades: A Collection of Contemporary Malawian Plays* (Zomba: Chancellor College Publications).

African Youth, Performance & the HIV/AIDS Epidemic
Theatre of Necessity

ESIABA IROBI

HIV/AIDS Virus: *I kill, therefore, I am*

The only time the world has seen anything like this was in the 15th century, during the Bubonic plague. One third of Europe's population died. (Bono, lead singer of U2, [Interviewed 28 November 2003 at HIV/AIDS Global Initiative Concert in Cape Town, South Africa])

Dolorous knot
Plead for me
Farm or hill
Plead for me
Stream or wind
Take my voice
Home or road
Plead for me
On this shoot,
I bind your leaves
Stalk and bud
Berries three
On the threshold
Cast your voice
Knot of bitters
Plead for me
(Wole Soyinka, *Idanre and Other Poems*, New York: Wang & Hill, 1968, p.23)

Unlike much postmodern theory, post-colonial theory often combines individual emotional commitment and outrage with defiant optimism. It is much more strident and activist than an acquiescent postmodernism. (Mark Fortier, *Theatre/Theory: an Introduction* (London: Routledge, 1994, p.136)

In this essay I want to examine the interface between theatrical performance as a life-affirming force on the continent and the challenge posed by the HIV/AIDS epidemic which has been projected to claim about 24 million African lives by the middle of the twenty-first century. By the year 2003 HIV/AIDS had already killed 17 million Africans, most of them children and young adults. As I write, 70 per cent of all the adults and 80 per cent of all the children who are HIV positive in the world are Africans. The most endangered are the 12 million African children orphaned by AIDS; those who have nobody, whose relatives, extended families and prospective guardians have already been erased by the virus, children for whom, 'what others make of life will pass them by',[1] as Derek Walcott, the Caribbean poet, puts it. The overall tragic prognosis is that these children are destined to die unless world governments, drug companies, politicians in both the rich Western countries and the impoverished African countries can work out a pragmatic programme for treating the infected, particularly the AIDS orphans for whom the beginning of life has now become the commencement of an agonizing death sentence.

My intention in this uneasy discourse is to light a candle, not to curse the darkness. By this I mean that I want to address ways in which African communities, especially the youth, are utilizing aspects of their indigenous festival and ritual theatre and much more contemporary performance forms such as theatre for development, popular music concerts, rap, spoken word, hip-hop culture, television drama, radio, the internet, video films, documentaries and the church – which now distributes rubber condoms to members of the congregation in many parts of Africa – to sensitize the world to the pain of a ravaged continent and also stem the onslaught of this dreadful plague by alerting other young people to the dangers that AIDS poses to their lives.

In her sensitive and moving book, *Playing for Life: Performance in Africa in the Age of AIDS*, Louise Bourgault pursues a line of interrogative scholarship by investigating how the positive aspects of globalization can contribute towards the reduction of the HIV/AIDS death toll in Africa. Globalization, she informs us,

> is the process of denationalization of a country's markets, labor, political and legal systems, and the rise of the global economy, greatly facilitated by supranational trade organizations and treaties such as the North American Free Trade Agreement (NAFTA), the European Union (EU), and the World Trade Organisation (WTO).[2]

In the humanities, she emphasizes, globalization refers to the process whereby individual lives and communities are affected by economic and cultural forces that operate world wide.

The question that now arises for the superpowers of the West is: Can Western nations value the quality of African life so much as to consider it worthy of being saved with the enormous capital presently diverted into military stock and warfare? What are the billions of dollars and medications doing in one part of a globalizing world when millions are dying in another part? Richard Schechner says that the question remains whether or not cultural globalization i.e. the hybridities and 'world styles' are really global. Are they the result of contributions made by many individuals and many cultures – or are they a sign of the increasing hegemony of the West, more specifically of the USA? And if the latter, is there anything that can be done about it? He asks: 'Will there also be a single value system based on 'human rights'? Will this lead to a general liberation or an ever-tightening interlocked surveillance and control operation – a kind of neo-medievalism? Is this global totalitarianism wearing gloves?'[3]

Bono, the lead singer of U2, the Irish rock group, and a tireless political activist, had this to say after visiting two South African maternity wards reserved for HIV-positive mothers and their newborn children – at the time of Bono's visit, neither mothers nor infants were on medication. They were all destined to die from HIV/AIDS:

> It is absolutely unacceptable on any level that we have drugs in the West, in Europe and America, drugs which cost nothing to produce, after the research in the laboratory, costs nothing, and there are thousands of children, women and men, nurses, teachers and farmers dying without us sharing these drugs - that have cost us little to produce – with them. What that says about us, I dread to think. And how history will judge us … And history may judge us hard … God even harder… This is an obscenity. It is like watching Jews being put on trains.[4]

The occasion was Saturday, 29 November 2003, at Greenpoint Stadium in Cape Town when Nelson Mandela had used his popularity as a prisoner of conscience and his prison number 46664 as a code to invite thirty musicians from all over the world to launch a global initiative aimed at raising global awareness to fight HIV/AIDS – the largest pandemic the world has ever faced. The concert played to a crowd of 40,000 and was beamed out to 2 billion people all over the world via television, radio and the internet. The money raised by the event went into providing drugs and medication to HIV/AIDS patients in South Africa. The musicians, apart from performing, made memorable comments about how the rich Western countries, the G8 and other superpowers have ignored the spreading epidemic. Bono commented that the last time there was a health crisis like this was in the fifteenth century, during the Bubonic plague in which one third of Europe's population died. He then asked: 'Imagine if the Chinese had had some sort of treatment for that Bubonic Plague and hadn't shared it out because it was difficult and expensive [to do so]. How would the history books judge the Chinese? How would we be reading about them, that is, imagining that they were us right now.'[5] Yvonne Chaka Chaka, a South African musician, said that 'AIDS is no longer a disease, but a human rights issue.'[6] Anastacia, an American pop singer said: 'I am embarrassed that we have let it get this far.'[7] Bob Geldof, the Irish musician who championed the concert to raise funds for victims of famine in Ethiopia in the eighties summed it all up in terms of how the AIDS crisis symbolizes the litmus test of the responsibilities of the rich West to the rest of the so-called developing world in the age of globalization. He said: 'Nelson Mandela whose life … represents the fight for justice through political action has come to the correct conclusion that AIDS is not a medical condition but a political one and that the only way the scourge can be defeated is by concerted political action.'[8] Bono concurred by saying that no matter how much money the rich pop stars pour into the fundraising for AIDS patients, the terrifying predicament needs governmental leadership all over the world. He mentioned names such as Tony Blair and George Bush.

Song, dance and music are now the primary media for sensitizing the world to what needs to be done to stop the plague. Addressing the HIV/AIDS epidemic through collective performance powered by music for a global community, as made possible by Nelson Mandela and a group of young South Africans in November 2003, is one such function. It is, then, with this theoretical insight and framework about the *functionality* of African performance and theatre, and the risks that children and the youth face that I will now give a brief summary of the techniques that artists, young theatre practitioners, community organizers, political activists and orphaned performers are using all over the African continent to combat the epidemic.

The Theatre of Necessity

Apparently what the AIDS crisis has created on the African continent is a Theatre of Necessity. This theatre is about survival. It is a form of performance which responds to a collective crisis. It draws its impulses and semiological constructs from the past – from elements and fragments of indigenous African ritual and festival theatre – in order to address, confront and transform the life-threatening situation of the present. It seeks to re-order dislocated worldviews and balm the fissures in culturally, psychologically and spiritually splintered minds, young and old, on the continent. It aims to heal the increasing wounds of modernity on the African psyche. Conceptually and performatively it is a world apart from what happens in the West End in London or on Broadway in New York. It is rather a theatre of cultural essentials in which puppetry, ritual, carnival, festivity, masquerades, quilts, music, dance, pop concerts, agit-prop, television drama and broadcasts, video documentaries, interviews and HIV/AIDS-ravaged bodies play far more important and efficacious roles than the theatre of 'dodge the furniture and say your lines', in other words, the theatre of cherry orchards and three sisters and mamma mias and lion kings and cats and the Jerry Springer Opera.

'Theatre of Necessity' is a term coined by Werewere Liking, the Camerounian theatre practitioner who lives in Côte d'Ivoire, to contextualize a contemporary practice on the continent which deploys indigenous African performance forms – children's games, funeral and coronation ceremonies, initiation rituals, festival structures, processions, healing rites, war chants, dances, storytelling, oral poetry, incantations, songs, music, drumming, mime, African epics – to address the vicissitudes of the present which include the cultural schizophrenia created by globalization and the HIV/AIDS pandemic. In an interview Werewere Liking explains the ethos of her work:

> I come from a culture where the role of the artist is not very different from that of the priest ... that's also why I am called a priestess..., I would hope that my art could intrigue the mind as well as clothe or nourish the body, excite and calm, provide a balm for broken hearts, as well as a piquant antidote against fear and those weak knees that fear always engenders... My first motivation is thus the awakening of consciences and desires for constructive action ... *in this African continent where*

> *everything is set up to maintain people, especially young people, in this state of frivolity and inconstancy which leads to consumption and dependency.*[9] (emphasis mine)

Werewere Liking is talking here about globalization and the culture of consumerism that it engenders on the continent. Having stated the purpose of her art, she goes on to say who it is for. It is for 'little kids, for weavers of cotton, for whiskered chins and hardened heels'. She now addresses the unique nature of the aesthetics of her art:

> My art is varied and open, eclectic and generous. This is why I speak of an aesthetics of necessity capable of including volumes for those who only have a sense of touch, scents for those who only have a sense of smell, colors for those who only have their sights, sounds for those who only have their hearing... *My highest priority needs are those of young people and more particularly those who are deprived.* There are the needs of their education, of culture, of knowledge, of new openings, as well as personal adventures susceptible to awakening other creative impulses in them in the face of my own, so that all of the young people and children here may be able to dream and carry out their dreams, to take off from their initial level to attain any level of their own thirst, knowing that in turn, they can create their own paradise or hell, that the choice is in their hands and they are therefore responsible for themselves... Necessity means progress: the necessity of taking responsibility for one's actions represents, in fact, a genuine power.[10] (emphasis mine)

Werewere Liking has created the Ki Yi Pan-African Centre for Training and Creation, an artistic commune, to train more and more young people and even the general public to make efficacious theatre, including theatre for development, which addresses issues such as the HIV/AIDS epidemic in Africa and uses performance to educate young people on how to stop themselves from being infected by the virus. The Ki Yi 'laboratory' (*Ki* means ultimate, *Yi* means knowledge) was started in 1985 and has laboured on since then with scanty and sporadic financial assistance from concerned individuals and organizations. It is now a foundation which allows African artists from different countries to have a space in which to live, to work, and to carry out permanent exchanges, enabling them to obtain a satisfactory level to compete on an international scale, yet be based in Africa. Werewere Liking's Ki Yi M'bock Theatre collective (*M'bock* means universal) has toured different parts of the world with productions written, devised and directed by Liking. A powerful and perhaps representative example of their work is *The Marriage of a Pygmy and a Tuareg* which uses performance art, multimedia, intertextuality and African ritual aesthetic to perform a fantasy of a marriage between a North African nomadic man and a Central African hunting/gathering woman as a catharsis for an ailing, morally dissolute, African body politic. These productions, it needs saying, are very complex, avant-garde, polyvalent, almost postmodern and have been compared with Artaud's, Mnouchkine's and Brecht's works. Liking explains that she had not heard of these European practitioners until her work was compared with theirs. She only read them thereafter and explains that her work derives from a lot of research into indigenous African ritual theatrical forms and epistemologies. In response to the question about how one can make the link between the African ancestral tradition as she presents it and that which we consider modern, experimental or avant-garde, she answered:

> When I observe things closely, I note that the past of Africa is the future of the world in matters of artistic creation. I say to myself, 'Ah that's it.' Our traditions are reborn elsewhere and are called modern. Which means, that for once, Africa is ahead. One finds the Surrealists in our oral and plastic arts for example. ... that's why I created the museum here in the village. In the teachings here, we call the museum our 'School of the Gaze'. We see in this school the audacity of the gaze as expressed in the objects of our traditional plastic arts ... we see fabulous, extraordinary forms, and we see that there was at some point a tremendous rupture between the universe inhabited by the creators of this art and the one in which we now live. And this rupture was all the more serious as it was a spiritual one ... we lost contact with the divine vibration that drove us towards our deep spirituality. This rupture ... was [caused] first of all [by] the slave trade, and then, colonization. This represents almost four hundred years of rupture...For Africa, this led to enormous repercussions in the relation to the divine. Our objects were emptied of their meaning. [11]

The discourse reminds us of the impact of slavery, colonization, modernity and now globalization on African cultures and African creativity. I have embarked on this historical and epistemological archaeology just to highlight that the Theatre of Necessity, as a postcolonial theory of African theatrical practise and performance is, both in conception and as practised by Werewere Liking and the Ki Yi M'Bock Theatre, philosophically profound and aesthetically sophisticated.

I emphasize this because, later, I extend the term Theatre of Necessity to include less complicated forms of performance that are used primarily by young people in Africa to respond to the HIV/AIDS crisis.

Werewere Liking continues:

> The teachings of the Ki Yi M'Bock which come from the Bassa of Cameroun, were, according to my great aunt, teachings that respond to a crisis. She explained that when she received this teaching it was already folklore, everything had been wiped out by colonization. It was all regarded as tales, ancestor's stories, oral art. It was necessary to rediscover the teachings, it took me four years to formulate and transcribe information that was entirely in my head. I had to reduce it to an essential minimum, to one concept per page with concrete examples. I am today the only person in the world who can perpetuate this 'ultimate universal knowledge'. ... I am therefore the *Ntorol Tchorot* or the one who wakens the stars. *The children who live here and who are given this teaching are the stars who, when the time comes, will transmit this knowledge to others.*[12] (emphasis mine)

Some of the children Werewere Liking talks about, who live and learn with her in the Ki Yi Pan-African Centre for Training and Creation in Côte d'Ivoire are, or may in the near future, become HIV-positive. Liking's hope and her super-objective is that by giving these children a holistic upbringing and philosophy for life: spiritually, politically, creatively and performatively, they will become vehicles of Ki Yi wisdom which are perhaps encapsulated in this quote:

African Youth, Performance & the HIV/AIDS Epidemic 37

> ... I would like humans to be more fraternal , I revolt against their quarrelling, their egotism, their lack of community spirit.... In the West, this type of organization is necessarily financed by the State. As for us, we threw ourselves into our work following our own need ... once more a case of necessity creating an aesthetic.[13]

A predominant aesthetic or indigenous African performance form that Liking utilizes in many of her plays is the traditional orature of the M'vet, the epic drama style of the Beti people of Cameroun. Apparently, in Werewere Liking's youth, there were great bards who would come and present epic poems in her paternal grandparents' courtyard whenever any major life event occurred. It was an art that fascinated her at the time. Later on she encountered the epic creations of other cultural regions as well as the work of African intellectuals who contemplated and studied the form. In her own words:

> I was also able to read the extraordinary M'vet stories of Tsira Ndonog and others. I can therefore affirm that I had many opportunities to become interested in the epic arts of various African regions and I find that they contain extraordinary riches in terms of imagination. *This is I why I continuously return to this source, because the youth of urban Africa are extremely disconnected from their roots, impoverished.* [14] (emphasis mine)

Other Forms of Theatre of Necessity on the Continent

In many other parts of Africa, the Theatre of Necessity, which is aimed at the education and rehabilitation of HIV-positive adults and children is less overtly philosophical, yet this urgent variation of Theatre of Necessity often created by young people, theatre groups, concerned artists, musicians, AIDS orphans and adults, originates from the same guiding principle Werewere Liking articulates above. This is theatre which is immediate and functional. It is far from the frothy opiates in the West which people pay large amounts of money to see, ensconced in plush seats and air-conditioned theatres, on Broadway or in the West End. It is a theatre which is about the recovery and redeployment of indigenous and traditional, i.e. pre-modern, African knowledge and epistemologies of art, performance and communality, as a response to a societal crisis, which, without this aggressive performative resistance, can culminate in the annihilation of an entire continent.

In Uganda, one of the East African countries heavily affected by HIV/AIDS – out of a population of 22 million people, one and half million are children orphaned by AIDS – there are two major institutions which use government funding as well as performance to fight the disease. TASO (The AIDS Support Organization) in Kampala takes care of adults living with AIDS by giving them medication, advice, support, since they are stigmatized and ostracized by the larger community, and space to develop a sense of community through performance. TASO has a choir which entertains people publicly at social occasions but all its members, mainly women, are patients living with AIDS in their individual homes and community. The coming together and singing and dancing becomes a Theatre of Necessity that affords the women some measure of solidarity and communal consolation as well as therapy to deal with the psychological trauma of living with the HIV/AIDS virus.[15]

The Meeting Point is another organization in Kampala, Uganda, also funded by a government organization, that looks after children orphaned by HIV/AIDS. The centre provides the children with rent, medication, education, adult support, and, most importantly, a forum for drama, theatre, performance via drumming, singing, dance, mime and skits which help the children overcome the trauma of loss when any of them succumbs to the virus. One of the most moving performances one can see at The Meeting Point, is a hymn to Death enacted by these orphans, imploring Death not to prey on any of them anymore. These performers range in age from 5 to 16 years old. Sex education is an intrinsic aspect of the training that the children acquire at the centre and cautionary lessons about premarital sex constitute a compulsory aspect of the primary school curriculum in Uganda today.[16]

In neighbouring Kenya, the major medium used to conscientize the youth about the consequences of contracting the HIV/AIDS virus is music. Both adult and adolescent musicians are putting out CDs and tapes studded with songs which warn against unprotected sex. Most powerful in the crusade has been rap music, an aspect of hip hop culture, that has had a pervasive influence on the lives on young people living in the country in the age of the epidemic.

In Mali, a country with a rich tradition of epics, griots, kora music, recitation and other forms of orature, the radio and television have been powerful media for communicating the messages about HIV/AIDS to a largely illiterate – in the Western sense – Muslim population. Cartoons have also been deployed to educate the literate – in the Western sense – middle class. But most powerful has been puppetry and street theatre which use animal characters and masks from Malian fables and folktales to dramatize how to avoid contracting the virus. Bourgault's book mentioned above, *Playing for Life: Performance in Africa in the Age of Aids*, deals exhaustively with the different techniques of performative intervention used in this West African country and is highly recommended as a reference.

In South Africa, a country with 250,000 AIDS orphans (Bourgault cites figures as of 2000) and highly developed traditions of both indigenous and modern theatre, numerous youth theatre and performance groups use the Zulu war dance, gum boot dance, bilingual songs, dramatic skits, full-length plays, television drama as part of the arsenal of Theatre of Necessity to stem the spread of the HIV virus. Popular in this campaign are Soul City Dramatic Television series; Eager Artists – a post-apartheid theatre group – whose *Free Birds* is a bi-national theatrical extravaganza addressing the AIDS issue; dramAIDE who introduce young audiences to comrade banana and comrade condom; men's singing groups who combine acapella music with fascinating feet and hands movements to deliver the crucial message of safe sex to both adult and young audiences; gospel choirs and pop groups whose stars feature in television programs, adverts and video documentaries, all aimed at galvanizing the society into confronting and reversing the onslaught of the pandemic.

The final example of 'Theatre of Necessity' on the continent focuses again on East Africa and involves the chronicles of Lynn Cottage, an African American playwright from Brooklyn, USA, during a recent trip to the continent. Her disturbing narrative gives us a deep and critical insight into the interface between the HIV/AIDS epidemic on the African continent, wars caused by arbitrary boundaries drawn inside pre-colonial nations by European colonizers, globalization, and the beauty of resistance through forms of performance that draw from indigenous traditions to address the existential crises of the present.

Cottage travelled to Central Africa in 2005 in pursuit of an idea centered around creating a play about the lives of women and girls caught in the middle of the devastating armed conflict in the Democratic Republic of Congo. However, a conjuction of unpredictable events brought her to Kampala, Uganda, where she wanted to see some contemporary theatre. She decided, alongside her husband and friends from the USA, to spend the night at the Buhoma Community campsite which is run by local villagers. They later discover that it is one of the sites where eight tourists and six park rangers were murdered in 1999 by Rwandan guerrillas. Later in the evening, amidst lively discussions and *waragi*, the local beer, she learns, from the Ugandan officials, about the death toll from both AIDS and the civil conflict in the area. As Cottage puts it, once she starts to ask the questions, their demeanor instantly shifts, a pall of darkness descends, and their eyes turn to stone. 'We used to go to a funeral once a day, now we go every other day, that's progress!'[18] is the response she gets from Bwiza Charity Joy, programme manager of the Forest Conservation Trust. Then, as if on cue, a parade of 50-odd orphan children, ranging in age from 4 to 18, dressed in rough-hewn traditional costumes, march in procession onto the campsite lawn, transforming the grassy space into a stage.[19] 'The orphaned children treat the tourists to a rather striking and unexpected theatrical event' consisting of 'beautiful praise songs, indigenous courtship dances, delivered with such pride, joy and exuberance that it is impossible to resist their charm'[20] or the resultant heave of emotions attendant to all such spectacles of beauty and the horrors of war and disease. After the performance, which lasts a little less than an hour, the children then exhibit their handicrafts. They are inmates of the Bwindi orphanage, where they are taught traditional handicrafts, as well as songs, dances and stories. The goal is to restore their self-esteem and preserve the history and performance traditions of the region.[21] Apparently the children are victims of war and AIDS from which their parents also died. Despite these terrifying beginnings, these orphans are representative of a professional performance troupe of 20 orphans called Children of Uganda who will tour the US to raise awareness about the AIDS crisis and funds for the Uganda Children's Charity Foundation.[22] After witnessing another emotionally devastating performance near Lake Bunyonyi, on the border of Rwanda, in a remote Batwa (pygmy) refugee camp, Cottage observes that the Batwa who had fled to the Ugandan side of the border after much of their clan was wiped out by Rwandan soldiers have been 'reduced to the lowest echelon of Ugandan culture and are now forced to beg and perform for their very survival.'[23]

The Batwa performance becomes an exercise in burial ground humour as well as a collective defiance to death. The dislocated Batwa community perform even though their elderly leader is freshly dead and buried beneath a massive pile of stones in the centre of the shanty settlement. The performance, energetic and powered by song and dance, is initiated by the elderly leader's daughter, who, with a single wave of the hand, insists that: 'The Show Must Go On!' And symbolic, if not symptomatic of the African continent itself, the performance goes on while the body of the Batwa elder and leader decomposes in a corner of the performance space. Later, Cottage and her friends are tempted to go and see a 'real' show at the National Theatre of Uganda but decide against it. In her own words: 'The idea of a conventional evening of theatre seems less than inspiring after all we've experienced.'[24] She, then, sums up the significance of the entire sobering, cross-cultural, theatrical experience:

> When all is quiet and the night sky complete, we're left to ponder our complicated feelings about the theatrical presentation(s). I can't quite place my discomfort. After a couple of *waragi,* I realize that it is because it is theatre of necessity, a kind of performance tradition that we don't often encounter in the United States. Theatre of necessity is a ritualized performance event designed for audiences seeking authenticity and purity of indigenous culture. Economic reality necessitates that indigenous people like the Bwindi orphans exploit their own culture in order to survive. Some aspects of traditional cultures will only survive because they have been theatricalized for audiences seeking authenticity. The reality of the situation is that certain indigenous rituals are exoticized and packaged for consumption and drained of their original meaning – but as in the case of the orphan children, that doesn't mean that the beauty and cultural resonance is entirely diminished. Theatre of necessity is perhaps the fastest growing and most prevalent form of indigenous theatre throughout the third world, yet it is rarely discussed.[25]

Why is it not discussed? It is not discussed in the West or its academies, first, because Western capitalism has made training for, and the study of, mainstream theatre practice the fulcrum of both the academic curriculum and cultural life in the West. Secondly, teaching or giving too much attention to theatre of necessity will open a window on to the complicity of Western governments and corporate organizations in the civil wars which are fomented and facilitated by gun-running officers of the CIA and other private businessmen from Europe and the rest of the Western world. It will reveal that both the ammunitions procured by the West and the worsening HIV/AIDS crises which the G8 and other rich countries of the West have ignored are all part of what a lot of African scholars suspect is the latent agenda of globalization, namely, to eradicate the continent of its citizens, exterminate their children, and impose Western control of the mineral and material wealth of the dark continent.

Salih Booker and William Minter of Africa Action attribute Africa's inordinate share of the AIDS case-load to being largely a consequence of the economic policies of the Western world, policies based on economic rather than human considerations.[26] Access to life-saving drugs and access to care for people with HIV, the two scholars argue, is largely a matter of race, class, gender and geography. Globalization, based on the ideology of free trade and the magic of the price mechanism, as they see it, is a device for minority rule of the world's resources.[27]

It fosters a double standard that guarantees human rights, including the right to health, only to a privileged few and denies such rights to the rest of the world. Africa, they insist, operates in a system of global apartheid. Forty-four of the fifty countries in the world with life expectancies of less than fifty years are in Africa. Minter, Booker and Bourgault conclude by telling us that the US continues to refuse to ratify key UN declarations and conventions in the international human rights order, despite knowing that recognizing access to medication in the context of pandemics such as HIV/AIDS is one fundamental element of the right to health. They underscore, significantly, that the US, a major proponent of globalization, has stood alone in its position against the almost unanimous vote in the UN.[28]

NOTES

1 Derek Walcott, *Selected Poems* (London: Heinemann, 1981), p. 34.
2 Louise Bourgault, *Playing for Life: Performance in Africa in the Age of AIDS* (Durham, NC: Carolina Academic Press, 2003).
3 Richard Schechner, *Performance Studies: An Introduction* (New York: Rouledge, 2002), p. 232.
4 Bono, lead singer of the Irish band, U2, gave this interview on Friday 28 November in Cape Town, South Africa during the lead up to the Nelson Mandela Foundation 46664 AIDS awareness concert.
5 Same interview, 28 November 2003.
6 Ibid.
7 Ibid.
8 Ibid.
9 Interview with Werewere Liking in Abidjan, Ivory Coast on 2 June 2002; interviewed and translated by Michelle Meilly of Harvard University.
10 Ibid.
11 Ibid.
12 Ibid.
13 Ibid.
14 Ibid.
15 See the section titled '*The Spirit of Africa*', in the DVD 46664: Concert, a video documentary about resistance to the HIV/AIDS epidemic in Africa produced by the Nelson Mandela Foundation. Available from www.46664.com.
16 Same video documentary, 2003.
17 See the CD-Rom accompanying Louise Bougault's book.
18 See Lynn Cottage, 'Out of East Africa' in *American Theatre*, May/June, 2005, pp. 26–7 and 66–8.
19 Ibid, pp 66–8.
20 Ibid.
21 Ibid.
22 Ibid.
23 Ibid.
24 Ibid.
25 Ibid.
26 Cited in Bourgault, p.260.
27 Ibid.
28 Ibid., p. 261.

Young People's Drama & Social Action in Northern Nigeria
A case study of the Zaria 'For Tomorrow...' Project

OGA STEVE ABAH
with FAITH, MAHMUD & NUHU

Introduction

This article describes the way Theatre for Development (TfD) has been used to address adolescent health issues in Nigeria. The article is organized in four parts. The first section gives a brief overview of the Nigerian Popular Theatre Alliance (NPTA) and the Zaria project, which forms the focus of the article. The project is titled, 'For Tomorrow: Adolescent Health and Education Issues'. In this first section, we outline the aims, method of work and outcomes of the project so far.

In the second section, we present one of the project's scenarios titled 'Jummai' and we discuss the practical use of the play to create awareness, involve audience in the 'writing' of the play and in generating the knowledge that makes informed choices possible. The play that the young people developed in the course of the project captures adolescent peer pressure and its consequences.

In the third and fourth sections, three young people who have been part of the project provide accounts of their personal lives, their involvement in the project and their vision for the future for young people in Nigeria.

In writing this article, we have played different parts. Oga Abah's role has mainly been to provide the background to the project, analyse some of the key issues emerging from the project and to try weave a narrative thread through the accounts of the young people's own stories. We acknowledge the contribution of Blessing Uzo, a Programme Officer with the project, who did the initial editing of the accounts by the three young people.

1. The Nigerian Popular Theatre Alliance and the Zaria 'For Tomorrow...' project

The Nigerian Popular Theatre Alliance (NPTA) was founded in 1989, at the end of a one-week workshop that brought together theatre practitioners, and cultural and communication workers in the Drama Village at Ahmadu Bello University, Zaria.

The mission of NPTA is *'the promotion of participatory development through the use of TFD and other communication strategies to build the capacity of NGOs, CBOs, women's groups and institutions'*. In order to do this, NPTA conducts research, runs training programmes and engages in community outreach workshops. All of these activities are for the purpose of contributing to, and influencing, transformative actions among its beneficiaries.[1]

Since its founding sixteen years ago, it has undertaken twelve major projects. These projects have been in different parts of Nigeria and were on community development, women's health, HIV/AIDS, capacity building, democracy and good governance, conflict and security, and poverty reduction. In the execution of these projects, two characteristics have been prevalent:

1. The approach was participatory, in which *animateurs* and the community shared knowledge, engaged in collective analysis and made drama on the issues together. The actors in these dramas were drawn from the membership of the communities where we worked.
2. The second feature was the use of Theatre for Development [TfD] as a tool of information gathering, analysis and discussion.

The 'For Tomorrow...' Project: Adolescent Health and Education Issues

The 'For Tomorrow...' project focuses on adolescent boys and girls in and out of secondary schools. It therefore has two groups of primary beneficiaries: students in secondary school and school drop-outs, or non-attenders as they are known on the project. The term 'non-attenders' is a less negative one that is less prejudicial than 'drop-outs', which has come to carry a whole baggage of connotations that are far from positive. 'For Tomorrow...' is a collaborative project between NPTA, the Second Chance Organization of Nigeria (SECON) and the Play House, a British non-governmental organization, based in Birmingham.

SECON is a non-profit national organization founded in 1996. The organization engages in the promotion of girls' education by focusing attention on factors that hamper girls and women's progress in society, such as traditional/cultural biases against girls, and unwanted pregnancies. One of its main actions is advocacy with schools and government ministries on the issue of giving a second chance to young girls and boys who have dropped out of school. Since its set-up in 1996, SECON's activities continue to include training on adolescent reproductive health, gender, peer counselling and advocacy skills for the adolescents themselves. It also runs workshops to educate the public on matters of concern for women and adolescents, especially the importance of education for girls. Prior to this project, it collaborated with NPTA to make a video film, *Onya's Passage,* which focuses on forced marriage, prostitution and AIDS. Although SECON is national in scope, its activities have so far concentrated in Kaduna and Plateau States. The organization has its headquarters in Zaria.

The Play House is a non-profit organization that engages in work in schools in Birmingham and other cities in the Midlands in England, UK. Its activities have largely focused on young people's health and safety. It delivers projects through its associated programmes, Catalyst Theatre and Language Alive! The Play House is Birmingham's first Healthy Living Centre.

The collaboration with the Play House had been gestating since 1992, when the first contact was made. Oga Abah was invited to present a paper at the Play House's first international workshop on theatre in health education, and since that time the two organizations dreamed of working together. This present project was conceived collectively, and funded by the Lottery Fund, UK, through the Play House.

The 'For Tomorrow…' project works in six schools in Zaria, Kaduna State, and four in Jos, Plateau State. In each of these locations, it works with one group of non-attenders. Overall, the project has three main objectives, with a further action agenda:

- To give young people access to correct information about sex, relationships and reproductive health.
- To train adolescents in peer education and peer counselling so that they can negotiate relationships and resist peer pressure that might otherwise lead them into trouble.
- To challenge the attitudes of parents, the school authorities and the educational establishment about adolescent health issues.
- In the action agenda, to engage in advocacy activities with schools, ministries and relevant social institutions for the promotion of sex education in schools and for the reintegration of non-attenders back into the school system.

The 'For Tomorrow…' project therefore taps into the range of skills and expertise between the three collaborating organizations. Both NPTA and the Play House make use of theatre as a tool, while SECON brings into the project the medical experience of its members in community medicine and adolescent sexuality. NPTA is well known as the premiere organization for the use of participatory methodology, especially its use of Theatre for Development (TfD). It has in the last sixteen years been using TfD as a research tool, as an instrument for generating debate through community performance and as a means of holding conversations across cultures and religions, that constitute both fault lines and conflict areas in Nigeria. On this project, NPTA has used the intervention technique in Forum Theatre, in particular to problematize issues of girls' education, reproductive health, 'dropping out' and subsequent reintegration into the school system. NPTA has done this with parents, teachers, religious leaders and government ministries. It has also explored the critical question of peer pressure and influence through the **c**hoices, **d**ecisions and **c**onsequences triangle [CDC]. In combination with Forum, CDC presents an elaborate system of exploration and analysis based on the understanding that in every situation there are **choices** to be made; **decisions** to be taken, and **consequences** to be lived through (whether positive or negative).

In working with the in-school students and the non-attenders, we would pick up on their stories of peer pressure to take drugs, alcohol or to engage in sex. The story is played out and brought to a point at which a critical decision is taken. The action is frozen and an analysis of the situation is undertaken. The different outcomes of the choices that the character decides upon are performed, debated and their merits examined. This is very much in the mode of Boal's 'Forum Theatre' (Boal 1974). This manner of processing the actions of the target participants allowed us to understand the issues and pressures the students face. We also came to appreciate why the non-attenders in the project dropped out of school. The technique is very participatory as it requires that participants engage in the debate of plausible alternative decisions, perform those outcomes and carry out an analysis of the situations. It is also a knowledge-creating mechanism as everyone involved begins to see new dimensions and perspectives to the many issues the adolescents confront.

The technique of Forum Theatre and 'jokering' combine neatly with the Theatre in Education (TIE) approach of the Birmingham Play House. Since its formation in 1991, the Play House has forged a reputation as a leader in this field. One of its main areas of expertise is Theatre in Health Education. The Play House devises interactive drama performances and programmes for children and young people. These programmes create dilemmas and raise questions on sensitive issues of concern to young people on drugs, sexual health or preparation for parenthood. Perhaps the difference in approach between NPTA and the Play House is that while the former engages with the beneficiaries to make their own plays, the latter takes the Theatre in Education (TIE) route. Nonetheless, the meeting point for the organizations are the issues and to a certain extent the interest in participation.

SECON constantly validated or demystified the medical truth or otherwise of the stories that formed the drama. The debate was around the myths that young people believed in and acted upon; and this debate also involved the larger groups that watched the performances in schools and designated community spaces. SECON was useful in the collaboration for its knowledge of, and experience in, health issues, education and gender inequalities that young teenage girls and boys face in Nigeria. The project's approach is therefore a synergy of experiences, knowledge and practices around adolescent sexuality that all three organizations have built over the years.

The training workshops in schools for (1) the students; (2) the guidance and counselling teachers; and (3) the non-attenders outside of the school environment, provided the ground for experience-sharing. For example, in each of the first two years of the project, Juliet Fry and Deborah Hull, both from the Play House, were in Zaria and Jos respectively. NPTA and SECON learned from them and they learned from both organizations.

Over the last two years, the project has worked with ten secondary schools and two groups of non-attenders in Jos in Plateau State and Zaria in Kaduna State. In each of the ten schools (six in Zaria and four in Jos), fifteen students were selected as the core group to be trained, totalling 150. It is this group that puts the drama together and performs for the school. The group in each school has further responsibility to train other students, and act as peer educators and counsellors. We worked with 30 non-attenders, fifteen each in Zaria and Jos. We estimate that the secondary beneficiaries, in and out of school, that the project has reached number about 20,000.

In selecting the students in the schools, we agreed on a number of criteria as follows:

- Students should be selected across the five years, i.e., classes 1–5. This was to ensure that the trained students still had a minimum of two years in school. Selecting students from each class was to ensure that students had someone from their own class to talk to whenever they needed.
- The second criterion was that students should be involved in the selection process. The project did not want the participating students to be merely the teachers' favourites but more importantly students that their peers trusted and saw as good role models, whom they could listen to and have enough confidence in to talk about their problems.
- Non-attenders were selected on the basis of their experiences and willingness to tell their stories so that other young people could learn from them.

At the time of writing we are entering the third and last year of the project from April 2005 to March 2006. In this last year, we will consolidate the gains of the first two years and explore strategies for sustainability. The external evaluation of the project done at the end of the two years suggested that there was a high level of buy-in by both schools and Ministry officials of the Ministries of Education and Health, especially in Plateau State. One of the key explorations in the last year of the project will therefore be the possibility of mainstreaming sex education in the school curriculum. The evaluation reveals that many students attest to the ways in which they have moved from a state of ignorance to that of knowledge on many issues around their sexual health and its interrelation with their educational career (Obono 2004). For this reason, the TfD methodology for knowledge and attitude change in the schools will run through the remaining period of the project.

Method of Work

In order to talk to our multiple audiences and stakeholders, the project has adopted multiple approaches. These are: (1) to investigate the issues of concern, i.e. the level of knowledge of sexual health information; (2) the incidents of dropping out and the position of schools on reintegrating non-attenders into the school system and (3) the general public's attitude to young people who have dropped out of school.

First, we began with a baseline survey using such techniques as focused group discussion, key informant interviews and participant observation. A number of notable facts emerged from the baseline survey that reflected the state of adolescent health and education issues in the two project locations:

- There was a general lack of knowledge of their reproductive selves by both young girls and boys;

- Parents were reluctant and very shy to discuss sex issues with their children;
- The prevailing attitude was that of a lack of sympathy by both parents and the general public to the plight of adolescents dropping out of school;
- The schools endorsed the draconian Ministry of Education rule that students who get pregnant should be expelled and that such students are no longer re-admissible in their own schools;
- The records about who had dropped out of school and for what reason were scanty to non-existent. The general attitude was that of good riddance to anyone walking away from school as the population was more than the schools had facilities for, anyway!

These were the key concerns that the project addressed in the training sessions, in the scenario development stages and at performances and the debates that followed. The training targeted three sets of stakeholders: the student peer educators and counsellors in the schools, the non-attenders, and the guidance and counselling teachers in schools. One of the skills learned at the training is drama-making, which provides the opportunity for all the participants to understand how to 'read' the situations, as well as make drama out of their experiences. In addition to drama skills, participants also learned other techniques such as 'letter-writing' about their traumas, 'hot-seating' – that is, the art of interrogating issues – and also 'jokering' from Augusto Boal's Forum Theatre practice.

The particular genres of drama we have used in this project have been a blend of TfD and Theatre in Education (TIE). These approaches are participatory as well as democratic in nature. The process of collective creation that characterizes TfD and the interactive interrogation of the Play House's TIE method means that all participants involved in delivering the project are active in making decisions on what the content should be. They are also part of analysing and remaking the drama. In this process, everybody counts, and what became prominent was catalysing and facilitation rather than a system of directorial ownership. As a result, everyone had an opportunity to contribute to the process. In addition to the practical delivery of the project in schools and communities, the decision-making process to determine the activities and assess the project's performance is by a steering committee drawn from all stakeholder groups. Herein lies the democracy of the process.

In the context of exploring sensitive issues around sexuality and of telling personal stories, both the in-school students and the non-attenders found the drama approach to be a protective forum in which to engage in dialogue and discussions with the facilitators and with each other. When their issues were fictionalized as objective stories about someone else, they generally felt safe in exploring the complex details of the events without fear that they were exposing themselves. We noticed that the two-step remove from 'I' or 'we' to the third person pronoun of 'he' or 'she' allowed both the students and non-attenders to tell their own personal stories. We followed the fiction of the drama and explored the events in the characters' lives with a mutual, but

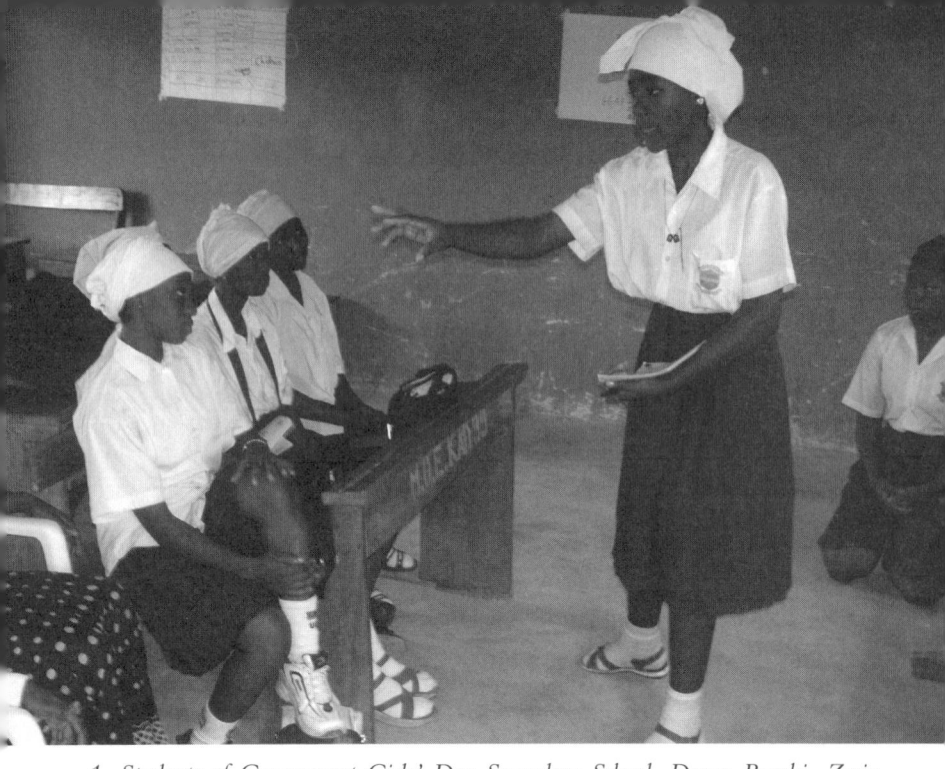

1. Students of Government Girls' Day Secondary School, Dogon Bauchi, Zaria performing intimidation and sexual harassment of students by teachers. (© Femi Douglas)

2. Two non-attenders, Nuhu and Ijudigal, introduce one of their friends to drugs. (© Oga Steve Abah)

undeclared, understanding that the stories were about the experiences of the adolescent participants.

However, in order to affirm that these were indeed the lived experiences of some of the participants, we always did a reality check on the fiction of the drama and asked for corroboration: Does this particular event we just saw in the drama happen in real life? Has any one here experienced something similar to what was in the drama? The answers we got were nearly always in the affirmative.

Drama performs several functions here. It builds confidence and promotes trust in participants. It also breaks down inhibitions. The characters are allies. What is critical and significant is the learning about themselves, their relationships and society's systems. This is embedded in the drama process itself: it proceeds from analysis through scenario-building to improvisation and performances.

The education and lessons learned come from the problematization of issues in which choices, decisions and consequences [CDC] are explored. An issue or problem is identified. The choices and options available to the protagonist are presented. The person then makes a choice and every choice has some consequences. All of CDC are played out in a drama skit. After this, the drama is thrown open for discussion and intervention so that all the other choices available in the circumstance are tried out and all the other consequences experienced. This process allows the participants to see the issue from different positions and to determine the most appropriate choice to make. The aim is to make the best choice in whatever circumstance one finds oneself.

2. The Play *Jummai*

The scenario that follows describes the drama-in-process approach rather than a finished product, either as a drama text or a performance. It is a combination of the Forum and CDC styles that generate debate and knowledge. The scenario is of the non-attenders' drama in Zaria. They devised the story by themselves from their personal life experiences. It was then toured round the project schools in Zaria.

The title of the play is Jummai:

Jummai is a young girl of about twelve just entering secondary school. She is beautiful, hard-working and full of morals and a determination to do what her parents had instructed. She attends class consistently and does all her assignments promptly. All these bring her to the attention of senior students, especially Talatu.

- Talatu is one of the key students in a gang of students who break rules and play truant to attend parties in town. She is the girlfriend of Kaballa Roller, one of the 'tough guys'. Disaster, another male member of the gang, is Kaballa Roller's friend. Talatu introduces Jummai to Disaster and pressurizes her to befriend him.

- Laraba (Larry Babe) is the most 'happening' girl in town. She throws a birthday party and the gang insists that Jummai must go, and takes her along in spite of all her protestations. At the party she is inducted into the lifestyle of Kaballa Roller and his group. She is prevailed upon to smoke cigarettes and marijuana and to drink. Because she is inexperienced, she gets drunk easily. Disaster takes her away and the rest of the story is easily imagined.

It is this imaginative rest and the implications that it has for Jummai that is explored in CDC and Forum. So what happens next? What happens next is the main concern of the drama, and it is during the interventions that this will unfold. That process of unfolding is the process of learning and sharing for adolescents.

Let us look at two bits of this exercise: We begin from scene one where Jummai has been introduced to Disaster. He turns on all his charm to impress her. Disaster invites Jummai to have breakfast with him (*Freeze and questions!*)

Question 1 – Should Jummai accept the offer? What are the *choices* available to Jummai now?

Responses from the audience:

In all the schools where this drama was performed and this system of interrogation of the issues was used, the replies we got aggregate to the following:

- To accept Disaster
- Refuse Disaster
- Join religious club
- To be alone
- Sever friendship with Talatu and her other friends

Are there any positive or negative consequences to each of the choices above? A whole range of answers emerged: If Jummai accepted Disaster, there would be the following *Advantages*:

- Jummai will enjoy a good life with Disaster
- Jummai will retain her friendship with Talatu
- Jummai will join the group of big boys and girls

Disadvantages:
- Jummai will no longer concentrate on her studies
- Jummai will become a bad girl
- Jummai may get pregnant or contract some terrible disease
- Jummai will lose her religious ways.

The joker/narrator carries the exercise to the next stage to let the audience know what choice Jummai has made.

Scene two of the scenario is where Disaster and friends cajole Jummai to the party and Disaster lures her into drinking and drugs. The choice that we see Jummai make in the drama (perhaps an unwilling choice), is to accept befriending Disaster and to attend the party in which she indulges in unfamiliar habits. Just before the last sequence of this scene, the Narrator asks: 'What do you think will happen to Jummai?' There are a number of responses:

- Disaster is going to rape Jummai
- Jummai is likely to get pregnant
- She might be infected with veneral disease or even HIV/AIDS

These responses highlight the consequences of Jummai's association with Talatu and her group of friends. It also paves the way for further discussion of the meaning of the drama. The issues that the participants always saw standing out as lessons from the exercise were the negative impact of peer pressure/ influence, bullying in school and the power play among students which indeed is the underlying factor of bullying.

'Hot seating': Questioning the psychology of misdeameanour

A further exploration of the issues in the drama was done in the 'hot seating' exercise. This is the exercise in which audience members pick on different characters and ask them questions about their motivation for engaging in certain actions in the play. In almost all the schools, the characters that the students wanted to talk to most were Disaster, Jummai, Talatu and Laraba who organized the party. Many of the questions were asked around what their reasons were, what they gained and how they felt about the different activities they engaged in outside of school work. The 'hot seating' exercise was very much a journey into the psychology of misdemeanour. Disaster, Talatu and Laraba all said that they wanted to have fun and that there was a lot of excitement in their non-routine school activities. Both Disaster and Laraba said they loved the power they had over younger students.

Forum Theatre: Challenging problems

At the end of this questioning of motives, Forum Theatre addressed how to challenge the issues of peer pressure and bullying, which led to alcoholism, drug use and incidents of unwanted pregnancies among students. A number of students went on stage and immersed themselves in the drama, acting out what they would do if they were Jummai. All the girls went on stage with the intention to reject Disaster's entreaties, to stand up to Talatu and Laraba. They did not always succeed as the 'bad' characters always put up brilliant performances and made sure they were stronger characters than those coming up to challenge their actions. However, some managed to reject Disaster's 'sweet nonsense' and Laraba's intimidation. Whenever a student in the role of Jummai defended her position and stood up against the trio of Disaster, Talatu and Laraba, her colleagues in the audience erupted into loud cheers of support and joy that a female had been assertive and not allowed herself to be deceived.

In exploring adolescent health issues, the reality that the CDC technique revealed was a mix of peer pressure, bullying, drug use, teenage pregnancy and dropping out from schools. We found that the process of discussion from inside the fiction of drama against the background of personal experiences opened the door to hear stories from students and especially the non-attenders. Nearly all

3. Yemisi, one of the non-attenders leading a forum discussion at a school performance
(© Oga Steve Abah)

of the female non-attenders the project has worked with, in both Jos and Zaria, dropped out of school because of an unwanted pregnancy. In the case of the male non-attenders, it was mostly due to drug use, getting schoolmates pregnant and some because of bullying other school mates or of being bullied. In Zaria for example, one of the non-attenders was known in the neighbourhood for laying in wait for girls to harass them. He also engaged in all manner of bullying his friends in school. The school authority was ready to throw him out when he left school of his own free will because he found no use for education!

Two factors constantly mentioned as being responsible for the mistakes of the young people are peer pressure and ignorance. We heard that the senior ones cajole many of the younger ones in the junior classes into doing things. Many such students are fresh from home where they have mostly been 'well-behaved' children listening to parental admonishment. So they often have few defences, and easily become victims.

The drama work, including the exercises of exploring issues and dilemmas through the CDC technique, Forum and 'Hot seating', also communicated with the parents and teachers, in addition to engaging the primary beneficiaries of the project. Very often, parents were ignorant of the pressures their children went through in school. Watching the performances and the follow-up exercises was enlightening for them. In June 2003, after a performance at the Government Girls' Secondary School in Samaru, by the non-attenders, one of the teachers exclaimed: 'I thought this girl was totally useless! I can't believe that this is Blessing! These girls must come back to school.' Blessing had fallen pregnant in her first year of secondary school and was expelled. The occasion of the performance of the drama by the non-attenders in her old school was the first opportunity to go back into the school in the two years since she left. Now she had the confidence to face staff and students in the school that had expelled her. She also came into the school with a knowledge that was different from her understanding as a first year student. It was this knowledge of the issues and factors responsible for the non-attendance of many girls and boys from school that she now came to share with her school. Blessing and her other non-attender group members became heroes in their former schools, not for dropping out, but for their bravery in coming back to tell their stories and to educate the other students and the school authority. In one of the secondary schools in Zaria one parent had made a confession before she realized when she said, 'So, this is how we have been neglecting issues concerning these children. God forgive us!'

These comments about Blessing are not so much about the acting abilities of the former student but about suddenly understanding the circumstances that led to the student's pregnancy and eventual expulsion. The project has begun to enlighten, change attitudes and draw out words of encouragement from policy-making institutions. A clear example of this was in 2003 when the Kaduna State Commissioner for Health after watching some of the project performances declared, 'I am an advocate of sex education in schools.'

3. Three non-attenders tell their stories: 'If we knew this before! But now that we know …'

Abah
Advocacy remains on a wish level. There is yet no official endorsement by either the Federal or State Ministries of Education for sex education to be taught in schools. Parents are still not sure whether the idea of sex education is good. The battle is between the morality of keeping young people clean and chaste on the one hand, and the reality that young girls and boys are taking actions on the basis of myths and half truths gleaned from friends and older people. There is also the confrontation between the belief that sex education promotes promiscuity among young people and the empirical evidence that indeed without sex education, young people are already engaged in sexual activities and that given the proper information, they would make informed choices.

This section provides accounts from three young people who dropped out of school for various reasons. Their stories describe a movement from ignorance to a more enlightened position and what they see as the gains from the 'For Tomorrow…' project. They wrote their stories themselves in a mixture of English and Pidgin. These were then modified and corrected. They have read through the corrected version, and they are happy that there is no distortion and have therefore endorsed them as their stories.

Mahmud's Story

Abah

Mahmud is now a 24-year-old young man. He quit his studies at Government Secondary School Idon Hanya, Kaduna State in Kajuru Local Government Area at the age of 15. He is from Kaduna State in the Northern part of Nigeria. As we will see in his account below, Mahmud was a well-known bully who was regarded as a monster by both the girls and boys in his school as well as people within and around his community. Everyone cried out against the terror meted out to them, their friends or their family members. Mahmud would waylay, Mahmud would rape, Mahmud would assault. According to him, by the time he heard of the 'For Tomorrow' project, he was already in a frustrated situation because there was nothing new to do any more. He was also frustrated because he lacked proper direction, good advice, firm support and positive influence. In his words, '*This project came just on time!*' A friend introduced him to one of the project staff who invited him for a talk and in the process introduced him to the project. At first he said, '*I thought they would send me back to school, train me and all. Contrary to my thoughts, they did not necessarily finance all of that. But I eventually got a lot more than that. The support and insight I had into the facts of life enhanced my desire to return to school. It also gave me a clearer focus not just for school, but for life*'. He says the drama method used for the project helped him to relax, learn lessons by doing things in the drama and it emboldened him to the extent that he became a drama facilitator at the end of the day. '*I found myself picking out the vices in my life by my own self. Nobody said Mahmud, you are a very bad boy.*' Mahmud now declares that he is a changed person. He tells us that even when tempting situations come around him, he finds that he can no longer recall those old traits and habits even if he wanted.

Mahmud

I dropped out of school in Junior Secondary III (JS 3) because I felt that going to school was a waste of time. When I dropped out of school everybody in the school was very happy because of how terrible I was at that time. Even the school authority could not control me; so everybody was very happy when I left the school. I smoked, drank, raped girls and did all kinds of bad things you can think of. At that time, the society could not even control me. My parents could not control me. I was just hanging around looking for trouble everywhere. Most of the people in my neighbourhood were against me and some of them were afraid of me. Even the police were tired of me. In short, before the project my life was in a mess. I was a very bad boy. Of course, I did not think so at the time. I saw it as being cool and that my mates who were not doing it did not know how to enjoy life!

What the project has done in my life
When this project was introduced to me, things began to change. Initially, I was taking it like a joke, but when I got to understand what the project was all about, my life started changing. I am now a changed person. I no longer drink

or smoke. I am no longer the way I used to be. The project has helped me a lot. From what I went through in the training and what I have learned from my personal experiences, I have touched many young people's lives.

After our presentation in schools, many young people have been coming to ask me some questions about the project and sometimes they come with their personal problems and I keep enlightening and advising them to stay focused to their studies. Those that have dropped out will reason with me and they would go back and continue with their studies.

I did not know whom I was quarrelling with at the time. Now I know that I was expressing my protest against society in the things I was doing, except that I could have done it more positively and channelled my energy and that of my friends into productive engagement. When I look back now, I think the protest was against the fact that the society always wanted you to do what it wanted, parents will say do this, do that! And, nobody asks what you want and how you want it done. However, I now know that I have to balance things.

How I have helped others
The 'For Tomorrow…' project has also allowed me to understand the problem of other young people like me. I have used this knowledge to help others. I have two examples of this. There is this girl who came to me with her personal problems because she knew that I am involved in the youth project. Her problem is that her parents tried to force her into marrying a much older man, whom she did not love. The man is about 45 years old and the girl is just 19 years old. Her parents wanted her to marry him because he is rich. However, the girl was not ready for marriage because she really wanted to further her education. Because she rejected the man, her parents stopped paying her school fees. They stopped taking care and doing things for her. She has been doing everything on her own. In 2003, she completed her secondary school level education. She is still working hard to make sure that she furthers her education. She tells me that the advice I give her from time to time are her source of courage to stand and work very hard. I strongly believe that she will be okay.

The other person I have been talking with is a young man like me who is always on drugs. He says that any time he does not smoke, drink or take drugs he feels like dying or he would be confused. I understand this young man because that is exactly how I used to feel when I was on drugs. He came to me and told me that he does not know what to do about his condition. To worsen the matter he dropped out of school at the senior secondary (SS1), that is in the fourth year of his study. I have been sharing my own personal experiences and how the project helped me to quit drugs and to enrol back in school to complete my secondary education. He tells me that he is willing quit his habit of smoking, drinking and drugs.

So, in summary, the 'For Tomorrow…' project has helped me to give up my past lifestyle. It has given me hope and self-esteem since I completed my secondary education. I have used the skills of peer counselling and what I learned from the drama to advise other young people. It has been a profitable project in my life.

Faith's Story

Abah

Faith's story is of a troubled girl in search of parental care. Faith is a 24 year-old woman who dropped out of secondary school at age 16. She is from the Benue State, in the Middle Belt area of Nigeria. She was born in Zaria where she attended the Government Girls' Secondary School, Samaru-Zaria. She dropped out of school due to an unplanned pregnancy.

She heard of the project from her cousin's sister. The antagonisms she had gone through from friends and family members made her reject the project at first. After much persuasion, she consented. By the time she attended one or two of the sessions, she became convinced and that was how we in NPTA and SECON got to working with Faith.

Faith has proved to be determined to live up to the values of the 'For Tomorrow' project. She freely tells us that she is not willing to go through her previous experiences again. Her desperate concern right now is education, and when it comes to her private life, she insists that she will wait for Mr Right!

Among other things, Faith says that she has learnt so much about negotiating skills. In her own words; '*I never knew relationships could be negotiated; but now I can use the choices, decisions, and consequences method to weigh things for myself and then take a decision. I am glad I came in contact with this project.*'

Faith

I grew up in a family of six, three boys and three girls. I am the youngest of the girls. We lived very happily with our parents, our Mom and Dad, until our Mom died. I was about 12 years old then. After she was buried, we stayed happily with our Dad. One year after, my aunty came from the village and told my dad that he was still young and needs somebody to be with him, so he agreed and married one woman. After a few weeks, she started maltreating us. She stopped giving us good food. She never made us happy. We were always unhappy and whenever we talked to her about showing us love she would say if our mother loved us so much, she would have stayed alive and cared for us! I was really very troubled. At that time, I was in Junior Secondary School (JSS3).

After my JSSCE Exams, my result was very good and I needed to proceed to the fourth and senior year. I told my dad this, but he never said anything to me and I asked him again and he said that he did not have the money. Then, all my friends had already started in the new class. I had a guy I was dating then. He knew about the problem in our house so I went to complain to him. He told me he would give me the money if I agreed to sleep with him. I refused at first; after some days I went back to him, I expressed to him my fears of getting pregnant but he assured me that nothing would happen. I was a virgin then. He had been asking me for sex before now, but I refused. He then used my predicament as an opportunity, and I had no other choice then than to do his bidding.

I agreed because I needed the money for my registration. I got the money, did the registration, and started going to school. I did not know that I was pregnant. Before I could know about the pregnancy, it was already about four months. I told my sister about it and she took me for a pregnancy test. In the lab, they said the pregnancy was four months. Before they could let my dad know about it, it was five months old. When my dad knew about it, he threatened to send me out of the house, but my sisters intervened and said that I had to stay in the house. That was how I continued to suffer alone with the pregnancy.

I felt rejected by my family and the society. Even until now whenever I am discussing with my male friends, and my dad sees me, he will say: 'The one you had has not taught you anything yet, you will still get another one.' My friends run away from me, people talk about me when I am passing. I did not have friends; I didn't interact with people. I stayed in the house alone. Nobody wanted to be close to me. Not even my own brother would talk to me. After delivery, I stayed for months before people started getting close to me because of the baby. They will come around just to help me carry her. My life was really a miserable one at that time.

After some years, my baby started going to school. It came to a point when everybody in the house would leave for school and I will be left alone at home. When they come back from school they will say *'Faith where is my food, where is my slippers, where is my notebook? I left it here!'* Every body is Faith, Faith! I was very troubled and I am the kind of person that cries a lot, so I would cry and cry and cry. One day through my tears I said, *'Even the baby I dropped out school because of is at school and she is also asking me where is this, where is that? I also want to go back to school so that I can come home and ask someone where is my slippers? Where is my food?'*

Young people have problems, because they are not usually educated about sex either at home or in school. Some of them are very young and so innocent that they don't know what their actions will result to. In my own case, I had never had sex before I got pregnant. That was my first time. The very first time I had sex therefore was the very first time I got pregnant. Many adolescents like me have learned that some parents do not have time to discuss such things with their children. Others do not even have the knowledge about sex to be able to tell their children because their parents did not educate them on such issues. However, it is very important for young people to be educated about sexuality.

The 'For Tomorrow…' project has helped me a lot in gaining knowledge and in my conduct. This project has changed my life. I was educated in the project to know what is good and bad sexual practice. I now talk to people about the project and educate them on sexuality. I learnt about listening skills and drama. I never knew I had any talent until I joined the project. This project had helped me to such an extent that I was able to go back to school and I wrote my senior secondary certificate examinations (SSCE) in June 2004. Now I have gained confidence in myself and can sit with anybody I feel like and discuss with them and I am not as shy as I was before. I never knew relationships could be negotiated; but now I can use the choices, decisions and consequences method to weigh things for myself and then take a decision. I am glad I was exposed to this project.

My friends have also benefited because I have shared information with them on 'For Tomorrow' and what I have gained. I now know some others like me need to be educated to let them know that they have a second chance to pick the pieces of their lives together again.

The best thing of all is that I was brave enough to go to my father and I apologised to him for what happened to me in school. He was shocked and at the same time happy. We have become father and daughter again.

Nuhu's Story

Abah
This third story is from Nuhu who reminisces about the benefits of the project for him against a background of struggles: '*I was hopeless and helpless thinking my life has gone astray and everybody around me thought I was very wayward and could not be reformed any more. But after undergoing a project like "For Tomorrow", I learnt about my past mistakes and I realized that there is life after such disasters.*'

Nuhu is a young man who is faced with two main difficulties. One is lack of parental care and extreme poverty. He is one of a family of six children, two of whom are disabled. The father is a low-income worker whose earnings cannot support all the needs of the family. To worsen matters, he has a lifestyle of drinking and of neglecting family needs. Nuhu's mother died a few years ago due to the burden of coping with disabled children, an abusive husband and financial difficulties. Some of the results of this family problem for Nuhu were that his schooling became irregular as school fees were not paid. He had no sense of family care as his father paid no attention to their needs. So Nuhu sought solace in joining a gang of youths who would smoke marijuana and drink alcohol. He eventually dropped out of school at the age of 13.

He has written the senior secondary school examinations once. The results were not so good. He has attempted once more and hopes it will be better this time. Nuhu's willingness to tell his story has inspired other non-attenders to share their experiences and this has allowed NPTA and SECON to offer appropriate advice and financial support, where possible. Nuhu continues to face the challenge of living a life free of drugs and of keeping away from friends who are likely to influence him negatively. When the family is not strong, the tendency is to find alternatives. His friends constitute a surrogate family in spite of the fact that their practices challenge his pledge to be on good behaviour. The consolation in this matter is that Nuhu understands the problems he has to face and is willing to tell the story and ask for advice.

Nuhu
The disasters in my life were two types. One was bad friends and the other was a difficult family life. There are six children in the family. Two of the girls are disabled, leaving a huge burden on my parents. It also did not allow them to have enough time for the rest of us. This was made even more difficult because one of my parents spends too much time drinking. Things got worse when my mother died. I looked for care and support outside the home, so I used to go about with my friends. I started to drink, smoke and taking drugs. In short, my

life was bad as I used to be arrested by the police. I also dropped out of school because I was not concentrating. In addition, my school fees were not being paid. Life was bad and I gave up.

My participation in the 'For Tomorrow' project has helped me in many ways to deal with my problems:

(1) Peer pressure: I was encouraged during the course of the project and enlightened, most especially about peer group influence and how to resist them. The drama exercises and performance were very educative and useful in this.
(2) Self-esteem and confidence: This was one of those things that I benefited from the 'For Tomorrow' project. With self-confidence I am able to stand everywhere and talk about my past life so that others could learn from it. Before now this could never have happened. Who was I to stand in the public and talk about my private life or myself? But, now I understand that once something has happened it is no more a secret but a lesson to learn about for the benefit of others.
(3) Pursuing beneficial ends: The project helped change my life in knowing things that are of benefit and those that are worthless. There are some things that when we see our peer group or friends doing, it motivates us to do the same. However, after doing it we will discover that there is no gain or benefit. Such things are things like smoking, drinking, and sex. My mother used to tell me not to have sex with any girl because of the consequences except I am ready to bear children. It is now that I understand!
(4) Making choices: We used the drama to talk about the consequences of the choice we make. It was very useful to see that there are things that would happen afterwards. They may be good or bad. We also saw that there are always alternatives for every decision. So we have to think well before doing anything. This means that we have to learn to abandon worthless things because the choice we make has a lot to do with our tomorrow, our future like school, hand works, business, etc.

4. Looking ahead: How we as young people see the future

Mahmud, Faith and Nuhu:
We want to conclude with some observations and a word of advice for young people. The issues of young people the project has been addressing are in three layers. One is personal, the second is family and the third it is societal. We begin by saying that we have not seen any coherent policy on the part of government that addresses the problems of young people. For example, the schools send us away when we make mistakes without giving us any opportunity to explain or be allowed to go back. Secondly, part of the problems young people face, whether they have dropped out or have completed their secondary education, is the fact there is no employment. When young people are idle they can easily be swayed to engage in anti-social activities. In general, the youth feel very strongly that they have been abandoned by government.

Our stories all reveal some level of family failures. What we miss is the adequate parental guide and love. While we do not want to impose blanket blame on all parents, we observe that many of them do not give enough time to their children. In some cases, and especially issues of sexuality, parents do not provide enough education because either it is not the usual thing in our society for them to do so or they do not know enough themselves. We also know that sometimes parents do not meet their obligations to their children because they do not have the means. The problem however is that there is no communication between child and parents so that there is mutual understanding. The problems are taboo, poverty and poor communication. As a result of all these, the personal lives of young people are very likely to go wrong. They look for love, support and company away from the home. The chances are that they will get into bad company and do the wrong things.

Our advice to young people is that they should not think that because the society is treating them roughly, because they may not be getting adequate parental care and so on, they should develop negative attitudes or drop out of school. It is important to work hard. They will surely make it.

You have the future, you have the talent and your destiny is in your hands. For your dreams to come through, you just have to believe in yourself.

We also advise parents and relevant authorities that the young ones are the seeds of tomorrow, and for this reason, they need to be looked after, cared for and treated well.

NOTE

[1] Brochure, Nigerian Popular Theatre Alliance (NPTA)

Faith is now a tailor as well as aspiring to enter University. Faith's daughter is now 6 years old and is enjoying going to school.

Mahmud is waiting to write the qualifying examinations to enter University. In the mean time, he has become a 'For Tomorrow' campaigner, working with adolescent drop-outs in Zaria.

Nuhu has written one of his Senior Secondary Certificate Examinations (SSCE), and is waiting to write the second one.

REFERENCES

Abah, Ogah S. et al, *Report of the For Tomorrow workshops in Zaria and Jos*.
Boal, Augusto, 1974, *Theatre of the Oppressed*, Pluto Press: London.
Nigerian Popular Theatre Alliance (NPTA) brochure.
Obono, Martin, 2004, *Impact Evaluation Report*, Development Resource Initiative, Kaduna Nigeria (DRIVE).

Promenade Theatre in a Sudanese Reformatory
Divining for Stories
The Cockerel & the King's Ear

ALI CAMPBELL with JANE PLASTOW
& a team of Sudanese practitioners*

Introduction

This exploration of the role of the facilitator in Development Theatre has in itself an interesting history which mirrors its subject: the search for an appropriate voice whereby an idea, a project, a set of techniques or a performance might be described, documented and evidenced. If one of the key principles of good and appropriate facilitation is a listening responsiveness to the contact group – a flexibility which allows for radical change right through the life of a collaboration – then how do I do justice, in retrospect, to the constant revising and adaptation this co-creative relationship demands, if it has been genuinely reciprocal and not tokenistic? I have to include the mistakes; changes in direction; redrafting, revising and even rejection of models, scenarios and approaches which have perhaps served me well hitherto, but which in this collaboration are superseded by what the group is not just telling me but *showing* me. Irrespective of the given content or theme of a Development Theatre project, I am being *shown* far more than I am being told in the formal stages of setting up meetings, taking on board the concerns of NGOs, talking around what I am intending to do and how and why. What is not said is as likely to move me forward as what is. A 'failure' might represent the moment in the collaboration where a working structure or set of assumptions, which served well as a kind of hypothetical scaffolding so far, is burned away in the heat of experience to reveal something truly of the moment which could have been discovered at no other time and in no other way than here and now in this group.

There is a cycle to how these discoveries are made.

First, many meetings occur, between performers, researchers, NGO staff, educators and, on this project, a huge number of Sudanese children. Then we open the 'toolbox' and in the imaginal space of the workshop the seeds of stories are unearthed, sifted and sown. Themes germinate. A language emerges. We translate, elaborate, narrate or interrogate until further questions trigger the need for fresh techniques with which to bring these to the place of embodiment and transformation we call the theatre.

It is in this space of search and re-search, vision and re-vision that our practice must risk transformation in a new creative process. It is here that one's own role, regardless of experience, is thrown wide open in the collective search for meaning by the group. As I discover, so am I discovered, and watched in the acts of my discovering.

How do we document this? How do we develop working principles which both stand the test of transferability to other contexts and handover to other practitioners? What we have really imparted in a process of Training for Trainers is shaped by the way in which we have imparted it.

> Human existence cannot be silent, nor can it be nourished by false words, but only by true words, with which men and women transform the world. To exist humanly is to name the world, to change it. Once named, the world in its turn reappears to the namer as a problem and requires of them a new naming. Human beings are not built in silence, but in word, in work, in action-reflection. (Paulo Freire: *Pedagogy of the Oppressed*)

The challenge for me in writing, after 25 years of this work, will always be to do justice to those unique moments in the process where this principle of true collaboration is fully embodied: transparent, vulnerable to failure and misinterpretation, yet wide open for the reader to connect to other experience. I strive in this work and its documentation for that writing to be both inspiring and practical: shedding light on collaborative Development Theatre techniques as experienced in one project, so as to show as clearly as possible their potential for meaningful and appropriate transference to another place, in the hands of another practitioner, open to the scrutiny of a group I will never meet in a context I can only imagine.

The context of the present discussion is Training for Trainers I ran in Khartoum in 2003 with Jane Plastow, Senior Lecturer in Theatre at Leeds. We were asked by the British Council to work with a group of Sudanese practitioners, from the North and South, Muslim and Christian parts of the country, all engaged as artists and teachers in work with young people displaced by 30 years of civil war. We were asked in particular to gauge the level of AIDS awareness among the groups we worked with and if possible to incorporate this into whatever performance, in whatever form, we might make in the Jirieff Children's Reformatory on the outskirts of the city as a pilot pointing the way to future work.

My aim is to give a practitioner's view of the two weeks we spent working through different techniques, looking for a style and a method and perhaps a story that we could take to the reformatory, where many of the young people were being held simply for their own safety as what was to become the horror of Darfur unfolded.

To do justice to the work of Sudanese artists who are not present, and to evoke and celebrate the journey undergone by these children, whose names we do not have, means that from the outset I must embrace failure. I must abandon the illusory retrospective voice which merely documents diaristically but fails to evidence what was really going on in the heat and risk of collaboration. I

1. Jane Plastow with trainees and children from the Jirieff Children's Reformatory, Khartoum, 2003 (© Ali Campbell)

must try to show the shifts in role between the facilitator as leader, moving things along, and as listener, increasingly changing direction in response to those who will ultimately continue the journey alone. I have to give the sense of wearing many hats (teacher; researcher; witness) and speaking in different voices (pedagogue; maker; diarist) whilst finding a device by which to orchestrate them, just as different roles or voices are used on any one day in the work.

To give a sense of this in form as much as in content, this paper was originally cast as a performance installation, comprising real hats to represent the range of roles we draw on. Plastow and I used dialogue as the most fitting way not just to describe but to model our own collaborative relationship. We were collaborators ourselves, and nothing less would do in relation to our Sudanese peers than transparency in the way we would choose this technique or that; supported each other in that choice; witnessed and talked about the outcome and what way forward it might show us. We would take turns wearing a hat, or sometimes fight over the same hat, or sometimes (as with Plastow voicing her perceptions as a parent) choose no hat at all.

The text of the performance installation, with the array of hats and (behind the performance) a display of images from the project was originally given at LUCAS, Leeds, May 2004, and again at Kolkata in Nov 2005 as part of Jana Sanskriti's Festival of the Theatre of the Oppressed. On both occasions the audience were free, before we spoke, to read the labels on the hats and make their own connections between these and the deliberately jumbled set of images on the walls on three sides. In addition to this was a glossary of the basic Arabic terms and phrases we picked up in the course of facilitating the Khartoum group for two weeks, some of them obviously pertaining to facilitation (such as setting up Boal's Stroboscopic Image) and some to the no less key business of managing a group of fallible human beings building creative bridges between each other in ever more uncertain times and situations. The audience had to make their own connections, and this opening was a direct appeal to the expertise of others: I trust that an open-eyed and open-minded witness will see in the performance installation what I myself only noticed with the help of my peers, such as the three key images of the HIV-positive man which triggered off in Fozia, a trainee, a profound connection with a traditional folk tale, *The Cockerel and the King's Ear*, which in turn became the vehicle for our final performances to young people and informed the crucial choice of promenade performance as a holding form. I had proposed a promenade on artistic, educational and even political grounds (as well as out of my experience in Eritrea, Uganda, Malawi and elsewhere) but it was Fozia's moment of connection in our workshop that made the choice a true and present one for our Khartoum group.

In writing this account here, dialogue has had to become a chorus of voices, orchestrated by an editing sensibility and contained in monograph form, in which the performative device of hats can still be discerned. It is the actual process of juggling hats and conducting the chorus of voices that is so challenging to convey, in its imperfection, open-endedness and comedy. I hope in what follows to appeal to an equivalent sense of active connection-making in the reader; between voice and hat; hat and role; role and group; group and context. And if this raises fresh questions about how this story raises and carries forward a principle, a new technique or a more universal significance, then this storyteller will for the time at least be happy.

Diarist

I want to tell you what we did in the Sudan: how we shared and adapted techniques; how we took a traditional story and made it into a grand, beautiful, funny, moving promenade performance with a cast of hundreds which lit up a dry hot day with unforgettable moments of learning, empowerment, discovery and downright fun.

I want to do this without saying: 'you had to be there' or giving the impression that we worked through an elegant sequence of games, exercises and pedagogical stratagems which express everything I believe in as a teacher and an artist. I want to explore the questions you must always cover if you are to structure a project that is appropriate to the brief, and to show that these, and the 'answers' we may or may not discover, are embedded in practice in a way that a reductive, sequential narrative would falsify and rob of their texture, their often chaotic reality. The questions, which frame every project I have ever engaged in, are:

WHO/*MINU?*
WHAT/*SHINU?*
WHY/*LE?*
WHERE/*WEN?*
WHEN/*MITEN?*
HOW/*KEF?*

People don't just want to know what you ended up doing. They are always hungry for the answer to *how* you decide what to make. Do you just turn up and say: 'I do community opera' for example, and so if it's an AIDS education project they know at least it'll have a lot of singing in amongst the condoms and awful statistics. Maybe even condoms singing the awful statistics! I know *that* we made a promenade performance, but *how* did we choose that form?

How do you impart those skills and tools and insights from your own practice in a way that is transparent, empowering and accessible to your peers in other cultures and contexts? *How* do you find a story that will resonate with young people? *How* do you choose a form of performance, which you desire to work with, but can hand over to adaptation and translation in a wholly different cultural context? *How* do I answer these questions with reference to one thing we did together, without making it seem that we had pre-decided what we were going to make and even what we were going to learn?

I want to talk about how we did find what worked, and in a way that opens up useful, transferable insight to my peers in this space and this context. But I want to do justice to how open-ended and uncertain our inexact art can be. I want to include what my Sudanese partners learned from working with me, and what I learned from them, and what we all learned from the young people, and the social workers, and the prison guards and the prison site itself, which we transformed into a temporary theatre just for one day. I want to show, not just tell, how important appropriateness of medium and story and style are, without sounding too sure of a method that works every time, because it is being honestly *unsure* that helps us find what is appropriate.

As a Diarist, for example, I might begin like this:
Day One. Nerves. Overly polite participants. Speeches and introductions. Practitioners on all sides of a weirdly smart conference table at the British Council in Khartoum, all secretly gagging to get up and *do*. Gradual relaxing and icebreakers and lunch and a swift realization that this group are hugely experienced, can make a play in ten minutes flat and a song even quicker, and do so daily. No problem discerning that all are eager for new techniques; especially issue-based and participatory performance. So we'll sample from the toolbox of Image Theatre and perhaps indulge in a little of what I call divining for stories: a theme, an issue or an existing tale that resonates with the group; that gives us the goosebumps; that makes us feel we're on the trail of something that will take us deeper into the task of finding appropriate ways of working in the reformatory next week.

How? Experientially. By walking the walk. By playing and sharing.

Yes: *How* do you find the set of techniques and the kind of piece everyone desires to make? It's appropriateness that seems most important, especially at the beginning, and yet it's the vaguest thing to try to convey in retrospect.

You listen, of course: to the group, to the whole room, to the streets of Khartoum outside, to the huge group of children we are working with alongside the training, to not just the prison staff but its geography. You listen to the spaces in between words and buildings: to the things not said and the places not shown, because the truth is so often found there. This might seem a rather fey and mystical aspiration, but it is precisely the opposite: we are working with human rights, with a silenced group; in a place no-one wants to visit.

You learn key facilitation words in Arabic: *Mahara* (skills).

You are eager to jump right in with a bunch of skills, but first, in this most formally polite of cultures, you say this:

A: *Salaam Alekum.* (Greetings)
B: *Alekuma Saalam* (Greetings to you)
A: *Garwa?* (Coffee?)
B: *Shokran. Mahara!* (Thank you. Skills!)
A: *Ay-wa.* (OK)
B: *Estaeed…* (Stand by…)
A: *Wahed, Etnen, Talata!* (One, two, three!)
Tutti: *Wagif!* (Let's go!)

Facilitator

I want to mark my own position as both teacher and student, in a relationship that is always transitive. In this context, at this moment in a workshop I know 'most', and in the street I will know 'least' of the members of the group, when we go out for a lunch I am unable to find or order by myself. In the reformatory, where we will be working these techniques with the children in parallel to the training, we will most of us know 'least' again about the stories waiting to be released by our agency but ultimately the authorship of others whose lives we cannot imagine. So although I am clearly learning the rudiments of facilitation in Arabic, what am I really teaching?

At one level of the work, I can answer this in a way that makes objective sense, in all contexts and in all languages. In the imaginal space of workshop or theatre, I am going to impart three long tried and tested techniques, each with a recipe I can write down on the flip chart in minutes, and which I can teach anyone to set up and run, wherever they are. They are what Boal calls prospective techniques, and although sometimes they yield dross and other times the gold of true story, I am confident in my ability to take any group through them, trusting that one or two will impact on people, differently, with varying 'success', but within a frame that I retain enough control over to discharge the facilitator's duty.

1/ Postcards

This is what we will do after our warm-up with the children tomorrow. We know there might be up to 200 of them, so it needs to be delivered with minimum words (or shouting) and the playback of group images needs, by simple arithmetic, to be possible in the short time we have. Here's how it will go, and although we aren't pretending to be children in this training, we will honour their point of view in the following sequence, and use this empathy to inform the language we need to use with them.

A/ Ali and Jane have never been in the Sudan before, and they have heard that you are from all parts of the country. In groups, each person will think of a place in Sudan, from the shade under your favourite tree to a whole province. Then, because they can't go there and only you know what that place looks like and feels like, we will send them human postcards. They can be walked round, listened to and brought to life, so they are much better than ordinary photographs. (Photography is forbidden in the reformatory)

B/ Now play these back and practice freezing, remembering where you are in the image and who is next to you; where your eyes/hands/body are. Don't tell us the place, show us.

C/ Now the audience can guess where these places are and tell Ali and Jane more. Sometimes two groups choose the same place, but show it differently; what might that mean? Sometimes there is a place that no-one recognizes, because only one person has ever been there. But we can see it! Now we might know it if we too go there.

On Day One we run this, along with an AIDS awareness quiz which reveals the young people's level of awareness and allows some content to rise to the surface, whilst giving them the first tools with which to explore that content in a mode one safe step removed from the personal. Some of the young women and girls in the group have been sex workers, and their hilarity is infectious as the quiz exposes popular beliefs such as: if you drink five litres of water a day you can't get HIV and using public transport is a good way to avoid AIDS. Jane and I don't laugh quite so long as the girls. But the making of images and the reading of them is a joy and huge excitement greets the show-and-tell: even the guards are riveted to the images of beauty, peace, chaos, work and flight that group after group reveal. We don't quite know what they all mean, but I feel that I am earning my keep in return for learning my Arabic!

2/ The stroboscopic image (Boal)

(The group makes three images, say of Sudan, and the audience open and close their eyes so that they see the images as a series of animated frames. Makes you look hard at what you see, and question what you think you know.)

Tomorrow we are using this technique to divine for stories at the reformatory, and today, to stay ahead of the young people (whose learning curve will speed upwards very fast, I think) we will try it for ourselves, in this context as a way of zooming in on story fragments already revealed in the reformatory work, or awakened in ourselves as artists in the time between then and now. There will be one or two which give the group the goosebumps; which are appropriate to the proposed content of AIDS awareness whilst imparting the expressive skills with which to address it.

A/ Take a story or a moment from the story. It might have happened to one of you in its entirety, or you may have heard of it happening to someone else (a lot of people affected by AIDS take this option.)

B/ Choose three images which really tell the story. Or if it is a composite story, negotiate what all are comfortable in showing others at this point. Practice these. Who will the protagonist be? The person the story is about? The person things are happening to, and who we might want to help change their situation? This should be as clear as the sequence of events itself. Practice this sequence and make it your own. Be ready to move smoothly from image 1 to 2 to 3.

C/ Playback! Audience close their eyes while players stand by (Estaeed) with Image 1.

Audience open/close eyes, (Efta/Ekfil) seeing only the frozen image for about ten seconds.

Repeat for Image 2 and Image 3; Estaeed...Ekfa/Ekfil...

D/ Audience: what did you see? Can you tell what is happening and who it is happening to? There are no wrong answers in this work: you might see an action movie or a fairy story or something that happened to you yourself, but that's not the 'wrong' answer. It is a connection, it is to do with what really happens to people, and how it feels, and how apparently disconnected events are often connected at a much deeper level, which we can't always put in words. That's why images!

The day we try this out, using group stories from the trainees, we go right to the heart of the matter, goosebumps and all, as indeed we must if we are to expect young people to follow not just our techniques but our example. Yasser tells a story:

> *Wahed!* A man who has just learned he is HIV-positive, with a whole queue of fellow-villagers behind him.
> *Etnen!* They spread the word.
> *Talata!* They ostracize him.

Maker

The images are visceral, unforgettable. Writing two years later I only need to close my eyes to see them. I am running the technique, so I don't get the benefit of the pure image when I open my eyes to each new one and feel its impact and theatrical potential. But I see something else, from my chair (its too hot to stand up today). I call image three, and all close their eyes, except Fozia, in the image as a doctor, who is looking right at me. The actors playing villagers have their backs to me: they are facing Fozia, making the image of a queue. Yasser is a tall, athletic man with true gravitas: he has never been inside a technique like this before, and hasn't experienced this way of either looking or being looked at. He moves swiftly and silently towards me, intent on moving from the second to the third images with silence and economy, as I have suggested. He isn't looking at me. He is looking to where inside himself the image is stored: not just the body memory of the initial choosing and sculpting of ten minutes ago, but somewhere deeper, further back, inward to where image connects to personal history, perhaps, and downward, into the collective history where all images have some source, where the doom of this imagined villager will inevitably return him. It is all of these directions and yet it is none of them: simply the place where the truth lies. He crouches, silently, beautifully, next to my chair. He covers his face with his strong, elegant hands. The effort of holding the image, until I call to open eyes, makes his legs tremble, and the tremor of this runs through his body like a fever. I can see his effort and his commitment, and in that instant I feel it, too. Dead friends are in the room. The temperature drops. I call out *Efta*! And I look away, to see what the audience's faces look like, while they look wide-eyed at Yasser, not knowing I am looking at them. Fozia sees all of this, of course.

Collaborator

These three images alone would make a Forum play. Or a ballad. Or a silent movie. But *how* do we work this choice out with our group, given our brief? *How* do we build a bridge between this devastating adult material and the place where the young people are, knowing that we do indeed need to look at exactly the same issues?

I open this up to the group and learn a new word: *Murarama*: compromise.

Diarist

Day Three. So far we've just asked as homework for people to bring in any song or story or fragment that might lend itself to a technique like the Stroboscope, or give us the basis for looking at issue-based work through traditional story. We haven't a clue that Fozia has already found the tale that will be the holding form for the huge promenade we will eventually make in the reformatory. This is the story Fozia brings, triggered off by what has come up on Days One and Two, through meeting and making with the young people, through opening up a style and content together and not least, through the Stroboscope.

Storyteller

There was a Farmer once, who had an old Cockerel in his employment. One day he said to the Cockerel; 'I'm tired of you. Your feathers are dull and mangy and your voice is cracked and weak. How can I expect you to warn off wild beasts when you look and sound like that? You're fired!'

The Cockerel didn't know what to do. In despair he left the farm he had lived in all his life, and made for the jungle. 'What shall I do?' he wondered.

2. *The cockerel rejected. Trainees rehearse, Khartoum 2003* (© Ali Campbell)

3. *The cockerel in despair. Trainees rehearse, Khartoum 2003* (© Ali Campbell)

4. *The cockerel seeks death in the forest. Trainees rehearse, Khartoum 2003*
(© Ali Campbell)

5. *Actor-teachers rehearse* The Cockerel & the King's Ear, *Khartoum 2003*
(© Ali Campbell)

'All my life I've just done this one job for the Farmer. Now there is no reason for me to live.' At that moment along came Tiger, looking for a snack. 'Why don't you just eat me, Tiger?' said the Cockerel. 'I'm no good for anything else, so I'm told. There must be a couple of bites left on me somewhere.' 'I'm afraid I can't do that.' said Tiger. 'Only the King can eat what's caught in this part of the forest.' 'Take me to him then' said the Cockerel. 'I just want to get it over with.'

And so they went to the court of the King, who as we all know is a magnificent Lion. To be honest, he didn't fancy the look of the Cockerel as a snack at all, and was just about to say as much when he was convulsed by a violent need to scratch his ear in just that place that no cat can ever reach. 'What's the matter, Sir?' asked the Cockerel, not wanting to drag his demise out further. 'This damned ear' replied the King, throwing dignity to the wind and thrashing about in a most unseemly manner for court.

'I can fix that!' piped up the Cockerel, despite himself. 'It's obviously a tick, and the cattle at my old place used to get them all the time.' Well before the court could get over their horror at the intimate grubby personal secrets of Royalty [some things never change] the Cockerel had hopped on the King's shoulder, rooted around in his huge furry ear and not only found but removed and eaten the tick. Yum.

The King was beside himself with relief and gratitude, and richly rewarded the Cockerel with a new home and the lifelong post of Keeper of the Royal Ear.

One night, not long after, as the Cockerel slept in his lovely new house, he heard a terrible roaring and howling in the distance, as of many wild animals about their ghastly business of carnage, theft and mayhem among the local farms. Imagine his surprise when suddenly at his door appeared his old employer, utterly distraught and begging him for forgiveness and mercy! For, said he, 'Wolves and hyenas and all kinds of ravening beasts have attacked my farm, and they're killing all the cattle and sheep, and I've no-one to frighten them away!'

'But I thought I was no use to you any more,' replied the Cockerel, in truth not feeling all that sympathetic.

'Oh please forgive me and help me!' cried the Farmer.

And so the Cockerel went to the King, and the King summoned the Court, and his soldiers drove all the predators away from the farmer's land.

The Farmer was so grateful he immediately offered Cockerel his old job back, but whether the Cockerel stayed at court, or went back to the farm he had lived in all his life, this tale, and this teller, cannot say.

Facilitator

I have used this technique in so many settings: interfaith work in Northern Ireland; bullying and peer education work on drugs in English schools; training artists to deliver human rights work in Brazilian prisons; helping young looked after people to develop strategies for looking at their lives and hopefully dealing with often unspeakable pain. But this jump from Yasser's three images is simply awe-inspiring. It is made through the series of handovers or removes without which this work only teaches us what we already know, and often unconsciously does little more than replicate the story of the facilitator, who has held onto the real power in terms of what does and doesn't get told. Were I to insist on a model for Forum Theatre, for example, this tale would probably be 'wrong': I would be inclined, as a Joker, to work on Yasser's original story (if he allowed me to) and celebrate the tale as a delightful digression; as process. But it is not that. From Yasser to Fozia, from both to me, from us to the young people tomorrow, this is the story that could unlock what we all agree we want to do, but in a way and a form that gives us a chance of actually doing it.

Collaborator

The Cockerel and the King's Ear is a gift to any development theatre project. There is clearly already the potential for a promenade performance, with different questions and tasks for the audience at each place they stop: Hot-seating the Cockerel with advice about re-training; Forum to enable the Farmer to see the error of his ways; a Health Education spot about orifices in general ... we will run the tale in the British Council studio, as preparation to marking out the whole thing at Jirieff, so that each of the trainees (15 or so) can place a different scene or moment at a different location on the site, enabling them to work up sections in a style that is celebratory, a form that is empowering and within a time-frame that is possible, while keeping the whole very tightly focused on the huge social and personal impact of AIDS. We will walk the story as well as talk it.

Dramaturge

But *how* does the choice of promenade arise from this story offered by Fozia? Dramaturgically, it is appropriate, as the audience will go on a journey with the protagonist. They will have to work for meaning. Some are displaced themselves. I can see the promenade form opening up experientially a resonance between MOTION, EMOTION and MOTIVE: the empathy we have with the protagonist that makes us want to move with the story; the identification with his labelling as redundant which is the dynamo driving us to risk an actual journey towards a solution; the choice the Cockerel has between simple revenge, and a forgiveness which opens up new possibilities and actions.

Collaborator

How do I check that this whole process, which is moving so fast and exciting us all with its promise, is indeed the culturally appropriate one? The answer can't be a final, fixed answer, coming from a post-dated point of expertise which I might adopt to sell, justify or mythologize such a wonderful moment as that which has passed from Yasser to Fozia to me ... and beyond. The answer is embedded in practice and articulated through relationship.

I am in a working relationship with Fozia. She has opened up a lot in the workshop, not least by coming out as a really strong feminist, and has offered a story that has come from a deep place in her, teased out by the divining process and the image work. I want to ask her where she thinks the story came from. Has something chimed with her personal experience? Over a cup of *Garwa* I ask why she alone among the female practitioners wears traditional African dress, suspecting that there is a story here in the complexities of Sudanese society over the last 30 years. I want to know her better as a collaborator. What she tells me throws all my preconceptions out of the window: she is a Christian, but her husband is Muslim. They attend Church and Mosque next door to each other, as do so many Africans who have not allowed the polarization of Islam versus Capitalism, authored by the West, to colonize their lives. Her six children will be free to choose their spiritual path when they are old enough. The only thing inconceivable to her and the rest of the group is that they might choose *no* spiritual path. Her life is *murarama*. Her traditional clothes do indeed suggest a traditional lady from the Christian South, but these are choices she makes and opens up to her children daily. She knows about the compromises each of us needs to make to function. We are walking compromises. This is the context for her choice of story: she is modelling change, flexibility and compromises all the time, as well as optimism and a rejection of crude polarity.

Pedagogue

There is only one sound methodological way to take this discovery back into the testing ground of practice.

We go back to the reformatory and in telling, setting and rehearsing *The Cockerel and the King's Ear* (Now paired with the Quiz as an AIDS awareness day) our own education takes another quantum leap.

Jirieff is an open prison, and many of the young people are only alive because they are in there. Some have been involved in the war as killers, and there is a shadow on them of terrible deeds done. Some, like the older girls, have been rescued from sex work and already have babies of their own. Many have been arrested selling illegal alcohol. They have a huge diversity of talent, experience and story. I hope the choice of tale isn't too patronizing. I'm pretty sure the choice of promenade isn't though, as the activity of walking through a story and having to move to find out what happened next is a hugely exciting thing to actors and audience alike.

The journey is circular and iterative, superimposed on the current settings in which this eager band of animated young people find themselves.

You have to earn the meaning. You have to identify with the protagonist, in this case the Cockerel, but can never quite share his point of view, preoccupied as you are with positioning yourself so that you can see what is happening, but always having to compromise because of the physical position of others, let alone their position as male or female, child or adult, inmate or guard. Where you are standing; where you are coming from: all of these things are in themselves the text and the meaning and the learning action of this promenade. You have to be aware that there are shorter people behind you. You notice that you watched the first part with the background of the Mosque; the second beside the Church (the prison has both) and the third where people wash and prepare the vegetables from the reformatory farm. And the way you walk is going to be part of what you take away as the meaning of the performance. And of course you have to look at your peers, and thus at yourself, through the filter of the story we are walking: at any point in the circular journey of the promenade, you are watching the action against a backdrop of this audience of your peers. They don't know you are watching them as they laugh, jostle babies on their hips, scratch their heads, and call out suggestions to the characters. The moments of rejection, exile, despair, discovery, transformation, forgiveness and questioning are all played out across the sea of faces opposite, with the actors (some of whom are your pals) mediating between you and the rest of the world you know. The frame of the story is your whole world and everyone you know in it. The meaning of the story is open to diverse interpretation as the changing reactions to it are multiplied and reflected by others' faces, and your own. At one point the guards sing and dance and join in. You will never see them in the same way again, after today. At another moment, in the hot-seating, a girl calls out a really good idea: really funny. Everybody laughs. You will always notice her from today on. The scene changes and you run ahead, trying to guess not what happens next exactly (you know the story already) but where? Where in the prison? And will you get a good view?

And who is this, stepping out of an air con land cruiser with War Child on the side?

Development Worker

I'm standing with the sponsors from War Child, led by the Dutch head of the charity. There is a huge crowd rather chaotically following the piece around the prison grounds. Sorry: reformatory grounds. They don't like to say prison. At any second in this spectacle I could take amazing photographs for the front page of the annual report: the audience is transfixed; is a creature and a character in its own right; is more than the sum of its individual parts; is brimming and bursting and indeed giggling with Social Capital: the transferable skills that devising, making, listening, cooperating, performing, critiquing and evaluating your work all require and galvanize; celebrate and deploy. These skills are all in play at once in this moment of heated performance. I can see the skills that making has required of the British trainers, their Sudanese peers, their young co-workers and the audience which all also belong to. I'd love to take a photograph but the last person to do so had the film confiscated. Maybe it wouldn't capture what this really is, anyway. It's a feast of live skill. I'd no idea so much could be going on in a play that Sudanese artists and social workers might make with such a large group of children. But reporting and evaluating to anyone not here will be a nightmare. Must follow the narrator puppet to get a better look. Pity it looks like a sex toy, but no one else seems to have noticed...

Parent (this hat and the voice it signifies was proposed by Jane Plastow and articulates her own experience)

I'd never worked anywhere quite like Jirieff before, where we found certain children were unable to participate because they didn't have anything to put on their feet and the sand was too hot to walk on – and consequently had to do a quick rummage in our pockets for money for flip-flops; and where I was introduced to a young boy aged 12 with a wicked smile called William. I'd left my own very similar looking William of the same age in England and the synchronicity has haunted me ever since. But what was important to the work was that William and a lot of other children not only learnt some theatre skills and some facts about HIV/AIDS, they also experienced the joy of creativity. More and more it seems to me that it is this joy in communally making, imagining and transforming that is at the heart of any benefit behind educational, development or indeed any old kind of performance work. Skills transfers and sharing of information are of course vital to development processes, but human development is also intimately related to human joy and achievement. Making the story of *The Cockerel and the King's Ear* was ever such fun, and when some of Jirieff's occupants were allowed out to the British Council to perform it in public and lead us in with their band they nearly burst with evident pride – not something they probably felt a lot of previously. Our time in Sudan was all too short, in an area of work where sustainability is enormously important. But we do know that Fozia and the other trainees, with the support of the British Council, have formed themselves into a local NGO to develop youth theatre work... I hope we get a chance to go back one day and play some more.

Maker

I have an image that is speaking to me still from the promenade. Our Sudanese collaborators have completely run with every idea we have worked on in our training for trainers. The piece has become huge, and a cloud of dust rises above the audience as they find their way back to the beginning, to ponder with the Cockerel what forgiveness might accomplish, and what revenge might. The brass band has vanished as quickly, if not as shockingly, as they appeared: where did anyone find the time, the instruments and the people to put together a brass band and create the King's magnificent retinue? All out of bin bags and feathers and two old trombones. I am humbled, and as the circular story takes us back to the shelter we have been using to work in, I settle where I can feel my own feelings and watch the audience. I notice two boys, still rapt in the performance and unaware that I am watching them. One has a perfect replica of a satellite dish in his hand. He has made it himself out of wire. It is exact, to the last detail, and based on those on the roofs of the expensive houses which we pass every day on the way here, which are placed for convenience near the airport. Who might be convenienced by a children's reformatory being handy for the airport? Me, I suppose. But working in the fields by the runway, which they could easily escape from if there was anywhere else in the Sudan to go, this boy must see limos and buses and green gardens with sprinklers and satellite dishes every day. Out of the blue I remember that half of the population of the world will never make a phone call. He catches my eye. His friend is pretending to write on a laptop: it consists of a decorated cardboard box on his knee and his mime, as in the workshops leading up to today, is as brilliant as ever. Between them they are recording the show and transmitting it somewhere. Where is that story going? What have they done to end up here, and where will the skills they are learning take them? I don't have the equipment to receive what they are sending today, sitting in the dust, one with an outsize Nike shirt and one in old men's pyjamas. There is so much I don't know.

NOTE

* Project run by Ali Campbell and Jane Plastow April 2003, with a team of Sudanese practitioners facilitated by British Council, Khartoum and the charity War Child.

First performed by Ali Campbell and Jane Plastow with hat installation at Performing Africa Conference, University of Leeds, May 2004.

This text by Ali Campbell, May 2004, with 'Parent' words from Jane Plastow.

Appendices

1. Hats

diarist
maker
2 students
facilitator
storyteller
dramaturge
collaborator
pedagogue
2 audience
development worker
parent
2 dunces

2. Participants

Abel Hakeem El Tahir
Athenasios Gideon
Fozia Daniel Paro
Hassan Ibrahim Ishag
Mahmud Mohammed Babiker
Mohammed Rahmatalla Ali

Monir Abdallah Hussein
Nadia Ahmed Zaid
Suleima Ishag
Walid Omer El Alphy
Yasir Mohammed Abdalla

Youth Theatre in the Displaced People's Camps of Khartoum
Kwoto

LUKE DIXON

Background

> *'Kwoto for me is everything, unity, reconciliation. It is like a key that opens for you a new learning of aspects of other ethnic groups of southern Sudan.'* – Omjuma Philip Ataron, from Eastern Equatoria[1]

The civil war in Sudan has been Africa's longest-running conflict of modern times. It is a complex conflict but the simplest and most visible element has seen the Arabic north of the country pitted against the black African south: Muslim north against Christian, animist south since the imposition of Islamic law in 1983. It was only in 2004 that a peace accord was reached in an attempt to bring to a close the last twenty years of warfare that has led to some two million deaths, widespread famine and huge internal displacement in Sudan. Millions have fled from the south to avoid the fighting and make a home in the relative security of the north. Khartoum, Sudan's capital at the confluence of the Blue and White Niles, has been the destination of most: black Africans seeking refuge in the major city of their Arab enemies. These people are not technically refugees because they have not left the Sudan; instead they are termed 'Internally Displaced People' and the camps they live in are called Internally Displaced Peoples' (IDP) camps.

Kwoto

> *'Kwoto for me is like an honest friend and a second family.'* – Amalia John, from Upper Nile State

There is a young people's theatre company working in these camps bringing song, dance and drama to the unknown numbers, perhaps millions, who live here in the most rudimentary of conditions. The company was set up in 1994 by Derik Uya Alfred, who was later joined by Stephen Affear Ochalla, to keep alive the song and dance traditions of the peoples of the south by giving performances in the camps. They describe their objectives as follows:

Youth Theatre in the Displaced People's Camps of Khartoum 79

- Strengthening the Southern identity through animation of their cultures artistically (theatre, music, singing, dance and puppetry) as a contribution to the national cultural identity.
- Adopting the Southern vernaculars as the medium of the theatre, with the notion of uplifting and developing these vernaculars.
- Collecting, classifying all the folk-tales, oral traditions, with the idea of utilizing some which are suitable for drama works.
- Making use of theatre as an open popular university which contributes to the social, economical development of the Southern Sudanese communities.
- Providing some entertainment, relaxation to soften the acute hardship burdens, created by the awkward displacement life conditions.
- Bringing back through the means of theatre the displaced Southerners to their roots, cultures, languages, customs and traditions.
- Creating a suitable atmosphere for young Southerners to exchange views, experience, interact and encourage enculturation amongst themselves.
- Offering opportunities to young gifted men and women of the South to promote and channel more artistically and scientifically their potential theatrical skills. As well as encouraging the spirit of creative playwriting, which will then find the way to stage and publicity.
- Posing the question of Southern culture through discussion, talk, seminars, research etc.
- Making use of the moving libraries (the elders) by offering them opportunities to share and contribute as experienced and knowledgeable storage of the local societies.
- Dramatizing some information connected with health-care, childhood and home economy to help raise the living standard of the displaced population. That is in collaboration with the institutions concerned.

The company operate from the *Kwoto* Cultural Centre, a bustling, well-organized lively collection of rooms (including a small but well-stocked library) around an open courtyard where rehearsals and performances take place. The building is in the heart of Khartoum. Performances are given at the end of the afternoon as the sun's shadows begin to lengthen and the heat becomes bearable enough for audiences to emerge from shade and shelter. Three performances that I witnessed on consecutive days give a snapshot of the group's work.

Square 42

> '*Kwoto is everything for me. It is my priority. It is exactly like school, where I learn many things*' – Emmanual Augustino Juma, from Bahr El Jebel State

After lunch a bus was packed with performers and equipment (some of it on the roof) and off we went to Square 42, a displaced area in Omdurman, which with Khartoum and Khartoum North is one of the three separate cities each on

1. Kwoto *musicians*, *Khartoum* (© Luke Dixon)

2. Kwoto *dancers*, *Khartoum* (© Luke Dixon)

3. Kwoto *audience, Khartoum* (© Luke Dixon)

4. Kwoto *audience participation, Khartoum* (© Luke Dixon)

a different bank of the Nile rivers, that make up the greater conurbation. It was a longish drive towards the desert with mountains on the horizon to Square 42, a cross between a squatter camp and a township extension. Some of the dwellings are tied together out of sticks and cardboard, others more sturdily built out of mud bricks.

The Catholic Church is the focus in these areas and this was true here. The building itself is a primitive structure. Benches were already out across the street of dried mud and as the performers got ready, a crowd grew, hundreds strong by the time things started. The performance opened with the group's anthem 'Kwoto Sossa', a salute to the audience written by Stephen Affear Ochalla. Kwoto is a sacred stone of the Toposa tribe brought, according to legend, by the ancestors from Najie to the banks of the Loovoro river where it remains as a covenant and a protection.

A devised piece about the scourge of AIDS started things off. Clear, witty, very funny and beautifully staged – a twenty-first century African 'La Ronde'. The audience whooped with joy, laughter and recognition. A generator had kept power going for a while but it gave up half way through the 20-minute play and so the dancing and singing began as soon as the play was over. The repertoire covers a wide range of traditional songs and dances from Southern Sudan and the Nuba mountains. Their themes vary from love, harvest, pride, war and peace-making to social teachings and positive criticism. One song had obvious resonance and was taken up by the audience. It was Baai, a song from the Dinka tribe of Bahr El Ghazal State in the Southern Sudan. It means 'Oh my land, you have been stolen'. Many of the dances would, in their home environment, have involved the naked performers whiting up their faces and bodies with flour. But there was no flour today, and no nudity, an unthinkable thing in the northern Islamic world. Instead the young performers, aged 16 to 26, wore T-shirts for modesty's sake.

The play has been in Juba Arabic, a simple, almost pidgin Arabic that is the *lingua franca* of the southern blacks and named after the main city of the south. The Arabization of the country in recent years is a major political issue. Unlike the drama, the songs though were in regional languages, vernaculars, and the sense of delight and recognition was palpable amongst the delighted audience. Ancient songs took on contemporary political overtones, old songs of love and courtship gleamed as new. There were songs and dances from many different ethnic groups, given with huge energy and commitment (no mean feat in temperatures of 45 degrees) by nearly 40 performers. At dances that they knew and loved people would come from the audience to join in, to compete, and with the older women, to show how it *should* be done. It was unbearably hot when things began, but as the shadows lengthened and a warm breeze came in from the desert, temperatures began to cool. The stomping dances kicked up a storm of dust as dusk fell. The dancers became shapes and noises in the gloaming, lost in dust and darkness.

The bus was packed in an instant and the group returned to base under the stars and with the odd lit candle to show that people were living out here without electricity or water (the only water comes from oil cans trundled around on donkey carts). The young performers played 'song wars' on the way home in the dark – each end of the bus vying with the other as to which could sing most loudly and most expressively.

The dances are learnt from within the group and from outside teachers. Or at times during a performance a woman will complain that there was no dance from her ethnic group. Then you must teach us one, she is told, and she is brought in to the centre to do just that.

Mayo

> *'Kwoto means to me the cultures of the southern Sudan.'* – Beach Louis Kual, from Lakes State

One afternoon is spent in Mayo, a displaced area on the edge of Khartoum. No one knows how many people are displaced, but these are estimated to be is something like 3 million in these camps around the city. They seem to stretch forever across the flat landscape, a labyrinth of little buildings built of sticks and mud, cardboard and cloth; whatever materials are to hand. Thousands upon thousands stretch into the distance in an endless vista, grey and dusty in the exhausting afternoon sun which dries the heat to 40 degrees or more. One larger mud and straw building is a church. It is, I am told by Derek the group's director, 'multi-functional': church, school, meeting room and refuge. Inside the group get ready and then, in their traditional costumes (plus T-shirts) dance around the neighbourhood to let people know there is a show on. Pied Piper-like they bring an audience back with them and a semi-circle forms around the dancers, three middle-aged women from the audience joining from the beginning. People struggle to keep their customs, traditions and cultures alive here just as they struggle to find food and water. The Kuku, Acholi and Lokoya from Eastern Equatoria, the Dinka and Jur Chol from El Ghazal, the Shilluk and Anywak from Upper Nile, the Bari of Juba, the Zande from Western Equatoria and the Kwalib from the Nuba mountains of Kordofan, all find their songs and dances alive in Kwoto's repertoire.

Wad Ramli

> *'Kwoto means to me many things: peace, unity and life itself, new life.'* – Santo Ahmend Jospeh, from Western Bahr El Ghazal

This performance, again at a church, starts with a drama called 'The Well'. A couple wearily draw the last water from a deep well and share it out. Then by a miracle the well springs with water. Everyone can drink. A soldier comes by on a bike and stops the celebrations. He pisses into the water and then shoots dead those who protest. The others take their revenge by strangling him with the rope that draws the water from the well. All beautifully staged like a Brecht parable with only the dust from the ground as make-up. The audience giggle and roar with recognition and appreciation. Stylized with no words and only drumming and homemade marimba behind.

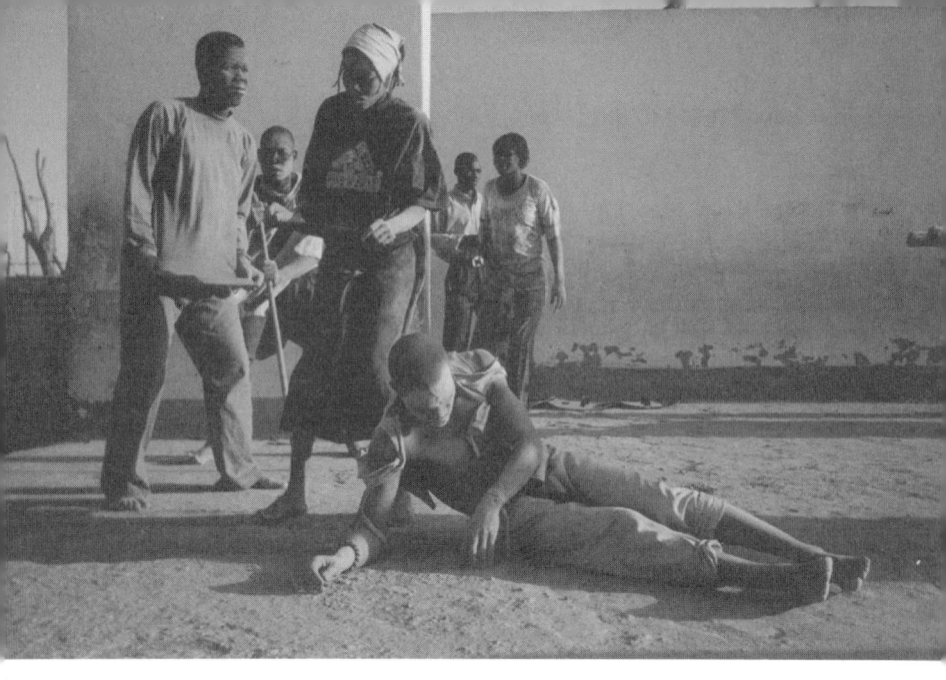

5. Kwoto *performance of* The Well, *Khartoum* (© Luke Dixon)

6. Kwoto *performance of* The Well, *Khartoum* (© Luke Dixon)

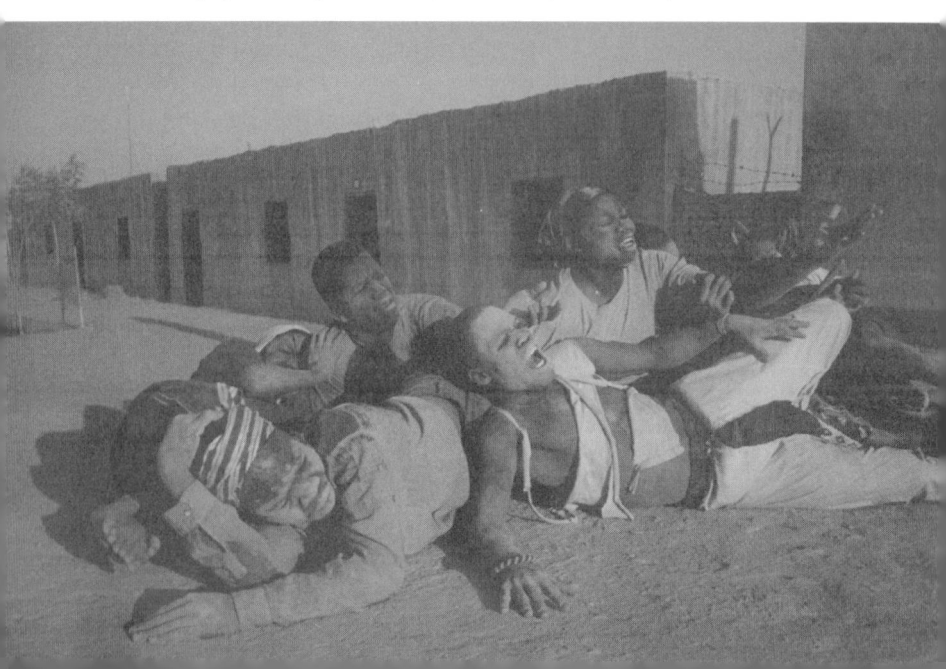

The Future

> *'Kwoto means to me the teacher, the guardian, the good brother and the brighter future.'* –
> Suzan Pascuali Karam

I talk with Father Bak and Derik Alfred about the desires of the southern peoples to return home if peace comes. Father Bak was the first priest sent by the church to the displaced people. Now he is one of a ministry of eight but still with so vast a congregation that he often drives 40 km between communions and speeds frighteningly around the desert in his four-wheel drive bakkie. Some, thinks the priest, will stay, others will send back one family member first to check things out, but most will want to go. Kwoto have already earmarked a site to build a cultural centre in the South when peace comes. The desert of the north is a foreign land to them all yet a land in which their cultures thrive in the dust.

Despite what is happening in Darfur, optimism is growing amongst the young people of Kwoto and amongst their audience in the camps. Focus is shifting from the past to the future and with their traditions strong, the group are looking to find ways of making new work as they and their country move forward.

NOTE

1 The quotations in the article are all from young people performing with the group, collected while I was with them. They show the geographical and cultural diversity within the membership and also reflect the joy and enthusiasm that animates everything they do.

Theatre with Street Children in Senegal

ROSA STOURAC McCREERY

Introduction: my work with children in Senegal

I am a performer, director and facilitator based in England. After two brief visits in 2004, I returned to Senegal for five months to work on various projects involving theatre and culture. I was given an Arts Council bursary with a view to supporting my own personal development as a practitioner. This was not funding for the many projects I was involved in. For this article, I will draw on all of these experiences, but I will particularly focus on my work with street children and children at risk. This includes the following:

- Running drama workshops for street children at two of the centres created by the NGO *Avenir de l'Enfant*, and more sporadically at the NGO *Empire des Enfants*
- Drama workshops and the creation of a theatre company at a primary school
- Drama workshops with children at *Ben Boy International*, a humanitarian and cultural association
- Devising and creating a play with children who participated in the Creative Workshops offered by the *Blaise Senghor Cultural Centre*
- This play was performed at the *Fest'Art International Theatre Festival for Peace*, where I also worked with the press and marketing team, the education team, and as coordinator of workshops run by myself and other theatre practitioners participating in the festival.

For the purposes of this article, the children I worked with will remain anonymous. *Avenir de l'Enfant* were very clear that they did not want me to identify the children I worked with there and taking images was also prohibited. I respect their wishes.

Finally, I created an exchange project, *Les Peaux des Esprits (The Skins of the Spirits)*, bringing together a performer and a mask-maker working in the Comedia Dell'Arte tradition in Italy, a Senegalese traditional leather artisan, an actor and musicians. The collaboration resulted in a performance, a joint exhibition, and mask and Comedia workshops which I helped facilitate. I was overjoyed to find that the audience of our first performance of this piece was largely made up of the young people I had worked with at *Avenir de l'Enfant* and the educators who work with them.

The performance began in the street, in a busy market area of Dakar hoping to attract audiences who might not often venture into our venue, the *Maison de la Culture Douta Seck*, or go to the theatre at all. At the evening performance, a group of five or six street boys followed the crowds to watch the performance inside the centre, stayed to look at the exhibition and watch the explanation of the masks and traditional Senegalese leather objects, and one boy even returned for the workshops the following day. The presence and participation of these young people in our project made it all the more worthwhile. Obviously my experience of theatre with and for children in Senegal is not exhaustive and I can only speak from what I did and what I saw in my time there.

Senegalese theatre: the context

In Senegal, as in most African countries, it is extremely difficult to make a living working in theatre. The professional actors I know either make most of their money on TV or on the comedy circuit, and the others...I honestly have no idea how they survive. There is no performing arts workers' union, and government funding for individual projects, never mind core funding, is very scarce. Obviously the big coup is to manage to take a successful production on tour internationally, either to an African theatre festival (which often loses rather than makes you money), or preferably to Europe or the USA where some income and recognition can be gained. Therefore, for most people who have large families to support, theatre is not the best career option. Theatre for children even less so: where is the money in that? That is not to say that it doesn't exist, only that resources, opportunities and initiatives are limited.

Most people, in fact, think that *theatre* is the Senegalese sofa dramas, and the Argentinian or Brazilian soap operas they religiously follow on TV. My name, Rosa, often caused particular admiration because of one such series, *Rosa Salvage*! So, for the majority of the population, including children, theatre happens every night on TV. When you begin theatre workshops with young people, changing this perception is one of the first challenges. Despite this, travelling around the regions of Senegal, I learned that almost every small town has its own theatre group, many of which are actively involved in using theatre to educate about health and social issues.

Another confusion is that in Senegalese culture, theatre and dance are virtually inseparable. There is a very strong culture of Senegalese traditional and contemporary dance, which was exuberantly represented during *Kaay Fecc, (Come and Dance)*, an international dance festival for which I also worked. Most traditional dances have some kind of narrative to them, and have recognizable characters. Some include masks and clown-like characters which mock the other performers or the audience. There are often improvised sections in the dances, when the codified dance language is paused, and improvised text and gesture provides a further insight into the narrative and characters. Therefore, when you talk about theatre many people also immediately think of dance.

Dance is one of Senegal's most successful cultural exports, alongside music and visual arts. The difference in audience attendance and funding for the two festivals I worked for underlined very clearly the preference shown to dance over theatre. Dance is very popular, and is part of all social gatherings and celebrations. It is a language that most children are very familiar and confident with. As soon as they hear a rhythm, they're off! This was at times helpful to my theatre work, since it meant young people were used to expressing themselves through their bodies, and did not have the same physical hang-ups that many Western people have. On the other hand, it sometimes became a hindrance, since during games and exercises, especially ones which included a rhythm, it took little for the whole group to suddenly be dancing, and the exercise to have disintegrated.

It was sometimes a struggle to convince the children to try doing things they weren't so familiar with, which would use their bodies in a different way, since they already knew how to dance, they didn't need me for that. This was sometimes reinforced by the other facilitators I worked with, as at times they encouraged the children to reproduce things they already knew. Of course, there is a place for this, reaffirming cultural practices and confidence, and recognizing the pleasure the young people find in dance, however, it is also an easy option, and doesn't always actively engage the children's creativity or teach them anything new.

I was lucky to learn some traditional dance during my time in Senegal. This gave me insights into the cultural forces of traditional music and dance, key to understanding many aspects of life. I was able to use this cultural reference point to my advantage: the children appreciated my awareness of their culture, and I could use it as a way into other exercises, which would ease the children into something less familiar to them.

How do most European children first experience theatre? At or through school is the most common answer. The Senegalese education system, as in most other African nations, is based on the old colonial models. Private schools with money, French-Senegalese and International schools are the exceptions. State schools therefore have strict, academic-based methods that rely on memorizing and repetition and leave little space for questioning, debate and creativity. Any creative or sporting activity linked to the school (and this does exist) is usually extra-curricular.

There is a strengthening initiative, mainly promoted by individual schools and artists rather than at a state level, to try to reinsert creativity into the education system. An example of this is an attempt in which I participated to create a theatre company in every school, even if it must, for the time being, remain extra-curricular. A colleague, Ibrahima Diallo, and I were put into contact with the Ibrahima Beye Primary School in the inner-city area of Fass-Colobane, by Babacar Fall, a facilitator and initiator of the movement to set up school theatre companies. He advised us to write a list of the resources we would need and make a budget for our own expenses and payment, to be passed on to the local council.

In my first meeting with the school's Headmistress, I watched her crease up with laughter as I mentioned this. She explained that the local council are supposed to be responsible for paying the school's electricity and water bills, but that they hadn't paid these for months. The school has had to find its own solutions, has run into debt, and has had to choose between water and electricity. They chose water, but having seen the toilets in the school, it still seems to be in short supply. Therefore, it is obvious that most state schools are a long way from having the kind of budgets that can include inviting artists and facilitators to come and work with them.

Similarly, most NGOs and other charitable organizations are on very strict budgets, and so creative work and inviting artists to contribute to their programmes is still a luxury. Of all the different projects I worked on in Senegal, the only one I received payment for was the workshops run with children at the Blaise Senghor Cultural Centre, which is state-financed. It is therefore easy to understand why there is a shortage of Senegalese arts facilitators and training in working with children. Many people who do that kind of work do so on a voluntary basis; but while their commitment is impressive, it is not consistent, since they can't always afford to give their time for free.

There are exceptions.

Azziz Gueye, an actor, is cultural attaché to a well-funded school in Dakar. I attended an inauguration ceremony for a new library the school had built, which included performances by Azziz's drama group. The young people performed sketches and poems, on a clear stage, with the odd prop or table, but there was certainly a budget for costumes. It was all in French, the children's second language, and sometimes you got the feeling that the children did not really understand the words they were saying. Not that they didn't speak good French, but the words were not their own. They had been given texts to read and work on, but in most cases, they had not made them *theirs*, and therefore, it did not seem that far from what they do in school every day, reciting the lessons the teachers have taught them. However, there were a few gems, a few brilliantly crafted characters and funny physical work.

There are also a number of new festivals for children's theatre. I was approached to take part in the pilot year of a children's theatre festival in Kaolack, another major Senegalese city, however it coincided with preparation for the *Fest'Art* theatre festival for which I was working, so I was unfortunately unable to attend. I heard that it went well, despite some organizational difficulties, and, as always, lack of funding, but it seems that here and there, initiatives and projects in theatre for young people are gaining strength.

Theatre with street children in Senegal

Doing theatre with street children has its own set of challenges.

When I first met with Moussa Sow, director of the organization *Avenir de l'Enfant*, he was clear about his interest in using drama within their work with young people, but also about the objectives and conditions he wanted to set. At one of their centres, the *Foyer d'Observation* (Observation Home), street boys are in theory temporarily housed while family mediation is underway, with the eventual aim of the child returning to his family, or while some other solution, such as a work or school placement is found. This is therefore a temporary home, where the children are housed, fed and offered classes in literacy and maths, creative workshops and manual work.

Moussa was clear that my drama work with the children should not counteract the centre's work in trying to help the children find a more permanent place. If they feel that they are integral to a process, like the creation of a play, and are enjoying this role, they may resist returning to more stable family life, knowing that those same opportunities will probably not be offered to them there. The drama should act as a tool for their self-expression, a way of sharing and validating their stories and experiences, and at times as an escapism, allowing them to enjoy themselves and think of something else, use their imaginations and the power of laughter.

In practice, despite it being a temporary home, there were children, generally the older ones, who had been there from the start of the project till I left. One of them was extremely bright, and had a real talent for drama. At the beginning he was invaluable, helping to reinforce what I was doing, and maintaining the discipline amongst the others, and was a real solid rock within the group. He obviously enjoyed the drama sessions. However, since other children came and went, and nearly every week there were new members of the group, he began to feel stifled and bored, and sometimes therefore became a distraction. I had to work hard to make the sessions challenging for regulars like him, and at the same time accessible and encouraging to newcomers who had less experience.

At the other centre, the *Foyer Familiale* (Family Home), children for whom family mediation was either impossible or would be a much longer procedure lived under the care of a Mum, with two children of her own, and either went to school or were apprentices of different trades. Here it was possible to lead a more continuous process and perhaps work towards a performance, since the children were there more permanently. There were other challenges. The children were younger and spoke less French.

In the early days of my time in Senegal, I often had to rely on working with someone who could help translate. At my work with *Avenir de l'Enfant*, I was supposed to have one of the permanent staff shadowing me at all times anyway, since one of the objectives was for them to learn from the techniques I used, and continue the work once I was gone. In practice this did not always happen. As I spent more time there, I began to learn more Wollof (one of the main local languages of the Dakar region), and therefore was able to communicate more directly with the children and understand them. Speaking Wollof was a key factor in facilitating relationships in many environments, but with the work with the children it was invaluable.

Thanks to my work with the children, I learned a lot faster, and again this was also important to my understanding of Senegalese culture. When the children realized I could speak their language and understand them (to some degree), discipline improved dramatically, and I believe they had more respect for me. I felt it was vital that they express themselves in the drama workshops in the language they felt most comfortable with, and this was usually Wollof. The play I made with the children at the cultural centre was all in Wollof, and was in their words. I sometimes did not understand everything they said, but I was more than happy to sacrifice a degree of my own comprehension for their creative investment and confidence in the work.

The *Foyer Familiale* had a particular dynamic. The children were mainly aged between 6 and 11, with one older girl of 15 and a boy of 16. The younger children were desperately in need of affection and attention. They adored the drama sessions, and were adept and quick to pick things up, but their excitement and enthusiasm could make it hard for them to focus and their concentration was often poor. The older children were double-edged swords, at times helping to hold things together, and at times becoming frustrated with the younger ones and disruptive, or too directive.

At both centres run by *Avenir de l'Enfant*, the work was sometimes hard but rewarding. Most of the children had been through very tough times, and had been deceived and let down by adults. Their confidence was sometimes very low. A street child does not have high status in society, and the level of education of most of the children was usually basic. Most of them had little or no experience of theatre. They came from a multitude of backgrounds, and even countries, since many street children in Senegal come from the surrounding, often poorer countries of Mauritania, Guinea Bissau and Guinea Conakry, the Gambia, Côte d'Ivoire and Mali. This meant they also spoke different languages and had different cultural traditions. I therefore had to make my introduction to theatre as accessible as possible.

I first began doing this kind of work with street children in Ghana in 2000, when I worked with my mother, an experienced facilitator, Kathleen McCreery, on a project with young people and staff at a number of centres supported by the charity Street Child Africa. We used the techniques proposed by Augusto Boal and the *Theatre of the Oppressed*[1] as the basis for much of our work, because it is designed for everyone, that is, people who are not necessarily trained theatre performers. These techniques are not culturally specific, and lead people to express themselves through theatrical forms without them being conscious that they are performing, so it removes the obstacles of embarrassment, or feeling that 'this is not for me'.

In Senegal I frequently drew on these techniques, mixing in other games I knew, exercises I had learned during my time at *L'Ecole International de Theatre Jacques Lecoq*, Paris, and some of my own invention. I would begin with general warm-up games, getting people moving, making them more familiar with me and each other, and putting them in a concentrated and creative frame of mind. Games to do with rhythm often proved quite difficult for some of the children. While they were good at songs or rhythms they were familiar with, new things often threw them, and would take some persistence to get right. I couldn't help comparing these young people with their English counterparts. We asked our primary school group to sing a song. They began to sing a traditional song, which soon turned into a joyous jam session, with everyone doing a solo, and dancing as they sang. Even those who were not the most confident of singers sang unselfconsciously. Try asking a group of 12/13 year-olds in England to sing you a traditional English song.

The children enjoyed the challenge of some of the physical exercises, and the boys at the *Foyer d'Observation* would practise them between sessions, but I often found them quite lethargic and lacking in physical discipline. The heat played its part in this, and the spaces we worked in were not always ideal; at the *Foyer Familiale* we worked outside in the dust and under the sun. I mention discipline recurrently because it is an important part of creating a respect for the work, which improves in quality when it is done with precision and specificity; with discipline. The participants therefore get more out of it, and feel pride and respect for themselves. It is a way of showing I expect a lot from the children. For much of their lives, no one expected much from them, and therefore they don't expect much of themselves. One little boy at the centre displayed a chronic lack of self-confidence. He would not even try a lot of the games, claiming that he could not do them.

The street children were good at improvising and problem-solving through drama. In fact, once they realized they had a creative freedom, and that I was expecting their input, and wanted them to engage their imaginations, almost all the children I worked with in Senegal turned out to be fantastic improvisers. This may be due to the very spontaneous nature of life on the street, and the need to be on your toes, to look out for and seize opportunities, in order to survive. The street children had defence mechanisms that usually made them either extremely extrovert or introverted. The extroverts were more obviously suited to drama, and tended to dominate, and sometimes distract, but the introverts often came up with surprising, and very thoughtful ideas, even if it took a bit longer to draw them out. In the work we did together, the children often tapped into cultural values and practices about which, through them, I learned a lot. I used a number of techniques to aid improvisation, many of which I picked up from Kathleen McCreery: one person sits on the only chair available, everybody wants the chair, and has to find ways of convincing the seated person to either leave or give them the chair. Once they got going, they could play this game for hours!

I was keen to explore conflict, as it is at the heart of all drama, and everyone has some experience of it. I felt sure it would have particular resonances for children who had left their families for many different reasons, and had been subject to all kinds of abuse and neglect. A partner game where the pair take on related roles, and decide on a conflict, then shout at each other for an entire minute, was quite revelatory. Parents and children, friends, bosses and workers all went to battle. Once these conflict scenarios had been created, we then dissected them, played around with them, and built them up into stories.

Perhaps even more effective was the 'still image' work I did with the children. From an exercise in which a pair create a series of random still images, I would pick one that had dramatic tension in it. We would then analyse the image together, decide who the characters within it were, and what was happening. From the basis of these images, many things are possible. You can make the characters speak, hear their thoughts, go back and forward in time, add new characters, bring the scene to life, and begin to build a narrative. The children enjoyed interpreting these still images, bringing their different ideas to what they saw, and helping each other find meaning and express emotion through the images. What is fantastic about this process is that there is no right or wrong answer. Every suggestion is valid, and can be as banal or dramatic as you like. That means that everybody's voice is valued, everyone can contribute. Naturally, through these images, the young people tend to reflect their own experiences. This was when the work really took on an importance in the context of what the organization is doing.

Every Friday afternoon, *Avenir de L'Enfant* would hold a 'Pedagogical Meeting' at the *Foyer d'Observation*, with representatives of the board of directors, outreach workers and the three centres, to discuss general running of the centres, special events or news, and individual case studies. Democracy is highly valued, and there is a policy of decentralization of decision-making. All matters are decided on by the staff who work regularly with the young people, however difficult that process sometimes is. My role in those meetings was to feed back observations I made through the drama workshops and also absorb information about the running of the centres, and the individual stories of the children I worked with, which would inform my work with them. This was fascinating. I was able to recognize within the 'fictitious' scenes the children created with me, elements of their real lives, like a boy who commented on a still image, saying that the boy being consoled by another boy was regretting having run away from the workshop where he worked. In fact this boy had himself run away from an apprenticeship set up for him by *Avenir de l'Enfant*. The fact that the story then created by the whole group revealed that the boy had been mistreated by the boss of the workshop, points to the common exploitation and ill-treatment these young people experience.

One session at the *Foyer d'Observation* particularly sticks in my memory. I predicted there would be a strange dynamic, since the children had just come back from a camp designed to facilitate the family mediation process. Many of the children from the relatively large group had thus rejoined their families. Those who were left were the cases where reconciliation was either impossible or more difficult, and this much depleted group was feeling somewhat despondent.

I wanted to make sure the workshop was a particularly positive experience, and would help them to find comfort in each other. I therefore proposed an exercise which involved complicity. First they walk in pairs, one behind the other, and observe each other's walks. Then they walk side by side, trying to find a common dynamic, stopping together, starting together, turning together, with no one leading, just sensing the impulse of the other. The pair then becomes a three, and gradually builds up until there are two big groups, like shoals of fish, which eventually merges into one. At first, you often find that some resist and do not 'listen' to the other(s), trying to lead, and set the other(s) right. Others will fall happily into a follower position. They will also tend to look down at their feet, trying to match their footsteps with those of their partner or group, and trying to predict the next movement, instead of feeling it. I encouraged them to look straight ahead, and use other senses to find the complicity. It took a lot of persistence and nearly the whole session, but eventually there was a beautiful concentration and sense of unity in the room. It was like something clicked, and you could sense the pleasure they were getting from doing these movements together. They went on and on, carried by their own momentum until, quite naturally, they all stopped. It was a very special moment. Any whiff of the sometimes strong competition and aggression between the boys had disappeared.

I felt it was important to recognize and reflect on the achievement together at the end of the session. We did not always do this collectively, but now we sat down and discussed what had just happened, and each boy expressed how the exercise had made him feel. One boy said, 'We are often very separate, and sometimes lonely, it felt good to do something all together, to be part of something.' We discussed the importance of individual responsibility, but also the support and strength you can find in solidarity with a group. We also discussed the importance of looking forward instead of down. One child pointed out that if you look down, you can avoid things on the path in front of you and not fall over them. I pointed out that looking ahead, you can see those things coming in advance, and do something in time to avoid them. These were all strong metaphors for life, and I used the opportunity to emphasize what I thought they were all capable of, and what progress we had made together.

Working with the children at the *Blaise Senghor Cultural Centre*, and the association *Ben Boy* was a completely different experience. These were generally not street children, although many of them who lived in the surrounding neighbourhoods came from families with economic and social problems. The first few months of workshops were manic. Ismaila Thiam had been running creative workshops at the centre every Wednesday and Saturday afternoon for a year and a half, and everyone was welcome. This was great in theory, but in practice meant that some weeks up to 80 kids showed up, and the next session there might be 20. This made it difficult to initiate any kind of process. There was a big age range, and lots of rivalries between children from different neighbourhoods. I sometimes found myself working without support with a group of up to 60 children. This made work with partners or individuals virtually impossible, and generally enforced a policy of group exercises in the circle, which meant that the creative input of each child was more limited, and it was difficult to develop exercises and hone skills. The days when the group was smaller bore more fruit, and we could really get somewhere. Then the Cultural Centre's creative workshops began, and I was asked to run the drama workshops. Despite organizational problems, in many ways this was an improved situation. Many of the children in the group (limited to 20, but finally numbering about 12), had been regulars at the creative workshops before anyway, and so knew me, but this group was far more focused, and had chosen to do drama.

We began with similar introductory drama exercises, but after a few sessions we soon built up a narrative for our play using the image theatre techniques I referred to earlier. I wanted the children to have as much creative input as possible, to make the main decisions and use their language to express themselves. I helped frame the piece and decided upon the theatrical forms, and did suggest a few story line details, but largely the narrative was created by the children and the text and characters were defined and improvised by them. The play, called *Batt Maam (Grandfather's Voice)*, was framed by a grandfather telling his grandchildren a tale: the story of how he met his now dead wife, won her heart, and overcame rejection from her family, due to his coming from a poor family and having seemingly few assets. The grandchildren take on the roles within his story, and the grandmother (whose spirit is evoked by the story telling), and grandfather, flit in and out. In my direction and design of the piece, I was definitely influenced by traditional performance practices and aesthetics, which I was absorbing throughout my time there. The intergenerational oral history element and educational role of elders, the place held by music and movement in the piece, and the pieces of the set made of found objects were all examples of this. The play was performed as part of *Fest'Art* International Theatre Festival for Peace, and at the culmination of the Centre's Creative Workshop programme. Music was provided by Moussa Niasse and Gabi Bâ on traditional instruments.

This was the first time such young children had performed as part of the International Theatre Festival, and the audience was largely made up of children: street children from the associations *Avenir de l'Enfant* and *Empire des Enfants*, and those who had just watched the other children's show within the festival, a puppet theatre company from Niger. I felt it was very important that children took part in a festival of theatre for peace. Once again, the road there was not easy: I had to deal with arguments within the group, inconsistent attendance, little real time for rehearsals and inappropriate rehearsal spaces. The children were also unused to the discipline of rehearsals; they thought that having done something once, they would not need to repeat it again, and did not always realize the importance of precision and detail. However, the children were proud of their performances (even if some were slightly overcome by being confronted by such a big audience!), and were very clear that it was *their* creation with help from me.

The evaluations I made with the different sets of children I had worked with were very interesting. The children who had performed in *Batt Maam* all wanted to continue doing drama, although some of the girls did say next time they would do dance workshops too. One little girl said, 'Theatre helps us to be wiser, and teaches us how we should behave. Our story tells us that love is the most important thing.' The 15-year-old who skilfully played the grandfather, said he would like to be in other plays, and his ambition is to write a solo piece to be performed by himself!

At *Avenir de l'Enfant*, ambitions were more modest, but the young people were very aware of the value of what we had been through together. One boy said 'Sometimes in this life you feel lonely. Next time I feel like that, I will think about the work we did with Rosa, and practise some of the exercises, and it will console me.' Many of the boys said they felt the physical benefit of the drama exercises, it made their bodies feel good. They recognized that they had shared their stories, and this took a weight off their shoulders. They all agreed they should continue doing drama work, and many said they now felt confident to do it without help, and would help each other to remember the exercises and work together.

Before I left Senegal, I met a number of other individuals and organizations keen to use drama to work with young people at risk. Ibou Diallo with whom I worked at Blaise Senghor and at the Primary school is currently doing a training course about working with young people. Azziz Gueye, Babacar Fall and Dramane Tandiane continue to use drama in their work with children, and the creative workshops at Blaise Senghor run by Ismaila Thiam continue. Organizations like *Lumière*, (another NGO working with street children in the south of Senegal), and *Sauvegarde*, an educational centre working for the prevention of juvenile delinquency, would like me to return to work with their staff and young people. Individuals and organizations are mobilizing creativity in the way they work, and recognize the value of theatre. This is vital in a developing country, but until creativity in education is made a priority, and there is more funding and infrastructure for theatre projects, for those individual people and groups, it is an uphill struggle.

NOTE

1 The book *Games for Actors and Non Actors* by Augusto Boal (London & New York: Routledge, 1992), translated by Adrian Jackson is a very good introduction to this work, and a source of games and exercises.

West African Child Rights Theatre for Development
Stories as theatre, theatre as a strategy for change

MICHAEL ETHERTON

Human rights, creativity and drama

My intention is to give an account of what some young Africans achieved, together with a small number of adults, in some Child Rights Theatre for Development (CR-TfD) training workshops. They took place in 7 African countries, between 2001 and 2003. I explore how young and poor Africans – children from 9 to 12 and adolescents from 13 to 18 – can meld a compelling performance aesthetic out of the process of claiming their rights and finding ways for them to achieve long-term social transformations. This is done in their way and in their own time.[1]

This work followed similar CR-TfD training with adults and children in South Asia, when I worked for Save the Children UK (SC UK).[2] When I left South Asia, the agency asked me if I would run occasional drama workshops similar to the South Asian ones in various African countries. The purpose would be to train SC UK's African staff in both child rights and in children and young people's participation in civil society, using this collaborative creative process.

My work in South Asia involved me working in the late 1990s with a group of South Asians to develop a particular kind of drama with Asian children that addressed the denial of young people's human rights. This work took place from 1998, starting in Bangladesh. We eventually extended the work to communities in India, Pakistan, Nepal and Sri Lanka.

SC UK has supported the work in South Asia and Africa. Those of us who developed CR-TfD all worked full-time for SC UK as development workers.[3] SC UK along with all the other agencies based their Child Rights work on the United Nations Convention on the Rights of the Child (the CRC). Children are defined in the CRC from birth to 18 years old. Our engagement was with 9 to 18 year-olds.

We were not theatre activists, although one or two had a background in theatre. I, for example, had worked in popular theatre in Africa; and two of my Bangladeshi colleagues in Save the Children were also involved in the emerging post-colonial Bangladeshi theatre.[4]

Although the process has become known as Child Rights Theatre for Development, the term represents an idea or concept that is confusing and alienating. Child rights, theatre, and development are three discrete areas of practice. Each represents a discourse that operates quite separately from the others. A great deal of my time has been spent dealing with the antagonisms that one or more of these terms provokes among different groups of adults. Part of the process in linking the separate ideas is to deal with these antagonisms, both theoretically and in practice.

Adults can recognize immediately when young people's drama and performances have great artistic quality. What they find more difficult to recognize is the need for young people to have creative autonomy and to be able to achieve artistic quality on their own, in their own aesthetic, in order to engage with adults. Adults need to learn to work with this youthful and productive autonomy that aims to impinge on their world of decision-making.

NGO adult activists working with young people should aim for good drama that is effective in performance. This effectiveness can be defined as an immediate response by a particular audience who find themselves seeing and hearing radical and compelling theatre. In a rights-based development context, adults who are invited to a performance by young people, and who probably come to a performance out of a sense of duty or obligation – even patronizingly, expecting to be embarrassed – should leave astounded. They should be amazed by the power of the performance they have witnessed. They should leave it with a transformed view of young people's creative abilities and the way the young people can focus a serious adult discussion.

For example, we began with a CR-TfD workshop in Liberia. Our premise was that even if just a few Liberian adults, who make decisions for young people, gain a greater respect for the independent abilities of children then change will begin. Adults need to see directly children's ability to transform their national society. To create a global movement of active young people in civil society we have to start with a few seeds of change. Community by community and country by country, young people could in time transform a continent. This is already starting to happen in South Asia and in Latin America; and CR-TfD has contributed to this new awareness.

The adults and children involved in CR-TfD are concerned, more generally, with the denial of human rights that poor and disadvantaged young people experience in their daily lives. Young people themselves are, of course, aware of the wrong done to them. Often, they can express it clearly, in general terms that are applicable to them and to very large numbers of other young people in their societies. However, when they express their understanding of their situation, they are not listened to, or even heard. Their dramas, and the detailed discussions with audiences that follow, together become a more compelling expression of their growing awareness.

When creativity and rights come together in a dynamic process, young people, from 9 to 18 years old, can create a new kind of drama aesthetic in performance. Within this age range, the younger children have an aesthetic different from older adolescents. This is only partly to do with the problems that they have to deal with. It is also, in part, the way they want to express their sense of themselves on the cusp of adolescence. Within this CR-TfD creative process the older adolescents learn to respect the younger children's ideas and the plays they create.

The performances – by older and younger children – flow into substantive discussions. The young people have prepared themselves to initiate discussions with those adults who are in positions of power. Adults find the whole process challenging but also compelling. The confidence and competence of young people in an adult world of decision-making is a surprise to the young people themselves, as much as it is to the adults around them in their societies. Young people feel that for the first time their own voices and their own art, expressing their own ideas, have been seen and heard. Sometimes, adults who hold the power can even decide to change their attitudes and behaviour towards children, in the light of what the young people reveal about their lives. The utilitarian aspects of this work have already been written up.[5]

What is developed here is an analysis of the aesthetics of this new kind of drama. There has been relatively little interest among development managers and policy-makers in the *artistic endeavour* that empowers young people to claim their rights. This is mirrored in the indifference, even antagonism, many theatre practitioners have to development processes. Far from TfD being an excrescence of either 'Theatre' or 'Development' – as theatre and development establishments dismissively see it – it should be seen as a radical new dramatic art, part of a whole new architecture of performance.

What evolved in the African CR-TfD workshops has been our adult understanding of the multifaceted artistic aesthetic of extremely disadvantaged and excluded young Africans. The denial of their basic human rights is now globally engendered. Their aesthetic is a distillation of their own globally aware culture, be it on sprawling urban streets, in impoverished rural areas, or in refugee camps. To climb up out of their poverty, boys and girls are evolving a whole range of expressive styles: in their own urban music, in drawing cartoons and graffiti, and in their own collectively created dramatic performances.

What we have discovered is that these arts of young people themselves cohere and flourish when they are linked to the business of fighting for their rights.

CR-TfD training workshop in Liberia

The first training took place in Liberia.[6] SC UK has an emergency relief programme in the country and also brings a commitment to child rights. This dictates the way in which this particular International NGO (INGO) disburses its aid and assistance. Training in child rights was already underway when I was invited there to run a TfD training workshop with the Liberian staff in the SC UK programme. The rights training was by Fred Kasozi, a Ugandan child rights trainer with SC UK. Subsequently he and I ran TfD training workshops in other countries together. In Liberia we also worked with Miatta Abdullahi, who headed the child rights section of SC UK's Liberian operation, and her Liberian colleagues.[7]

The Indian sub-continent[8] is much further on in respect of child rights activism by adults and young people. Young local activists in parts of South Asia now lobby for their rights within civil society. Child rights agencies in Lesotho, South Africa and Liberia had for some time been keen to develop an expertise in promoting rights among its staff and, more significantly, with children and young people themselves. In Africa in 2001 this conscious move to empower young people was exceptional.

In terms of the aesthetics of performance, I returned to the popular theatre work I had been involved with, in Nigeria, many years before.[9] That earlier work was with adults. It sprang out of Augusto Boal's Forum Theatre. There, we focused on the deliberately uncompleted play, and made extensive use of irony, paradox and contradiction. In writing up this work then, Brian Crow and I introduced these ideas as a new kind of drama aesthetic, as much as a mechanism for social or political change.

We had found in South Asia that these elements had enabled the young people and the adults working with them to confront a deeper reality in their lives, as they perceived that reality, in drama. Many of the young Africans we worked with seemed to be able to develop a much longer story of their collective lives than their Asian counterparts. The young Africans then only dramatized parts of their stories. Much more than the young Asians, these young Africans' sense of *incompleteness* in their lives and in their stories seems to be organic to their worldview.

In all our work with NGOs there is, first, a workshop with the adults. This is usually with SC UK staff members. They go through four days of experiential learning to make and perform dramas, and to develop analyses of significant issues. We undertook this in Liberia. Even the British expatriate Country Director took part in the experiential workshop.

After we had completed the adult training in Monrovia, we left the capital for one of the Sierra Leone refugee camps in Liberia near the border with Côte d'Ivoire.[10] Sinje is a small Liberian town in the west of the country that now hosts several refugee camps. These house refugees who had fled from the fighting in Sierra Leone. The tents and other temporary structures of the camps march over the forest-cleared hills. Their temporary inhabitants surround and swamp the Liberian community living in Sinje.

Some of the adolescents in these camps have been child soldiers, boys who shot people and even cut off the arms and hands of other children. Many of them have witnessed terrible atrocities.[11] In this workshop we worked with 18 children between the ages of 13 and 17. We had six facilitators who had done the initial training in Monrovia. There was also a group of six other adults, three from the Sinje office and three from the local community, working in the camps. There were an equal number of Sierra Leonean boys and girls from the camps. They were selected from the clubs in the camps that the SC UK adult team had already set up. In addition, six adolescents who came were Liberians from Sinje.

We went to Sinje on the Friday, the day before we were due to begin the workshop. Fred and I were accommodated in the tiny office, in little rooms, on mats on the floor, under treated bed-nets; our co-facilitators were billeted with local Liberians in the town. Humidity by day gave way to rain, lightning and continuous rolling thunder by night. The workshop was due to take place in the nearby Liberian secondary school, in three classrooms that opened up to form a school hall. They were filled with heavy and cumbersome iron desks and benches.

On the Saturday from about 7.00 am a couple of us facilitators, together with three children, moved the iron desks and tried to sweep the filthy echoing space. We intended to begin at 8.00 am. Hardly anyone was there, in this brick-forlorn Liberian secondary school, except a hymn-singing adult evangelical group, in a classroom across the yard, which, to my surprise, went on for most of the day. I marvelled at the faith needed to sit in a dirty classroom behind an iron desk, clapping hands and singing hymns all day.

Between 8.00 and 9.00 am we went from hardly any participants to twice the number we had invited to attend. Eventually we achieved the right number, and were able to lay down sturdy plastic – conned off UNHCR – on the dirty floor. In the workshops adults and children sit on the floor together. It is a levelling-off between the ages.

The workshop in Sinje went on for four full days. The adults and the young people participated from 8.00 am until about 4.00 pm. After this, the adult facilitators did another couple of hours of facilitation training with me, and also some further training on their own, or in pairs, ready for the next day. The adolescents were divided into three groups: there were two groups of younger adolescents and one group of older adolescents. Each group created a drama and developed an analysis of what it was they wanted to communicate to other people about their lives. There was a fourth group of adult participants doing this creative work for the first time within their development careers, who also developed their own drama about what they wanted to say. The issue they focused on was HIV/AIDS, but eventually their drama – and the subsequent discussion – was more on the total denial by adults and officialdom in Liberia of this scourge than about the causes of AIDS.

All of the four plays had artistic merit. They were also full of meaning – but devoid of messages to any kind of an audience. All deserved to be recorded in one way or another; but unfortunately they were not. The Sinje performances existed in our minds, collectively, both in terms of some vivid scenes and also in terms of the dilemmas they portrayed; and we spoke about them subsequently. One of the adolescents' groups went on to perform at least one of their plays again in the camps.

There is a problem, in fact, about the ephemeral nature of the artistic achievements of young people. This is not simply a matter of finding some means of electronically recording the performances, but of maintaining a balance between the creative process and electronic evidence of significant discussions between children and powerful adults. Young people the world over want to be able to go on creating new plays on their own initiative. They would also like to have digital video records of their collective artistic achievement. The purpose of a performance event is not to make a video of it, but expensive equipment and technicians can dangerously make it so.

A more detailed description of the creative and analytical process within one of the groups may indicate the significance of the interaction between young people and adults. This was on much more of a level playing-field between adults and young people, in a more open atmosphere than is usual between children and adults. The facilitation aims always to challenge young people to think things through, sorting out cause and effect, without either seeming to be threatening or judgmental of their views and attitudes.

One of the plays was built around a situation identified by some of the adolescent girls as being a significant problem in their lives: teachers having sex with their female students. The INGO adults, once they had got over their shock that this was in fact frequently happening in Sinje, initially assumed that, typically, male teachers were abusing the girls. The girls were rape victims. The teachers were using their status and power over them to satisfy their lust.

'No,' said the girls in the group. 'That's not what we are saying. It's just unfair.'

'Unfair?' We adults were confused.

'Yes. Very unfair,' the girls and the boys insisted. 'Often, it's not very bright girls. Actually they're useless at the lessons. They sleep with the teacher in order to get very high exam marks. They could never get those marks on their own. They just don't have the ability.'

'So you're blaming the girls?' asked one of the SC UK adults, incredulously. 'Not the teacher?' One of the facilitators asked, 'Why are you blaming the girls?'

'Not just blaming the girls,' says one of the girls, emphatically. 'We are blaming the teacher, of course. The teacher is to blame because he should grade the exams properly. According to whether the answers are correct or not.'

'And sometimes,' another girl adds, 'the teacher promises to give you high marks if you sleep with him. But I can get high marks anyway. I fully understand the lessons. If the others come to know that I've slept with him – the teacher – they will not believe that I earned those high grades. This is the unfairness of it, you see.'

The others agreed. There was more discussion and they agreed that the best thing would be if teachers could be publicly exposed in the school when they had sex with pupils. They understood the situation quite differently to the adults. The real problem was the credibility of the examinations on which their futures depended. Sex between older men and teenage girls, including rape of the girls, was also a serious problem and they were concerned about it. But the two issues should not be confused.

The drama they developed eventually went even further than this. It focused on the girl's father – not on the teacher, nor the girl who had complicit sex with him. They portrayed the father as a traditionalist: sons should be educated, not daughters. Daughters should be married off as soon as possible. They portrayed the girl in the play as a very average student, certainly not an academic highflier. But she was determined to get herself an education and not to be married off as an ignorant young woman. The father used her poor marks as a reason to stop her schooling; and for this reason she agrees to have 'sex for success' with the teacher. The twist in the story is that the father himself is having sex with a young adolescent girl. What's more, this girl turns out to be the daughter of the teacher – with the inevitable pregnancy. The drama made the most of the irony and paradoxes in this situation to expose adult double standards, and the unfairness to all the students of the teacher's behaviour, as well as the behaviour of their parents.

The play was incredibly funny. One scene flowed into the next. Dramatic ironies played havoc with the audience's expectations. It was also well acted. The drama this group created did not have a conclusion. Nor did it seek to try out alternative statements or behaviour, as you might get in Boal's Forum Theatre. The group presented their evolving piece to their co-participants in the other groups for critical commentary on both the personalities involved and the situations into which they had dug themselves. The initial audience, made up of their workshop colleagues, told them what they understood from their drama. If this was different from what they intended, the group had to go away and re-do their scenes. This sharpening of the focus is an integral part of this particular TfD process.

This was just one of the four plays created in Sinje. The others were equally interesting and intellectually fresh in their interpretation of problems. The deepening awareness among all of us was the gift that the young people gave the adults in the workshop.

The plays take audiences into the deeper reality of the issues affecting their lives. It is not enough just to consult children and adolescents. Many adults who claim the authority to speak on behalf of children and young people see such consultation as sufficient in order to say what is to be done. They miss what is really significant. The way young people understand their lives and the world they will inherit *emerges through their dramas and other creative media*. Then it is further defined by the on-going discussions that these performances excitedly lead onto.

I contend that in order to get to this deeper awareness there has to be a serious creative purpose. The whole process of understanding the lives of, and our interactions with, young people can be underpinned by a coherent aesthetic of improvisation and dramatic performance. The problem is that adults working in development, who focus on child rights, do not regard children's creativity as a vital ingredient of claiming their rights or of being directly involved in social change, both in the short term and the long term. On the other hand, adults who are more focused on children's collective creativity, especially in drama and theatre, don't automatically become part of the global movement for children that the child-rights side of the development industry has now begun to usher in.[12]

This workshop in Sinje was followed by another workshop back in Monrovia. This was with Liberian children and adolescents from 9 to 18 years old, from some other parts of the country outside of Monrovia that were still able to reach the capital. This third intense workshop in a row was exhausting for the facilitators, but there were two outcomes that were significant. The first was the successful performance of four short plays to an invited audience of Liberians from other INGOs. These adults were amazed at the quality of all but one of the performances. They imagined that they had been scripted by adults, learned by heart and directed by adults. The fact that they were the stories, ideas and concerns of the young people continued to be met with disbelief. Adults working in development will always know when a performance succeeds in being truthful and convincing. But they expect this level of artistic achievement to be achieved only by adults and within the framework of scripted and rehearsed drama. Adults imagine that novices cannot achieve good performances. Most also believe that improvisation and spontaneity cannot achieve them either.

This workshop demonstrated to the participants unambiguously that improvisation by young novices, resulting in four plays of 15-minutes each, can achieve an effective level of artistic creation. The work immediately engaged the audience. It sustained this engagement right through to the end of lengthy discussions which, in small groups, flowed for about 45 minutes after the four performances had been staged. They reflected a level of analysis that gave new insights into problems already identified by adults. Young people had succeeded in making adults think differently about some important issues. In fact these key issues related to the ways in which young people perceived the denial of their basic rights.

The Save the Children adults, particularly the managers of the agency's operation in Liberia, commented, at the conclusion of this third workshop, that taking the plays of the three workshops together, the perceptions of young Liberians about adult Liberian society were very bleak. Adults unremittingly pursued quite selfish ends. The family, as a positive, nurturing institution, had disintegrated.

The play by the younger children – pre-teens – showed step-parents to be hugely traumatic. A child's status in the family of her biological parents may seem tough to the outsider and not much different when a stepmother arrives with her children. But to the child, the transformation of her status in her father's home is cataclysmic. She goes from being a child of the family to a slave without hope in the house that has been her home. Ad hoc calculations from known statistics suggested that perhaps as many as 60 per cent of children in Monrovia and its environs had one step-parent.

Sierra Leone

The training and the workshops in Sierra Leone took place nine months after the Liberian training in TfD. In the interim, Fred Kasozi and I had completed a two-week training programme in Mozambique.

As we reflected on this work, Fred and I realized that our Liberian and Mozambican colleagues, together with the children with whom they had done the workshops, had transformed this CR-TfD process to the particular culture and dynamics of creativity in their country. We had engaged with the drama-making abilities of young Africans. This was specific to the complex cultures of, first, Liberia (West African, American-oriented and largely Anglophone) and, second, Mozambique (Southern African, ex-Portuguese colony and Lusophone).

In Sierra Leone, the children and young people were in especially impoverished and tricky situations. In 2002 Sierra Leone was just coming out of its civil war. The UN peace-keeping presence was to ensure the process of reuniting the country and supporting reconstruction in the war-battered countryside.[13] Children and young people were returning to their families and communities from their refugee camps in neighbouring African countries, as well as from internal displacement within Sierra Leone. This return was not always something that the young people wanted for themselves. We had learned from the Liberian workshops how dreadful, sometimes, their homes could be for them.

The Sierra Leone cultural emphasis was in the languages used in the workshops, in the songs and music created within the performances, and in the Sierra Leone adolescents' personal style: the music they listened to, their clothes, gestures, movements, aspirations. The context of this youth culture was the recent civil war, internal and external migration, repatriation, and grinding rural poverty. The workshops gave this rather nebulous teenage sub-culture some sort of recognition among adults who were working in development. The essence of the culture reflected keen powers of observation and an ironic stance.

This teenage style is, in essence, similar to other countries in Africa whose populations are now emerging out of long civil wars into fragile peace-making. The ghetto language may be different, but the attitude is very similar. The Angola CR-TfD workshop a year later revealed a similar ghetto adolescent culture. It was based in modes of dress, gestures, and, above all, in the new rap /hip-hop music in Portuguese patois. These young urban Angolans were more observant and ironic than their rural Sierra Leone counterparts, but their attitudes were very similar.

In fact, these urban youth, living among guns and poverty, were much more liberated, aware and critical of Angolan officialdom than the Angolan adults. The 30 to 40 year-old adults who were working with the young people belonged to a generation that had only known civil war. The social oppression on both sides of that dreadful ideological war had left its psychological marks on them.[14]

In Sierra Leone, in order to engage with this teenage subculture, we needed to enable the adults to interpret their collective creativity within their own post-conflict culture. These are adults who work in the development sector. They were starting to focus in their development work on child rights, as set out in the UN CRC. SC UK would like their staff to be able to work more effectively with young people in those countries where they have development programmes to benefit children. The staff needed to acquire a range of skills to facilitate the participation of children and young people in decision-making. A training programme for them in TfD techniques might possibly provide them with the skills to enable young people to be effective in communicating with adults.

These first TfD training workshops therefore, in 2001 and 2002, were commissioned by the agency on a trial basis. The senior management was not yet convinced of the appropriateness of this particular kind of creative empowerment of young people. Role-plays were okay, as were message-laden plays. But handing over the initiative for action to young people was another thing altogether.

It is necessary to analyse, first, the aesthetics of improvisation with *the adults* in the development industry whose management of development projects impacts on the lives of young people.

Most of these adults do not have any significant practical experience of the art of drama and performance. They have no experience at all of improvisation in its artistic, dramatic sense. What they may have is experience of short role-plays around specific messages within the development agenda. In so far as this is drama, it is a 'message-laden' theatre. So unequivocal are the messages that they might just as well be displayed on a good poster.

This kind of role-play, beloved of development agencies, demonstrates good and bad behaviour for the education of audiences who are usually forced to watch it. Role-play is used as an alternative method of teaching in NGO workshops. Participants are usually told to 'act out' characters with good and bad attitudes. It is meant to show the problem under discussion 'directly'. The acting is merely illustrative of a pre-determined learning outcome. NGO 'role-plays' and 'message-skits' lack merit, either as art or as development – though sometimes they are given a little Boalian dressing-up, by way of a couple of alternative 'outcomes'.

For adults working in NGOs, who are about to venture into improvised drama that engages with human rights, the role-plays of their NGO world are, however, a starting point. In four days they move a long way away from that starting point. The TfD process they go through is experiential learning for them; it works at their adult level; and it works collectively. People learn from each other. The problems they work out together in a dramatic form, and which they subsequently perform to their colleagues in other agencies, are problems they have identified that matter to them. They are realized artistically, as a shared awareness. These plays open out to further analysis of their causes and complexity.

The issues are different for men and for women. Younger women and older women, younger men and older men, have different ideas of the problems of working for an INGO in Africa. There is a problem with managers, with the conflict between the demands of work and the demands of their homes and their families. These personal problems are strongly contextualized for very poor people by the wider national tensions of living and working in what Oswaldo de Rivero called *non-viable national economies* or, worse, *ungovernable chaotic entities*.[15]

There are no simple, pre-ordained solutions; and for nationals on US dollar salaries whose work is in poor communities, among the shattered lives of their compatriots, the contradictions are often overwhelming.

The contradictions are often better confronted through fiction. Powerful stories have their own truthfulness, made up of ironical elements, paradoxical elements and contradictions. They generate surprise and suggest honourable compromises that are the least bad options for most of the protagonists. Turning these stories into effective dramas, through collective improvisation, building up the fiction scene by scene, will turn the story into something more than just a story. It becomes an animated and unfolding present that calls both the past and the future into active questioning. We want to know what happens next. If it is not what we expect, but more significant than what we were expecting, we are amazed. We see its roots in a new interpretation of the causal past of the story.

We are part of the drama that is unfolding, but it is more than a part of us. It makes us a part of common humanity. Together, actors and audience are confirming what it means to be human.[16] When I watch young people from many different cultures, in many parts of the world, improvise their collective experience, I strongly sense that they too are discovering a shared humanity between adults and young people.

The adult training workshop in Sierra Leone led the adult participants into this drama aesthetic in performance. They discussed the extraordinary experience of the single performance of the plays they had developed with their colleagues in other INGOs and Sierra Leone NGOs. What amazed them, and what they found inexplicable, was that the dramas had no messages, were incomplete, and presented no obvious solutions to problems that had not previously been expressed in public. Development managers and workers have to believe in solutions; their projects are designed on the basis of impact and achieving positive change.

The dramas peeled back this layer of certitude and developmental determinism. They exposed the doubts about projects and what they actually manage to achieve. As a result, they generated an informed, animated discussion in small groups among the audience members. These discussions went on for an hour after the performances. The discussions were not about the plays – though tangentially a scene or a character might provide an apposite reference – but about their lives, work and country.

This was a large workshop with 21 adult participants, 20 of whom were new to drama and improvisation.[17] Three dramas were developed. One of the plays was set in a rural community and a story evolved concerning leadership in the community, male pride and ambition, the sense of belonging, family strife and the dashed hopes of the next generation.

Once a basic story was turned into scenes through improvisation, it started to evolve in other directions. Various TfD exercises – mirror exercises, improvisations in pairs, trios and fours, 'hot seat'; 'status'; 'sculptures' – resulted in a growing intensity in the characterization and a deeper complexity in the dilemmas. The play developed as a result of exposure to criticisms from the rest of the group – whose own plays were then subjected to close scrutiny.

Like the other two plays, certain vignettes were so deeply embedded in irony and so well acted that they developed an iconic status for the duration of the workshop. One example was the short scene, over almost as soon as it started, in which the overbearing and ambitious father insisted that his 16-year-old son wear the ugly boots he had bought him. The 'boy' – played by one of the adults – teetered on the brink of rebellion, but did not quite know how to prosecute it. Mother and sister urged restraint; but the bottled-up compliance led to a greater revolt later. The boy wanted some fake Nike shoes; the father accused him of undermining African tradition. But the tradition the father upheld was nothing but negative and destructive self-interest, expressed through an arrogant patriarchy.

That little scene had been spontaneous. It had not been planned in any way. Yet it seemed so true to life that it immediately struck a chord with us. The offending shoes – there, physically, in the acting arena – laced their way through subsequent scenes and became a metaphor for a complex cultural transformation that was taking place between the generations, finessed by the civil war that had been ended by foreign intervention.

Two further points need to be made about the adult training. The first concerns the language and registers used in the workshop and in the dramas created. The second concerns the notion of 'acting'.

Sierra Leone's national language is Sierra Leone Creole.[18] There are a number of other languages spoken by certain communities in Sierra Leone, but the linguistic dynamic is generally between a fairly standardized English and Creole. Although the workshop itself functioned in fairly standard oral English, the players spoke in Creole. Except, that is, for the one native British participant, who played a tribal chief but spoke in standardized English that was both simple and robust. One of the people from Côte d'Ivoire could not speak any English.[19] Her role in the drama she helped create took account of this. Actors spoke in a register of the language they felt most comfortable using in improvisation. As the workshop progressed the plays became linguistically rich. Actors became increasingly subtle in the ways in which they used both language and their bodies. This led on to a further semantic subtlety as startlingly appropriate words, suddenly used in the improvisation, were then discussed.

A similar subtlety in the acting developed over the four days of the workshop.[20] Most of the participants who have never done improvisation are terrified of it. They are encouraged in the early exercises to concentrate on the situations and the dilemmas, on the time of day, on the details of each situation. They are specifically discouraged from self-consciously 'acting', taking a role, as though they were trying to become some rather stereotypically 'other' person. They are encouraged to think in terms of images, rather than texts. They are led to discover that their bodies are naturally expressive, without even trying to be. The situations, and the scenes collectively created, are discovered to be energising. After some practice at improvisation, most of the participants find the situations that they are developing surprisingly comfortable. They expected to be discomforted doing them, yet they aren't. They begin to enjoy contributing to the overall creative effort.

The Freetown Workshop that trained the adult facilitators was followed by three simultaneous workshops with young people in different parts of the country. The report on all four workshops was produced by many of the adult participants. They used the opportunity to comment on their experience of being a participant and then a facilitator of TfD with children. The following is part of the commentary by one of the men from the field who participated:

> Before Lakka [Freetown], TfD was, to me, mere child's play. I had never, before then, been enthused by the glamorous impressions people gave me about it. I had studied drama during my first three years in college. We made novels into drama, staged plays and even acted a movie. 'What ... would be new to me?' was the question that engaged me all through.
>
> But when we started the mirror exercises, imaging and discussions on issues, I became a different person altogether. The impact of those exercises and the attendant ripples on my imagination were extraordinarily overwhelming ...[21]

Francophone West Africa: Burkina Faso and Mali

The final TfD training in West Africa took place in Burkina Faso and Mali in January 2003.[22] The first training workshop was conducted in French; the two subsequent workshops with adults and young people were bilingual, using French and Fulfulde.[23]

Nine small 20-minute dramas were developed into performance in the three workshops. There were three plays in the initial adult training in Ouagadougou; three plays in Dori and three plays in Sevare (in Mali). Every one of the plays generated a great deal of discussion during and after the workshops around the content of the dramas and the dilemmas that they each raised. Some of the plays provoked interesting commentary on the artistic achievement of the particular play and on the way in which the whole event – three plays, songs, interludes and discussions – was creatively handled by the whole group.

The discussion was about the relationship of NGO-type content to the performance art that framed it. The typical NGO issues of poverty, oppression and abuse were, probably for the first time, being brought into the lives of those adults whose paid work was to deal with those issues in the lives of poor people. This required a new level of creative achievement to communicate it to colleagues. Some of the participants began to understand the paradigm shift they needed to make.

One of the dramas in particular demonstrated this fusion of artistic achievement with a profound understanding by young people of the problems in adult civil society that affected children. This was a drama created by a group of boys in the Dori workshop. The boys were all very young gold-miners, except one of the group who was the only boy at the local secondary school. It

The Gold-Diggers

On the stage, which is either an apron stage with audience on three sides, or theatre-in-the-round, are a group of young boys. They are young gold-diggers, working a small gold mine. Many such workings dot the countryside in northern Burkina Faso. These lads are mining gold underground under the intermittent supervision of an adult 'Patron', whose office is on the other side of the stage. His relationship to whoever owns the mine is never clarified. The Patron may or may not own the concession. If he doesn't what does it matter to the lads who are risking their lives there. His supervision of them is ad hoc, haphazard and unpredictable.

On a flat stage, the boys create a convincing image of shafts and tunnels, dirt and supervision.

As the mining continues another scene emerges, this time off the stage, in the middle of the audience. This scene depicts a very poor farming family, laid low by successive droughts: a mother, a father and a son – all played by boys in the group. The farmer tells his family that there is no crop, no seeds, no food and no money. He will have to work on the gold mines. The young adolescent son says no, he is the one who should go and get the work on the mine. The mine owners prefer boys to grown men because they can work in the smaller shafts and seams. He has heard this from one of his friends.

The father says no, it's wrong for young boys to work in the mines. It's too dangerous; and anyway, boys should try to get some education – that's the one thing that will stop them becoming poor farmers! As they are discussing all this, within the audience, we see on the stage the mine and the boys labouring 'underground'.

The father treks to the mine where he meets the young miners sitting above the shaft. What chance of work, he asks them. You're too old, they reply. But I'm strong – look, please talk to your Patron to hire me. The boys agree and the scene shifts to the other part of the stage which is the Patron's office, where the man himself has all the while been vacillating between bureaucracy and booze.

After an exchange, the man is hired as though he is just a boy. The risks are on his head. Gold digging continues, with the boys instructing the farmer and 'lowering' him down on a rope into the shaft. The inevitable happens: the shaft collapses and the man is buried under a heavy fall of earth. The boys frantically scrabble to dig him out. But he is dead.

The Patron reacts by distancing himself from the tragedy and by making the boys go and tell the family. This adult task of consolation is even more difficult for the boys than gold mining. The farmer's son blames himself for not insisting on taking the job rather than letting his father do it. Back at the mine, the young gold-diggers try to extract some small compensation for the family out of the Patron. He sends them back to their work while the son, aged 14 and now fearful of the mine, decides to head off to Abidjan to try to survive somehow through city work or even prostitution – to support his mother.

was his specific and emphatic choice to join the gold-diggers, even though he was the outsider there and was actually wanted in the other groups. He was the only boy who spoke both Fulfulde and French; the gold-diggers only spoke Fulfulde. In the end everyone praised his acting, his identification with the other boys and commented how convincing he was as a gold-digger. Outside the drama, however, but still within this group, he played a vital role as translator, subordinating himself completely to the much more disadvantaged boys in the group.

Opposite, in a box, is an English prose version of their performance. A number of the scenarios that have been developed in the subsequent workshops by the young people exist in a similar English (or French or Portuguese) prose form. These 'stories of the dramas' have evolved over the workshop and represent the version of the plays that the young participants who made them consider to be the most appropriate to translate into English. The final English translation is checked with the young people.

The boys in Dori made up a much longer story initially; and then turned it into a drama by themselves. My sole contribution was to suggest that they put the scene with the farmer's family actually into the middle of the audience, instead of crowding it onto the stage. They grasped the idea immediately and loved doing it.

The boys had asked the adult facilitators to invite the District Government officials – the local bigwigs – to the performance of the plays. The officials agreed to come; and they were amazed at the quality of the whole performance event. After all plays had been performed the actors in the three groups divided up the audience and conducted a discussion with them on issues that had informed their plays. The facilitators offered training during the workshop in how to prepare for the discussions and then manage them. What was to be discussed was left to the local groups themselves.

In fact the discussions with the audience continued from those raised by participants from Day One of the workshop. In the workshops, facilitators enable the participants to interact with each other, make stories, turn them into scenes and whole dramas, and to facilitate discussions and analysis. They do not set the agenda or pass judgement on any issue that is raised. The structure of the workshop is designed to enable all kinds of views to be properly represented, analysed and agreed upon, all within what is clearly perceived to be a safe space.

The young gold-miners seized the opportunities that the workshop provided and prepared themselves very well for the discussions they hoped to have with District Government people after the performance. Since most of the boys were illiterate they drew the issues as they saw them in great detail on flip charts as an aide memoir. Their subtle drama and imaginative performance had the effect of becoming a highly significant 'platform' for their lives and their acute awareness. The audience as a whole responded and gave them great applause.

When they confronted the officials they had a great deal of confidence and were very focused. The boys had even intuited that the officials wouldn't – or probably couldn't – speak Fulfulde and so they had set up the schoolboy in their group who also spoke fluent French to interpret for them. They asked him to translate from Fulfulde into French exactly what they were saying; and to translate back into Fulfulde exactly what the officials were saying to them. They would not let the adults fob them off with simple 'solutions' that were no solutions at all. In fact, they did not seem to be heading for immediate solutions: they wanted the government officials to see Burkina Faso as they saw it. They wanted them to see what the country and its future looked like from the bottom of a gold mine, be the miners adults or children.

The story their drama told was full of irony and paradox. For instance, it is not a child who gets killed in a cave-in, it's an adult. The truly painful thing is to see the young boys going to the dead man's home and comforting his bereaved family. This is, surely, 'inventing the human'. The boy who didn't go down the mine goes to Abidjan. In the longer story, the part they couldn't dramatize in the time, he contracts HIV/AIDS.

The problem of getting any kind of formal education was also interesting. One of the boys told the government officials how his friend had to leave school because his parents had no money for the fees. He immediately went to the gold mines, got work and saved up the fees. By the time he could afford to go back to school – his adolescent ambition – he was no longer an adolescent and his body had deteriorated.

When the officials suggested they took the manual skills training, the boys pointed out that it was only available in the District town and they couldn't easily get in to the town. There was a charge they couldn't afford; and when they qualified the only place they could go and use their skills was in the capital, Ouagadougou. Otherwise the exploitative milieu of Abidjan in Côte d'Ivoire and child trafficking beckoned. In fact, two of the other dramas in this workshop had focused on this.

Commentary

Burkina Faso, Mali and most other countries in Africa have recent traditions of TfD with adults: Forum Theatre, popular theatre and theatre with young people. TfD is not new. It has been generated mainly within the universities in Africa and Britain, but particularly in Anglophone West and East African Universities. It has been written up extensively in books and journals.[24] To a much lesser extent, it has also been sponsored by development agencies: INGOs, local NGOs, and occasionally even by bilateral donors like the British DfID or Swedish SIDA.

There are three ways in which the work loosely referred to as Child Rights TfD differs significantly from Augusto Boal's Forum Theatre. It also differs from the adult TfD that has emerged from African popular theatre that has been sustained by the universities, who have nurtured new kinds of participatory political drama within the context of a vibrant new African theatre in English, Creole and Pidgin.

These three differences are, first, that the work is located within the development sector. More specifically, it is deliberately situated within an

INGO that is itself increasingly focusing on Child Rights and children's participation in governance. Secondly, there is an equal emphasis, or focus, on creativity and analysis. Unlocking young people's creative abilities is equalled by the trainer's – or facilitator's – insistence on the development of a strong reasoning capability.

Thirdly, the work reflexively transfers the facilitation and the structure of the process to the participants. It does not just transfer ownership of new drama skills and social content to the participants; it transfers the whole agenda and the very purpose of the work.

How does a vision of Child Rights TfD fit in with African performance traditions?

In the early years of popular theatre in Africa, in the eighties, there already was a kind of deconstruction of drama expertise. The emphasis in, for example, the work of Ross Kidd's *Laedza Batanani* in Botswana was on 'rough theatre'. In effect, the art of drama and the art of performance were subordinated to the campaign's social or political purpose. Quite deliberately, theatre was applied to social change. In these circumstances, theatre or drama did not require an expertise; but good development certainly did. The art of theatre, of drama and of performance was not so much deconstructed as simply set aside.

In Forum Theatre and its many offshoots in political theatre, almost the reverse seemed to occur. A new aesthetic of theatre of the oppressed was consciously developed. It evolved out of the audience's participation in the art of performance and in how that collaboration created meaning. The purpose was the jointly created dramatic performance, by and for those whom theatre normally alienated or excluded. A new kind of performance expertise was realized; and serious Forum Theatre activists needed to acquire this expertise. Conventional development expertise, that usually focused on the project cycle, log-frames, baseline surveys, monitoring and evaluation was irrelevant.

The TfD process with young people in Africa attempts to link, as equally important components, rights-based development with artistic achievement. This is the vision. The artistic aesthetic is not seen as being compromised by rights or by development practice. Child rights, an integral part of human rights, is not undermined by artistic endeavour. The one area of expertise is not diminished when pursuing skills in the other area. Rather, combining these different areas of expertise actually enhances young people's chances as adults in the dangerous global market place.

The different approaches of the various African political drama traditions and global CR-TfD are not in a hierarchy of relevance. One is not better than another. Children have entered the arena of adult theatre and performance with their own playmaking; and they tend to complement the existing cannon. The art of drama and performance as young people shape it, now finds a role to play within the liberation movements that continue to shape humankind. The abolition of slavery, the struggles for workers' rights, the fight for independence and against colonialism, and the women's movement, were all adult movements that enabled oppressed adult groups to claim their inalienable human rights.

The notion of an autonomous global movement for children is new.[25] In different parts of the world, groups of impoverished and socially disadvantaged children are starting to acquire the skills that will enable them, by themselves, effectively to claim their rights as they define them.[26] TfD puts the art of creative drama and the art of performance at their disposal. It is located in the acquisition of negotiation skills, in skills of advocacy and lobbying and in technical media skills.

Situating TfD within development agencies

Child Rights TfD differs from a more conventional adult TfD and children's theatre in that it has emerged out of NGOs that work in civil society.

In South Asia, and subsequently in Africa, this TfD process has originated in Save the Children UK, as a child-centred INGO. The work has found its audiences within the framework of NGO activism within civil society. The training has been of adult development workers, who are not theatre or drama people. The creativity that CR-TfD promotes among children and young people is enhanced by ways in which the NGOs work within civil society. For example, some of the best NGOs in different parts of the world have first pioneered gender awareness in the agency's own field staff and managers as an integral part of their work with poor and oppressed women in urban and rural communities.

This is an institutional and personal reflexivity. That is to say NGO staff work on their own attitudes and prejudices as an inherent part of the project work they initiate with women in very impoverished societies. This personal and sustained critique of themselves indicates to the beneficiaries a sincerity that evokes a positive response from poor and vulnerable women. As a result of the cumulative success of this approach, some NGOs have been able to develop comprehensive and innovative training programmes in gender for their senior management.[27] In addition, this has led to institutional transformation as a way of working. It has taken root in good NGOs and led to much better development practice.

NGOs may therefore have been the right place to begin creative drama within the child rights framework. A number of development-oriented NGOs have within the last five years started to engage comprehensively with human rights. To do this effectively, they have expanded their range of skills at all levels of their operations. These new institutional capabilities are legal expertise, skills in advocacy and lobbying, expertise and strategies for democratic access to the new media. They have begun to challenge governments and big business in innovative ways. They are proving themselves effective and they are starting to have a much greater impact.

CR-TfD has started to contribute to a radical idea of children's and young people's participation in civil society. A number of excellent training packages have been produced: on rights, on children's participation, on children and citizenship, and on youth-led strategies for change.[28]

We have attempted to introduce into SC UK a training process that included the art of drama and performance intended for adults and children, working together. In some ways this insistence on an artistic standard, as much as on the already high standards of adult practice in working with children within development projects, is even more radical. We have tried to locate young people's creativity and artistic achievement within the institution.

Developing creative and analytical abilities together

Two particular capabilities – creativity and rationality – are as innately human as is our ability to learn to use language as a child, both our mother tongue and other languages.[29] The assumption behind this is that children of four years can *talk*, so they must also be able to *reason* and they must be able to *create*. This suggests that *reasoning and creativity* are inextricably bound up in *talking together*. The language capability of very young children confirms the innate ability to be spontaneous yet rational. It is the combined spontaneity and rationality that finds expression in dramatic improvisation.

We can all improvise within fictional situations. We can do this precisely because we are human. We all can and do relate, with great intensity, to collective improvisations as they evolve. This is true of children. It is also true of adults. Adults and children, who are improvising and creating together what are for them significant dramas, do not see any false adult-child relationship in this creative process, no distinction of humankind between them. We are all experts in spontaneity, once we see it in action.

We all have innate rational ability. Children have the ability to reason at the age they can talk. Linked to this is the emergence of an evolving moral sense that develops throughout childhood and adolescence in what are described as moral dilemmas.

The CR-TfD training process has as its overall purpose the empowerment of groups of individuals to link their creative abilities with each other's; to link their reasoning ability with the reasoning abilities of the others; and then to link together these two areas of innate human capability. Workshop after workshop that has used the process has revealed to the facilitators that people do indeed have skills and understanding they never knew they possessed. The facilitators and the structure of the workshops have no other purpose than enabling the participants to discover they can do things they never thought they could do. They can do these things both rationally and creatively as the young people in the African workshops have shown.

CR-TfD places a strong emphasis on the process by which young people realize their reasoning capabilities and analyse their situations with logic and frankness. But the motor for analysis within the workshops is *fiction*. However, it is not an abstract notion of 'fiction'. For the workshop participants it is the stories and the dramas they collectively make. Through the tools of irony, paradox and contradiction – and, of course dramatic irony too – the scenes they create begin to have a life of their own. The plays they have made develop an independent existence that now accompanies the groups that created them.

Both the adults and the young people enjoy the relationship between themselves as creators of the drama and the seemingly independent power of the play they have created. This perhaps explains why most improvisations go through a continuous transformation and then, at some point, they become fixed, completely stable, almost a 'text' (even though it is certainly not a written text). It is as though a moment of startling collective awareness was suddenly achieved during the improvisation process. Thereafter, the group seeks to repeat that moment of enlightenment, to capture that instance of awareness with new and different audiences.

The NGO ethos contributes to the analytical tools in the TfD process. There is a hankering in many NGOs after an ever more convincing explanation of the ways in which macro forces – economic and political – impinge on the micro level of lives lived in obscurity and unfulfilled potential. To translate the hunger for a more convincing explanation of why there is injustice and suffering, to the level of children and young people is both startling and persuasive.

Unfortunately, though, NGOs are very much addicted to 'messages'. If we are to link creativity to rational analysis we need a Rights-based TfD which is the opposite of 'message-laden' drama. Adults in NGOs, especially, find it hard not to slip into a teaching or preaching role, even though they do this with the best intentions in the world. The facilitators, be they adults or children, continuously point out that messages will close off both the creativity and reasoning that is currently going on in the workshop. Young people usually welcome the absence of messages in the plays that they create.

The process delivers plays that make a great impact on their small audiences. They then conduct discussions with their audiences that make sense. Children and young people actually enjoy the alternating activities of playmaking, concentration games and reasonable discussions. However, NGOs as institutions find it very difficult to commit the very core of their work to such extreme dialogical processes.

Transferring the structure and facilitation of the process

This TfD process with young people also insists on transferring the structure and the facilitation of the actual process itself to the participants. This handing over control of the process entails a deconstruction of the notion of expertise, both in 'theatre and drama expertise' and in 'development and human rights expertise'. The purpose of such a deconstruction is to transform our understanding of what constitutes expertise.

Both development agencies and Child Rights groups have started to extend the expertise needed by their professionals. For development agencies, including the bilateral government agencies and the multilateral UN and EU agencies, it is now *de rigeur* to include some form of participatory rural appraisal (PRA) in the process of project formulation. A range of useful tools has been developed: transept walks, mapping, Venn diagrams, and analyses of power relations at the micro level. A participatory expertise has, like a palimpsest, been overlaid on the more traditional development expertise.

An expertise needs experts. 'Expertise' suggests that there is a correct way to do something. Often it then becomes the *only* way you can do it. An orthodoxy develops. Those who previously worked in these areas in their own way begin to feel disempowered. However, creative drama linked to child rights tends to shift the emphasis away from an idea of expertise that trains us to do things in a specific or professional way, and towards the recognition of the innate skills that are in all of us. Unfortunately, our socialisation often leads us to suppress or negate these capabilities.

For the next phase of the training – taking young people and other adults through the process experientially – the facilitation is handed over to the adults of the first workshop. They become in effect trainee-facilitators. At the end of the children's workshop, it is also possible, if the young people want to do more, to hand the structure over to them and to encourage them to experiment with it. Adults practise facilitation skills as they facilitate this kind of TfD and experiential learning with other adults and children. In turn those young people learn facilitation skills and facilitate the creative and rational process with other children or young people.

What holds this all together is the perceived integrity of the drama or other art forms – music, dance, drawings – that have been created during the four days of the workshop. The way artistic integrity and rationality emerges, and is recognized by participants and facilitators alike, is itself capable of scrutiny. The participants can scrutinize every stage of the process, and understand how the whole process achieves artistic integrity.

In the workshops in Africa it is too soon to say if the young people have developed their own drama workshops. There have been a couple of examples of independent initiatives by young people within their communities, particularly in Liberia, Sierra Leone and Nigeria. After the Mozambique workshops, the children organized their own performances of the plays they had developed without any adult initiative. In fact, their subsequent performance, followed by discussions, was on a much larger scale than the one we had arranged with them. Following the Lesotho Training Workshops, some of the young South African adult participants immediately initiated a workshop in the Free State in South Africa with young people in their projects. They felt sufficiently confident to carry out a training in their way. They had taken ownership of the process. In the Luanda ghetto, in Angola, the young people took their drama about sexual abuse and corruption in schools actually into a school. Although the young people themselves asked for, and arranged, this performance, they did it under the protection of those adults who could ensure a positive outcome for them. It brought out into the open a number of problems that adults in education needed to address.

In Asia the work has gone much further, with young people setting up their own theatre groups, particularly in Nepal, where they contribute to advocacy for their rights. In various places in both North and South India the drama work is part of a much broader activism among young people that marks their independent engagement in adult civil society.

Adult NGOs have their own agendas, be they in development or emergencies or in human rights. They have to say what they are going to do; and then they have to do it. Many would find it impossible to raise funds if it were otherwise. NGOs might in the end not be the natural home for this work, even though they encouraged it initially. Perhaps the time has now come for children and young people to set up their own organizations, their own NGOs, their own kinds of institutions. In South Asia and Latin America, for instance, young people are doing precisely this. [30]

What constantly amazes us adults is the quality of the drama the young people create in the process of defining the infringement of their rights. In country after country, in culture after culture, children and young people have a beautiful sense of dramatic improvisation. Young people's art in all kinds of creative media, coupled with their struggle for their rights in an unfair world, stands a good chance of changing the future in ways we adults cannot now imagine.

NOTES

1 The ages of the young Africans were mainly 12 to 16 years old, although there were some children as young as 10 and one or two 17 and 18-year-olds.
2 Within the global Save the Children Alliance there are a number of national Save the Children organizations. Save the Children UK is the oldest and the largest. It was set up in 1922.
3 This work is written up in M. Etherton, 'Child Rights Theatre in South Asia' in R. Boon and J. Plastow (eds) *Theatre and Empowerment* (Cambridge University Press, 2004).
4 See Syed Jamil Ahmed, *Acinpakhi Infinity: Indigenous Theatre in Bangladesh* (Dhaka: The University Press, 2000). See also his *Theatre for Development and Cultural Identity*, University of Warwick, MA dissertation, May 1989. Professor Jamil was linked through his Drama students to our first Save the Children workshop in Bangladesh.
5 A number of SC UK Reports, some of which are internal. Others are more widely available. See the Table in the appendix and the references at the end of this paper. These Reports have focused on Save the Children's programmes in the various countries, of which this work was supposed to be an integral part.
6 Liberia: In 2001, Charles Taylor, warlord and the then President of Liberia, controlled Monrovia, the capital, and only parts of the country. He was removed from office and out of Liberia in September 2003.
7 These included Edwin Dobor and Emanuel Paivey, who were co-trainers on the subsequent Sierra Leone TfD Workshops. It also included Doris Mansarray, who was also a co-facilitator in the later workshop. She is a Sierra Leonean, but at the time was working in the Liberia Programme. Doris co-facilitated with me in Bo in the Sierra Leone Workshop.
8 South Asia, the Indian Sub-continent, comprises, from south to north, Sri Lanka, India, Bangladesh, Bhutan, Nepal, Pakistan, Afghanistan. Afghanistan is sometimes linked geographically to the Middle East. CR-TfD training workshops have been held in Kabul and Mazar-I-Sharrif in 2004.
9 See M. Etherton, *The Development of African Drama* (London: Hutchinson, 1982); and M. Etherton and B. Crow, 'Ideology, Form and Popular Drama' in R. Kidd and N. Colletta, *Tradition for Development* (DDS, Bonn, 1981).
10 During the workshop (July 2001) the emergency situation in the north of the country, where rebels were successfully challenging Taylor's authority, became much worse, resulting in

another wave of internally displaced people. It is difficult to know the scale of the killing and displacement; SC UK estimates about 30,000 internally displaced people .
11 SC UK has a small office and team stationed in Sinje, on the edge of one of the camps. Save the Children world-wide is effective at family tracing and in reuniting children with their families; and they do this in Sierra Leone. The agency is also concerned about children's education in the camps and in HIV/AIDS. The TfD training is subordinated to the SC UK operation within the camps.
12 The Global Movement for Children gained momentum in the preparations for the UN Special Session on Children in New York in May 1992. After the Special Session for Children, the various agencies concerned with children's rights and with their participation in decisions affecting them focused on a number of specific country initiatives, such as the National Plans of Action for Children. The term Global Movement for Children now loosely refers to these initiatives.
13 SC UK operations in Sierra Leone supported family tracing and family reunification, in the context of returning young refugees from Liberia and Côte d'Ivoire. Work involving the rehabilitation of children and young people encompasses a number of sectors: child protection, HIV/AIDS, education (both formal and non-formal), and sexual and reproductive health.
14 This is written up in an internal document of SC UK in Angola: 'We Are Speaking – Are you Listening?' which had collected individual and collective commentaries from children concerning their present and their future. It is to form the basis of a much wider publication.
15 Oswaldo de Rivero, *The Myth of Development, Non-Viable Economies of the 21st Century* (London: Zed Books, 2001).
16 Harold Bloom, in his recent study of Shakespeare's plays, describes how Shakespeare 'invented the human'. See Harold Bloom, *Shakespeare: The Invention of the Human* (New York: Riverhead, 1998).
17 Edwin Dorbor, Emmanuel Paivey from Liberia and Doris Mansarray, Mike Charley from Sierra Leone were co-facilitators. Among the adult participants were senior managers – Sierra Leonean and British – middle managers and field workers who were all Sierra Leonean. Two of the participants were from Francophone West Africa, from Côte d'Ivoire. Sixteen of the participants were from the SC UK operation in Sierra Leone: this more or less closed down the office for four days and was a huge commitment for the agency to make. In addition, in terms of office hierarchy, two of the facilitators, Dorbor and Paivey, were quite junior to some of the participants they were instructing. This was, in fact, a training that broke all the written and unwritten NGO rules.
18 A Creole is a Pidgin or contact language which has become a mother tongue, a fully formed language. Like any other language it may be acquired as a second language by speakers of other mother-tongues. SL Creole is a language in its own right. The national language in Liberia is American English.
19 She understood most spoken English. Translation during the workshop when she needed it was handled by her colleagues on a one-to-one basis.
20 In connection with acting and improvisation, I have been much influenced by Viola Spolin and Keith Johnstone. Viola Spolin, *Improvisation for the Theater* (Illinois: North Western University Press, 1963 & 1983); Keith Johnstone, *Impro: Improvisation and the Theatre* (London: Methuen, 1979 & 1981).
21 Abu Kokofele, in *Draft Report, Sierra Leone Theatre for Development Training Workshop, April 13–25*, 2002, SC UK (unpublished), p. 23.
22 These workshops did not involve Fred Kasozi. He continued with training in Child Rights in Nigeria, Liberia and Sierra Leone. But it did involve Roger Djiohou from the SC UK Regional Office for Francophone West Africa as my co-facilitator as well as other participants from Côte d'Ivoire and also from the Ghana Regional Office for Anglophone West Africa who were able to operate in French.
23 Only a minority of the facilitators and participants were bilingual in these two languages. All the adults spoke French but only some could also speak the language of the Fulani or Peul diaspora. Some of the children could only speak Fulfulde, because this was the mother tongue of the two areas in which we had located these workshops, Dori in Burkina Faso and Sevare in Mali.

24 See, for example, Martin Banham, James Gibbs and Femi Osofisan (eds), *African Theatre in Development* (Oxford: James Currey, 1999).
25 Child Rights, and the Global Movement for Children, are not the main focus of this paper. See the references at the end of this paper for the key publications that communicate the concepts and strategies of this new global movement for children.
26 See, for example, the following websites that share information about the nascent institutions of young people's activism:
 <http://www.crin.org> [Save the Children Alliance]
 <http://www.hrw.org/children/> [Human Rights Watch: Children's Rights]
 <http://www.ohchr.org/english/bodies/crc/> [Office of the UN High Commissioner for Human Rights: The Committee on the Rights of the Child]
 <http://www.boes.org.wap> [Multilingual Human Rights/Children's Rights Across the World]
27 Oxfam GB and Oxfam International developed important institutional gender awareness during the 1990s. At the same time, this was mirrored in the independent gains made by women in societies in, for example, the Indian Subcontinent and in Latin America.
28 See CD ROM, *The South Asia Child Rights TfD Training Manual* (Kathmandu: SC UK, Regional Office for South and Central Asia, 2001).
29 See Steven Pinker, *The Language Instinct* (New York: Harper Collins, 1994).
30 See The Concerned for Working Children (CWC) and Bhimha Sangha in Karnataka, South India; email address is cwc@pobox.com

REFERENCES

UN and UN-related Reports on Special Session on Children May 2002.
The UN Convention on the Rights of the Child [CRC].
The UN Special Session on Children: A First Anniversary Report on Follow-up, Global Movement for Children, Child Rights Caucus and UNICEF, June 2003
Child Friendly Version of the Outcome Document: A World Fit for Children, Save the Children, September 2002 (44 pp).
Dictionary (for use with the Child Friendly Version A World Fit for Children), Save the Children, September 2002 (6 pp).
A Young Person's Guide to: The 2002 United Nations Special Session on Children, Save the Children, September 2002 (8 pp.)
A Tool for Change? Reporting to the UN Committee on the Rights of the Child, Save the Children UK, October 2003 (author Daniela Baro).

Appendix

Table 1. Reports from Child Rights Theatre for Development Training Workshops in Africa 2001–3

Date & Place of Workshop/s	Title & Author	Source & Copyright	Status
2-14 July 2001 Monrovia, Sinje & Monrovia	**Liberia TfD Training Workshops Report** (Michael Etherton & Fred Kasozi)	SC UK Office Monrovia, Liberia	Final
12-27 Nov. 2001 Maputo & Mopeia	**Mozambique TfD Training Workshop Report** (Michael Etherton & Fred Kasozi)	SC UK Office, Maputo Mozambique.	Draft
12-26 April 2002 Lakka (Freetown), Dara, Bo, Kambia	**Sierra Leone TfD Training Workshop Report**[1] (Michael Etherton, Fred Kasozi & Others)	SC UK Office, Freetown, Sierra Leone	Final
May 2002 Kaduna,	**Nigeria TfD Report** (Asif Munier, Samina Sardar & Others)	SC UK Office, Kaduna Nigeria	Final
15-25 Nov. 2002	**Lesotho/South Africa TfD Training Workshops Report** (Michael Etherton & Selloane Mokuku)	SC Regional Office, Southern Africa, Pretoria, RSA	Final
20-31 Jan. 2003 Ouagadougou, Dori (Burkina Faso) & Sevare (Mali)	**Burkina Faso & Mali TfD Training Workshops Report** (Francophone West Africa) (Michael Etherton, Roger Djiohou; trans. French & English by Andre Nkiema).	SC UK Regional Office, West Africa, Accra, Ghana	Draft (English & French versions)
17-31 March 2003 Luanda, Hojy-ya-Henda, Huambo	**Angola Child Rights Training** Child Rights TfD Training Workshops Report (Michael Etherton, Sally Griffin, & Etelvina da Cunha)	SC UK Office, Luanda, Angola	Final
	'We Are Speaking, Are You Listening?' Preliminary Report (Gillian Heubner)		Internal
15-20 June 2003 Mtwara District	**Tanzania: Mtwara District Education Training Workshop on Children's Participation in Education Provision**:[3] (Report by Michael Etherton)	SC UK Office, Mtwara, Tanzania	Final

Notes

1. The Sierra Leone Report contains some general analysis of new tools and ideas, both in terms of adapting tools to African specifics, and to programme relationships. Although a large number of people have already contributed to the Report, it awaits a final edit and layout before formal publication.
2. The Angola Training Workshops Report and the Voices of Children Preliminary Report are the most significant in terms of programme integration and follow-up.
3. The two Reports of the Tanzania Workshops situate participatory Rights-based work within a major sector, Education.

The Impact of Child Rights Theatre in Sierra Leone
Umo is talking

PAUL MOCLAIR
with MIKE CHARLEY & children in Daru

Introduction

Umo is talking.
'I felt very good because that was my first time to actually stand in front of a crowd and act. I felt very good and was not ashamed.'

She looks us calmly in the eyes, talking in measured tones, confidently steering the conversation where she wants it to go, despite the fact that I am asking the questions.

Five years ago Umo wielded an AK47 in the ranks of the RUF.[1] But she is not talking about her prowess on the battlefield. Rather she is recalling the transformational effects of a Theatre for Development [TfD] workshop she attended in 2001 in the nearby town of Daru.

Playing devil's advocate I suggest that TfD is good fun, but of little consequence. Umo smiles patiently at me.

'Before it, I was blind, but now my eyes are open and I'm bold.'

'What did it open your eyes to, Umo?'

'At first I was shy, but I'm no longer shy, no longer afraid to talk to adults.'

That Umo seems to regard standing before adults as a laudable act of courage brings us to the heart of an ugly paradox. She has survived aerial attacks by helicopter gunships and skirmishes with the Sierra Leone Army [SLA]. Here as in many other countries, children are firmly excluded from civil society and from decision-making that affects their futures. But their participation is eagerly sought in war and prostitution and all that is dangerous and debasing. The consequences of this have been devastating for Sierra Leone.

Ben Hirsch, GOAL and the Save the Children TfD Training in 2002

I should begin by declaring my own interest. I was in the country to do a three-month project with a local non-governmental organization [NGO] called *Ben Hirsch Women in Development and Child Care*. Ben Hirsch, as they are known, are based in the town of Kenema, where they provide care for 370 disadvantaged children, many of whom are sex workers and/or street children. When I first visited them I found a culture of relentless rote-learning and corporal punishment. By national standards, though, Ben Hirsch was a marvel, providing the only safety net for these children. The bankrupt Ministry of Social Welfare was unable to perform its duties and was passing many of its responsibilities for local homeless children onto the organization.

Ben Hirsch had recently signed a partnership with Irish international non-governmental organization [INGO], GOAL. The partnership agreement aimed at changing the culture at Ben Hirsch to one where children participated in all decision-making that affected them. It sought to build up the capacity of these severely disadvantaged children so that they might advocate for their own rights. I hoped to bring about this change in culture by training the staff in TfD.

Essentially the training worked in two different directions, inward and outward. In the 'inward' phase we used games, creative activities and drama exercises to help the children identify and analyse their problems. Through a progression of role-plays and improvisations we explored the frequently contradictory aspects of those problems. The second 'outward' phase involved devising plays based on our earlier exploratory improvisations. These plays, which we devised as questions and not as answers, were to be performed in front of an audience of adults who had power over the children. The performances would sensitize adults to children's perspectives and challenge traditional attitudes.

The overall aim was to raise children's confidence levels and improve their analytical and communication skills. By basing the training of adult staff on joint adult and children's workshops we hoped that the medium [TfD] would become the message: children's and young people's participation in decisions affecting their lives. It sounded wonderful in my project proposal. Deep down though, I struggled to repress panicky thoughts that it might all be a fit of academic ecstasy. In the middle of my project, with my thoughts turning towards formulating an exit strategy and to ensuring sustainability, I felt the need to confront those doubts.

That's where UNICEF's Mike Charley comes in. Two years previously, as a Save the Children UK [SC UK] worker, Mike had helped facilitate a seminal TfD workshop in the town of Daru for children affected by the war. I wanted to find some of those children and ask them what they remembered of the workshop. How had it affected them? Had it changed the way adults treated them? Had it given them the skills they needed to negotiate with adults? Or would they merely recall it as a bit of harmless fun? I was hoping that their memories and conclusions would help guide my own work with Ben Hirsch to a successful conclusion.

First though, we had to find the children. That's how we came to be perched on Mike's trials bike early on the morning of the first local elections to be held in 30 years. The normally teeming markets for once were empty; only the vultures had shown up for business, perched above the deserted stalls like hanging judges in a closed court.

We race through a landscape of forest, banana trees, elephant grass and towering termite mounds. On any drive in Sierra Leone you cannot miss the endless signposts and placards put up by international and local NGOs advertising training schemes, income generation schemes, workshops, women's groups, children's groups, activity centres, skills training centres, craft centres, handicapped centres. They seem almost to constitute the only activity in the country outside of the markets. There are few alternatives by way of services or infrastructure. They are like hundreds of steel surgical pins holding together a shattered limb in the desperate hope that the bone will knit.

Lost to our thoughts, I am racing forwards through time, to the children we hope to find, to the end of my project and beyond. Mike is racing backwards, to a night four years before when burning buildings and broken heads had convinced him of the need to rethink attitudes to children. To a night during the emergency period of disarmament and demobilization in 1999 to 2000 and to an interim care centre [ICC] for 300 children run by Save the Children UK [SC UK] in Daru. Some of these children had become separated from their parents as part of the chaos of war. Others were ex-combatants or children associated with fighting (numerous enough to be given a widely used NGO acronym – CAF).

Daru then was the only safe enclave in the district. Defended by the CDF, it was entirely surrounded by rebels. The children at the ICC were former rebel soldiers. The local children came from Kamajor families. This made for an understandably inflammatory situation. With weary understatement Mike recalls the atmosphere. 'It was trying.' Friction between the children at the camp and the village children had seen violence flicker on and off. But one night an altercation between a child and a staff member had erupted into a riot. The camp was burned down and one member of staff seriously injured. The riot proved a turning point. SC UK took a strategic decision to change their methodology, and introduced a programme of TfD, which they wisely named 'Working Better with Children'. These are the children we hope to find.

Just when I think I will never recover feeling below the waist again, we ride into Segbwema. Every building in the town is freckled with bullet holes. After paying our respects to the village chief we find Mr Banks, a mild-mannered schoolteacher who agrees to help us trace two children. That's how we come to be sitting in this dark house on the edge of a hill overlooking the shattered town.

Umo

Umo is talking and we are listening. She is recalling life in the camp.

'We were in booths. I remember the booths which housed us. There was a place to wash, a bathroom, and there was also a *barrie* (meeting room) where we held workshops and also I remember that the boys were in a separate place from us girls.'

'What was the best thing about the camp, Umo?'

'The food was good, the toilets were clean, the *barrie* where workshops were held was nice, even the booths were good.'

'What was the worst thing about the camp?'

'The plastic sheeting. It was cold inside when we were sleeping. When it rained the roof leaked.'

That Umo is talking and we are listening is in itself an astonishing state of affairs. It is pointless going any further without positioning Umo's speech within the context of the national culture. Children and young people in Sierra Leone have no voice. Like women, they are the possessions of the man of the house, to be put to work and beaten. They are utterly excluded from all decision-making. Power resides entirely with the elderly. Children are silent and invisible, remaining disenfranchised well into their twenties. Half of the population is aged below 15. The average life expectancy is 37. So extreme is this generational apartheid and the intense frustration that it generates, that it is now widely acknowledged as one of the main reasons for the war.

The pointless destruction of community infrastructure by the rebels, the endless 'own goals' in terms of ruined health-centres and village amenities, calls to mind the inwardly directed wounds of the adolescent self-harmer, or the remand home prisoner smashing up his own cell. Tragically, the war seems only to have exacerbated the division between the generations. Many elders now look down on the youth with renewed contempt, as being solely responsible for the destruction of the war years.

Since the end of the war, children's participation has become a politically charged term that politicians and many adults working with children are eager to pay lip service to. Scratch away at the buzz words however and you rarely find much of substance. I believe that TfD is the perfect tool for shifting this stubborn paradigm. I am eager to see what effect it has had on the lives of Umo and her brother Mohammed.

Umo is talking about the camp in Daru.

'And what happened in the workshop?'

'A plastic sheet was spread on the floor. Everybody sat on the tarpaulin and they told us to stand up and we prayed.' A smile rolls out across her lips. 'Then we played *Zip, Zap, Boi-ing*. There was a break and we all ate and then we came back to the workshop. They asked us to draw anything that happens at home. So I did a drawing although, you know, I am not perfect at drawing. And everyone explained their drawing.'

'Can you remember what you drew?'

'I drew a pregnant woman with a baby on her back pounding rice. There was another child sitting beside the mortar and pestle.'

'And how did you explain your picture?'

'I explained the difficulties that women go through. This woman I drew had lost her husband during the war and was pregnant. She had a child on her back and another sitting by her side. I was trying to explain the difficulties that women go through. Later we made the drawings into a play.'

'What was the play about?'

'I'll tell you about my part in it. I was with the child, but my husband was not around, he had gone to the bush. My husband's friend came and told me that he had heard firing in the bush. He asked me where my husband had gone

I explained that he had gone to the bush. Then I heard the shots too and my belly started catapulting. We were trying to decide what to do, whether to run away or not, when the rebels arrived. They took the children from me.'

Time and again in Sierra Leone I am struck by the grim realism of the stories that children tell to adults when they are permitted to do so. Harsh, pragmatic and brutally honest, they are markedly at odds with the playful and foolish tales that adults enjoy telling children. With folklore and children's tales, adult narrators are trying to pass on the wisdom of the tribe, to impart ethical values and outline ideals. The stories are apocryphal, legendary and anonymous. Children's stories, with their unconscious honesty, often recount the failure of these ethics or highlight the hypocrisy of adult value systems. They are individual testimonies and are overwhelmingly personal.

I ask Umo if she thinks there are differences between the stories that adults tell children and the stories that children tell adults.

'Yes, there is a difference. Because the big people, what they have learnt in the past is what they tell in those stories. But the kids, they tell stories that come from themselves and from a combination of what they learn, bits and pieces from big people.'

When adults tell stories to children, they do so to educate as well as to entertain. The harsh realities of the adult world are deemed unpalatable for children. We sugar coat them with fantasy and displace malevolent realities with symbolism and codifications. But these children have had the warm mantle of childhood ripped from their shoulders years ago. Our softly-softly approach to story-telling is one more symptom of our reflex underestimation of children's capabilities. Sigmund Freud, quoted in an introduction to Joseph Campbell's deconstruction of mythology, *The Hero with a Thousand Faces* had strong views on the matter. Commenting on the myth of the stork as the bringer of children he observed:

> (The child) hears only the distorted part of what we say and feels that he has been deceived; and we know how often his distrust of the grown-ups and his refractoriness actually take their start from this impression. We have become convinced that it is better to avoid such symbolic disguisings of the truth in what we tell children and not to withhold from them a knowledge of the true state of affairs commensurate with their intellectual level.[2]

Our reluctance to confront children with the cruel messiness of life is understandable. Perhaps, too, our story-telling models with their fondness for neat symmetries and pat solutions are informed by our sense of shame at our inability to provide answers. 'Just do your best and you'll be all right.' 'Work hard and you won't have anything to worry about.' 'Honesty is the best policy.' These are the maxims we pass on to our children. And though they are admirable sentiments, they are next to useless in the sort of society the children in Ben Hirsch have been thrust into, a society of endemic corruption and unemployment where hustling is an essential life skill. The stories that these children are often told amount almost to a betrayal.

But if story-telling has been part of the problem it also provides the best chance of a solution. Story-telling is a key tool both in reconditioning our own habitual perceptions of children and in empowering children to name their own world. Allowing children to articulate their view of the world in Sierra Leone is a radical step. The most natural way for them to do so is through story telling. It is simply by listening attentively to their stories that we most convincingly demonstrate our respect for children as partners and help redefine them as fellow travellers rather than troublesome luggage. The simple fact of being heard springs a child from the prison cell of adult preconceptions and releases her from passivity into action. It gives her the creative freedom of portraying her world, however tragic, through play and story. With this power comes a rapid growth in confidence and self assurance.

Mohammed

Mohammed is talking.

He has experienced the opposite extremes of being subject and object in his life story. He begins by recalling the year before the workshop.

'Our mother took us to Wilberforce Barracks in Freetown and we were there until 6 January 1999. On 6 January the rebels invaded Freetown. One of the rebel commanders, a lady, told me and another boy to stand near a mango tree and wait. She said she was going to kill us. Another rebel passed and told her to release us because he knew the boy's mother.'

We move forward two years to discuss his time at the workshop.

'How did you feel when you were told you were going on a Theatre for Development workshop? What did you think would happen?'

'I didn't have any specific feelings, but when I got there I was a little shy.'

'How did you feel about acting?'

'I felt fine. I felt it was a nice thing and it was the first time I had done it. And I could boast to my companions about what I was doing.'

'Did the workshop help you or change you Mohammed?'

'It has helped me a lot. For example, some of my uncles came here to Segbwema with a dance group. They came to us children and asked who could dance. And then because of that workshop I didn't feel too shy to say, "Yes, I can dance!" So it has really helped me a lot.'

In later interviews I met children who had attended other workshops where adults had pre-selected issues for discussion and where the plays seem to have been little more than vehicles for putting words and ideas in children's mouths, for preaching at them, rather than listening to them. The story of Umo and Mohammed is more encouraging. Crucially, Save the Children had helped set up a network of Children's Clubs where the children could continue to tell their own stories and perform their own plays without any interference from adults. This seems to have engendered a ferocious sense of ownership, of independence and even of artistic integrity, as evidenced by Mohammed.

'Have you done any acting since the workshop, Mohammed?'

'I acted in some plays after that. Then I came to the Children's Club. My sister is part of the Children's Club and she told me that now I had to pay a registration fee of 500 Leones to join the club. But I rebelled. I said I wouldn't pay a cent because it was our club. We started that club in Daru. So why should they now ask me to pay? So I linked up with some other children and formed a breakaway group.'

'And has the breakaway group performed any plays?'

Mohammed goes on to outline the convoluted plot of a drama in which he played a would-be Lothario attempting to string two girls along at the same time. In the end they both beat him up and left him.

'Who did you perform the play for?'

'We cleared a space and built a small buffer or fence and invited some people from the police and some parents to come and watch the play.'

This matter of finding an audience is of central importance. Too often TfD projects aimed at ensuring children's participation culminate in a play performed in front of an audience of NGO workers and civil servants, all with a prior interest in children's rights. This amounts to little more than preaching to the converted, or indulging the adults with a glimpse of some idealized future. Nothing will change until the actual oppressors of children constitute most of the audience. Mohammed's decision to stage his play in front of the local police is much more valid. We need to remember that TfD has a real role to play in advocacy and lobbying and reformulating public perceptions of children.

Peter Hansilles works in Freetown for the Dutch NGO, 'War Child', which seeks to address the psycho-social problems of war-traumatized children through creative therapy and the arts. By way of illustrating the cultural difficulties of working for child rights in Sierra Leone he told me that some members of the newly constituted Street Children Task Force on which he sits had suggested categorizing children by how dirty they looked and how badly they smelt. Peter had retorted that his own children would often fall into both categories after a day's play. Even where there is a will, he warned, there is little history in Sierra Leone of working on social welfare issues. 'It is not yet part of them,' he told me.

Hansilles went on to emphasize his firm belief that drama can really help adults in Sierra Leone to see children differently, and to begin to value them. It has a legitimate role to play in revising how youth are perceived. Amidst all my own doubts about the validity of my own presence there, I found this deeply reassuring.

The longer I stayed in Sierra Leone and the more I listened to children, the more I became convinced of this, of TfD's ability to help bring about the increased participation of children in their own development. It involves training them to analyse the forces that keep them oppressed, to articulate their concerns and to channel potentially destructive emotions into creative outlets capable of affecting both inner transformation and challenging damaging adult perceptions. The inward phase is initially straightforward. It is in the outward phase of attempting to persuade adults to increase the participation of children that you meet a brick wall. In this TfD process you learn to rely on the young people's own resourcefulness to break it down.

At the end of our training at Ben Hirsch we devised a play on the inadequacies of rural responses to rape. We wanted to make the audience question the merit of traditional 'punishments' in rural areas, where rapists are fined or made to marry their victims. The local Child Protection Committee wanted to see rapists being put through the court system. In our play we wanted to show that both traditional and progressive viewpoints had compelling arguments that could not be dismissed without thorough exploration.

We spent the whole of the first act building up the character of Mbalu, the raped girl, to show what a unique and talented individual she was. We did this both to engage the audience's attention and so that the magnitude of the crime would be felt more keenly when it eventually happened. In a similar vein we needed to look at the rapist's motives, so that he wasn't merely a two-dimensional tabloid monster.

To that end we came up with a single short scene in which Kpana, the rapist, was working in the fields with his father who had taken him out of school. Kpana pleaded with his father to let him continue his education, saying that without a qualification he would have no chance of a decent job or a good marriage. His father mocked him and told him he would have neither. Kpana stormed off in a fury, later running into Mbalu and raping her. After the play had been performed, a representative of the paramount chief stood up, thanked us for our work and said that the play clearly showed that if we kept the boys back from school there would be consequences.

Of course it is easy for northern development workers to blame the exclusion of children in Sierra Leone entirely on African culture. It is easy but dishonest. Northern adults are often as frightened as anyone by the practical implications of empowered children. It is unhelpful to pretend otherwise. Quite simply, our culture seems to lack any inspiring examples of children taking control of events and directing them successfully towards a fruitful conclusion. Rather our minds are haunted by shadowy impressions and half-memories of empowerment tapping into the dark side of children's psyches. At school we are introduced to the feral brats of Lord of the Flies, almost as a cautionary tale. Thereafter we struggle to repress nightmarish media images – of prepubescent Red Guards hurling teachers out of fourth floor windows. Or of 10-year-old Khmer Rouge prison guards attaching electrodes to genitals in Phnom Penh's Toul Sleng prison. Even the horror movie industry knows how much more frightening an evil child is than an evil adult. Children, it is suggested, are potentially destructive agents who need to be restrained and muted.

These are the stubborn cultural perceptions, buried deep within us, that keep our hands clenched knuckle-white on the steering wheel and which prevent us from relinquishing control. We have to acknowledge these fears if the concept of children's empowerment and participation is ever to spring free from policy papers and conference speeches and take root in working practices and living projects. Too many adults deny this fear instead of confronting it.

I am sitting in on a meeting between an INGO and a local children's charity somewhere in West Africa. The INGO programme director is newly arrived from the States. It is early afternoon and the heat is intense. The fan pushes the muggy air around in thick waves, lulling us into a post-lunch torpor. A perspiring man is going through the clauses of the children's charity Governing Instrument. His words seem to be receding into the distance. Eyes begin to glaze over. Outside the window two dogs lie dazed and dozing in the dust. Up under the ceiling a trapped moth is dying of heat exhaustion. The man's voice comes to me as if through a blanket of sleep. Somewhere far away he is describing the constitution of the charity's steering committee. 'It is comprised of six children and four adults.' Suddenly the American programme director sits bolt upright as if hit by an invisible bucket of iced water.

'Wait a minute!' she shouts. She has that look of nascent panic that flits across a passenger's face when it first dawns on her that she has boarded the wrong train. 'Wait a minute! In my understanding a Steering Committee actually runs an organization. It makes the decisions and decides on policy and staffing.' The smell of adrenaline has revived us all now. People are beginning to sit upright.

'That's right', says the children's charity representative.

'But you can't have a steering committee with more children than adults' she gasps.

Her mind is racing to throw a lasso around the runaway logic of it all. 'They'll spend the money on something silly!'

There is a long pause broken only by the sound of a ripe mango landing in the dust. Many of the children that we are discussing are hustlers and sex workers. They have plenty of experience in harsh business realities and negotiation skills. She asks how the children are to be elected onto this committee. The representative informs her that they are to be elected from among the student body. Instinctively she turns to me for support as a fellow Westerner and product of the Enlightenment.

'But Paul, you know how that'll turn out. The most violent children will rise to the top. It'll be like the Sopranos!'

The sad irony of this is that if we, who profess to have the best interests of children at heart, are unwilling to engage their active participation, there are no end of malevolent forces only too happy to call our bluff and put them in positions of real authority. Mike Charley provides bleak evidence of this:

'You know, those children there were with the RUF. They were RUF children. And Mr Banks was their commander. That man was RUF through and through.'

I will myself not to blush. Mike continues. 'You see the RUF relied solely on kids. The kids have access to so many people and places. They used to brand them with big positions, like commander. The children felt very big and their confidence increased and so they did everything they were asked to do without questioning. So the children were a really big asset to the RUF because what the adults cannot do they can do. They can pass off as innocent children. For instance they can walk into a town unnoticed, find out who the local CDF are and then report back to the rebels. The children were the ones that really they put on the front line.'

'So in a very perverse way, the RUF practised complete participation with children?'

Mike stubs out his cigarette and pauses to consider that.

Rosa Lita

Back on the motorbike, Mike and I are headed for the home of Rosa Lita. He has told me how her last exam results were the second highest in the country. 'She's a straight 'A's student,' he says, the phraseology of suburban America as out of place here as a credit card in the local market. At Rosa Lita's house there is no Volvo in the drive. There is no drive. The smell of coffee does not waft out to greet us. Inside the house nobody is practising the piano or taking cello lessons. A gaggle of half-dressed kids sit around a ramshackle yard amongst the chickens. Rosa Lita's foster father strolls out to meet us, belly spilling out over stained shorts. Rosa Lita follows in his wake.

We sit in the yard and chat about her childhood. Wide-eyed and willowy with a rich musical voice she exudes restraint, considering questions carefully before answering, always seeming to hold something back. Rosa Lita was born in Liberia. In 1991 she and her mother fled the fighting there and crossed over into Sierra Leone. Rosa Lita was captured by the RUF and taken to Kailun. She was six. Two years later the Sierra Leone Army freed her and took her to Freetown where she was cared for by an uncle. When the RUF stormed Freetown she was recaptured and taken north again. She deflects questions about how she was treated with such well-practised evasions that one can only guess at what memories might lie behind her slowly batting eyelids. In 2001 SC UK found her and took her to the ICC in Daru.

There she was selected to go on the TfD workshop. She recalls games like *Zip, Zap, Boi-ing*, the *Mirror Exercise* and *Paint a Problem*. And a play about foster parents mistreating an adopted child.

'In our play the mother was treating her son better than their adopted child. But in the end the boy who was adopted was the child who came out best.'

I tell her that the previous week in Ben Hirsch the children devised a similar play with the same ending.

'After the workshop we went to Freetown for the UN's International Day of Peace. There was a presentation from different ICCs from across the country. We raised the UN flag, the Sierra Leone flag, the Liberian flag. In the process we sang the various anthems for the flags. After that the chairperson gave a presentation. We sang more songs then had a discussion about disarmament, what will be the process of disarmament. We were sensitizing people. Then we sang two peace songs.'

Unbidden she launches into the first.

'Bye-bye war, no more killing, no more fighting, we want peace, for mankind is one.'

Buoyed up on the memory she segues into the second.

'We have to stop the war and forget about the fighting...'

Before we leave I ask her how she rates TfD as a way of working with young people.

'I think it is good. In TfD people are trained how to sensitize each other, even by the way they present the drama in public. People seeing the play will learn how to cope with some things and how to avoid others.'

'What would you say you learnt from the workshops?'

'I learnt that during that time people were abusing children's rights. They were exposing children to separation, child abuse, raping the girls. In the workshop we were taught that if anything like this happens to us we are to report it and the NGOs will do something about it. So that sensitizes people on how to take care of their children and how to relate to children.'

'Has that knowledge of children's rights helped you?'

'Well you know, I learned about the rights of the child, then it happens that I am around someone who is abusing a child I will immediately intervene and advise that person.'

'Has that ever happened?'

'Even here my younger sister was about to beat the very young one, so I stopped her because by beating that child maybe it will happen that the child will become dispirited. It is not right. It is better that she go and report the child to the parents.'

'Are there any other ways that the workshop made changes in your life?'

'*Yes!* By now I can control my temper. I will not just react to anything that happens now. While then I didn't know what was right, I would just take action into my own hands without reporting the issue to any elderly person.'

'Do you really think the workshop helped you control your temper, or is it just because you're getting older?'

'The workshop. It was the training that helped me to control my temper. Theatre for Development helped teach us that. At that time we had just come from the bush. They told us not to react violently if someone hurt us, but to lay a complaint. So if you lay a complaint you don't just react. You know, maybe in your reaction you will do more than the person did to you...'

My work at Ben Hirsh CBO and the *Musa Wo* stories

We have been using improvised Forum Theatre at Ben Hirsch to try and improve the children's analytical abilities and to guide them away from the unrealistically pat solutions and folksy maxims so beloved of NGO teaching plays. It is an ideal form for demonstrating to children that, rather than solving problems, our well-intentioned actions usually serve only to displace them. As the improvisation unfolds it is the facilitator's job to challenge unrealistic endings and propose alternatives.

If, in the context of the improvisation, a child complains to a teacher about the behaviour of a bully, and the teacher punishes the bully, the action cannot be allowed to end there. The facilitator might 'fast forward' to later in the day, placing the bully in the path of the victimized child as he makes his way home. Thus we are training children away from the parroted certainties and truisms that rote-learning thrusts on them, and encouraging them towards an individual analysis of cause and effect, enabling them to foresee the likely consequences of various courses of action. In doing so, we are guiding the stories away from unrealistic and dishonest happy endings towards a starker conscientization. As adults we owe children this hard honesty.

Not all adult story-telling is unhelpful. In our attempts to increase children's participation at Ben Hirsch we found an apt cultural totem within Mende folklore, in the figure of Musa Wo. Musa Wo is a classic West African trickster in the tradition of Ananse the spider. A mischievous boy constantly getting into trouble, his adventures form a sort of oral tradition soap opera. Any temporary victory that Musa Wo accomplishes only results in a fresh quandary. The stories have no proper ending, they are never fully resolved. Rather they lead into a new tale, like an endless game of cliffhanger. The flow of the narrative surges on and on, continually renewing itself and is never dammed artificially with deadwood formulae such as 'And they all lived happily ever after.' The cyclical nature of his travails has even suggested a Mende proverb, *Musa Wo domeh*, meaning literally 'It's like a Musa Wo story' but more helpfully translated as 'There's no end to it' or, possibly, 'It's just one damn thing after another!'

The Musa Wo stories are not in any sense cautionary tales. Rather his feisty anarchism is held up as a source of admiration and fun. In his book on children's participation in the civil war in Sierra Leone, *Fighting for the Rain Forest: war, youth and resources,* Paul Richards makes the following observation:

> Musa Wo stories serve to remind Mende elders not to neglect the energy and cunning of the young. Rather the challenge is to harness these skills for the greater social good.[3]

Unfortunately the lesson of the Musa Wo stories appears to have been forgotten by the Mende elders and the tragic consequences are everywhere on display in the detritus left by eleven years of war. But it is within this very wreckage, in the razed buildings and the amputated limbs, that we might just find hope for the future. Government ministers and NGO programmers, working from a rights-based agenda, position children's participation within the context of the CRC. But there is a grimmer subtext of *realpolitik* lurking in all those strategy papers. Everybody knows that if serious violence is to reappear, its most likely source will be these marginalized rural youths. The bottom line is to integrate the children or risk facing more of the same.

Hawa, Johnny, Senesi and Moses

Mike Charley and I are walking towards a large patch of open ground the size of a football field on the edge of Daru. Mike's pace quickens as we draw nearer, the way you speed up when you spot an old acquaintance you want to greet. He strides away from me, down corridors of personal memory where I cannot follow. Eventually he emerges from his reverie.

'This is where the camp was,' he says. He points to patches of grass, reconstructing the order of things in his head. 'That's where we held the workshop! That's where the booths were! That's where the fire started!'

I look at the wind-flattened grass, unable to make out the ghosts that have entranced Mike. Outside a house a few hundred yards away stand a group of children who provide corporeal evidence of the Daru workshop. Mike introduces me to Hawa, Johnny, Senesi and Moses. They are all in their late teens.

Hawa is talking. She is recalling the day when someone from Save the Children asked her to attend the workshop.

'And when they said, "Will you go on a Theatre for Development workshop, Hawa?" what did you think that would mean?'

'When I heard the word *theatre* I thought it would be just acting, play acting.'

'And did you think it would be a good idea or did you think it would be silly?'

'No. I thought it would just be light-hearted.'

'And did you want to go on it?'

'No. I didn't want to go at the beginning. But when I went I quickly grew interested and so I attended the other sessions. It went on over four days.'

Like Mohammed and Umo before them, these children describe a process in the workshop where problems were identified through painting exercises, analysed and discussed and eventually put into play form. I'm keen to hear their views on the matter of children telling stories to adults.

'So, usually adults tell children stories. With TfD children get to tell adults stories. But the sort of stories big people tell children are very different from the stories children tell big people. Do you think that's true?'

Johnny is first to answer.

'When adults tell a story, what we feel is that adults are like the voice of experience, so whatever they tell us in stories is like gospel truth because they are speaking from experience. For most adult stories it's also part of advising kids on how to proceed in life in addition to being funny. But children's stories are very practical. For instance, if there is no peace in the home children can bring the mother and father together and tell stories as a way of bring about peaceful coexistence once again.'

'Is it a difficult thing for adults to listen to children?'

'We ourselves are now telling stories to the adults and they are listening, because they have been exposed to a lot of workshops telling them that the voices of the children also matter. Because of this our parents are now listening to what we tell them. Now there is a lot of gravitation towards participation. For instance, the members of the children's club have been invited to be part of the Child Welfare Committee and the local Child Protection Committee so we are there to participate on equal terms.'

All this is very encouraging, but I'm worried about whether it can be sustained without NGO input and financing. From Hawa's answers, it becomes clear that the impetus can come directly from the children, they do not need prompting or guidance by adults. What they do need though is financial support.

'Hawa, I can understand that what you have said is true in a town where there are a lot of NGOs. But if you go out into the bush where there are no NGOs, do you think adults will listen to children easily?'

'Initially we had a fund and we used that fund to set up other clubs for children. We used to go by ourselves and organize our colleagues to form children's clubs. But in the process we spent all the money. So now it's difficult, particularly when SC UK is not around. Those clubs would develop plays which the adults would come and look at. The plays let them teach the adults about their own views. Adults interacted with the kids. But this is not happening any more.'

I remain stubbornly sceptical and with good cause. In the 1970s I was a school child in Northern Ireland where many well-intentioned adults tried to reconcile children from the different communities with 'arts based' approaches, such as having kids release hundreds of orange and green balloons simultaneously. It made great television but lousy community relations. Therefore I ask them if the workshop was just good fun, or if it taught them anything of lasting value.

Johnny is first up to the stump.

'The workshop taught me to live within my own community.'

'Did the workshop *really* teach you that Johnny, or was it just a case of you getting older and more mature?'

'It was the workshop, because when I came back from Liberia…' [where he had fled the fighting] '…I behaved very differently.'

'How?'

'In Liberia we children were on our own and we did everything by ourselves. We had no respect for adults. But when we came here we were taught to respect authority and not just to do whatever we felt like.'

'Do you think you'll do any more acting in the future?'

'I've been in lots of plays lately, particularly those related to HIV and AIDS. Also a play about peer pressure. I also help devise some of them.'

'What do the rest of you think? Is TfD a good way to work or is it just a bit of harmless fun?'

'We think it's a good way to work,' says Senesi. 'It teaches people a lot of things, such as what really happened to refugees in Liberia.'

Hawa jumps in next. 'It's a good way of working, particularly for girls, because there were a lot of girls in the workshop and they learned about early marriage, early pregnancies, unwanted pregnancies and how to avoid them. It was very useful.'

Moses has the last word. 'It showed us how to advise our companions to control their anger and not to react angrily to situations.'

Before I travelled to Sierra Leone I was passionately convinced of the need to increase children's participation in their own development. I was much less sure about the role of Theatre for Development in achieving this. Part of the problem lay with that very name, suggesting as it does the inappropriate export of effete and self-indulgent European art forms to a country where people are struggling to survive.

In order for Theatre for Development to have any validity it would have to result in meaningful changes to oppressive political and social structures. I bought into a criticism that I had inherited from others i.e. the charge that all too often TfD only leads to more TfD, but conceded that in the course of a TfD workshop you would inevitably help participants improve their confidence and communication skills. However, I had dismissed those to the status of secondary outcomes.

It now seems absurd to me that I ever entertained such notions. I now believe that TfD's ability to empower a child to stand up, fix an adult in the eye and voice an opinion is its most inspiring strength, and that acting as a corrective balance to years of rote-learning is its most compelling function. I was always over-sensitive to the mockery of friends who imagined TfD to be the sort of post-hippy day-dreaming encapsulated by those clouds of orange and green balloons floating impotently over Belfast's parks. But it was the speed with which local people saw the potential of TfD and the readiness with which they employed it that most convinced me that my early concerns were hollow.

Two of GOAL's social workers came to observe the workshops at Ben Hirsch. In an illuminating conversation they later told me that previously their counselling had been limited to a sort of benevolent, avuncular finger-wagging. They would engage children in a paternalistic chat and warn them of the dangers of smoking. Let's not even pause to consider the absurdity of identifying cigarettes as a danger to children who sleep rough on the streets in fear of the police, and who survive by stealing and by selling themselves for sex to lorry drivers. These men knew the limits to their methodology. They were not trying to conceal them. They wanted a better approach and they recognized it in the creative arts-based approach of TfD. These are two middle-aged men who have survived an eleven-year civil war and decades of debilitating poverty.

And what of the criticism that TfD *only* leads to more TfD? True, TfD on its own is not going to stop the IMF in its tracks, persuade the US to ban landmines or engineer a peaceful revolution in Burma. But I saw it make life more pleasant and meaningful for 370 frightened children. If TfD does *only* lead to more TfD, how is that deemed a valid criticism?

Within Sierra Leone as elsewhere, it is the norm for frightened children to sit at their desks parroting whatever comes out of their teachers' mouths. Children are not expected to have an opinion, let alone express it. And the concept of a child harbouring or giving vent to an opinion that is either hostile or critical of the adult word is unheard of. Children soon learn that such opinions are rewarded with violence.

The TfD workshops that I took part in, and those that I learned about from the participants, moved children off their benches and onto the floor to sit as equals with adults; to share opinions and stories and work together to examine solutions. If 'all' TfD does is to spread those ripples further, is that deemed a valid criticism?

Mike Charley and I are standing up and thanking Umo and Mohammed and saying our goodbyes.

We emerge, blinking, into brilliant sunlight and start walking across the fields to where Mike has left his motorbike. Mohammed accompanies us, holding onto my hand. With a grimace I climb back onto the narrow seat, knowing that within five miles I will once again feel as though I have been administered an epidural. Mike starts up the bike and we ride off down the track. Looking back I see Mohammed running home. Mr Banks is ambling down the hill towards the schoolhouse. And outside the house three adults are standing listening to a skinny girl and smiling at what she is saying.

Umo is talking.

NOTES

1 The Revolutionary United Front (commonly referred to as 'the rebels'). In their struggle to wrest power from a succession of governments and juntas based in Freetown they were opposed physically by the national army, the Republic of Sierra Leone Military Force (commonly referred to as 'the army' or 'the Sierra Leone Army'). Public faith in the army suffered amidst persistent allegations of corruption and of collusion with the rebels. This led to the formation of locally recruited militias that sought to protect their areas from rebel onslaught. These militias were known as the Civilian Defence Force (CDF) (commonly referred to as 'the Kamajors').
2 J. Campbell, *The Hero with a Thousand Faces* (London: Fontana Press, 1949).
3 Paul Richards, *Fighting for the Rain Forest: War, Youth and Resources in Sierra Leone* (Oxford: James Currey, 1996), p. 59.

Sewit Children's Theatre in Eritrea

CHRISTINE MATZKE & JANE PLASTOW

The study of Eritrean theatre history is still relatively new. It began during the 30-year liberation struggle against Ethiopia (1961–91), but most of this research has remained unpublished to date and little is available in an international language. This article is part of a larger enterprise by the writers who have sought over the past decade to make some of the extraordinary achievements of Eritrean artists available to a wider public. We are thus most concerned not with issues such as innovation in an international context, but with recording how children's theatre emerged in Eritrea, and how *Sewit* is carrying forward that development. Throughout a considerable part of its modern history Eritrea was substantially isolated from an international exchange of ideas. Theatre artists have therefore developed their expertise within a very particular, separate, socio-political context. This paper seeks to help readers understand that context while celebrating the contribution *Sewit* is making to developing performance work with children in Eritrea.

Our article outlines the history and activities of *Sewit* Children's Theatre in the Eritrean capital Asmara over a period of ten years, from 1994 to 2004. It is divided into three parts: a) a brief introduction to the context of children's theatre in Eritrea (Christine Matzke); b) the history of *Sewit* and a run down of their various activities (Christine Matzke), and c) a case study of one play, '*Gesa, Gesa* (Home, Home)', which is currently being produced for the children's programme of the national television station, Eri-TV (Jane Plastow).

The material on which this paper is based was collated over a period of four years, from 2000 to 2004. It comprises documents and visual material provided by *Sewit*, but largely depends on interviews, field notes and practical experience with the oldest and most accomplished children's theatre in Eritrea.[1]

A thumbnail history of children's theatre in Eritrea

Children's theatre in Eritrea is a relatively recent affair. While the long-established performance forms of the country's nine nationalities[2] have always also included the young, records of theatre exclusively *for* children are available from the last decade of Italian colonisation (1931–1941), particularly for puppets shows. Given the rigid race segregation established under fascist rule, however, these shows were almost certainly not accessible to Eritrean children. This was to change with Italy's defeat in the Second World War, when the country came under British Military Administration (1941–1952). For children's theatre, it also marked a change of paradigm; from theatre *for*, to theatre *for* and *with* children. Local schools, closed under Mussolini, were reopened and pupils were encouraged to get involved in drama productions, often at the end of the academic year. Notably adaptations of English classics such as Shakespeare are remembered by former students; all of them male, as the few girls privileged to receive schooling had been either too shy or feared the social stigma often associated with women performing. Religious schools were also known for an on-going tradition of putting on plays to mark church festivals and holy days.

While British influences undoubtedly had a catalytic effect on children's theatre in Eritrea and while a considerable number of theatre veterans attributed their life-long love for performance to their first encounter with drama in schools, English classics soon gave way to local productions on filial/parental relations, literacy and the country's development, particularly after Eritrea's federation with, and subsequent annexation by, Ethiopia (1952 and 1962 respectively). As time passed, more girls were encouraged to join the end-of-term plays and other performances.[3]

While schools continued to produce drama throughout the period of Ethiopian rule (1952–91), a new development occurred during the Eritrean struggle for independence (1961–91). Children's cultural troupes were established by both liberation movements; the Eritrean Liberation Front (ELF), the first armed liberation movement, and the more successful Eritrean People's Liberation Front (EPLF) which had split off from the ELF. Both established cultural troupes in the late 1970s; *Tsebah* (Early Morning) under the auspices of the General Union of Eritrean Students (GUES) of the ELF; and a cultural troupe at the EPLF's *Sowra* (Revolutionary) School which later developed into the *Keyahti Embaba* (The Red Flowers). While *Tsebah* eventually broke up, due to the virtual disintegration of the ELF as a fighting force in the early 1980s, the *Sowra* School group prompted other schools to start their own cultural troupes which were immensely popular with adult audiences. These troupes were commonly known as The Red Flowers; the colour red symbolizing the revolution, with flowers being a wide-spread term of endearment for children at the time. After the strategic retreat of the EPLF in 1978, children from various Red Flowers joined the *Sowra* School to form a gigantic cultural troupe. The new Red Flowers, however, were soon reduced in size to be trained and supervised by professional fighter performers. Tom Killion notes that the Red Flowers were dispersed in 1983 to help fight the Seventh Ethiopian Offensive; latest research however suggests that they were re-established in 1987.[4]

All these groups imitated the influential adult cultural troupes of their respective organizations. Above all, they copied the common performance pattern by staging variety shows lasting several hours and comprising songs, poetry recitations, local dances and educational skits. This formula has to a large extent survived until the present day, albeit modified and modernized for a post-independence context. While during the struggle the groups' main asset was often their emotional appeal at a time of intense patriotism (Alemseged Tesfai 1983), today the emphasis is more on children and their creative development.

The emergence of *Sewit* Children's Theatre

When in December 1994 two EPLF veterans – Esaias Tseggai, a well-known Eritrean poet and writer, and his colleague, Feshaye Yohannes 'Joshua' – decided to set up a children's theatre, they had a number of motivations. Firstly, their experience in the liberation struggle had shaped their belief in the power of the performance arts. Secondly, they wanted to pass on their skills to the young. And thirdly, there was a growing sense that with *de facto* self-rule in 1991 (and formal independence two years later), life in Eritrea had changed rapidly and that work-wise they needed to move on. From 1991, Esaias and Joshua[5] had worked for the new Ministry of Culture and Information – Esaias first as head of the Tigrinya theatre group, then as staff member for the newspaper *Hadas Eritrea* (New Eritrea); both were then sent to Asmara University to join a management programme. In 1994, now with the cultural section of the Ministry of Education, they chose demobilization over work as 'fighter'-civil servants. This was then not an unusual choice; indeed most performers, particularly musicians, preferred to work on their own, rather than for an official cultural organ.[6] However, the motives of the founders of *Sewit* seemed to differ from those of other artists, some of whom, it was alleged, had been keen to enter the rat-race for money and fame. In the spring of 2000 Joshua and Esaias explained:

> *Joshua:* We wanted to work with children. There were actors, singers, and dancers in Eritrea, but they were not professionally trained. [...] We also wanted to be in charge of ourselves. We wanted to be independent. And if you want that, this was the only possible way to do it. If you work with adults – all these groups are with the government or the PFDJ [People's Front for Democracy and Justice, the EPLF-turned-civilian party after independence]. There were no independent organizations. (Interview, 5 May 2000)

> *Esaias:* I had been working with adults since 1982, I think. They are not as capable of learning as much [as children]. Of course, I have learnt a lot from my colleagues. I appreciate that and I honour them for the things they taught me. They have inspired me tremendously. But now I was a grown-up person, so I too could teach people. [...] I did not want somebody to tell me what to do and what not to do. So I decided to work on my own. (Interview, 15 March 2000)

Like all beginnings, the initial period was fraught with difficulties; financial, structural, and personal. But there was hope that something extraordinary could be achieved. This was also expressed in the name chosen for the new organization: *Sewit* – the 'ear of grain [or] pod (of peas, beans, etc.), still green but ripe enough to eat'[7] and hence particularly delicious. Once official permission was granted, some eighteen children aged between ten and sixteen were selected from various schools and given drama and music lessons, each adult working in his own field of expertise. Three further adult members came to support the group in 1995; Aaron Teckle, a medical lab technician and former member of an EPLF cultural troupe, as well as David Isaac and Yohannes Bereket. Two 'handymen', Hamsa Abdulkadir and Yeergalem Aberen, followed in 1996, serving as puppeteers and technicians. A constitution was then written to 'legalise the theatre association' (Esaias Tseggai 2004: 1). Its objectives were a mixture of didactic, patriotic and entertaining elements, summarized by Esaias as follows:

1. To fully acquaint children with their culture
2. To help children love their country and their people
3. To upgrade children's potential in the arts and help create qualified actors, writers, singers and musicians
4. To help children grow up well-mannered, respectful and appreciative of education
5. To create an environment for children to speak their own languages and enjoy their leisure time irrespective of their sex or their ethnic, social or religious backgrounds
6. To help establish other associations with similar objectives.
(Esaias Tseggai 2004: 1).

Initial support was provided by the PFDJ and the government in the form of a rehearsal room and some musical instruments; yet at first conditions were basic. 'The hardest task', Esaias notes

> was the start, the implementation of duties; developing the actors' basic knowledge by providing them with elementary theatrical and technical orientation and organizing cultural shows for children in different parts of Eritrea by preparing dramas, songs and dances. Regardless of the shortage of money, rehearsal sites and musical instruments we were able to make a start. (Esaias Tseggai 2004: 1)

One obstacle was the bad reputation performers suffered with the public. Consequently, all monetary matters would have to be made particularly transparent; but there was also the perception to fight that theatre artists were often believed to be drunkards or to otherwise behave disreputably. For the financial aspect, an umbrella body was found in the Ministry of Education which would supervise their transactions, without however funding the group. (This has been achieved through commissioned work, NGO support and private donations. It should be noted that all of the money is directly used for *Sewit*. None of its adult members makes a living out of the theatre group; instead they work as freelancing artists, journalists, and in other professions).

More problematic was the initial reluctance of parents to let their children, especially girls, join the new theatre association.[8] There were fears that school performance would suffer, but also concerns about the children's personal wellbeing and safety. As Joshua explained:

> You must understand that during the Derg period [the period under the Ethiopian military government of Mengistu Haile Mariam, 1974-91], a lot of girls were gathered, apparently to join cultural activities, but who were then abused by the Derg. Therefore everyone who joins a cultural troupe – well, it is still in the mind of the people. But if they trust you, if they see that we act as their fathers, we don't have any problems. (Interview, 5 May 2000)

Safeguarding their charges continues to be a top priority for *Sewit*. In March 2004, Meseret Ainom, one of the early members, now a college student and assistant director-cum-administrator of the group, emphasized that they were still taken home after evening rehearsals despite the rise in the cost of petrol; and that they were well looked after when on tour:

> Esaias is very dedicated to his work. He is Eritrea's most famous poet and could easily work with all the stars, but he does not care about the fame and prefers to work with the children. He even went to Sawa [military training camp] when some of the older students were there, and to Assab and Gahatalay to support them. He never wanted us to work in nightclubs or sing at weddings. Once you are used to the money you no longer care about developing your art. It will also spoil your reputation. Singers in night-clubs and at weddings drink a lot, and they go with prostitutes. Esaias even looks at the children's home work and their school certificates to make sure that they are doing well and don't neglect their academic studies. I am very grateful to what he has done for us. (Interview, 28 March 2004).

To date Esaias remains the strongly committed director of *Sewit*; and he has indeed seen the group through difficult times. All other founding members have had to discontinue their work. As a result *Sewit*'s activities were suspended in 2001 when Esaias went to Leeds for postgraduate theatre studies. Several children left the association. That year the group also lost access to its previous rehearsal space, Cinema Croce Rossa, an old, centrally located Italian cinema, though they were later given a hall on the Expo ground – better known as the 'Coca-Cola building' for the huge advertisement sprawled across its walls – on the outskirts of Asmara. Buildings are allocated centrally; and the group is happy to have been granted a new space in which to resume their work.

In a recent report to the British Council, one of *Sewit*'s funders, Esaias summed up activities in the year of the group's inception. It is the spirit of commitment shown here that has enabled the group to stay active and alive; and which seems to have inspired new children's groups to emerge in recent years:[9]

> The first year was a year of organizing and preparing the children for the big task ahead. Thereafter we were able to write and rehearse creative works which were relevant to both children and adult audiences. We presented our first show in a

kindergarten school named *Aghi*. The group was excited and came to believe that it was capable of doing something big. With the initial help of *Save the Children* (Swedish and UK) we managed to recruit more children and continued our effort with more commitment. (Esaias Tseggai 2004: 1)

Sewit's *Activities and Performance Training*

Given that Eritrea has not only emerged from a thirty-year liberation struggle against Ethiopia but also suffered another, so-called 'border conflict' in 1998-2000 with devastating economic and human consequences, it is indeed astonishing that *Sewit* has continued its work with only one interruption over a period of ten years. While music and theatre training had always been core elements of their activities, a more serious music education programme was established in 1999 by recruiting two professional musicians as trainers. These classes went on for eighteen months, with five of the original eight participants becoming the group's musicians. Indeed, most members quoted their love of music as the main reason for joining the group (interviews, 19 September 2004). Since 2003 a further fifteen children have been taking regular music lessons; in autumn 2004 a new course was started with Mohad Suleman and Senait Fitwi from the National Marching Band, focusing on vocal performance.

The group has also recorded a number of children's songs on video and audio cassettes, but so far no sponsor has come forward to help produce and distribute their work. Once again, funding is a major problem. However, some of the songs are now being filmed for a *Sewit* children's programme on the national television station, Eri-TV.[10] To help lower the costs, most lyrics are written by Esaias Tseggai, most melodies by two well-known Eritrean composers, Simret Kebede and Mesfin Tesfagergish 'Maabel', who are happy to give their support.[11] As yet, none of the older 'children' – young adults, in fact – has contributed songs to *Sewit*, but some have started to write lyrics under their teachers' tutelage. 'We are still learning', tenth-grade student Efriem Kahsay explained (interview, 19 September 2004). From the very beginning, one unusual factor in the theatre group has been the involvement of well-known local theatre experts, such as Maabel, the singer Kedija Adem and the actress Nechi Fesehatsion, the most quoted female role model for aspiring actresses. This has helped *Sewit* to provide an exceptional training environment in the Eritrean context where there has never been any professional long-term tuition in the arts. The children draw a lot of encouragement from their encounters with local experts, as they feel they are being taken seriously; and generally there is a great sense of loyalty and commitment to their association. As a result, members of *Sewit* have been called for professional engagements, particularly in child roles in video films, while NGOs and ministries have commissioned educational plays and video dramas. The focus of their work, however, is still on live performance. *Sewit* usually presents new shows on national holidays, such as Independence Celebration and Martyrs' Day, in commemoration of those who gave their life in the liberation struggle; they also go on tour regularly. In early 2004 Meseret Ainom explained that most of their shows are toured in the countryside, despite the better theatrical infrastructure in Asmara and other towns. 'Shows in remoter areas are more rewarding', she explained. 'Often people have never seen a cultural show in their lives and they are very appreciative. You get huge crowds for one show' (interview, 28 March 2004).

Theatre training is one of *Sewit*'s main concerns. All of the now twenty-two members have participated in elementary theatre lessons, including theatre history (world and Eritrean theatre), basic acting and technical skills, and the uses of theatre (Esaias Tseggai 2004: 3). The theoretical background, basic as it may sometimes be, serves as a starting point for practical work. Main rehearsal times are from 8 to 12 a.m. on the weekends when there is no school, but the schedule is flexible according to individual students' availability. As children in Eritrea are taught in two shifts at school, you can easily find those from the afternoon sessions practising music in the mornings, or those from the morning shift at work on a play in the afternoon. For many, the Coca-Cola building has also become their favourite hangout. This is particularly important given the lack of recreational opportunities for children and young adults in Eritrea, with the exception, perhaps, of the amenities offered by the National Union of Eritrean Youths and Students (NUEYS). One rarely enters the premises of *Sewit* without encountering at least a small group of youngsters working on something, chatting or drinking tea. As Semrawit (II), a member since 2001, succinctly put it: 'It is like a second home' (interview, 19 September 2004).

Although *Sewit* works with music, dance and drama, as is usual in Eritrea, they are seen as separate entities and are not usually combined in performance. While music is geared towards the modern urban styles of the two major ethno-linguistic groups, Tigrinya and Tigre, dance focuses predominately on the traditional forms of various Eritrean nationalities; mostly Tigrinya, Tigre, Afar, Hedareb and Kunama. There have been few attempts to develop modern (indigenous) dance forms in Eritrea. Dance performances usually go together with elaborate ethnic costumes and hair styles which for the group are part of the fun. The music group normally performs in uniform – a relic perhaps from older theatre associations, particularly Ma.Te.A. (*Mahber Theatre Asmara*, the Asmara Theatre Association), which introduced this style in the 1960s. Later, it was also taken up by the cultural troupes in the liberation struggle. It also reflects the current practice of wearing school uniforms in Eritrea and thus helps create a sense of common identity among the young adults and children.

The third, and perhaps most diversified, performance form practised by *Sewit* is their drama work. The main staple is short, mostly educational pieces, not unlike *Gesa, Gesa* discussed below, with the occasional 'longer' play of 30 minutes to an hour. In addition, the group has worked on local fables and anthropomorphized animal stories; they have also utilized puppetry for commissioned campaign plays.[12]

Most of the shorter plays directly relate to the experience of Eritrean children, others address their families, with titles like *Meebeya* (Upbringing) or topics like under-age marriage. All plays are written by the adult members of *Sewit* or based on traditional stories, though 'our ideas are also considered', as sixteen year-old Hannah pointed out (interview, 19 September 2004). Previous attempts by one of the early associate members to use simplified plays or adaptations in translation, such as Henry James' *The Marriages* or Saint-Exupéry's *The Little Prince*, were soon discarded and deemed irrelevant for the local context, even if interviews with the then actors suggest that they enjoyed working with non-Eritrean texts and were able to relate to their content. Perhaps this was due to differences of opinion among adult staff; but there has always been a general wariness among Eritreans towards foreign influences as a direct result of their nation's history.

Sewit has also produced a number of commissioned plays which are both an income generating activity and a creative challenge. In 1999, a play on the integration of disabled people, *Mistir Nayta Kofo* (The Secret of the Grain Basket) was commissioned by the Ministry of Labour and Welfare which toured in five of the six regions of Eritrea and was seen by an estimated 35,000 people (Esaias Tseggai 2004: 2). Later, it was turned into a video and aired on TV. The play is centred on a young disabled boy who is hidden away in a grain basket as a result of common shame regarding disability. He is in fact the bread winner of the family, painting beautiful pictures the father sells as his own. When his sister is about to get engaged, she eventually insists on bringing the secret out in the open.

A second commissioned work was a puppet play on condom use as part of a national HIV awareness campaign in 2000. Here, after a brief courtship, a (human) couple is seen going to a local pharmacy where the health workers and pharmacists (two cows) demonstrate how to use a condom. All this is commented on by two gossiping rabbits which provide comic relief. By using puppets instead of actors the group was able to create a distance between real-life events and the graphic instructions on stage, thereby deflating potential embarrassment among an audience where public discussions of sexual matters would normally be unthinkable.

Finally, the group produced a piece on landmines, *Mekalf* (Hindrance) as part of an international project on Mine Action Education (MAE) organized by national and internal organizations.[13] Two adult members of *Sewit* were trained in mine awareness and then commissioned to undertake Mine Risk Education (MRE) in local communities with songs and theatre. The result was a play about a young bright boy in a landmine infested area who lectures his parents on local dangers. Despite his intellectual ability, his parents refuse him permission to attend secondary school in the capital. When he eventually loses his life in a landmine explosion while herding livestock the family is devastated, and deeply regrets not having sent him to Asmara. The message seems somewhat ambiguous and judgemental as in older traditions of heavily moralistic drama; yet an estimated 40,000 people watched the play and it was deemed a great success.

Despite financial limitations and a shortage of staff, *Sewit* has already achieved more than any other children's theatre before in Eritrea. Most important, perhaps, has been the personal impact on its members. Meseret Ainom now helps Esaias run the group, but there are others whose development has been less spectacular but equally significant. Many children appreciate the music and drama education they receive (interviews, 19 September 2004); and the group makes a conscious effort to include the mentally or physically challenged. When asked about what the work with *Sewit* has given her personally, Semrawit (I), a seventeen year-old female high school student in 2000 replied:

> I can only say that I benefited. If I had continued in school, I wouldn't have acquired so much knowledge. Here we learn music and theatre. It also helps you in your studies, it does not hamper your school performance. I also used to be too shy to speak in front of an audience during my first time in school. Now I no longer feel shy because we practise such things in *Sewit*. It has given me confidence. (Interview, 1 April 2000)

Gesa, Gesa

Over New Year 2003 I flew out to Eritrea to mount a production of *Macbeth*. Perhaps the dreadful curse carries over to Africa, but insuperable problems with the translation meant that it was impossible to put the play on. I was looking, therefore, for something else worthwhile to work on while I was in the country when Esaias asked me if I would like to come and help him develop his newest play, *Gesa, Gesa*, with the children of *Sewit* Theatre Company. Since he had by then been asking me to come and look at *Sewit's* work for the best part of a decade, and I had never previously managed to make even one visit to their theatre, I jumped at the invitation.

That weekend I went over to the Coca-Cola building in which *Sewit* are based to watch a small performance of dance and music. The band have a range of electronic instruments which they play to a thumpingly rhythmic beat in uniforms reminiscent, to European eyes, of the 1970s, with two-tone colour schemes and wide lapels. I have to admit I have never been a fan of Eritrean music, either traditional or modern, so such performances are always a bit of an ordeal. The band was followed by some beautiful Eritrean traditional dance in bright costumes setting off the children's grace and love of the movements they performed. Esaias had organized a New Year treasure hunt for the children, and we were all then treated to tea and cakes. I was to return the next week to start rehearsals with the children in the afternoons and at weekends.

Many of the children I found myself working with were quite new members. The company had been in abeyance for a year while Esaias was studying with me in Leeds, and he had had to recruit a number of children who were notably shy, not only of me as a stranger working with them, but also of acting at all. Esaias had already written the play, a short, 20-minute piece, addressing fathers' responsibilities towards their families, and two alternative casts had begun working on the piece. This would mean that not only would more children have a chance to act, but performances would be easier to arrange round children's varied school and family commitments. As is common in so many African countries, playwrights often direct their own work in

Eritrea, so Esaias and my collaboration on *Gesa, Gesa* was a little unusual, though entirely in keeping with his ruthlessness in involving any passing talent he can rope in to helping the children develop as performers. To my knowledge adults always write the plays for *Sewit*, certainly devising is a relatively unknown means of making theatre in Eritrea, and though Esaias would be delighted if his students developed playwriting skills none has developed in that way yet.

Gesa, Gesa begins with children playing a game of 'house', hence the title of the piece. They play at being various animals, until mutual teasing becomes too much and the game breaks down in sulks and accusations of unfairness. Such play was immediately believable, though the young actors found being playful and extravert with the fantasy of the game embarrassing at first. While his sister sleeps, the brother moves into a long soliloquy about how he would like life to be. This would be difficult for any young actor, and the increasing aplomb with which the actors were able to command attention was arresting. At this point 'real' life breaks in, and we are in domestic scene with not squabbling children but quarrelling parents, and a father in particular who takes no care to understand his children and seeks to run away and drink with his friends rather than support his family. Eventually, in the moralistic style common to so much Eritrean and Ethiopian theatre, which surely claims direct descent from the preaching of the powerful Orthodox Church, the children lead their father to see the error of his ways.

For me what was interesting about the play was that it sought to move beyond the dominant realist mode in Eritrea. The children's play introduced an element of fantasy from the beginning, and the boy's speech was a direct address to the audience. Later on we brought in a mime sequence as children surrounded the men in the local bar reminding them of responsibilities while their fathers were spending all the family money on alcohol, and we then cut between scenes of domestic reality and more stylized bar sequences.

The children were all enormously willing to try things out, a testament to their confidence in Esaias. I tried to teach them about looking to make dramatic stage pictures and the importance of pace and energy in the performance. Since a certain lack of these is a criticism I have made of quite a lot of Eritrean theatre over the years I am unsure whether these issues were particular to the culture; quite as likely they were to do with working with many relatively novice actors, and they are certainly issues which often arise in making theatre. What was notable was that Esaias did not want his performers to blindly follow direction. He wanted me to explain, to talk more widely about my ideas behind making theatre in the way I did, and to involve the children in discussion.

Sadly I had to leave Eritrea before the first public performance of *Gesa, Gesa,* but I am delighted the play has been on to Eritrean television. And Esaias won't be having to ask me for another ten years before I go to work with *Sewit* again.

Acknowledgements

Christine Matzke gratefully acknowledges the financial support of the AHRB, the *Cusanuswerk* and the German Academic Exchange Service, DAAD. For administrative and office support she is indebted to The British Council Eritrea directed by Negusse Araya. Thanks also to her Eritrean colleagues, Mussie Tesfagiorgis, Tesfazghi Ukubazghi and Yakem Tesfai for helping her with the interviews.

Jane Plastow gratefully acknowledges the support of The British Academy.

NOTES

1 Christine Matzke recorded *Sewit*'s activities from 2000 to 2004 while researching theatre in Eritrea; Jane Plastow was invited to work with the group in January 2003. Most of the written documents were provided by the founder-cum-director of *Sewit*, Esaias Tseggai.

2 Today Eritrea acknowledges nine ethno-linguistic groups which are generally referred to as nationalities. They are divided into two dominant peoples, the Tigrinya- and Tigre-speakers, and seven minorities: the Bilen, Kunama, Nara, Rasheida, Saho, Hedareb (Beja), and the Afar. In this paper we will mainly refer to the two dominant groups, the Tigrinya and Tigre.

3 By the early 1960s, for example, girls comprised half of the two hundred participants involved in the public performance of Students' Music Day arranged and directed by two well-known artists, the hugely influential Alemayo Kahasai and his colleague, *memher* (teacher) Asres Tessema (Asres Tessema, 9 August 2001); Matzke (2003: 84-6).

4 Killion (1998: 318); Matzke (2003: 149-50, 172-5, 253-6). Today, a number of (second-generation) Red Flowers are in the state Marching Band; others, mostly first-generation performers, have become music teachers at the Asmara School of Music or work as actors and performers. The British music educator Sarah Maidlow has conducted research into their work; her findings are awaiting publication.

5 It is common to address Eritreans by their 'first' name, the second being the father's name rather than a surname in a Western sense. During the liberation struggle, fighters often used 'nicknames' or *noms de guerre* rather than their given names. *Noms de guerre* were part of the reinvention of people's identity in the liberation movement, but also a means to avoid easy identification by the enemy forces. Fighters of the liberation war still tend to prefer them to their civilian names. First names and *noms de guerre* are therefore used in this paper.

6 That they are still administered by, or report to, an official body – be it one of the ministries, one of the national unions (Youths, Women and others) or the PFDJ Cultural Affairs (the cultural section of the party People's Front for Democracy and Justice) – is an Eritrean peculiarity and has to do with the centralized, state-controlled organization of Eritrean civil society.

7 Thomas Leiper Kane, *Tigrinya-English Dictionary*, Vol I (Springfield, VA: Dunwoody Press, 2000), p. 757.

8 Interviews with members in September 2004 suggest that 10 years later this is no longer a main concern. With one exception, none of the children had faced objections from their parents; indeed, most had been encouraged to join the group (interviews, 19 September 2004).

9 Apart from various groups under the National Union of Eritrean Youths and Students (NUEYS), which are mostly run by young people themselves, a new children's cultural troupe by the name of *Asr* (Footprints – meaning those who follow the fighters) was established by the Ministry of Education after the latest military conflict with Ethiopia (1998-2000).

10 The programme started to be aired in early September 2004 and is shown Sundays from 2 to 2.30 p.m., with a repeat on Thursday afternoons. In late September 2004 Esaias explained that Eri-TV had been very co-operative, assisting them with cameramen and transport while leaving the artistic responsibility to *Sewit*.

11 According to Meseret Ainom, the financial administrator of the group, commissioning a piece of music may cost between 1500-3000 Nakfa in Eritrea, approximately €150-300 per song.

12 For a list of activities see Appendix.

13 Among others the UNMEE MACC (UN Mission to Eritrea and Ethiopia Mine Action Coordination Centre), UNICEF and the Eritrean Ministry of Labour and Social Welfare were involved. See bibliography for various online sources.

BIBLIOGRAPHY

Note that all Eritrean sources are cited with the author's ('first') name first, not the father's name ('surname'), as is the custom in Eritrea.

Alemseged Tesfai, *Drama*, mimeograph, transl. Tekeste Yonas (n.p.: EPLF, [1983]).

Esaias Tseggai, 'Brief Account Concerning Sewit Children's Theatre', unpublished report for the British Council, 2004.

Human Rights Watch, 'Eritrea: Landmine Monitor Report 2002' available online at http://www.icbl.org/lm/2002/eritrea/ ; accessed 18 June 2003.

James, Henry, 'The Marriages', adapted for Television by Helaine Michaels-Klein, in *Design for Drama: Short Plays Based on American Literature*, by Helaine Michaels-Klein, Reading Proficiency Through Play Reading, For Students of English at the High Intermediate/Advanced Level (Washington, D.C.: English Language Programs Division, Bureau of Education and Cultural Affairs, United States Information Agency, repr.1991), pp. 1–13.

Kane, Thomas Leiper, *Tigrinya-English Dictionary*, Vol I (Springfield, VA: Dunwoody Press, 2000).

Killion, Tom, *Historical Dictionary of Eritrea*, African Historical Dictionaries, 75 (Lanham, MD: Scarecrow Press, 1998).

Lawrence, Willie [lawrencew@un.org], 'Subject: UNMEE MAC Newsletter, Date: Fri. 15 June 2001 10:12:12+0300; UNMEE Mine Action Coordination Centre Update', available online at http://www.univ-lille1.fr/pfeda/Ethiop/Docs01/0615macc.htm; accessed 15 January 2004.

Mahalingam, Suba, 'Education: Protecting the Rights of Displaced Children', *Forced Migration Review*, 15 (Oct. 2002), 22–23; available online at http://www.fmreview.org/FMRpdfs/FMR15/mr15full.pdf; accessed 15 January 2004.

Maidlow, Sarah, 'An Account of Music Education in Eritrea', unpublished paper, June 2003.

Matzke, Christine, 'En-*gender*ing Theatre in Eritrea: The Roles and Representations of Women in the Performing Arts', unpublished PhD thesis, University of Leeds, September 2003.

UNICEF, 'UNICEF Humanitarian Appeal for Children and Women Jan – Dec 2002', available at http://www.relifweb.int/w/rwb.nsf/0/cb701c82b8aa3c6f85256b5f006df242?OpenD; accessed 15 January 2004.

UNMEE MACC (United Nations Mission in Ethiopia and Eritrea Mine Action Coordination Centre), 'UNMEE MACC Weekly Update: 15 February 2002', available online at http://www.mineaction.org/countries/_refdocs.cfm?doc_ID=849&country_ID=498; accessed 18 June 2003.

INTERVIEWS

(Professions, if stated, are those at the time of the interview).

Aaron Teckle, lab technician, Head of Haematology. Recorded interview in English, 28 April 2000, Asmara, Eritrea. Interviewer/transcript: Christine Matzke.

Asres Tessema, retired teacher, musician, playwright. Recorded interview in English, 9 August 2001, Asmara, Eritrea. Interviewer/transcript: Christine Matzke.

Awet G/Tsadik, Mulugeta Berhane and Hannah Kifizghi, members of *Sewit*. Recorded interview in English/Tigrinya, 19 September 2004, Asmara, Eritrea. Interviewer: Christine Matzke, translation: Meseret Ainom, transcript: Yakem Tesfai.

Efriem Kahsay and Daniel Mussie, members of *Sewit*. Recorded interview in English/Tigrinya, 19 September 2004, Asmara, Eritrea. Interviewer: Christine Matzke, translation: Meseret Ainom, transcript: Yakem Tesfai.

Esaias Tseggai, director of *Sewit* Children's Theatre. Recorded interview in English, 15 March 2000, Asmara, Eritrea. Interviewer: Christine Matzke, transcript: Mussie Tesfagiorgis.

—— Recorded interview in English, 2 May 2000, Asmara, Eritrea. Interviewer/transcript: Christine Matzke.

Erena Afewerki, Thomas Asefaw and Luam Tekeste, members of *Sewit*. Recorded interview in English/Tigrinya, 19 September 2004, Asmara, Eritrea. Interviewer: Christine Matzke, translation: Meseret Ainom, transcript: Yakem Tesfai.

Feshaye Yohannes 'Joshua', journalist, co-founder of *Sewit*, demobilised fighter. Recorded interview in English, 5 May 2000, Asmara, Eritrea. Interviewer/transcript: Christine Matzke.

Meseret Ainom, high school student, member of *Sewit*. Recorded interview in English/Tigrinya, 7 April 2000, Asmara, Eritrea. Interviewer: Christine Matzke, translator: Tesfazghi Ukubazghi, transcript: Mussie Tesfagiorgis.

—— college student, now assistant director and administrator of *Sewit*. Unrecorded interview in English, 28 March 2004. Interviewer/notes: Christine Matzke.

Semrawit (I), high school student, member of *Sewit*. Recorded interview in English/Tigrinya, 1 April 2000, Asmara, Eritrea. Interviewer: Christine Matzke, translator: Tesfazghi Ukubazghi, transcript: Mussie Tesfagiorgis.

Semrawit (II), Winta Berhane, and Alex Tseggai, members of *Sewit*. Recorded interview in English/Tigrinya, 19 September 2004, Asmara, Eritrea. Interviewer: Christine Matzke, translation: Meseret Ainom, transcript: Yakem Tesfai.

APPENDIX
A list of Sewit's activities

Year	Place of performance	Number of audience	Additional information
1994–95	Aghi school, Finland Mission and Delukus Club; all National Ceremonies and the cultural festival, Massawa	More than 20,000	
1996	Tour in the big towns of Zoba Debub (Southern Zone) and Northern Red Sea Zone	Around 32,000	Relationship between parents and children
1997–98	All elementary schools in Zoba Maekel (Central Zone), Massawa and Ela Beried; all National Ceremonies	More than 43,900	
1999	A long tour in five regions of the country, 16 sites	Around 35,000	Disability and community-based treatment
2000–2001	Most war-affected areas, 14 sites; all annual National Ceremonies	Around 40,000	Mine and HIV/AIDS awareness
2002	The group had no place to resume its activities.		
2003	1. The countryside of Zoba Maekel (Central Zone), 15 villages. 2. Independence day and cultural festival.		Awareness of children's need for attention

(Esaias Tseggai 2004: 2)

Project Phakama: Stories of South Africa, London & Lesotho
Landscapes of the Heart

YVONNE BANNING, CAROLINE CALBURN &
LUCY RICHARDSON

Introduction

We often talk about *young people and not* with *them* (*Facilitator, Project Phakama*)

This paper describes the working processes, relationships and performances of Project Phakama, an educational arts network of young people, arts educators and theatre practitioners that operates across South Africa, in the SADC region of Southern Africa, in India and in the United Kingdom. But unlike most descriptions of such projects, this account offers views expressed directly by the participants themselves.

It speaks their experiences in five residency projects between 1997 and 2004, which brought together people from a wide range of geographic, cultural, linguistic and social communities to live and work together to create a community-based site-specific theatre performance in various locations across the participating countries.

Compiled by a small team of participant editors, it is organized round each of the projects chronologically and thematically, rather than as a linear narrative, so that readers can encounter the fragmentary, sometimes contradictory, always passionate, and above all, feeling responses that characterize the Phakama experience.

How can we tell the stories?

These stories speak in the voices of people who, together, are Project Phakama. They speak to you (from other times, places, continents) of the varied experiences, values, beliefs, dreams, hopes and memories of a diverse collection of people separated by all kinds of geographic, cultural, social, linguistic and ideological differences. There is no single Phakama story, only a vision that is both theatrically, socially collective, and also uniquely personal to each of us.

This account of the work of Project Phakama is a compilation of views expressed by the participants (young people, facilitating tutors and audience members) on five selected projects that were created and performed as part of Phakama's ongoing arts education programme.

The small team of compilers (who are all themselves Phakama participants) wanted all these voices to speak for themselves, unmediated as much as possible by any single authoritative editorial voice. We wanted to capture the diversity of cultures, experiences, perspectives and debates that characterize the processes of living and working in the residency projects which comprise the central nodes of our programme.

So this is a collection of fragments, each of which refracts a particular hue and intensity within the whole spectrum of the rainbow that is Phakama. The various projects are organized chronologically; and within these sections we have used thematic headings, to create a loose conversational structure, so that voices speak to each other and to you, often passionately, sometimes disputing, changing the subject, or contradicting each other, much as we do when talking among friends.

We do, however, precede each section with a short description of the particular project. These derive from the more formal writings of funding proposals, publicity documents and so on that Phakama teams have produced over the years. And we begin with a brief general description of Project Phakama – its aims, mission statement and history – in order to map out the terrain. But it is the textures of feelings of the participants' voices that transform the map into the real landscapes of the heart of Phakama. The editorial insertions are marked in the text by the use of italics, and a full list of all the major national and international projects is appended at the end.

Phakama is ...
Mission statement
Project Phakama is an ongoing arts education and cultural exchange programme between practitioners from across South Africa and internationally. The Phakama network currently extends across South Africa and the SADC region (Namibia, Botswana, Mauritius, Mozambique and Lesotho), India and the United Kingdom.

We are committed to the practice of cultural exchange and celebration of shared experience by promoting a participant-centred and non-hierarchical educational philosophy through the medium of the arts.

We believe that cultural exchange, arts activities and arts education are central/key to the empowerment and development of young people and communities. We believe that cultural exchange takes place when different cultures exchange their beliefs, values, customs and arts willingly in a spirit of equality and trust through a process of negotiation.

Our approach is driven by a common desire to make high quality, creative theatre and we adhere to Article 31 of the United Nations Convention on the Rights of the Child; that is, that 'every child has the right to rest and leisure, to engage in play and recreational activities appropriate to the age of the child, and to participate freely in cultural life and the arts.'

Aims and objectives
- *To empower young people to explore and validate their cultural identity via high quality arts education and training;*
- *To bring together artists, educators and young people from diverse backgrounds in a spirit of exchange to promote and celebrate cultural diversity;*

- To foster a participant-centred philosophy to further the creative potential of every individual participant;
- To establish a network of arts practitioners sharing a philosophy of arts education based on the principle of giving and gaining.

I saw young South Africans from around the country living and working side-by-side, building a community, and collaborating to create powerful site-specific theatre. This type of community theatre allows for unique cross-cultural interaction, because it brings youngsters together behind an artistic goal.

Journeys, literal and imaginative have always found their way into the themes of each of our projects. Whether it's shoes for walking, suitcases to carry, walking the road to freedom, or the journey into the self, Phakama has been a continuous journey.

Phakama has been inside me from the day I was born. This very new, very different way of working towards a goal feels very familiar, and very indigenous to my soul.

It's always difficult to describe the way Phakama ticks. People have to be part of the tick in order to understand the nitty gritties.

In the middle of a warehouse caught up in the exuberance and excitement, I knew exactly why I was there, and why I had to stay.

This is how Phakama works: the principles are enacted more than talked about.

Beginning the story

From conversations about where South Africa was, post 1994, the idea of creating an arts education exchange between teachers, community arts workers and young people in South Africa and Britain grew. Its aim would be to develop expertise in organizing, implementing and creating multi-cultural arts education projects in schools and communities, using the medium of drama for conflict resolution and reconciliation.

And so Project Phakama was born in a month-long residency in Benoni, a mining city outside Johannesburg. In the coldest winter of that decade, 17 South Africans and 4 Londoners met and worked in an old empty garage.

Isolation to inspiration

I come from a region that one might call one of the forgotten areas in theatre. I was doing backyard work with young people, without any access to professional assistance. Phakama was my first contact with professional artists both black and white. The pain of working in isolation came to an end.

It was a rare opportunity to meet and work with teachers, theatre practitioners and government workers from across South Africa. This network has been a source of inspiration.

Could it go on? Was it worth the cost? There was no more than the smiles on the faces of the young people to reward us.

A sceptical audience of local officials realized that a new community could be born out of an arts process based on risk and innovation.

Over the next six years, Phakama worked on a dream and a shoestring, bringing facilitators and young people together from first Britain and South Africa – and later India, Mozambique, Lesotho, Botswana, Mauritius and Namibia – to continue developing the principles and values that make Phakama.

These have been forged by *the work* that is created, by the *relationships* that have formed, and by *the contexts and situations* that we have found ourselves in.

Living the art of Phakama
With a Suitcase in My Hand, Seshego 1997 and Cape Town 1998

Sixty young people from across South Africa created an unusual performance that took audiences on a physical journey through a transformed warehouse in Seshego (Limpopo Province). They witnessed stories about suitcases; histories forgotten and deeds untold.

In Cape Town 120 young people and tutors from across South Africa and from London joined Western Cape participants for a two week residency to explore stories and responses to a series of cultural visits made in and around Cape Town, to Robben Island, District Six and Cape Point. The performance focused on memory and reconciliation.

Living together, working together
Phakama's educational aims are fulfilled precisely because the work is embedded in the daily social experience of differences that come with sharing, eating, laughing, talking, celebrating, suffering and sharing together – from *living* as well as *working* together.

Phakama almost invariably has an accommodation crisis.

We stayed in a scout hut in the middle of a field. About 40 teenage boys squeezed into one room like an army barracks. To get to the toilets you had to go outside. The South African boys were laughing and joking, pushing their bags under the beds and settling in.

The UK boys were horrified at the lack of privacy, the absence of personal space, and there was nowhere to hang up their clothes.

In the old part of Pune [in India] there were 30 facilitators living and working in the marriage hall. I shared a room about 4m by 4m with five other people. There were two squat toilets and two showers between 30 of us. We lived like this for three weeks. I can't now imagine how we managed. But we did!

We have the tuck shop going now. Much joy. Liesl bought lollipops for it, with whistles in the stems. Big mistake!

In Seshego it was over-crowded. There was no public space that was not a bedroom. Teachers' planning sessions happened in the lounge, which was bedroom to nine students. The situation could have led to enormous stress and tension.

New bonds are formed, knots are tied and circles are created if you participate in Phakama.

What is it that sends one off on these potentially trying and often unimaginable missions?

There's a level of trust and intimacy built up that is just not possible when everyone goes home at night. I've always felt richer because I've had to share.

In a creative process, often the most important moments happen not in the middle of a workshop but in the queue for food, waiting for the shower, in conversations over dinner or breakfast.

Learning to live with difference

We didn't just learn about cultural differences, we lived it in life as in our theatrical work.

To overcome language barriers, the young people developed their own way of greeting each other: one word, '*tchoborops!*' If all else failed, 'tchoborops' was there.

The young people saw interracial relationships in action among the tutors.

Life into theatre, theatre into life

Everyone built dream homes or shacks out of matchsticks. Each person had built beautiful, wonderful dreamscapes of calm paradise around their shacks, where animals could shelter, friends could come and flowers could grow.

Although I'm still young and never experienced the pain of living under apartheid, the mood, the smell, the scenic views of Robben Island brought the past years back. I lived the moments.

In the warehouse at Seshego there was a complex and vivid tale of *muti* [medicine, sometimes with magical properties] in a suitcase that was used to create rain ... at the time I barely knew what *muti* was but I did know rain.

An allegation of misconduct was made by one of the young people against an adult tutor. In the performance the 12-year-old participant enacted her own private reconciliation with the tutor. There's a sequence where each participant collects a stone from the fire circle and offers it to a member of the audience. This young person spontaneously offered her stone to the tutor.

One group chose Hamza's story to enact. At the end Hamza ran out of the room. [I] followed and found him crying outside the door. He kept repeating 'What am I doing to my mother. I never knew what I was doing to my mother.'

We would not have achieved our performances without the contexts that the project provides: the holistic merging of theatrical and social; personal and collective; symbolic and real; trusting and daring.

Finding yourself on foreign soil
Be Yourself, London, LIFT 99

This three-week residency culminated in a performance in the Tricycle Theatre in London. It was an insider's and outsider's view of London, that told of its pain and celebrated its diversity. The project involved twenty young people from South Africa and ten from London.

Cultural exchange is painful

How were we going to cope on foreign soil?

I have mixed feelings about London. For the first time I came to grips with the tortures of cultural exchange.

South African facilitators were concerned about the change that the South African young people were going through – that they were looking at London and its way of being as what they wanted to become. It caused huge anxiety and tensions.

Tears, hurt and I want to go home everywhere.

Many of the facilitators expressed anxiety at working with London youth: that they were more outspoken, more articulate more savvy than we are; that we have nothing to teach them.

The London kids complained about the food, the lack of free time – it felt like they were complaining about everything. But they were just being themselves, doing what they would do if they were on a project in London. It took us all a good few days to realize this, to let it be.

Discovering my self

I started this project as a total stranger to others and to myself.

My own little world became more and more cramped as this project opened more doors that led me into a new world. It was a journey of self-discovery for me.

People have accepted me for who I am, not who I fake to be.

One young man is very fearful of being returned to Sierra Leone. He feels very vulnerable and disguises it with street swagger. Only in Phakama sessions has he ever really shown the kid in him.

Until you spread your wings you will never know high you can fly.

> If only I knew
> His past, his now, his future
> Would I understand   (*participant's haiku*)

Tony put his arm around Kabelo and told Kabelo's story; how his mother had been detained during the Struggle; how she had given birth to him while in solitary confinement. When Tony finished, Kabelo broke down and wept in his arms. Hearing his story being told by someone else to the group, it was as though he was able to shed a lot of the burden carried with him. Kabelo died a year later from a very sudden heart attack.

Call Me Not a Woman really taught me to treasure and respect my life.

I give myself different roles to play in different projects. I always try to come back a different person.

I felt a growing awkwardness as the village spokesperson addressed all his remarks to me as the only white adult amongst the group. It was a clear reminder of the cultural barriers that exist in simply being who we are.

It is through being in another country, working amongst another culture that we come to discover who we are. And give insight into what we do. And why we do it. And this process is not comfortable.

If I tell you that one of the most moving, exuberant and visually stunning shows to see in London is a youth production devised and performed by a group of South African and London teenagers, you will probably be sceptical. But *Be Yourself* is really terrific ... It is an exhilarating and truly brilliant achievement.

Giving & gaining
Call Me Not a Woman, Genadendal & Mmabatho 2000

This provocative exploration of women's lives, which took place in Mmabatho, in the North West Province of South Africa, led to a performance by 70 young people set in two domestic houses on either side of – and including – a four-lane national highway.

It is important to acknowledge that everyone, no matter how young, has something valuable to give to the project – and that others can learn from them.

The Phakama sun

We use an exercise called Give and Gain to establish what skills and knowledge participants feel they can give to the performance, and what they hope to take away with them.

It's not about everyone doing the same thing; it's about everyone doing what they can – that's what Phakama is for me.

Tutors go through this process too. The end result is a huge sun shape, made up of orange strips showing what each person hopes to gain, and yellow strips showing what everyone feels they can give to the process. It's very useful because it immediately becomes possible to see where the group's skills lie. And where there are gaps.

Taking the plunge

How many times has Phakama asked us to jump, and we *have* jumped.

I had to organize the residency in Mmabatho. I lacked experience. What if the residency failed, that was the biggest risk I was facing and I was scared to death.

The Phakama process has allowed me to have extraordinary faith and to take the most horrendous risks.

Trusting others

I trust that things will fall into place if I am gentle and wait.

It's about working out when to intervene, and when to let things go.

I trust that others will take responsibility, and that their method, though different to mine, is often more effective.

I'm not scared

This discovery that you are not alone is critical for young people in the developing world.

I think that I enabled participants to take real responsibility with adequate support when they needed it.

When this support works, it's extraordinary; when it doesn't, it's a long way down.

The process is thinking about 'we', not 'I'. No following the leader. Everyone celebrates together. No muddles, because, for child and adult, freedom comes with responsibility.

The young people of Porter School are considered law offenders. The project helped remind them they are still young people of this democratic country.

I performed and I was not scared. And I was not tired. I was talking. People were cheering for me. I was so happy because people were happy and it was a first performance for me.

Alternatives in learning and leadership

Phakama shows people that there are alternatives to the oppressive systems of schooling that dominate most education systems around the world.

Ja neh!!! There were times when kaal-voet laities[1] like me used to sit around street corners and do nothing. Now times have changed for the best since joining project Phakama. I am now volunteering and coaching the Mafikeng goal-ball team for the Blind. I am also volunteering with Love-Life [2]... ek se Jou!!!

The young people expressed things they are not usually allowed to say in a formal education context ... Many of the young people said 'if they could be like this in school they would never fail'.

We have to accept that this work will empower them, even if it is not in ways that we like.

Looking back, looking forward

Enacting what it was like living through apartheid brought to light human suffering in a way that celebrated the future as well as remembering the past.

I carry the Phakama vision of a shared future in every play I perform in, every production I direct and every class I facilitate.

> Only one picture
> Controls where I go from here
> My life is a door   (*participant's haiku*)

I started a small group. Everything Phakama gives me, I go and share with my group.

It has given me a huge faith in my country and its people, and the opportunity of dealing with the ugly monster racism.

The young man said 'It just widens my horizons, I learn new things all the time. I mean, take us talking, I've never spoken to a white woman before.'

Journeys
The Freedom Project, Robben Island 2001

Commissioned by the Robben Island Museum, this was the first public performance by young people to take place on the infamous prison island off the coast of Cape Town. Four months of devising between artists, ex-prisoners and young people from around the country culminated in a performance on the island for South Africa's Freedom Day. The young people explored the concept of freedom, using the history of Robben Island to investigate their own stories and their own experiences of freedom.

On 27 April (Freedom Day) 2001, some 35 young people from five provinces in South Africa present a single performance at a number of sites on Robben Island. The event begins at sunset. Audience members travel among these sites on foot carrying small hurricane lamps, and in buses.

It was maps, maps, maps. What route were we going to take? What journey did we want the audience to experience? Could we organize buses? Was the walk too long? Would we all arrive at the end together? If we didn't, what were we going to do? It felt as though this performance was just another transport nightmare!

How do we get there?
We've had accidents, relief vehicles driving out into the unknown, flight problems, cars stuffed beyond capacity, overbooked ferries. The journey of simply getting to a Phakama project can be our biggest challenge! And getting there doesn't always imply we can get home!!!

If I have to walk from one end of the village to the other *again* today…

Participant travellers
During the three-month process the participants listened to stories from ex-prisoners and quite literally walked in the footsteps of all the people who have lived – and died – there over the past three centuries,

Armed with a desire to explore, off you went for the day's adventure … Things of familiarity suddenly became fascinating; you began to look at things differently, strangely, curiously.

We drew a large outline of Robben Island on the floor and asked the young people to tell us where all the places we had visited were. It was as though they were dragging their minds back along the footsteps they had taken.

Pogiso came up with the idea of journeying people sitting down beside the side of the road to tell different stories related to suitcases.

Sites: passports to landscapes
It was beautiful, the movement from place to place – it created a sense of ritual, incorporating the audience.

It was the first time that I worked in a theatre – both exciting and scary.

It has been a strange experience working in theatre and I don't feel entirely comfortable about it – it doesn't feel right for Phakama.

Standard theatre is not the place for us. How did we get away with water in the auditorium? Drumming in the foyer?

The production takes the show into the audience: you feel as though you have been thrust into the very heart of the city, into its smells, sounds and sights.

The children have chosen to take their audience on a journey. The tragedy of out-of-work miners is depicted in a dusty street.

In *Call Me Not a Woman*, two houses on opposite sides of a busy road served as a theatre. During interval the audience was escorted across the road by rows of performers, singing, dancing and carrying lanterns.

Genadendal is a small village, and the boundary between drama and reality blurs too easily.

It was exciting, watching the young people realize how the site transformed their ideas. The oddity and ordinariness of spaces produced a style that veered from the surreal and extra-ordinary to the very real.

Audiences as travelling companions

How would we transport the audience? Anthea drummed up every tractor, trailer, lorry and donkey cart in the village. And that is how 300 audience members travelled.

It is as though the travelling provides a way into the performance for the audience – makes it theirs, makes it their journey.

It's like one of those airline maps in which you see lines connecting all across the world.

On the first evening, the police arrived in bullet-proof vests. They joined the audience. The irony of the performance became frighteningly clear.

Moving from spot to spot, the audience is constantly surprised by the show's simplicity in structure, its sweep of imagination.

I was not expecting to walk so far: a long walk to freedom.

I asked an elderly woman in the audience if she'd like a lift in the kombi. She replied, 'I wouldn't miss one step of this pilgrimage.'

A huge bird arrives. Viewers are asked to attach their 'wish notes' to its wings before it 'flies' off. You feel the magic in the night.

Audiences were extremely shocked at the subject matter: rape, brutal violence, pain, sex. I think they were expecting a nice play – but that's not what the work is about.

The cast come around with bowls of water and offer to wash the audience's hands. The washing away of guilt? Or a kind of atonement.

We all meet up again to walk back to the harbour. Small boats, each carrying a tiny candle, are launched onto the water. They drift across the harbour until they sink or are lost to view. We board the ferries waiting to take us back to Cape Town. Those remaining on the island sing us on our way. The performance ends. Or does it?

...the impossibility of getting the audience to go home afterwards.

Landscapes of democracy
The Child I Curry, Lesotho 2003

Fifteen facilitators from Mauritius, Lesotho, Mozambique, Namibia, Botswana, South Africa and Britain worked with 66 young Basotho to create a performance in Morija, Lesotho, about children's rights and how, despite adults' hopes and dreams for them, we manage to destroy their childhoods. The next phase is to take place in Botswana after intensive work at a local level in each of the participating countries.

'Follow the Bird. Follow Your Dreams' chant over 60 Basotho young people. They circle us with paper birds, and then, as a flock, escape through the windows and out into the garden beyond. And so begins our journey.

The Child I Curry (The Child that Curries Me) is a project that explores what makes a young person and what a young person can make. It will be a critical exploration of social justice, good governance and human rights. It will allow young people and facilitators to make new discoveries about their histories and find the confidence to act on their discoveries within their own countries and social context.

We follow, into a garden where children's imaginations have run wild.

Making images

I was armed with the most important tool for any artist – the spear of creativity.

Michael, a boy from Ethiopia, covered everything in his bedroom with white fabric. The bed, the TV, the table, the carpet, the chair. He sat there in a white robe reading a white book. He said it was his room of calm and silence, a place where he could study, make up for his lost learning and become a genius.

There's a drawing exercise where you draw the outlines of people on a huge sheet of paper, one over another. When the paper is full you stand back and look at the spaces. The task is to find the unexpected. We were trying to look for animals in these abstract spaces. And nothing was happening. I was on the verge of giving up when one of the boys said, 'There's a chicken.' Everyone looked at him. With a huge grin he says again, 'There's a chicken.' Sure enough, in the space between two feet, an elbow and someone's back there was the outline of a chicken.

We spent an afternoon decorating these domestic spaces with poetry and everyday objects associated with women's lives.

... whispered secrets from mouths haloed by oil lamps; a rainbow canopy surrounded by raging fire ...

A small team of us built a 'rain cloud' out of hose pipe and fixed it in the gloomy rafters. The *muti* man threw a handful of dust in the air and called down the rain; we turned on the tap; there was a long pause, and then the rain came – a sprinkle, then a shower, then a downpour. There was a moment of madness as audience members started dancing in the rain, clapping, shouting and catching the rain in their hands.

The Phakama process is as fragile as it is brilliant.

Children are up on branches decorating the Tree of Life, and painting motifs on its trunk. And what are those boys doing with a plywood crescent? Why, it's a blue moon with silver spangles!

There are moments when I was made to feel like a magician, because I'd created something no-one believed was possible.

A young boy stands sentinel over a miniature group of beaded dolls, playing a handmade tin guitar. Another is up a tree, sprinkling water on a woman standing beneath an umbrella. But as we are led further into the garden we leave innocence behind.

Practicing democracy

We often talk *about* young people and not *with* them.

Sam said to me, 'Democracy doesn't work.' We began a conversation about that, but had to stop to go off in the taxi. Pity.

The facilitators were wise enough to let us set down our own rules.

The four youngest facilitators gave me a new perspective on young people as leaders and decisions-makers.

When young people are given the freedom to express themselves, they speak with profound words, and I begin to believe in a brighter future.

It's tricky working democratically in theatre.

I found it much easier to ask questions when I was working side by side with someone.

I learned to recognize the importance of allowing space for the local team to deal with local politics and customs.

We are the same, no-one says I am big, no one says I am small. We are so happy about our working. We play and sing together; no-one is angry.

It was difficult to introduce Phakama's ethos into an environment that seemed to be very authoritarian in structure.

If you ask young people about the things they really want to talk about, it will be what they see around them, the world they come up against. They needed to raise those subjects publicly. But it wasn't negative. There were very moral tales that explored options, rights and wrongs. They created energy and optimism out of the problems they faced … finding hope in what most would see as a bleak future.

Conclusion

Landscapes of the heart

We are each other's tutors. You cannot get more democratic than that.

I never thought that so many different cultures can be mixed and exchanged in just one project in so little time.

I've been an artist, composer, dancer, director, an actor, a photographer, a learner, a facilitator, poet, singer, a host, a friend, but best of all, a member of Phakama.

These young participants should be the new ambassadors in the world.

A sense of magic
A sense of pageantry
A sense of occasion
A sense of healing
A sense of empowerment.
A deeply moving experience.
All the things theatre should be.
Truly South African.

NOTES

1 An Afrikaans colloquial phrase meaning 'a barefoot youngster'.
2 Love-Life is a national programme for educating young people about HIV and AIDS.

APPENDIX
Major Phakama Projects 1996–2004

1996 **Bulang Dikgoro – Open the Gates**
Benoni
Inspiration for this came from a combination of surviving the realities of life in the suburbs of Johannesburg, and the young people's aspirations for the new South Africa.

1997 **Izimbadada – If I were in Your Shoes**
London
20 young South Africans came to London to work with 20 young Londoners from Lewisham Youth Theatre in a three-week residency. This resulted in a dynamic show at the Albany Theatre in Deptford, one of the undisputed highlights of LIFT '97.

1998 **Ka Mor Walo Ka Seatlang – With a Suitcase in My Hand**
Seshego
In a week long residency in Seshego, Limpopo, a team of South African and British artists worked with 70 young people from the North West, Gauteng, Western Cape and Limpopo Provinces. The performance of stories out of suitcases carried by migrating people took place in a large disused warehouse, and played to audiences from the local community and surrounding informal settlements.

1998 **Met 'n Sak Onner die Blad**
Cape Town
A total of 100 young people from across South Africa and London joined Western Cape participants to explore stories and responses to a series of cultural visits made in Cape Town; to Robben Island, District

Six, and Cape Point. The performance focused on memory and reconciliation.

1999 **Wololo! Y2K Kom Verby**
Cape Town
40 young people, over a period of three months explored moments in their lives which were like gateways – when their lives changed crucially at such moments. This site-specific performance ended in celebration dances round a fire.

1999 **Be Yourself**
London
As part of LIFT '99, 20 young South Africans chosen from 300 young people across the country, worked together with 10 young Londoners over a three-week period. After an intense exploration of the city, from Stephen Lawrence's memorial to Selfridges, an astonishing performance was created in London's Tricycle Theatre.

2000 **Call Me Not a Woman**
Genadendal
Through oral histories gathered by 40 young people from around the Western Cape, a provocative and celebratory journey of women's lives was created. The 300-strong audience for this performance travelled by donkey cart and tractor, as well as on foot from a house in the village to a newly erected house on the village outskirts.
Mmabatho
Set in two domestic dwellings which were separated by a four-lane national highway, 70 young people from around South Africa continued to unravel the lives and experiences of women.

2001 **The Freedom Project**
Robben Island
Commissioned by the Robben Island Museum, this was the first time that the infamous and sacred island was used as a site for performance. Four months of devising among artists, ex-prisoners and young people from around the country culminated in a pilgrimage performance for Freedom Day.

2001 **Walking Home**
Cape Town
A celebratory processional performance with lanterns, a flying carpet and fireworks through the oldest part of Cape Town – the Company Gardens – on Heritage Day.

2002 **The Phakama Way**
Pune

This month-long training project in Pune, hosted by Prithvi Theatre in Mumbai, introduced arts education practitioners from across India to Phakama's methodology. This included creating a magical site-specific performance with 199 young people from Pune.

2002 **Spices**
Cape Town
A five-day project that involved the training of young facilitators who created a performance with 25 young people. Set in various spaces in the grounds and buildings of a school, the performance took the audience on a spice journey that ended around a cauldron of chai.

2002 **Soul Food**
Nelson Mandela Gateway, Cape Town
In collaboration with the Robben Island Museum, Soul Food researched the lives of people who have inhabited Robben Island over the centuries. The young people created an installation of the sources of inspiration that have kept people going while living on the Island.

2003– **The Child I Curry**
2006 Lesotho, South Africa, Botswana, Namibia, Mozambique, Mauritius
This ongoing project, celebrating the lives of children and their contribution to civil society, brings together young people and practitioners from SADC countries as well as Britain and India. Local performances have been given in each of the participating countries, and international residencies have taken place in Morija (Lesotho) and Gaberone (Botswana).

2003– **Strange Familiars**
2004 London
Developed in London this project is in response to the increasing numbers of isolated young asylum seekers in the city. Weekly workshops over a ten-month period resulted in a week-long residency and performance at the National Children's Home as part of LIFT's Family Friendly Season and a collaboration with Lewisham Youth Theatre at the Horniman Museum.

Approaching Theatre Work with Children in Zimbabwe
'Share what you have'

ROBERT MSHENGU KAVANAGH

'The child at the centre'

CHIPAWO means literally 'please give' or 'give also' in the Shona language of Zimbabwe. In essence it means 'share what you have'. Originally it also stood for Children's Performing Arts Workshop. CHIPAWO was founded in 1989 with the following objectives:

- to ensure that our children know and appreciate our own culture – Zimbabwe, Southern Africa, Africa
- to ensure that through the arts our children learn, develop and grow up as balanced, harmonious, whole human beings who in turn help to make a balanced, harmonious, whole society
- to ensure that our children enrich and improve the performing arts of our country and in many cases find fulfilling employment in the arts and related fields
- to involve our children in a participatory, creative, learning process which is dynamic, gender sensitive and democratic and in which the child is at the centre and *every* child is precious – boy/girl, rich/poor, town/country, able/disabled

It can be seen from these objectives that CHIPAWO's intervention was designed to tackle some of the root causes of the crisis in arts education – and in education itself.

CHIPAWO calls its core programme, arts education for development and employment (AEDE). This programme has a syllabus and a method, guided by its own pedagogical, aesthetic and ethical framework. In its arts education programme, drama, along with music, dance and media (video and television) is a component. The object of the AEDE is as its name implies to engage children in arts training as a vehicle for their education, development and, where appropriate, future employment. However, obviously, performance, though not an end in itself, is an aspect of the method. Thus drama performance in the AEDE is part of CHIPAWO's work in theatre.

In addition to the AEDE programme, CHIPAWO also has a Performance Programme. In this programme, performance is not just part of the process but the end itself. Here children and youth from the various centres are selected by audition to become members of the Harare Junior Theatre (roughly equated to the primary school) and the Harare Youth Theatre (roughly equated to the secondary school).

Another centre where performance is accentuated is the all-girl Girl Power Centre, where the power of performance is an essential strategic component of the centre's effectiveness with regard to advocacy for the girl child.

As CHIPAWO has developed and its children leave school, it has had to adapt to new circumstances. The major development in this regard was the establishment of the Zimbabwe Academy of Arts Education for Development, which offers diplomas and certificates in the performing and media arts.[1] Other responses to the needs of CHIPAWO graduates include the CHIPAWO Performance Company, the Musical Ensemble and the New Horizon Theatre, this last being an initiative of the graduates themselves, though it receives non-financial support from CHIPAWO.

At the outset it needs to be stressed that because of the nature of CHIPAWO's method the CHIPAWO child and the CHIPAWO graduate are versatile performers, all of whom have acquired a wide range of musical and dance skills with many of them having had experience of television and video work.

Before taking a closer look at CHIPAWO's theatre practice, perhaps we should take a closer look at CHIPAWO, where it comes from and what it is trying to do.

'Captivating children's minds'[2]

Before majority rule came to Zimbabwe in 1980 as the result of a bitter and protracted struggle, arts education was the prerogative of the white minority. In the pre-colonial societies of the region there existed various forms of arts education but with the advent of colonialism they broke down and the activities of the Christian missionaries and the new values, dictated by survival in the colonial capitalist economy, to a large extent undermined the status of the arts in general.

The same forces dictated that the education system in place at the time of majority rule would be yoked rigidly to examinations and as a consequence the pedagogy or teaching methods that prevailed in the classroom would be based on rote learning, drilling and top-down, autocratic relations between teachers and children.

This meant that in the years after 1980 when a new society was being constructed and democracy came for the first time to the people of Zimbabwe, children were being educated in a system that had little time or respect for the arts and in which there was very little scope for discussing, questioning and challenging, for imagination, creativity, originality and democratic freedoms in the classroom. Few in the education system at that time conceived of children as having the capacity to contribute to their own education.

Their lot was to be *taught*. Few conceived of children as having rights. They simply had duties.

Yes, it is true that Government considered that Education was a right and not a privilege. This was evidenced by the massive investment in education in the years after majority rule. Children had a right to education but not education about their rights.

In the former white schools (Group A) the arts were given greater prominence – on the tacit understanding that the arts meant the European arts. In the classroom there was art, music and verse-speaking – all Euro or rather Anglo-centric. In the extra-curricular timetable there were Speech and Drama, Ballet and, depending on the school, lessons in piano, violin or some such instrument. Zimbabwean or African content was virtually taboo. In some high schools there were annual productions of Shakespeare and Gilbert and Sullivan. There were no Shona drama clubs as there were in the former Group B schools and even introducing Shona into the classroom curriculum in Primary Schools was strongly resisted.

In addition to this, many teachers entertained a number of negative attitudes to the arts, which exacerbated the situation. Many felt that the culture – and this included the arts – of traditional societies was unchristian. Others saw the arts as an activity that captivates the children's minds and takes them away from their academic studies, in other words, examinations.

As far as arts education and pedagogy are concerned, the family in most cases mirrored the school – autocratic and either uninterested or negative towards their children being involved in the arts. Many Christian parents, like the teachers, disapproved of traditional arts and culture. One of the consequences of the social changes brought about by colonialism was the collapse of indigenous social recreation systems. For many children and young people in the new Zimbabwe the only forms of recreation were playing together, listening to the radio or watching television, listening to recorded music, going to church and/or cinemas and (night) clubs. And here the impact was devastating, particularly in the urban areas. Music and even dancing played a very big part in their recreation but it was all foreign – from the United States to be specific. It was foreign not only in its origin but in its culture, morals, manners and vision.

It should be clear from the above survey of the context of arts education in Zimbabwe in the period after majority rule – and very likely in the region as a whole – that the arts, arts education and the state of education itself were, and are still, in crisis. Another factor affecting the arts and children was the extreme compartmentalization of the apartheid-style colonial society in which government policy based on race intensified the class divisions prompted by capitalism. Thus in the period after the coming of majority rule not only did different races and cultures not mingle but neither did town and country nor high-density (former black) and low-density (former white) dwellers. The school system did little to break down the divisions – in fact with the exception of certain former Group A schools, which were attended by children from both high and low density backgrounds, it largely reinforced them. White children were rapidly spirited off to private schools along with the children of the new black middle class. Children grew up and developed in their respective boxes.

Starting with one centre consisting of 60 children between the ages of eight and twelve, following a programme of dance, music and drama, CHIPAWO in the fifteen years since its founding steadily expanded its operations. Seventy-eight centres following the CHIPAWO method and pedagogy are now to be found all over Zimbabwe and in the region of 3,000 infants, children and young people of all backgrounds and abilities are involved in its programmes. Its performances by many different groups of children have been seen widely on national television, in many parts of Zimbabwe and in countries such as Kenya, South Africa, Mozambique, Finland, Denmark, Germany, China and Japan. It manufactures musical instruments and costumes and produces television programmes and videos as well as providing training and services of all kinds. It has an Academy that offers diplomas and certificates accredited by a Zimbabwean university. All in all CHIPAWO now employs 28 full-time staff and trainees and 83 part-time Arts Educators. CHIPAWO is registered as a Trust and is currently working towards establishing a Children's Arts Development and Entertainment Centre (Mntwana Centre).

The drama of arts education

The aims of CHIPAWO have determined its pedagogy and that in turn has shaped its aesthetic. This is especially true of drama. How and why it is being taught determines what kind of drama is practised. This is not an aspect that needs to be explored in any detail as this concerns the teaching of drama in the context of arts education as opposed to the main focus of this paper, which is the practice of drama in the context of performance.

In CHIPAWO's publication on its pedagogy, aesthetics and ethics, *Arts Fit for Children*,[3] three crucial maxims are proposed:

1. Child at the Centre
2. *Mwana anokosha* (Children are important)
3. Child as Child

If the child is to be at the centre, the value of the child has to be recognized. The child at the centre is seen as precious and important. But just as important this maxim must apply to *all* children. By *all* is meant the full and equal inclusion of disabled and even mentally handicapped children, the poor and disadvantaged and talented as well as not so talented children.

The child is at the centre, both precious and important. This must refer to all children – but it must also refer to the *whole* child – not just that part of the child that is involved in arts education. Is the child hungry, abandoned, orphaned, not doing well at school, too poor to pay school fees, being abused, needing a job after school? In other words, the child as child not only as arts learner.

These three maxims encapsulate the essence of arts education for development and employment.

In brief, CHIPAWO's arts education theory and practice produces a drama that is developed from the children's own thoughts, opinions, stories and experiences with their full, critical participation, often on issues that concern the rights or welfare of children. Plays will provide exciting performance opportunities for as many of the children in the cast as possible. Those who are struggling to master their parts are not replaced but assisted to do the best they can with the children helping each other. Plays will tend to include lots of music and dance and the performers will probably act, play marimba, drums or *hosho* (shakers) and dance. Girls will not be disadvantaged and there will be no gender stereotyping.

The drama of performance

The change from drama in the AEDE programme to theatre performance in the performance centres is dramatic. CHIPAWO is at pains to advocate that this difference be explained thoroughly to the children otherwise they can easily be upset and discouraged. The arts education session now becomes a rehearsal and the arts educator becomes a director. The pace and intensity of the work changes. Now a performer who cannot master a role, a dance, a piece of music is assisted as is any performer but may also be replaced by one who can. This is a fundamental diversion from the pedagogy but obviously performance has its own exigencies.

However, though the transition from drama in arts education to theatre as performance is a big leap, the basic aesthetic characteristics developed by the CHIPAWO pedagogy as well as the nature of the training offered in arts education still influence strongly the nature of theatre as performance both in the CHIPAWO performance centres as well as among the graduates. CHIPAWO has always been strong on communal or collective creativity and performance rather than solo performance. For instance, the marimba band is an ideal medium for involving children in making music. A basic set has six pieces, some of which can be played by two players, but these can be added to depending on the availability of the instruments, Other children will be required for drums and *hosho*, yet others for clapping and singing – and depending on the tune being played – there may also be scope for dancers. In this way the marimba band can actively involve up to 25 children. If further percussion is added, this can be even more. In comparison learning the guitar would involve an instructor devoting time to fewer children.

Then, as mentioned above, the integrated syllabus of the CHIPAWO arts education programme means that a CHIPAWO child or graduate is an all-rounder, with the ability to act, make music, perform modern dances as well as numerous traditional dances. The arts training they have received, many of them from an early age, also means that they are very receptive and quick to master new choreographies, compositions and dialogue. With a cast of CHIPAWO children it is possible to knock up an exciting Christmas Show in a week where the same programme might take months with children who have not experienced the CHIPAWO arts education programme.

It remains a fact however that CHIPAWO has been conspicuously less successful in drama than in music and dance. Drama training and performance throughout the organization has always been relatively weak. The performance centres have been able to transcend this weakness to a great extent but even then many of the performers will be more at home in dance and music than they are with dialogue. This is a matter of concern to CHIPAWO and it is something that CHIPAWO is struggling to address. Almost anyone can put together an improvised sketch. However training dramaturges and directors to be able to transform the material into an original and powerful script and then the action into a genuinely dramatic performance seems to be a problem not only in CHIPAWO but in the country as a whole.

The development of a pool of CHIPAWO graduates who are full-time professionals and are available for intensive drama rehearsals has created a new dimension. As they are able to concentrate on their acting, without constantly dissolving into dancers, drummers or marimba players, has led to a marked improvement in their acting skills and the way in which they handle dialogue. They are a new breed of actors in Zimbabwe.

Acting in Zimbabwe, even by the best, has hitherto been characterized by a tendency to improvise and thus script work is weak and actors tend not to learn their words. They feel that if they get the general drift they can get along paraphrasing in their own words. In Harare – the situation at theatres like Amakhosi in Bulawayo is different – direction has been weak and actors do not expect to be directed. They either prefer to direct themselves, perhaps believing that if anyone says you need directing they are implying that you do not know your job as an actor, or direct each other – even though there may be someone nominally 'directing'. The result is that plays lack precision, words are muffed, the balance of lines, pace, ensemble and of course even characterization, suffer.

Working with the 'new' young actors who have graduated from CHIPAWO can be a refreshing experience for a Zimbabwean director who has previously had to work with the old school. Here are actors who learn their words, understand the rigours and discipline of a rehearsal and rehearsal schedule and have grown up accepting the need for a director. Of course they have also grown up expressing their own ideas, challenging the director and collaborating in the creative process.

Layiti theatre

'Layiti' is the CHIPAWO word for 'infant'. Layitis participate in the CHIPAWO programme at pre-school centres and at other school-based

1. Mangwende and his donkey in the Shona comic opera, **Mangwende's Donkey**
(© CHIPAWO)

2. Amainini, the younger wife in Jari Mukaranga
(© CHIPAWO)

3. The father in Cry Thinking *showing off his new baby to a friend, not knowing the baby has been born deaf*
(© CHIPAWO)

4. *'Getting out of the box' – a deaf child begins to communicate in* Cry Thinking
(© CHIPAWO)

centres where Grade 1 and 2 are considered layitis. At other centres the whole spectrum of ages is to be found so each of these centres will have a layiti group, junior groups and often a youth group.

When CHIPAWO first started working with infants in the pre-schools, the arts educators were guided by the theory and practice of the women who worked with them. Generally there was a belief that if you can get infants to do anything at all it is a great achievement and it is extravagantly applauded. And this remains the belief and practice at most pre-schools when parents are invited to concerts. The infant 'performers' have been taught a line or two which a teacher has written for them. They are shunted into a line and then the teachers will prod and whisper until the children do as they have been told. The teachers all the while will be onstage moving from child to child pushing them into position and prompting them – and going so far as to prompt the audience to clap for them at the end as they shepherd their little charges off the stage. The infants have endured the performance basically standing rather gormlessly gazing at the audience or at each other and waiting to be prodded and prompted.

Experience of what small children are able to do for themselves elsewhere seemed to indicate that this approach to infant performance could be improved. Two alternative approaches suggested themselves. One was to create an environment in which the children 'played' – after all I believe that one of the origins of drama is in play. Small children soon come up with dramatic situations which it is possible to help them develop and standardize – and because they have originated it and it is in a form very closely related to their own play, they are able to perform in an independent and uninhibited way.

The other approach related to scripted plays. Generally speaking the CHIPAWO method involves a greater degree of script-writing by arts educators for infants, less for juniors and even less for youth. CHIPAWO has developed a number of acting scripts for infants – and these are collected in an in-house publication titled appropriately *All by Ourselves*.[4] All of these scripts have been acted by infants at public performances such as the Zimbabwe International Book Fair, National Book Week or various concerts organized by CHIPAWO as well as in CHIPAWO television programmes. Plays such as *The Hyena and the Children* and *Mabiko* were based on children's *ngano* or folktales. Others such as *Sabhuku and the Book* were developed in response to requests by developmental organizations for plays on specific themes.

It was during a rehearsal of *The Hyena and the Children* that the breakthrough was made. I was assisting the children's arts educators with the preparation of the performance and after some time watching the usual approach with all the 'mothers' onstage and the children standing and looking blankly at the audience, I asked all the 'mothers' to leave the stage and sit in the audience. I then sat down with the children onstage and asked them whether they knew the story. Of course, they all said they did. So I asked someone to start telling it. The little raconteur started and then froze. I asked if anyone would like to continue it. Someone did – until eventually the children had collectively finished telling the story. I then praised them and said they knew the story and

I am sure they could act it out all by themselves. By now they were beginning to believe in themselves and they said with one voice that of course they could. So I said I am sure you can too. Go ahead. I then joined the others in the audience.

So they started acting the play again – all by themselves. It wasn't long before they stopped and looked about them for help. Of course the 'mothers' in the audience were behaving as if they had ants in their pants. My role was simply to sign to them to stay seated and keep quiet. When the children saw that no help was forthcoming, they starting talking among themselves and the play cranked back into action. And so it went on – with much anguish in the audience but growing confidence onstage until they got to the end and they had done it – all by themselves. From then onwards the old shunt shunt, prod prod method was abandoned and the main reason these days that one of the pre-school teachers comes onstage is to make sure that the audience realizes that these confident, independent little performers are hers.

A thrilling vindication of this method was a performance by a pre-school group at an international conference of anaestheticians in the Harare International Conference Centre, the largest and most overawing venue in Zimbabwe where the children gave a flawless performance, full of confidence and professional panache, looking the audience straight in the eye from the moment they hit the stage.

It is also extraordinary to observe infant actors participating in the film process. Everyone knows how demanding filming is, with its numerous takes and re-takes, its fragmentation of the action and the script and its total lack of respect for chronology. My feeling that infants can do virtually anything if you ask it of them, explain and leave them to do it all by themselves may not be accurate but I believe it is closer to the truth than the opposite belief – and it is definitely very much more empowering.

Junior theatre

In CHIPAWO by 'Junior' one is referring to children from approximately Grade 3, the year after the infant school, to Grade 6 or possibly 7, in other words from about the age of eight to twelve. The bulk of CHIPAWO's children fall into this category and therefore the bulk of CHIPAWO's drama.

In terms of developing scripts in Junior Theatre the children themselves are assisted to identify and develop their own material. The following, taken from *Arts Fit for Children,* illustrates the pedagogy in operation in the development of plays with Juniors:

> …the creation of a script for Christmas called Father Christmas in the South Pole. In this case the drama leader began by discussing with the children the fact that we needed to prepare material for the CHIPAWO Christmas Show. He started by asking questions.
> LEADER: What do you think of when you think of Christmas?
> CHILDREN: Presents.

LEADER: Where do these presents come from?
CHILDREN: Father Christmas.
LEADER: How do you get presents from Father Christmas?
CHILDREN: Write a letter to Father Christmas.
LEADER: Where is Father Christmas?
CHILDREN: In the North Pole.
Now up to this point the leader has been simply drawing out the creativity of the children. Now the leader begins to guide. He would like to pose the question why should children in Zimbabwe, in the Southern Hemisphere, depend on a Father Christmas in the North Pole? The leader then contrives the story so that it becomes impossible to write to a Father Christmas in the North Pole. He puts an obstacle in the way. The obstacle is intended to stimulate originality. The children have to search for their own solution and use their imagination. This technique eventually encourages the children to imagine a Father Christmas in the South Pole and a magic scotch cart which the children travelled in all the way there along with the fantastical and totally original ending to the story.

The above technique demonstrates not only how children at this level are involved in creating the story but also how they are prompted to be original and true to their own identity.

Although universally in Zimbabwe, in schools and in theatre groups, the dominant tendency is to improvise and not to script, CHIPAWO has found that this habit is in fact one of the major causes of the relative weakness of theatre performance in Zimbabwe. Starting with infants CHIPAWO practice requires that after plays have been devised and developed with the children, they should be written down, usually by the children themselves, and a script produced. Of course, the script is open to development during rehearsals but such development has to be agreed and included in the script.

The following are five examples of Junior plays that have been developed in CHIPAWO and performed either by CHIPAWO AEDE centres or by performance centres at local and international festivals or on public occasions. Some of these are available in another in-house publication titled *The Fruit of the Muonde*.[5]

Chipo and the Bird
Jari Mukaranga
Mutongi Gava (Judge Jackal)
Chibhomutiti and the Beautiful Girls
Tsitsi
Dhongi ra Sabhuku Mangwende (Mangwende's Donkey)
Cry Thinking

Of these all were original scripts except for *Chipo and the Bird*, which was adapted from an award-winning children's storybook about life at Great Zimbabwe. A performance of this play was staged in Kenya at the Harvest of Plays Festival in 1994. *Mutongi Gava* was based on a traditional story about the leopard who falls into a trap but when released breaks his promise and declares his intention to eat the young girl who helped him out of the trap. The Jackal comes along and tricks the leopard into getting back into the trap. *Chibhomutiti* was an original story on an environmental theme about girls who meet a strange monster on their way to the river to fetch water. *Tsitsi* was developed for UNICEF from the children's own experiences of HIV/AIDS. *Jari Mukaranga* and the opera, *Dhongi ra Sabhuku Mangwende,* were developed from popular songs. *Cry Thinking* is a play that was developed with an all deaf cast and based on the children's own written answers to the question: 'What is it like to grow up deaf?'

Perhaps the way in which *Tsitsi* was developed illustrates best the CHIPAWO method. UNICEF had requested a play by children on the impact of HIV/AIDS on children and women. A staff officer from UNICEF and the then Child President of Zimbabwe came to the first session and talked to the children. With their guidance they come up with a storyline. However I felt that with greater input from the children we could come closer to what children are really experiencing with regard to AIDS. So I asked them what they knew about AIDS and if any of them had been affected by it and how. Then I asked them to think about it on their own and then come back and tell the others what they had experienced. We then chose three or four of their testimonies and they acted them out. We then began to weave them together, using some of the material that the discussion with UNICEF had produced, to come up with a play that incorporated their actual experiences.

The development of plays from songs is now a common technique in CHIPAWO, perhaps predictably seeing that drama is offered along with music and dance to all children. It all began when one day I attended a CHIPAWO AEDE session at one of the centres and found that the marimba session being taught by Clency Gwaze[6] was working on playing the popular song, 'Kachembere kegudo', which features an old lady baboon who was climbing the mountain looking for food and stopping from time to time to scratch herself. I found out from the traditional dance educator, Elizabeth Takawira,[7] that there were mimetic actions that normally accompanied the song. So the children were taught this. They thus could sing it, dance it and play it on marimba. I felt the next step was to make a play out of it. Following the question and answer method cited above, we developed a situation and characters to explain why the old baboon was looking for food, why she had so many children to look after, what the others were doing while she was looking for food etc. We soon came up with a story and an exciting adventure. The whole thing was then put together to produce a play which acted out an exciting and amusing context for the song while featuring the song itself, the dance and the marimba-playing.

The same technique was used for developing the play, *Jari Mukaranga*, which was successfully staged in Germany at the World Festival of Children's Theatre and later at the World Expo. The song, 'Jari Mukaranga', is a popular song in which a senior wife laments the fact that she has given so much to her marriage with her husband but, now there is a younger wife, he no longer has time for her, buying a *jari* or rug and giving it to the younger wife and not her. The context of the song is *barika* or a traditional polygamous marriage. Because the group was concentrating on bringing to life the context of the song, they were not intent on any message or illustrating any prejudged prescription on polygamy. The result was a context that is refreshingly fair to the institution in the sense that before the fatal mistake, namely the giving of the rug to the younger wife, the two-family situation was characterized by what many writers and witnesses have attested to about polygamous households – whether traditional or Muslim – namely that they can be very companionable and happy. However it also brings out the inherent potential for conflict, jealousies and tensions which can eventually lead to disaster. The factor of poverty intercedes as the husband, Baba Bhoyi, might well have been able to maintain the balance and preserve the contentment of his polygamous family if he had had enough money to buy two *jaris*.

The stilted, contrived and therefore ineffective nature of most campaign plays that have a prejudged 'message' and then manipulate situations and characters to illustrate the 'message' and so 'teach' the audience, has become a blight on the development of theatre in many parts of Africa. The method of developing a play described above may be one approach which could bring back honest and whole depictions, which at one and the same time, explore a topic, suggest conclusions and refresh the audience with real-life human behaviour.

Two developments from *Jari Mukaranga* were in the direction of opera and Africa's own version of Augusto Boal's Forum Theatre. The opera was *Mangwende's Donkey*. The children of the Harare Junior Theatre chose to develop a play from a popular song by Steve Makoni about a donkey that ran away while it was on the way to the mill with a heavy load of grain on its back. The donkey belonged to a Sabhuku (Headman) called Mangwende. However this time I decided to vary the exercise by asking the arts educators working with the children and the children themselves to see whether they could go one step further. Instead of a dialogue play based on a song, could we make a play in which all the dialogue was set to music? The result was a comic opera in Shona named after the song, *Dhongi ra Sabhuku Mangwende*. The arts educators themselves struggled with the concept until my fellow director, Clayton Ndlovu,[8] a talented choreographer, turned out to be an equally gifted composer. The children, the arts educators and I developed the plot and the lyrics while he set it to music and added the choreography. The whole performance was backed by music from an orchestra that consisted of marimba, keyboard, drums and *hosho*.

The plot was developed from the basic question: 'Why did the donkey run away?' The answer was that although the Sabhuku was popular with the villagers, his wife was very discontented with her lot. She complained that though she was the wife of the Sabhuku the wives of the other villagers had nicer things than she did and she cited one who had a lounge suite, another a television and a third prettier *doeks* than she. She saw her only hope of getting rich in the donkey. As a result she gave both her husband and the donkey no rest. However, the family dog, Machena, whom the wife particularly disliked, was a great friend of the donkey and together with the other animals on the farm and around, the cows, the rock rabbits and the birds, greatly sympathized with the donkey and feared the Sabhuku's wife. Finally the dog comes up with a way of fixing her. And it was this plan that the donkey puts into operation and in the process exposes her folly in front of the village. The opera gives a touching and amusing insight into life in rural Zimbabwe, all through the medium of music, dance and song.

The opera was performed in Shona in Toyama, Japan, at the World Children's Theatre Festival and was a great success. It was revived last year in English to an enthusiastic reception. There are plans to take it further as in its way it is an extraordinarily original piece and the music is exceptional.

The other direction mentioned above is participatory theatre à la Boal.[9] With the Harare Junior Theatre, we took one of UNICEF's educational publications for children in the Sara series, called *The Trap*, which shows a Sugar Daddy or older man, who tries to seduce a schoolgirl. In the original, the girl and her friends together trap the man in the forest when he comes to meet her – a highly unrealistic solution to the problem of girls being seduced by Sugar Daddies. We adapted it in order to set up a participatory discussion of the problem with schoolchildren in which the audience would be able to express their ideas or questions by joining the actors onstage and acting them out. For this reason we decided not to use the questionable ending as depicted in the book and instead opted to leave it open for the children to explore their own solutions. In its finalized form the play was called *Kunaka Kunze*, meaning 'nice or sweet on the outside'.[5]

Cry Thinking was devised with and performed by children from CHIPAWO's centre at Emerald Hill School for the Deaf. The title was taken from one of the children's written efforts to explain what it felt like to be deaf. She wrote that every night before sleeping, she used to cry thinking about it.

Not having had any special training in theatre of the deaf and there being no sources of information in Zimbabwe, the challenge with this play was to explore how to communicate powerfully the experience of growing up deaf in Zimbabwe with deaf actors. They had a tradition already of quasi-realism in which they either used Sign Language – where the audience was deaf like themselves – or exaggerated gestures and mime. Using this method they acted out a story that had been developed. But this did not seem to be appropriate and it felt that there must be more powerful ways of communicating their experiences. I started doing mime exercises with them – though deaf, they still had to be trained in mime. One of the exercises involved being trapped in a box. As they worked, the power of their stillness and concentration immediately impressed me and then it seemed that being in a box is a very apt and expressive image for deafness. The play then opted to tell the story by alternating the biography of the deaf child with a series of mimes in which a central *mimeur*, echoed by a group, enacted the progress of finding a way out of the box, discovering that getting out of the box would not help unless one could communicate. The learning of Sign Language brings comparative freedom but the fact that hearing people cannot understand and speak it is the final barrier. Thus the play transcends the expression of the deaf experience to become a challenge to the hearing – learn our language and set us free.

The deaf children were asked to write down their thoughts or experiences on the topic 'Deaf Child'. The play is based on their writings and sets out to convey to those who hear, what a child feels who cannot hear. It also explores Zimbabwean cultural practice and the ideology of deafness. Finally, it affirms the capacity of deaf children to rise above their inability and assert their humanity and power.

The play collages a series of mimes on the experience of deafness and episodes in a deaf child's growing up. Though many of the experiences are painful, the intention is not to paint a picture of gloom but to bring out the capacity of the children to live positively, express themselves and have meaningful relationships.

The deaf child who goes through all this is the one who 'cries thinking' that she is the only child who is deaf. When she goes to a school which caters specially for deaf children, she is overjoyed to find out that there are other children like her. She is no longer lonely. With the ability to speak in sign language she is now no longer 'silent'. She finds that she is good at her school work and her mother and family are proud of her.

A deaf child is not stupid – breaking the silence becomes the challenge not only for the deaf but for others who share the world with the deaf. Why is everyone not taught sign language, for instance? The play poses a challenge to everyone – a challenge in which it is not the deaf who are the disabled and disadvantaged but rather the rest of us.

Youth theatre

Another example of the use of participatory theatre involving CHIPAWO was the Wills and Inheritance Laws Campaign in Zimbabwe in 2002–3. Funded by DFID for the Ministry of Justice and master-minded by Titus Moetsabi, a co-author of the SADC publication *Handbook on Participatory Rural Communications Appraisal*,[10] this campaign sought to raise awareness and bring about change in behaviour and practice by making use of absolutely every one of the arts, including theatre, as well as a vast range of other communications tools such as the internet, newspaper advertisements and cartoons, posters, calendars, CDs, radio, television, T-shirts, caps and stickers. It was significant that of all the communication media used in the campaign, theatre communication, along with radio, was one of the most effective.

A cast of youth from CHIPAWO performed three of the four plays evolved for the campaign, namely *A Woman's Will*, on the difficulties facing a woman who decided to stands up for her rights as provided for in the new Wills and Inheritance legislation.[11] The plays were *Tsika Dzemandorokwati*,[12] on the abuse of traditional practices relating to inheritance, and *Guarding the Guardian,* about the problems faced by children, especially when a trusted guardian, who is a family member, abuses his trust and helps himself to the money. The youth company performed the play at schools in Harare, Bindura, Chinhoyi, Gweru and Masvingo.

As many of the children who are able to attend CHIPAWO while at primary school go on to boarding schools out of town or find themselves no longer able to access a CHIPAWO centre, almost all the drama work with youths has been done either with the very first Youth Group or with the later Harare Youth Theatre. I have selected two productions, one from each, to look at, namely *Chill Out* and *Mbira*.[13]

The first youth group was formed when it became clear that the older children no longer wanted to attend joint sessions with infants and juniors and were dropping out. This would not be a problem now but in those early days attitudes were different. Their adolescent dignity – or 'pose' as they put it– was at stake. For this reason a separate centre was set up for the youth in quite a different venue. The first CHIPAWO Youth Group was quite an amazingly talented and original crowd of young people and the work they produced would have taken them places if they had not been working in Zimbabwe, where the critical and promotional structures in performance, especially at that time, are both underdeveloped and also less connected to international performance networks. Though, as with CHIPAWO itself in its founding period, many of the group's members were the children or relatives of the founders of CHIPAWO, the majority were not and the mark that they have made since leaving CHIPAWO speaks for itself.[14]

Chill Out, as the title implies, was a play created in the idiom of a certain section of Zimbabwean youth, namely largely those who live in the middle-class suburbs and went to former Group A (white) schools, which was the dominant composition of the Youth Group in the early days. Naturally the idiom was US American. However the play interrogated precisely this phenomenon. Set in a former Group A school, the play depicts Tinovimba's conflict over her identity – as in this speech from the beginning of the play:

> Hi, I'm Tino, short for Tinovimba. I hate my name and I hate my parents for giving me such a name. Sounds like I come from the rural areas. And I might as well live there the amount of times we go visiting there. Why can't I have a name like Anne or Catharine? I mean – they're everything I want to be – pretty, popular. They may not be all that smart but they have guys crowding round them all the time. I don't know – I used to be all those things and more a few years back but now I'm just 'Tedious Tino', the class bore. They – Jackie, Cherry and Emacula – they all have something I don't have. I don't know what it is but I wish I had it too.

The play goes on to explore many of the little insecurities, doubts and crises of self-esteem which can make teenage life so anguished. It also looks at culture, particularly the attitudes of the youth to Zimbabwean culture. One of the teachers starts a traditional dance club at the school and of course the 'in crowd' have nothing but derision for that. To everyone's amazement the school lover-boy, David, who has all the other girls swooning at his feet, makes a play for Tino. He takes her dancing but then she feels his hands are wandering too far and pulls away. She also refuses to drink anything but diet Coke. When he presses her she says: 'I do like you, David. It's not that. But right now I don't just feel right about what you are trying to do. Maybe later when I get used to things – to you. Or maybe not. I don't feel ready. Can't you try to understand that?' David abandons her saying: 'Call me when you catch up with the real world, babe.'

By the end of the play however Tino finds that the other girls she so admires and who have always mocked her, begin to appreciate her and they become friends as in this extract from the end of the play:

> **Tino (to Jackie)** Is there something bothering you, Jackie?
> **Jackie** I was just feeling a bit bad about the way I ditched you for Anne and her crowd. You seem to have got yourself a whole new crowd of friends. I am just wondering if there is space for little old me.
> **Tino** Sure, Jackie, there always was. But tell me, Jackie, is life always going to be like this? One minute you are up, the next you are down. One minute you are in, you are hip. The next you are out cold. I just wonder if the heart can take it, year after year.
> **Jackie** Well, let's see what happens. Let's see what life has in store for us
> **Tino** Will it get happier? Or sadder?
> **Jackie** Probably both.
> (*Song*)

The play's plot and dialogue reflect the crisis of identity facing sections of the urban youth – one of the main reasons for the founding of CHIPAWO. The language is a kind of US television hip hop jargon and so are the sentiments. The characters are young people who live surrounded by the realities of their parents' Zimbabwe but who cannot or do not want to identify with it. They yearn for something they feel is better – and that means less 'Zimbabwean', more US American. But the endless doubt, insecurity, low self-esteem and the cruel competition to be 'in', 'cool', 'hip' take their toll.

The second play, *Mbira*,[15] is so different it is hard to believe that it was created and acted by youth from the same country, let alone from the same organization. The fact that *Chill Out* was a product of the early 1990s and *Mbira* of the new millennium – it was especially prepared for an aborted Youth Festival to be held in London to coincide with the millennium – partially explains the difference. The other key factor is that the members of the Harare Youth Theatre in 2000 were with a few exceptions from the so-called 'high-density' suburbs of Harare and were attending former Group B (black) schools. It was also a testimony to the influence that CHIPAWO was able to exert on the question of youth culture and the degree to which traditional culture, music and dance gained acceptance.

The theme of the festival that was never to be was 'The Challenges Facing Youth in the New Millennium' – and this is what the Harare Youth Theatre set about addressing. The topic was discussed and then the cast went away and wrote essays in which they tried to write about their hopes and dreams, what they wanted to be or do in the future, and what were the main constraints, what did they fear might get in the way. Most of the youth were from the

Chitsere Centre in Mbare, Harare. The Chitsere Centre is the first Bursary Centre[16] and Mbare, then Harari, the oldest black ghetto in the then Salisbury. It is still very poor, crime-ridden and overcrowded. The youths from Mbare expressed their hopes that they would somehow rise above their environment and make something of their lives but they cited the numerous problems they faced – from poverty to early pregnancies, sugar daddies, AIDS, violence and abuse. The play set about trying to depict their hopes and fears, place them in context and develop a vision for their future.

The structure of *Mbira* consists of four juxtaposed scenes, like beads. The thread that binds them as in a necklace is the *mbira*-player, who is there at the beginning and moves, almost mysteriously, from one scene to the next and is there at the end. The first scene is set in pre-colonial times. What would have happened if a modern Shona-speaking youth (the *mbira*-player) were to enter the homestead of a Shona-speaking family at some time before the coming of the whites. She arrives when the elders are holding a *bira* in one of the dwellings while the youth are outside passing the time in front of the fire. The youth get to talking:

Youth What is this you need to get a job? There are always plenty of jobs.
Mbira-player O, like what?
Youth Herding cattle.
Youth Milking cows.
Youth Ploughing.
Youth Building houses.
Youth And cattle pens.
Youth And granaries.
Youth Making baskets.
Youth Pots.
Youth Grinding corn.
Youth Cooking.
Youth Hunting.
Youth What do you mean it is difficult to find a job?
Mbira-player We live in town. Those are not the jobs we look for. We want to be a doctor, a teacher, a hairdresser, a bank teller.

The next scene is set in the here-and-now. It is a function in the Sheraton Hotel, being attended by a different kind of modern youth, the 'yuppies'. The third scene is on the street and depicts street youth waking up on the anniversary of independence amongst their cardboard boxes and rags. The fourth is called 'Hot-seating' – referring to a solution adopted to accommodate more children in schools whereby half the school attends classes in the morning and the other half in the afternoon. This scene is set in one of the high schools in Mbare. The play ends with the *mbira*-player recalling the youth her *mbira*-playing dream journey has brought her into contact with. As she remembers them they appear before her. The *mbira*-player's name is Tapfuma (literally, 'we are wealthy'):

Tapfuma Another young person – another music. Music from a box. Music from a

plug in the wall. Mbira. What will become of mbira? Mbira!
Chokoto girl Music of the spirits.
Dancer Spirit of the past.
Streetchild 3 Lead us ...
Tapfuma Somehow. Lead us.
All ... into the future.

While the juxtaposing of the scenes makes its own meanings about the youth and their experiences, the music and dance in each scene is another conduit of contradictions and paradoxes. In the first scene we have the traditional use of the *mbira* and *mbira* music as it is an integrated part of the *bira* ceremony. Outside the youth dance the *Chokoto* dance. However the *mbira*-player teaches them a dance, *dinhe*, which in modern Zimbabwe is considered to be a traditional dance:

Youth Can you play?
Mbira-player Yes, I can play dinhe.
Youth What?
Mbira-player Dinhe.
Youth Let's see.
(*She dances. The others all laugh.*)
Youth You are not dancing. You are pretending to work in the fields.

In the corporate function at the Sheraton an *mbira*-player has been hired – to be followed by a traditional dance group. The motivation that corporate institutions like the fictitious Anglo-Magnesium might have in hiring traditional performers to a function of this kind in an upmarket venue is complex but the scene subtly probes it. Then, towards the end of the scene, reality dissolves into an eerie evocation of the real dance culture of traditional society when the *Jaka* dance begins as if it is being performed for Anglo-Magnesium but as the lighting changes and the costumes become authentic, the audience sees the origins of the dance in the strange and awkward loping movements of a pack of baboons as they move about the great bare mountains typical of Zimbabwe's scenery.

In the next scene the youth living on the streets dance the *jiti* or *kongonya* dance of the liberation struggle, where the contrast between what independence has brought them and the hopes of those times emerges powerfully through the music. At the high school, of course, the music comes from a ghetto-blaster and the dance is hip hop. As in the social mores and culture of the play's juxtapositions so in the dance and music, it is the *mbira* and the spirit of the *mbira* which must hold it all together – or the centre will not hold.

Professional theatre

The CHIPAWO graduates, some of whom are now performing for a living, also do music and dance performances. Their drama performances have been to date a direct result of the initiatives of Stephen Chifunyise.[17] These initiatives have been intimately associated with a project of CHIPAWO's, namely to establish a Zimbabwean repertory theatre at the erstwhile exclusively white Harare Playhouse.[18] Though the graduates have performed other plays in collaboration with Chifunyise, I propose to look at two of them, namely *Vicious* and *Soul Sister Comes to Africa*. Last year the group set themselves up as the New Horizon theatre company.

Staging programmes at the Reps Theatre is a very recent development for CHIPAWO. The first breakthrough was a Gala Fund-raising Concert for the children of Emerald Hill School for the Deaf, who were taking their play, *Cry Thinking*, to the 7th World Festival of Children's Theatre in Lingen, Germany. The response was so positive and the experience so rewarding that CHIPAWO decided to build on it. In October 2002, CHIPAWO then staged Stephen Chifunyise's play, *Vicious*, and revived *Cry Thinking* for a second performance at Reps.

The response to this programme both of the audiences and the press encouraged CHIPAWO still further. In 2003 and 2004 longer runs were attempted, with *Vicious* revived and then *Soul Sister Comes to Africa* premiered.

Vicious must be one of the masterpieces of Zimbabwean theatre, a classic example of Zimbabwean realist theatre. Originally written by Stephen Chifunyise for the United Nations Food and Population Agency, it is a tragic portrayal of the prevailing poverty in Zimbabwe where even middle-class families with a good income are drawn into poverty by the needs and suffering of their relatives, who come to live with them in town or remain, many dying of AIDS, in the countryside. Owing to the desperate plight of others in the extended family, such families end up housing, feeding and educating a whole horde of children and various unemployed or sick relatives in their houses and can no longer afford the basics for themselves or their children. The predicament is made worse by the fact that culturally it is very difficult if not impossible to refuse to take up such responsibilities.

Though the realities of the situation are heartbreaking, the play was written and directed – by Chifunyise himself – in such a way that *Vicious* comes across as comic though all the time pulling us in the direction of the tragic (in contrast to Chekhov who wrote comedies which others presented as tragedies). The young actors were up to the material and produced very human, moving and professional performances.

Chifunyise's next play, also staged at Reps Theatre, was *Soul Sister Comes to Africa*. This is a satirical play which analyses marriage in Shona culture and contrasts it with marriage in the West. It is the story of Chenjerai who marries an African American wife (Gloria). When he tells her he is going to visit his family in Zimbabwe, she insists that she wants to come with him. He flatly refuses, telling her, with examples, that there is no way that she, with her background and culture, will be able to understand and accept that of his family. Ultimately she prevails on him and they travel together to his rural home in Zaka. Gloria discovers that many cultural aspects were not properly explained to her while her in-laws had assumed she knew everything. The ritual approach of the bride, completely covered, the trials and tribulations she suffers at the hands of various relatives and the processes she must go through as she inches her way towards the village, turn out to be – as Chenjerai knew full well in the beginning – too much for her. Scandalizing him and everyone else, she throws off the sheet she is covered up in and demands to be taken back to Harare where she says she will 'discuss' the issue with her husband.

Of course, this is an evergreen theme in African theatre – the most celebrated example that comes to mind being Ama Ata Aidoo's *The Dilemma of a Ghost*. *Soul Sister Comes to Africa* is a Zimbabwean treatment of the theme and produces lots of laughs – and much to think about, for both Zimbabweans and African Americans.

Challenges

From the above it should be clear that CHIPAWO can talk of much that has been and is being achieved in terms of drama. However there remain some serious challenges ahead. The relative weakness of the drama component in the AEDE programme is one such. Others include training for directors and scriptwriters, creating a paying theatre audience, finance for the initial stages of establishing a repertory theatre and publishing the many useful playscripts that CHIPAWO has developed. Drama on television has great potential and CHIPAWO has an unending supply of material as well as the expertise and equipment at its Media Centre to make television dramas and feature films. Unfortunately, the Zimbabwe Broadcasting Corporation cannot pay and so sponsorship is essential but not easy to source, Finally CHIPAWO needs to do more to popularize its theatre work outside the country as well as producing films and television for the region and internationally.

NOTES

1. See www.zimartsed.co.zw
2. For a full account of the strategic history of CHIPAWO, from which much of the following account is taken, see Strategy Document www.chipawo.co.zw\library (documents)
3. For full text of *Arts Fit for Children* go to www.chipawo.co.zw\library (publications)
4. For download go to www.chipawo.co.zw\library (publications). For hard copy e-mail info@chipawo.co.zw
5. Contains *Jari Mukaranga, Mutongi Gava (Judge Jackal)* and *Chibhomutiti and the Beautiful Girls*. For download go to www.chipawo.co.zw\library (publications). For hard copy e-mail info@chipawo.co.zw
6. Clency Gwaze lived just up the road from the Chitsere CHIPAWO Centre in Mbare, Harare. He used to hear the music and came along. Since then he has become an expert marimba player and an instructor in great demand. He is a Senior Arts Educator in CHIPAWO.
7. Elizabeth Takawira was a member of the National Dance Company established shortly after independence. She joined CHIPAWO as a traditional dance instructor when the organization first started. She has been with CHIPAWO ever since and is now a Senior Arts Educator/Trainer. For her story and that of other women and girls in CHIPAWO see the in-house publication, *Vasikana ve CHIPAWO (The Girls of CHIPAWO)*. For download go to

www.chipawo.co.zw\library (publications). For hard copy e-mail info@chipawo.co.zw
8 Clayton Ndlovu started teaching modern dance in CHIPAWO when he was a student at the Zimbabwe College of Music Ethnomusicology programme. He is a Trustee of CHIPAWO and on the staff at the College of Music. He was Consultant Director of Performances in CHIPAWO for many years and has been responsible for many of CHIPAWO's most brilliant performance choreographies.
9 A note on Forum Theatre in Africa: There is a long and extremely robust tradition of theatre in Africa that uses radically participatory methods of animation, dialogue circling and empowerment – not only in the traditional or pre-colonial context but also since political independence in the form of theatre for development and more recently theatre communication.

Theatre for development in its most advanced practices – Kamlongera (Malawi), Mlama (Tanzania), Mda (Lesotho) – applied many of the techniques associated with Forum Theatre for the simple reason that these techniques, formalized by Augusto Boal in his seminal publication, *The Theatre of the Oppressed,* derive from the work of Paulo Freire, after whose publication, *The Pedagogy of the Oppressed,* indeed Boal's *Theatre of the Oppressed* is named.

Paulo Freire has, independently of Boal, been a great influence in Africa, not only in education but also in theatre and cultural politics – note the enthusiastic espousing of his ideas by Steve Biko and the Black Consciousness Movement in South Africa in the 1970s. The pioneering theatre for development practices in Botswana, which Ross Kidd popularized in the publication, *Laedza Batanani,* are almost unthinkable without Freire.

Theatre for development was itself further improved and 'developed' from those early beginnings and Freire's influence came to be fused with other dialogic and participatory methods derived from indigenous African theatre as African practitioners increasingly came to lead the theatre for development movement.

In more recent years, largely in the framework of development work quite divorced from theatre, the concept of participatory communications has developed. Clearly working with concepts relating to democracy, respect for cultures, gender-sensitivity, participation of the beneficiaries, empowerment etc., which it shared with advanced practices in theatre for development, the Participatory Communications strategy provided a natural home for that most effective tool in the context of African urban and rural communications – theatre. Hence participatory theatre communication.

In the light of the above, it is difficult to understand why African theatre practitioners would attempt to reproduce Boal's methods in Africa when perfectly good ones are to be found in the indigenous traditions.
10 Anyaegbunam, C. et al, *Handbook on Participatory Rural Communications Appraisal* (SADC Centre of Communications for Development/FAO, 1998).
11 These plays have been published in the following collections: (in English) RSC Zimbabwe, *Act Alive* (Harare, 2002) and (in Shona) RSC Zimbabwe, *Chandagwinyira* (Harare, 2002). For hard copies contact RSC Zimbabwe at mshengu@mango.zw
12 Published in *Act Alive* as *Inheriting a Wife?* but literally meaning 'the real or genuine tradition or custom'.
13 For hard copy e-mail info@chipawo.co.zw
14 David Chifunyise is a nationally renowned singer and composer. Chiwoniso Maraire is an international mbira singer. Both are recording artists to boot. Chipo Chung is acting in the British theatre, having trained at Yale University and RADA. Danai Gurira did drama at her university in the States and is now starring in the States in a two-hander on AIDS with a black American woman. Thando McLaren is an increasingly successful writer and illustrator of children's books and published a book on Islamic Art, with another, *From My Sisters' Lips,* on young women in Islam, coming out this year. Philemon Gezi is a musician and has his own audio-visual recording studio. Thulani Sandhla is managing State-sponsored national gala concerts and Conrad Zvinindiramba works for CHIPAWO as a national Field Officer and a leading member of New Horizon theatre company.
15 *Mbira* was performed by the Harare Youth Theatre at the *meetingplace 2000* Theatre Festival in Slagelse, Denmark in 2000.
16 The CHIPAWO Bursary Scheme, funded by SIDA, supports children at eight bursary centres in disadvantaged communities in Harare, Bindura, Chitungwiza, Domboshawa and

Marondera. It also assists 50 children who cannot pay their fees at other centres.
17 Stephen Chifunyise is a well-known theatre personality in Africa and arguably Zimbabwe's foremost playwright. His career spans two countries, Zambia and Zimbabwe. He is a founder of CHIPAWO and Chairman of the Board of Trustees. Currently he is Principal of the Zimbabwe Academy of Arts Education for Development.
18 A note on the Harare Reps Theatre: Little Theatres, sometimes called Enclave Theatre, are the theatres established by the colonial populations in Africa for the entertainment of the European community. They were invariably amateur and their repertoire usually consisted of light entertainment from the metropolitan stage – English, French, Portuguese, whatever the case may be. Though more serious theatre might have been performed from time to time, including Shakespeare, generally the repertoire consisted of comedies, musicals, pantomimes and revues.

Over the years the Little Theatres either collapsed or were slowly liberalized and eventually integrated. Gweru Theatre was summarily annexed but it then ceased to function as a regular theatre venue. The Courtauld Theatre in Mutare and the Charles Austin Theatre in Masvingo slowly saw the increasing involvement of schools, community theatre and so-called 'Township' theatre groups. But over the years, Reps hardly budged. The powerful white community in Harare maintained it and sustained it and a bitter debate raged. Those involved in the Community Theatre movement, in the Association of Community Theatre (ACT), subsequently to become ZACT, the Faculty of Arts Drama at the University of Zimbabwe, the Zimbabwe Foundation for Education with Production (ZIMFEP) and other individuals pointed to the equipment and facilities at Reps, which they could not access. Zimbabwe is now independent they said and reserving all this stuff for a small white community when the people out there were making theatre and couldn't use it, was not acceptable. There was even talk of taking over Reps and turning it into a national Zimbabwean theatre.

Meanwhile established theatre critics and spokespersons for Reps pointed out that the theatre was a private club. It received no public subsidies and it had every right to do whatever it wanted with its own private property. No door seemed shut more tightly than that of the Reps. And as the years progressed, the door showed few signs of opening – despite developments in other parts of the country.

It was a hot issue, I can tell you. It was one of the issues that kept arguments and squabbling going for many years between ZACT, the University, the Ministry of Education and Culture (depending on what the name of the ministry in which Culture had been dumped was called at the time) and the National Theatre Organization and the Little Theatres on the other. CHIPAWO only noticed that the situation had begun to change a couple of years ago. There was a distinct difference in the way in which Reps was operating and in its attitude to organizations like CHIPAWO.

On the Making of Journeys: Young People's Theatre in Zambia
Tansitha, Safe-T-Child & others

DAVE PAMMENTER

This paper is about journeys undertaken – metaphorical journeys – with young people through projects in Zambia between 1998 and 2003. It will raise as many questions as those it seeks to find answers to. The journeys were with different groups and organizations concerned with the needs of societal transformation. When we embark on this kind of a journey with others, we collectively engage in dialogue with others to determine our path and chosen destination. We analyse the context in which our journey is to take place. We pose questions to ourselves and others; and in this process of redefining the self in relation to the other, we are concerned with questions of identity through our developing conscientization. We consider what we are and what we are becoming.

Some questions which arose from these journeys.

Why is my life story as it is?
Why is your life story as it is?
Why does my story disturb you?
What does our dialogue achieve?
Why and by whom are our voices silenced?
Why is our world as it is?
Where does our path lead?
Why is power and control as they are?
In whose hands are our realities?
Who or what is determining our futures?
What must we change?
How do we make transformation?

To begin at the end

In the closing moments of a play, the central character is standing alone. She is wrapped in a death shroud and sinks to the ground and is still. The other actors remove their character head-bands and are no longer actors. They stand in a semi-circle around the corpse and each light a candle and speak the name of someone known to them who has died of HIV/AIDS. They place the lighted candles in large bowls of sand placed either side of the body as they speak the name.

They quietly sing as the central character whose story we have witnessed removes the death shroud and her character head-band, lights a candle and places it in the sand, speaking the name of another who has died. She moves with an outstretched hand to the audience offering a candle and in silence invites them to light it and place it in the bowl speaking the name of another who they had known. The singing, music and rhythmic drumbeat continue. One by one, members of the audience take the extended hands of the women, light a candle, place it and speak the name of another who has died. We join the women and begin to sing with them and as the song changes we are led into a dance. The dance which had begun as a dance for the dead, leads us into changing partners, changing spaces and to the holding of different hands.

We speak our names and talk as we dance. We ask questions, tell stories about the death of friends and family and begin to share our views and realities about our individual and collective contexts.

Food and drink arrive and we have become a group sharing our identities. It is impossible from the outside to tell what our roles are or were. The actors and audience are now indistinguishable but are becoming a kind of community. Dialogue continues and more and more questions emerge. They are open kind of questions, enquiries and conversations about things that we are often too 'polite' or too 'restrained' by our status or our social roles to ask. The disturbing questions of identity and different realities posed within the play that had culminated in a reflective 'Dance for the Dead', had themselves become transformed into shared questions of our collective realities and understandings and of our purpose in the present. Contemporary contradictions and other perspectives were being spoken about and resolutions collectively sought. This took us back to the start of the project which had also begun with the sex workers, the actors, telling their stories.

This kind of ending is not new and is similar to traditional endings for popular theatre, for example the culminating dances of 7:84 or the interventions at Dario Fo performances. This practice of sharing, of questioning, of collective participation is central to many kinds of events in different cultural contexts.

This ending was planned but it took off in an unpredictable and highly energized way. The participants were sharing detailed stories of the events in their own lives, about their friends and families and, in sharing, they were seeking help and advice in finding ways forward.

The ensuing dialogues lasted longer than the play. This was a key element in the expression of the young sex workers who felt an inner identity as a human being, rather than as a prostitute. They were conversing with others as critically creative citizens instead of finding themselves ignored and marginalized, which was normally the case. What is more, these collective experiences in communicating and questioning realities were occurring in a public space where such voices are usually unheard and often chased away in the bid to silence them in the name of 'public order'. The dominant culture's silencing of voices was being confronted and the real articulation of the 'self' and the recognition of the 'other' were being constructed. This counter cultural ownership of space and articulation was a useful start to developing cultural action as social transformation. The end of the play was the beginning of different dialogues about different futures.

History and context

The play was devised, written and performed by the young women of Tansitha, an NGO in Lusaka. The project and play were titled Respect (Research Peer Education and Community Theatre) which took place in the year 2000. Respect came into being as a result of meetings with the management and the women of the NGO during 1999. It was part of a six-year period of collaboration in Theatre for Development with regional and national partners. These projects were involved with education, training of trainers, project planning and delivery with theatre groups and NGO organizations concerned with street children and community organizations. Many of the projects were concerned in some way with formal and non-formal education. Partners included Mapode and Fountain of Hope street children's projects in Lusaka and the Safe-T-Child project in Mulifira in the north of Zambia. We also collaborated with the Kamoto theatre group and the University of Zambia (UNZA) on some of these projects, for example Voice to the Marginalised, a project that included the creation and touring of a play and performances devised by disabled children about the cultural and social realities of their lives in a compound near Lusaka. The Voice to the Marginalised project, which was sponsored by the British Council, was a series of training workshops spanning a three-year period.

The work was, in different ways, concerned with informal education and training in TfD and dealt with the areas and issues of self-esteem, confidence-building, advocacy, ownership and identity, plus the generation of skills and theatre events in the pursuit of articulating the voice of the marginalized in pursuit of change. The projects were about developing collective and individual skills in creating and constructing public events as forms of cultural action for transformation. These collaborations were concerned with theatre both as an artistic medium for communicating human experience and as an educational and social force in constructing dialogue and meaning. This is human development for social and cultural transformation.

Respect

The Respect project began with meeting the sex workers who wished to develop their skills and capacities in using theatre and performance. There had been a brief history of Tansitha members performing plays written by others which carried cautionary messages to audiences warning or advising them to avoid following the path of the sex worker. The approach of these plays was rather didactic and moralistic which was consistent with the original aims of the NGO which, from its inception, had been concerned with notions of 'reform' of the commercial sex workers. The organization has since dropped its focus on reform but when the project started it still remained an ambiguous area within the organization's operation.

A project proposal, developed from a needs analysis workshop, was prepared in collaboration with Sian Long from Healthlink UK and sent to the management of the NGO but unfortunately this was not shared with the intended project participants and neither was it responded to. It subsequently became clear that there were real problems with the operation of the management in that while the rhetoric was that of a dynamic 'bottom-up' NGO, the reality was that of a 'top down' organization, that lacked dynamism and organizational capacity. There were clearly questions of how contradictions were dealt with, who was in control and, crucially, who was being silenced.

On our arrival at the project's base we negotiated our aims and planned our work with the participants. The project was to last three months. Our aims were concerned with developing creativity, criticality, the personal and collective resource development in theatre skills, drama skills and methodologies, confidence building, articulation and advocacy. What became clear was that despite the internal organizational culture, the young women had something to say and the determination to say it through the form of theatre.

One of the many aspirations of the women was to conscientize the ever-increasing numbers of young women, girls like themselves and children drawn into the sex industry. Most of these young people are exposed to violence, abuse (physical, sexual and psychological) and accompanying exploitation. This was not seen as an intended 'don't do it', or moral agenda, but simply as a question of survival: 'If you are going to do this work, then here is how to do it better, more safely, with less risk, more control over the situation and more power over you own lives....'

This aspiration was also linked to the desire to change the common public perception of the commercial sex worker and to achieve their legal recognition and protection from harassment. The participants, most of whom became sex workers as children were concerned that they were also citizens, artists and educators with something to contribute to the much-needed cultural and social transformation of their position and that of others. Our collective task was to develop the understandings and skills needed to liberate their potential as theatre workers, cultural activists, peer educators, trainers and teachers.

It quickly became clear that the embryonic project had gathered considerable local interest and support from a number of individuals and organizations including women writers, theatre workers and NGOs. Evidently the project had a potentially significant contribution to make both to the continuing self-development of the participants themselves and to the social and cultural position of sex workers and children. It also became clear that the work could make a real contribution to public and community consciousness of safe sex practice. This also included HIV/AIDS awareness.

Both the sex workers and the children from the street children's projects, which I discuss later, have been marginalized by mainstream Zambian society. They have generally a low status and often low self-esteem. They tend to come from the poorer sections of society and increasingly from families destroyed by death and from the fragmentation of extended families caused by poverty and changing patterns of industrial development. They have received, at best, a low level and useless formal education. They have little or no support: financial, social, spiritual, apart from their peer groups or support organizations such as NGOs. Their human and civil rights are ignored or violated and they are not accorded the status of citizens in Zambian culture and society. What is clear from all statistical evidence is that their numbers are growing at an alarming rate.

With this in mind, we were faced at the start of the project with clear questions, the answers to which would begin to shape and structure our workshops and the direction of the project. What was to be our starting point? What was to be our methodology? Who was to be in control? How would we work together? How would we assign and evaluate leadership? What would be our democratic procedure? How would we individually and collectively take up and deal with responsibilities in terms of power, democratic principles, questions of sustainability, questions of accountability and reliability? How would we determine the areas of our enquiry and what would the content of our theatre be? Where would our programme lead?

We collectively agreed that learning springs from the need to know, that if knowledge is power then the marginalized know better than most what needs to be done to change their situation and to develop their theoretical and practical knowledge which could assist them, through subsequent action, in gaining the power they need. Who better to develop the voices of the marginalized than the marginalized themselves? Who better to develop the skills of cultural communication, advocacy, education and intervention in pursuit of social change and community development than those with the greatest need and perhaps the greatest clarity? Who better to develop and pursue a Human Rights-based agenda than those with very few or no rights at all?

In order to construct theatre, performance, meaning, cultural action, dialogue, it is necessary to research the context, to reconsider what we think we know and to re-examine our understanding and the connections we make between ideas, realities, histories and social or cultural assumptions. We have to start from where we are. There can be no other starting point for our journey, individually and collectively. Both the sex workers and the street children, our participants, already knew a great deal and most of it empirical knowledge.

The extension of our knowledge would be tested as practice through

- becoming articulate
- the confidence in articulating our research into ourselves and others
- the conscious and deliberate sharpening of contradictions
- the making and sharing of meaning in participatory performance.

The practical and tested extension of our creative capacities in finding the interconnectedness of ideas and realities would create change in ourselves and others. We could not change and transform the realities of our context without first changing and transforming ourselves.

> Clearly the starting point for any 'subject' has got to be the experience, skill and talent of the author or creators. We must never fall into the trap of trying to make mechanical theatre, with lumps of ideological meccano. A person, or a very small group of people, has to be the human imaginative dimension through which the work is explored, mediated, created. (John McGrath)

The realities

The stories from which the devised piece eventually emerged were largely narratives of rural girls whose family circumstances had forced them into going to Lusaka and subsequently into the sex trade there. There was a particular scene in one of the stories which summed up their situation. A girl in her teens whose parents had died from AIDS was taken in by her aunt and uncle. In a scene without words the aunt was depicted facing the audience preparing the evening meal while behind her, the girl was being raped by her uncle. The girl's face is visible throughout and the scene finishes with her running from the house, pausing only to pick up a small bag that contains all her possessions. Her flight to the city was captured in that single, minimal *gestus*. The girls in the workshop, though habituated to such moments in their working lives, were reticent about the depiction because they had thought themselves back to their younger, innocent selves; in Stanislavsky's terms, the emotional memory transformed them into the state of mind of the character at that moment, regardless of whether or not the particular incident had happened to the actor who chose to depict it. There were many things which initially the women did not want to talk about or share. This was a consequence of their low social status, where all oppressions are internalized and all identities foisted on to them from outside apparently accepted, and because they did not wish to offer any excuses for themselves and their lives. They are who they are.

The children in the projects in the NGOs Safe-T-Child, Fountain of Hope, Voice to the Marginalised and Mapode were similarly occupying a place at the bottom of the hierarchy as children in families, local communities and street children, which impacted heavily upon their self-perception. Many of their stories were about the consequences and the feelings evoked by being at the base of the pyramid. Everyone 'helping' them is doing them a favour; their whole existence is by the courtesy of the 'goodness' of someone else: cousin, uncle, NGO worker. As a result they are continually operating in response to oppression and coercion. The feelings of these groups could have been exacerbated by the presence of a white male middle-aged facilitator and I had to counteract this by playing low status and working through processes that did not place them at a disadvantage. A lot of attention was paid to movement and space, to simple low key dialogue and conversations. The sex workers in particular had an acute understanding of space and its significance in defining relationships. There was a concentration on mirror work, balance work and dance. Above all, this work was about building and developing trust and confidence.

The official reforming agenda of Tacintha as an NGO may not have been quite how the organization worked in practice but nevertheless this created difficulties in the initial stages when the participants placed the facilitator within the agenda of the NGO. To move from understandable suspicion, despite the participants own decisions in constructing the plan of the work, to being prepared to talk about moments of truth in their lives required a slow, patient, cautious and low-key approach grounded in the building up of the kind of trust which is not a regular feature of their lives. One example of such a moment was the story of one of the girls who had gone out with her friend and two clients one evening. Her friend and one of the punters left the car they shared and went off into the night. The friend was later found murdered but the girl did not dare identify the murderer for fear of injury or fatal reprisal. Instead she had carried this truth around inside her, festering until the moment she chose to speak of it in the life-map exercise undertaken in the workshop.

Self imposed silencing is thus second nature to those obliged to live by the grace and favour of those more powerful: this is the reality of Freire's 'culture of silence'. Altering this ingrained habit of silence is a painful and awkward process. A range of alternatives to words were needed to assist the articulation of the emotions being given off from the stories like hot breath in a winter morning. 'What sound goes with this moment? What colours?' Sound pictures and drawings, simple gestures were employed to piece the moment together. It is neither 'theatre' nor 'improvisation' but a representation of an inner reality by any means available to the participants.

This was an essential process to enable the sex workers and street children to reclaim some long-lost confidence before they were able to make effective use of the story-telling phase of the process. The process was conducted through the device of life-maps which were frequently re-visited and re-examined as the details and key turning points in the participants' lives became more clearly identified and articulated. The life-maps were initially conducted in the security and intimacy of small groups. When these groups came together as a single group, key words and pictures from the stories were posted on the walls around the space. They were then asked: 'What is held in common?' 'What do you recognize in these words and pictures, these colours and images?' The shared answers to these questions provided the platform for the collective journey that the group undertook. The answers tightened the focus by enabling agreement on the key themes and issues we collectively felt were important in constructing a narrative. The 'drawing together' was an important stage, because it involved making decisions. What had been useful from the life-maps in terms of understanding each other and articulating our own identities had now to be analysed in the creation of a narrative that sought to piece together the contradictions and questions with which we wished to confront our audience.

What interconnections did they need to find in order to disturb their existing understanding of the seeming normality in their lives? What key issues and considerations did they need to experience in our play in order to move consciously towards change? From the many stories and concerns we focused on those at the centre which we wished our audience to examine and respond to. We were devising a planned disturbance. This process finally led us to devise a story which became a journey centred on a single central character placed at the core of the intertwined narratives. This proceeding journey led to the creation and presentation of a collectively devised depiction of the shared – and now analysed – realities of being a sex worker, through a process where the girls owned and created everything. Scenes took shape in answer to the question 'What happened that made you so unhappy?' 'What did you do?' 'What could you have done?'

One such moment underlined the girls' command of movement and space. When they were asked to show how they entered a room, they replied that they did not immediately enter but waited until the client had gone in and then remained in the doorway, the only way out of the space. Then they looked round to locate something that could be used to hit him, the place of the window to call for help and where the light was. Physical movement and spatial awareness are not aesthetic options but matters of survival, hard-wired in the instincts and the bodies of desperate human beings.

One of the girls told a story which she said was that of a friend who had a 'madman' among her regular clients. She had missed him for several weeks when he suddenly appeared before her in the market place and thrust a bag of money into her hands with the words 'This is for your funeral. I've got AIDS.' They were invited to explore the motivations and understandings which underpinned that moment. How did the girl respond? What of the wife of the man? How can such feelings find expression? These girls without power had to negotiate what could and could not be said: to take on the gap between feelings and words. This story became an important moment in the performance of the final play. This, in the end, was the pedagogical – transformative – achievement of the process. The participants consciously and confidently felt able to articulate their truths and identities unmediated by considerations of status and safety.

When, after the performance of the play in a public space, which was in effect the final product of their devising, they became indistinguishable from their audience, this reflected not only changes in themselves but also a transformation in their audience who had come to patronize them as types of sex workers but stayed to recognize them as fellow human beings. It became possible through the truth of their presentation and enquiry strung across the poles of creativity and criticality.

The street children

There were similar experiences with the Safe-T-Child, Mapode and Fountain of Hope workshops; the well-meaning and supportive NGO was in one sense teaching street children to pray and be grateful; to keep their real feelings and actual experience locked up inside them. Like the sex workers, the street children inhabit two worlds and the workshop process was itself not exempt from that reality. In some cases, rehearsals were interrupted by the children's need to hide from the police, avoid the baker from whom they stole or the trip into town centre to pick a passing pocket. But they always returned to the workshop simply because the wanted to. They had something to articulate, to make sense of; driven, in Freire's telling phrase, by the 'need to know'. They were also drawn to the work because they placed a value on it and developed a relationship of trust with the facilitators.

In some contexts the presence of the foreigner, automatically associated with what some saw as a self-serving NGO, provoked the question 'What's in it for us?' We had to make it clear that we were not here to dispense free gifts in return for grateful patronage; that we had nothing to offer that was outside ourselves. We always played low status; participating, playing, buying the odd ice-cream if we met in town and above all sharing time with them. The women dressed me up in local style clothes which they sewed from cloth from the local market. I think I looked absurd but the process provoked dialogue about how the clothes and the costumes were made, where the cloth came from, about appearance in my culture and theirs. Equality was being built over time and trust was developing in both directions. Stick drawings, sound pictures, depictions and games with simple improvisations were used to communicate with each other, as well as language about England and Zambia and our respective realities. The process was one of posing questions. 'What do you really like?' 'What don't you like?' 'What makes you smile?' 'What makes you unhappy?' We listened to and heard each other's answers. Exchange was the key in responding to such questions. The children's answers reflected their lived experience and their treatment at the hands of others, including the zealous well-meaning Christians, as they strove to articulate feelings both awkward and essential to the realization of their identities.

The facilitator role was not about making things happen but about sensitivity towards the moment; realizing the significance of a sign, a word, a transaction. The worst moments for the children were when telling of jobs like cleaning and collecting firewood which reminded them of their low status and oppression within the host family or group. Their best moments were to do with inclusion and recognition of themselves as humans. This was often experienced only within their own peer group. One of the stories centred on the difficulties the children faced when attempting to bury a friend of theirs, another street child who had died. They created a piece of theatre depicting the reality of them being chased away by adults who wanted nothing to do with the dead child or the problem presented to them by his surviving friends.

The children performed to an audience of local people, family members and NGO workers for the little festival of plays. At the end of the workshops and improvisations they led participatory discussions. The audience understood and were disturbed by what this child-led practice had produced. They knew what was going on with this work and their recognition and acceptance of what the children felt and articulated about their circumstances and oppression became the starting point for a modest transformation in attitude and behaviour. The event which the children organized, hosted and led created a dialogue with the adults about what things should be re-considered and changed. If this was possible after a short workshop, what might a six-month process, grounded in the precepts of Illych and Freire, produce in terms of capacity and altered consciousness? What could be achieved through the practice of an Arts as Education collective cultural policy open to all local people?

Ways forward

What did our practices teach us about planning and delivering a participatory, rights-based agenda based on the pedagogy of Illych and Freire? How can informal education through the capacities of TfD achieve understandings and transformation beyond the reach of formal educational processes which require children to wear the mask of the one being educated? How will we examine and explore the key notions of power and equality in relation to education as opposed to training? What do we propose as a different kind of practice?

If questions of being and becoming, of education, of identity, and of development both individually and collectively are conditioned only by the cultural and educational schooling of the dominant, then we must first, in our resistance and building of the counter cultural, begin with a clear understanding of the theory and practice of the dominant discourse and its purposes. We must ask and identify how the neo-liberal order emerged, what its purposes and structures are, and how it is normative social and cultural schooling strategies operate. We must grasp, understand and ultimately reject its theft of the areas of culture and communication, its control and theft of public spaces and its marginalization and silencing of the truth of our realities. We must identify its owners, controllers and agents and their often invisible yet concrete effects on us and on our own sense and experience of becoming.

As cultural activists, educators and development workers, we need to identify the road we are on and determine whether or not its destination and structure is of any use to those other than the architects of the dominant social order. Having determined our goals we should, with those on the journey with us, try to liberate and own the pedagogy and structures of co-intentionality and we should struggle in pursuit of our collectively agreed and named objectives. The dominant order exists in opposition to other ways of being and alternative visions of the future. Our 'inclusion' and that of young people as place-occupiers and servants within the dominant narrative will only serve the agenda of those who have already placed the poor in the position of the marginalized.

This requires imagination. It is centrally concerned with creativity, criticality and the development of our ability to seek and find the interconnectedness of ideas, conceptual frameworks and realities. It enables us to locate and analyse events from history in the present and is therefore key in developing our capacity to participate in creating the future.

Artists, educators, theorists and community activists in pursuit of social, cultural and political intervention and empowerment have long been aware of the need to forge a humanizing curriculum which places the naming and making of the people's world in the hands of the people themselves. For Vygotski, Illych, Bruner, Freire and many others, pedagogy and its ownership has been at the centre of how transformation occurs. How do people understand their world? How do people learn? What is the content and context of their learning? Who determines the purpose of their learning? What is the difference between 'schooling,' 'education' and 'training'? Who determines what is achievement? Who determines the answer to these questions? Is what passes for education simply a means by which the teachers fit the children into the values and structures of the dominant? Are the needs and the rights determined by the government, the teacher or the learner? How do we develop compassion, respect, responsibility, imagination, the understanding of difference and of the values and ethics which underpin our own decisions and actions in the world? How do we become conscious of our rights and the rights of others, and how do we construct practical and analytical frameworks for the achievement, protection and expansion of those rights and responsibilities?

Culture is not only the product of social experience it is also social communication. Communication is crucial to society's development because it articulates social relations among people. It is central in developing the conscious interconnections between issues, understanding and ideas. It is therefore of key importance in the making of cultural and social change, both in terms of individual and collective transformation. How communication happens, what it contains and how it occurs, crucially affects the purpose of education. The way a social group sees itself, the way it sees and upholds its ideas, its values, its ethics, its rights and responsibilities, is embedded in its system of education. This is the case whether or not such systems are formal or informal in nature.

Education and communication are central cultural components which human groups have always been dependent on in terms of their own sense of identity and history. It is this sense of identity which conditions both their own self view and consequently their world view. It is also one of the conditioning factors of how others see them. It produces consequences in the form of actions, events and new realities. In this sense, the questions of ownership of self and collective transformation are a vital contribution in terms of development. Who is developing who and for what? Whose interests are being served and who is in control?

In educational terms it is essential that the relevance and necessity of the work and its practice is achieved by evolving a dialogical curriculum based on the principles of Freire's 'horizontal pedagogy' where the learners and teachers, participant artists and cultural creators share a co-intentional participatory educational practice. Learning must be rooted in the notion of our agreed articulation of 'needing to know'. The content of the learning experience should be derived wherever possible from the starting point of lived realities of the learners. In this sense, the teacher is both learner and teacher and the learner is both learner and teacher.

Our intention must be, in essence, the creation of processes which focus upon the education and training of people who, through the skills and perspectives of good facilitation, can in turn offer dialogue and practice to the education and training of others from the community itself. This process of self-development through and with the development of others will help ensure the sustainability of the work and the increased capacity for the articulation of rights and needs by the community on its own behalf. This is, in part, the role of advocacy. We should seek to ensure that our shared principles of education as cultural action will generate processes which lead to people's own self-determined transformation and become a mainspring of people-centred development.

We should engage at every level those agencies and elements in civil society which we have access to and construct our own where we do not. We should seek and build associations and programmes for change with those elements in civil society and help develop the capacities of those individuals and groups concerned with education, the arts, communication, public policy etc. in order to expand our collective resource base. Through expanding our collective cultural capacities and responsibilities we will redefine and construct our own political programmes and practices in order not just to withstand the dominant but to transcend it.

If we do not engage in this way we too shall watch our purpose and our future becoming marginalized and silenced and we will inherit the 'anger of the damned'.

APPENDIX
The Voice to the Marginalised

[Excerpt from 'The Road to PPP: a personal account of a public journey into TFD' available at http://www.cdcarts.org/ppp]

The Voice to the Marginalised project (sponsored by the British Council) was a series of training workshops spanning a three-year period. The first phase involved a series of workshops which introduced community activists and performers to the concepts of participatory performance practices (PPP). The second phase of workshops in Lusaka emphasized a fusion between Participatory Rural Appraisal (PRA) techniques and those of theatre as research. This created a process whereby a performance group could subdivide into smaller groups and work as facilitating artists for different agencies or with different target groups within a single community, addressing related issues. This was the path taken by Kamoto Arts after their members attended the first phase when they used PPP with a group of mostly disabled young people in the Ngombe compound on the outskirts of Lusaka.

Phase Two developed Kamoto Arts' work with the disabled group in the Ngombe compound. After detailed research Kamoto had fostered a series of performances by the group (which also included some able-bodied members) in and around Ngombe. Through the performances the group had been enabled to speak for themselves about their own social reality and in particular about the rebuttals they received on applying for jobs. Their plea was to be perceived as ordinary people.

The outcome of this was a series of interventions with different sectors of the community, which culminated in a mini-festival of performances at the local school.

The disabled group performed their play, which had not been seen by the school children. Members of the workshop worked with three groups of children and a mini-festival of performance was arranged in the school precincts. The children performed their own plays that depicted how they used to taunt, bully or otherwise spurn their less fortunate counterparts. This was the first time either group had shared such an exchange of views. The able-bodied children felt that they would no longer be so callous while the disabled group were glad of the frank, friendly and, they felt, fruitful exchanges.

Hopeful Youth Drama in Kibera, Kenya

PHAN Y LY

Introduction

In November 2004, as part of my MA course in Theatre and Media for Development at University College Winchester, UK, I was required to do a three-month project that would extend the knowledge and skill that I acquired during the course. For me, that should be a place where there is demand and need and 'hunger' for new skills.

I avoided contacting large, well-known non-government organizations, because they are traditionally structured and hierarchical. I was looking instead for a community who can decide for themselves and negotiate directly with me. I was focusing on the African continent, simply because I had never been there. My keywords for searching on Google were 'theatre, drama, community, development, Africa'. It was like a search for a needle in a haystack, not only were this combination of key words hard to find, but also the results that actually matched only showed the well-established organizations whose concerns are more about funding than new skills, and the decision-makers are definitely not those who are hungry for what I could offer.

My luck arrived when www.comminit.com offered a wonderful directory of differently categorized organizations for each region of the world. Among them is the list of 'Community Organizations' in Africa, and I found this:

Kibera Community Youth Programme
A youth programme formed and run by youth from the slums of Kibera, Nairobi, which aims to educate youth and slum dwellers about drug abuse, illegal firearms, domestic violence, child abuse and HIV/AIDS, using sports and dramatic arts and via networking with other organizations.

The link to their website produced both excitement and admiration. On the computer screen was a very simple web page with basic information about the group's vision and activities. Despite the amateur feel of the site, the commitment and determination of the young people clearly shone through. One would not believe the website was set up by those living in the slum.

1. KCYP office where the group meet to discuss, plan and rehearse, Kibera, Nairobi, December 2004 (© Paul Moclair)

2. Living space: view from KCYP group leader Frederick Ouko's house, Kibera, Nairobi, March 2005 (© Phen Y Ly)

'Edutainment' was repeatedly mentioned in the programme page. They also called it 'Theatre for Development' where they go out in the community with skits and plays to act in the community based on a particular theme: 'This is used as an edutainment approach where we pass information while entertaining the audience.' Beside funding and equipment, the group also described 'new skill' as one of the areas they have been seeking to develop. Fredrick Ouko, a 23-year-old coordinator of the group, proved his determination through a series of articles he wrote and submitted on many other development websites that I later found.

My request to work with them on the use of theatre in community development was greatly welcomed. We exchanged about four emails each day for three months, explaining our situations, hopes, fears and expectations. Every time I expressed my concern for their lack of financial stability and questioned their commitment, Fredrick would end his reply email with 'I am sure I won't be the one to disappoint you, and you can mark my words. It is hard to trust someone having not worked with him/her in the first place, just get it from me that I respect your comments and look forward to close involvement.'

Because the group has a great passion for using arts in their work and have been performing self-written plays for two years, and because they believe in 'edutainment', my 'secret' plan was to give them a 'push' to try out Interactive theatre and Forum theatre in the community. I did not openly discuss this with Fredrick because I wanted the situation and opportunity to speak for itself. On 5 February 2005, I arrived in Nairobi, Kenya and went to Kibera for the first time.

Kibera – 'A dirty secret along railway embankments...'

Kibera can't be found on a tourist map or any other map. It's an illegal city and nearly a third of the population of Nairobi lives there. The name 'Kibera' is a Nubian word meaning 'bush'. The 'bush' has been forgotten by the government, and yet is has been around for nearly a century. Following successful service during World War I, the British colonial government awarded a wooded hillside outside of Nairobi to a group of Nubian soldiers who eventually settled there. The soldiers built homes and set up businesses, all without any legal rights to the land.

Unfortunately, the British never gave title to the land to the Nubians, so the residents of Kibera do not qualify for any government assistance. However, title never stopped the refugees from coming. And come they did, pouring in from not only the Kenyan countryside as villagers seeking employment, but also from neighbouring countries. One could type the keyword 'Kibera' in a search engine and find thousands of articles on the world's second largest slum, all describing it as 'a forest', 'pile of rubbish – a clutter of cardboard and cloth on a damp pavement', 'a cramped and filthy squatters camp', 'a dirty secret along railway embankments' where '... the Nairobi police are reportedly too afraid to patrol', 'nearly half of the population is young people' and 'approximately one quarter of Kibera's population is HIV positive'.

... Or not

'In one of the largest slums in sub-Saharan Africa, Kibera, where the majority live below the poverty datum line, everyone would expect to meet frowning faces with lots of despair, this is not the case', said Fredrick, 'there is a ray of hope coming from a group of energetic and innovative youth who are ready to go an extra mile in serving their community needs.'

'It was after great concern that we youth came together, to form the group: Kibera Community Youth Programme. We were not represented and therefore had nobody to listen to our voice or our cry. The need for coming together was necessitated by the fact that, we had common problems that called for unity towards addressing them,' expressed Merab Florence Adhiambo. She is 25 years old and has been with the group for the past three years. 'With lack of employment, there was a need to engage ourselves in different activities that would make us occupied and self-reliant as opposed to letting the adults do it for us.' Merab's and Frederick's personal contributions to this article are included at the end.

The group consists of 25 regular members with the youngest being 18 years old and the oldest being 25 years old. There are ten women and fifteen men and the numbers are not fixed as there are always more new members coming. Commitment is one of the criteria for being accepted in the group. Approximately 60 per cent of the population in Kibera are young people who can't continue to higher education because of financial constraints. These constraints in turn exclude them from official employment.

According to Fred, 'KCYP is therefore trying to engage youth whom it recruits as volunteers/members in self-reliance activities that enable them to stay afloat and meet some of their essential basic needs. There are five programmes that form the bulk of KCYP's work, these are: youth development and empowerment, reproductive health, arts for development and social change, environment and sanitation, and special programmes.'

Right from my first day visiting and attending the group's performance and rehearsal, I could see the passion and talents that each member possesses. As with my experience of their web site, I noticed the same combination of amateurism and determination in the group's drama performance. KCYP was partnered with Population Service International (PSI) and performed plays in different communal areas in Kibera. As required by PSI, their plays had to give clear and spoken messages of 'Abstinence', as well as promote the slogan 'Chill' (which means not having sex before marriage) to the community. Every afternoon the actors gather at their office in Kibera and walk together to the performing area pre-selected for that day. These places are often markets, large empty spaces with many passers-by, or even crowded roads; depending on where it is, sometimes the actors may have to walk as far as 5 km.

3. *Mask work by Mill, a group member, KCYP office, Kibera, Nairobi, April 2005*
(© Phan Y Ly)

4. *Warm up to reggae music from solar-powered radio, KCYP office, Kibera, Nairobi, March 2005*
(© Phan Y Ly)

KCYP's office-cum-rehearsal place is a humble shelter made of mud, tree branches and a tin roof, located in so-called 'upper class Kibera' which means less mud, more street vendors, bigger lanes, stronger houses, and with spare electricity. The group members told me they wanted to develop 'drama' and 'self-evaluation skills' so that they would not have to rely on PSI's TfD expert to come twice a month and point out their mistakes. They also dream of becoming famous actors and actresses and that their theatre group will earn lots of money.

It was never too late...

The group members had a great passion for acting, with surprising theatrical and musical talents. However, despite being together for two years, they have never had a drama training or team-building workshop. Those with good English and imagination write play scripts which the team would then rehearse. Theatrical techniques for them were as simple as speech, songs and poems.

We decided to have an intensive training on theatrical and facilitation skills. While leading them through the exploration of different story elements, theatrical forms and techniques, the focus was on team-building, self-awareness and improvisation. Setting a 'holy ground' of Trust, Love and Respect for working together, the training was carried out three days a week, for three hours each day. Each day had a different objective but it was built on the following principles:

- At least a third of the content of the day had to be carried out by a volunteering member
- Whenever possible, the importance and different aspects of Trust, taking care of each other, or 'respecting others value' was emphasized
- Theatrical exercises were intertwined with personal life experience
- There is no 'impossibility'

At first, the actors were led through a series of discussions and exercises to open themselves up and start sharing their life stories in a safe and natural way. The exercises can be about sharing the most precious items and analysing each owner's reaction and emotion during the telling of the stories, or can be sharing moments of oppression while learning about the power of still images. On Valentine's Day the actors could have a discussion on Love, or debate different conditions for Trust and link them with the trust they want to establish with the audience. Amazingly, the actors, through the 'excuses' of 'discussion' and 'exercises', were slowly revealing their personal values and sharing their life experiences. Shy members started to open up, theatrical exercises were an opportunity for them to show they also have talents.

After three weeks, Martin, an actor who has been with the group for three years, told me 'It is amazing! Before if we asked the group to think of a play, they would say they have nothing to think of, or that they have no idea! Tell them to act and nobody would stand up! And now, after 15 minutes even the shyest members have a very creative play!'

In the second month, March 2005, we had two days of life-story sharing, called 'Life Map'. From an impressionistic drawing of the ups and downs in each of our lives, we then shared the story of those moments. One by one people came up to tell the group about his/her life. *SHOCKING* is the word I would use to describe the experience. Everyone was brave, everyone was protective and trusting. Everyone was crying. The atmosphere was heavy and tight. The actors sat close and hugged each other, some looked far away, some of them covered their faces. For two years, their laughter and 'work' were playing out the duty of burying the painful truth in each member. As close as they were to each other, none had had a single opportunity to share a truth about what they went through in life and why they ended up in Kibera. It was shocking to discover how much strength they had, and it was more than shocking to realize how well they have been keeping their lives so 'top secret'.

With permission of the authors, the group chose two stories to build two plays. The authors did the casting and directed the plays as an exercise on the power of 'truth' and 'simplicity'. But, more than that, each actor gained insight about him/her as an individual and about the group as a whole.

Later, relatives and the group members shared the following comments with me:

- 'She [one of the actresses] said it was a very painful day, but she is so happy that the group was given that opportunity. She always regarded herself as mean and miserable and thought no one was as miserable as her. But now she knows there are other people with difficult lives, and she has to go on, she is now very confident'
- 'Now I know why she [another member] behaved that way … I didn't know what she went through.'
- 'It is so good that finally we have been able to speak it out and let it go.'

The underlying value

Perhaps the one thing that is repeated most frequently in the training is 'Respecting different values'. How would the actors facilitate transformation in the audience, if their way of doing it does not show a real understanding and respect for the different values the audience have? Every day discussion on this topic led the group to an agreement of not 'lecturing' the audience through the performance, but simply creating a condition where the audience can debate and question each other's point of view.

Meanwhile, the group was still performing 'abstinence' plays for Population Service International in different areas of Kibera. They started inserting new drama techniques in these plays where appropriate. The interesting thing is they had two contrasting approaches to compare and analyse. One was the lecturing plays with slogans given by the Population Service International that they were performing every day in the community, the other was the agreement to be 'neutral' that they had reached among themselves in the training. The topic of 'being a neutral facilitator' was a hot topic, spread over three weeks! Every day a member would have a new concern for the ability to be 'neutral'. Perhaps this was drawn from their actual experience with the PSI plays.

Each day an actor would volunteer to start the training by leading the recap and warm-up section, and end it by facilitating a 20-minute discussion on a topic given on the previous day. This way not only could an individual member prove him/herself independently in a safe environment, but also the facilitation provided a practical example for the group to examine and express their view of what a neutral facilitator should be. In the feedback session, group members also shared practical tips with the facilitators, from body language, voice, eye contact, timing, the arrangement of the seating, to questioning skills, conflict management and neutrality. As they gained experience of 'facilitation', their analysis of the challenges and contradictions of a facilitator went deeper:

- 'A facilitator can only mention fact and not personal opinion, but a fact can support one team and not other, how does s/he then still maintain the neutrality of facilitation?'
- 'What if the group comes up with "wrong" conclusion, should the facilitator "shut them up"?'
- 'If you nodded for the answer of this person then you should nod for the other person's too!'

Without my knowing, the group employed this facilitation method with a section of KCYP called Group Therapy, which was outside the training. During one Group Therapy session, a facilitator volunteers and leads the group through a discussion on a given topic, for example 'On what criteria will you choose your life partner?'

At the same time, 'Accepting each other's ideas' was an important principle that we agreed on. This actually came out of the training on improvisation skills. 'In order to make a story flow, you need to accept your partner's idea and build on it.' From the 'magic' of 'accepting ideas' tested in their theatrical exercises, the actors applied the principle to the group etiquette. Even the shyest members now can respond: 'Remember? Accepting ideas!!!' whenever his/her suggestion is neglected. This was not easy for the actors, yet they made a 30-minute play with the actors having no idea what was going to happen next, and when asked 'how did you understand your partner so well?' the actors proudly said 'we just accepted the ideas and went with it!'

This principle of improvisation was also accompanied by 'always act as if on stage'. This was intended to sharpen their professionalism and improvisation skills.

'A facilitator has to challenge the audience to bring out what is inside them' *(Martin Oduor – group member)*

The idea of 'facilitator' was compared to the role of an 'MC' (Master of Ceremony) in their performance. Their performance in the community was then compared to the discussion in the training. That was how Forum theatre in KCYP was formed. Before we could begin to build a forum theatre structure, the actors debated and requested everybody in the group to change the title 'MC' to 'facilitator'.

The actors had had their discussion activity in the training, forming their own 'model' of a 'neutral facilitator' and were very happy with it. However, when it came to applying that to Forum theatre where the audience could debate and actors are facilitators ... everyone was a bit hesitant:

- 'We perform in the community where the audience are not settled like in a church or in a school, this kind of performance needs thorough participation'
- 'It requires the facilitator to talk a lot ... in open air...'
- 'You know this is Kenya, and the audience are adults, sometimes old people, sometimes drunk... we can't just make them clap their hands and do games and ask them to participate.'
- 'How can we act if we have not prepared beforehand?'

These concerns were converted into topics for group discussion. If one day per topic was not enough we would continue it until everybody was happy with the result.

My actual involvement in the training was less and less as the seventh week of the training arrived. Every day, for theatrical exercises sessions, the actors would divide into two teams and give a performance after 15–20 minutes of discussion. A new facilitator in the team would be assigned to lead the Forum theatre. Each team would pretend to be the audience for the other. The actors mixed and matched and tested different theatrical techniques and through success and failure drew out their own Forum theatre style. A facilitator would be criticized if she or he tried giving hints to the audience on what is 'good' and what is 'bad' in the play. An actor would be commented upon as 'less challenging' if his or her character accepted the criticism and insults from the audience too easily.

'A facilitator has to challenge the audience to bring out what is inside them', said Martin.

From this point of view, the actors had formed a unique Forum theatre style where theatre is a platform for dialogue to take place between the audience and the characters, among the audience themselves, and within an individual audience itself.

In an unrealistic setting like a dramatized play, it might be easy for an audience to criticize or insult directly, for example, a female character who has sex with her boyfriend. But not where, instead of accepting the accusation, the character demands the questioner for justification, or explicitly and bluntly states her belief and point of view. In this situation she is now able to challenge the audience to get into a deeper and more truthful discussion.

Often when Forum theatre is mentioned, people think of a play where an audience can give thoughts and solutions. If we are not careful, Forum theatre can be a place to reinforce oppression and superficial 'moral lessons', because it is often much quicker and easier to criticize something or someone based on a shallow crowd-pleasing view without much analysis involved. In the above example, it is easy to say that the female character is spoilt and she should not have sex until marriage. But how easy is it to make such a comment when the character says she believes in having sex before marriage and that she would not marry at all?

Being provocative, blunt and honest are methods that the actors adopt for their characters during hot-seating, and this triggers the audience to think, and forces the silence to burst out and wipes away superficial responses.

A 'result' - or 'a solution' - is not a 'must-have' achievement in this kind of forum theatre. The actors discussed and agreed that it is the process of thinking and reflecting in each person that is important, not the ultimate consensus solution, because, as one of the members said, 'each person makes a different solution for him or herself'.

Each performance would start with a warm-up activity for the audience, which could be dancing and singing with drums. The facilitator then would introduce the style of theatre used in the performance and ask for the audience's support. The play is prepared by the actors before the show, and it would 'freeze' on the critical decision-making moment. The facilitator then would ask for the audience's consensus on what happened in the play, what they think was the 'problem', if it is something realistic, and whether they would like to have a conversation with each character. The audience will often choose the most controversial character that they 'hate', and the most common question is 'Why did you do that?' The characters would bring the audience to reality by giving honest and blunt answers on the reasons he or she did something. The audience often wants to know how the character feels and what she or he would do next. They would test the character's reaction on certain decisions that other characters would then make.

Sometimes the audience gets into an argument among themselves and this is where the facilitator intervenes.

After the audience has finished with their 'interview of characters', the facilitator will ask the audience if they have any advice as to who should do what to make the situation better. The actors would carry out the next scene. This kind of Forum theatre show often takes about an hour and a half.

The first time the actors tested out this form of theatre was in one of the slum markets. In contrast with the actors' fear, the audience – street vendors, school children and passers-by – was fully involved in the show, even leaving their shops unattended. The audience members laughed or were silent, depending on the character's reply to their question, and even argued with the characters on certain issues.

5. Community performance in an outdoor market in Kibera, May 2005. The audience are street vendors, passers-by and children. The clothes belong to a street vendor but are used as a prop in the play (© Phan Y Ly)

When asked if they would like to continue this form of theatre, Fred and the actors said they will definitely change from a typical message-driven play into an interactive one that involved the audience. The group members then took on my role of designing and facilitating a training day and carried out the workshop themselves.

The following letter from Fredrick explains further KCYP's future plans:

> Hi Ly, I have gone through your mail and the only activity I can be able to take stock of is the performances in the community, the increased willingness of people to take art as a serious thing, plans to make documentaries is becoming evident with the group. Martin is submitting his application to Care Kenya to see if he will be taken as a trainer on TFD. International Medical Corps had a meeting with us today with a view to engage us in using forum theatre to promote TB/HIV prevention here in Kibera. We'll be networking with them henceforth. From the TFD training, participants are now taking another training on Filming just to actualize the skills. Plans are still underway to get the routine inhouse training going on, based on the TFD skills acquired.

The silver lining…

The group members come from different areas of Kenya such as Lamu, Mombasa, Kisumu, Siaya, and belong to different ethnic groups such as Kiisi,

Luo, Kikuyu, Luiya. Some of them came from other countries like Tanzania and Uganda. Some were born in Kibera itself. None of them have a university degree.

I have quoted Martin earlier. Martin's family moved from Siaya in Western Kenya to Kibera, Nairobi when he was a little boy. His father's death in 2002 made him and his three brothers orphans, 'but life has to move on', as Martin would say. His younger brother, a 23-year-old, gets up at 6 am every morning to go and teach mathematics in a primary school in Kibera. One elder brother is married to a woman he met in Kibera, and they are now a small family with three children, their humble home is also in the slum, but with electricity.

When I visited their home, Martin was teaching his little nieces and nephew to count in Kiswahili and English. 'Education is important', Martin said; and I could see that on the mudded wall hung an old and broken piece of wooden board, with careful child's writing of A,B,C. Martin said it is not that he does not know the life outside the slum 'My other elder brother owns a proper house not in the slum, I used to stay with his family.' When asked why he moved back to Kibera, he shrugged: 'Well I have my own life too.'

Besides being an actor and group member of KCYP, where he gets the income of roughly 2,000 shillings a month (60 shillings can buy a meal in the slum) from contracted work with organizations like Population Service International, Martin is also a peer educator and is often invited to give a speech on HIV/AIDS, Voluntary Testing, and so on in universities. I followed him one day and found to my amazement that Martin was having a great time interacting with more than 200 listeners who are first year students at Nairobi Teacher Training College. No-one would believe that the talented and knowledgeable speaker had only graduated from high school and was living in Kibera. Martin said he did the work for free because his friend – a student of the university – had invited him.

Martin's ever dying wish is 'to be back to school' and 'learn what you are learning now' he told me. We actually sat together in front of a computer in an internet café and browsed through different scholarship opportunities given by local and foreign governments. After an hour of screening every single word in every single document online, Martin looked like he wanted to cry because all the scholarships for university were reserved for 'government officers'.

Fred Ouko, whose own piece is written to conclude my article below, is one of the founders of KCYP. He is now the general manager of the initiative. He is currently the director overseeing the functions of the management board and has been instrumental in creating communication links, in programme design and in starting up new programmes, in addition to his other day-to-day activities. He grew up in the Western part of Kenya and belongs to the Luhya tribe, came to Kibera after his completion of high school in Mombasa, and then the idea of forming an organization came up:

> I have been a leader since my school days; on coming here I found friends who were welcoming and we talked about many thing, it happened that we were all youth and the idea crouched in my mind that there is indeed something we can do together as

young people living in Kibera. There was a need for young people to express themselves, I saw lots of injustices being meted to young people in other projects and decided that I could not mourn about this but try my best to provide a solution, we joined hands with friends and the rest is history.

Living in a thatched house in Kibera and still managing to travel to work every day on two crutches, Fred has been supporting himself and his family with the different allowances he gets from volunteering.

> I have been doing some consultancy work though not as a profession, people ask me for ideas in disability and this gets me some meagre income, there are some sorts of allowances that can be gotten from volunteering in different projects which I normally do including KCYP.

Like many other young people coming to Kibera in search of jobs and income generation opportunities, Fred sends money home to support his parents whenever he can spare some. 'I am in fact assisting with the education of my younger sister who has now come to Nairobi and she's in High School, and my brother who is in Form Three at home as well.'

Planning to stay in Kibera for the 'whole of his life', Fredrick said his dream is to lead a vibrant social movement that will stand the test of time. He wants the whole world to know that indeed disability is just another kind of ability, and said that would be his greatest achievement. 'You can dream, you can have the strategies in place, but with no money; things are just wishes. It has been difficult to find support for what you believe in, few people trust young people and what they have to offer.'

Andrew is the computer expert in KCYP. He comes from Western Kenya. His parents and sister are back home, while Andrew came to the city to 'be independent and find a job'. He has been in Kibera for five years. Kibera was chosen as his second home because it is cheap. Sometimes his father would visit him in Kibera and even give him some money, or else he would not have anything to eat or dare to go anywhere for weeks! Andrew has been supported by an American friend to study Computer Application in one of the very best centres in Nairobi. Showing me the exam results, Andrew was disappointed at getting 'only 98% for this paper ... because I was sick the day before.' I told him that 98% is high but he shook his head 'I know, but I am aiming for scholarship from this institute so I don't have to pay...'

Andrew is passionate about media and design. He taught himself how to use a video camera. He came to see me any time I was free so he could practice movie editing on iMovie! On the day I left Kenya, Andrew completed his first media product of a two-hour film which was shot and edited by him. The film was about the graduation day celebration of the first university student in Kibera. Andrew's dream is to have his own studio where he can develop his creative abilities in media and design.

Merab, whom I quoted above, is 25 years old and has been with the group for three years. Her commentary on our work together in the group for this article is below.

Commentary by Merab Florence Adhiambo (KCYP member)

It was after a great concern that we youth came together to form the group Kibera Community Youth Programme. We were not represented and therefore had nobody to listen to our voice nor our cry. The need for coming together was necessitated by the fact that we had common problems that called for unity towards addressing them.

With lack of employment there was a need to engage ourselves in different activities that would make us occupied and self-reliant as opposed to letting the adults do it for us. The first move was to mobilize the youth and inform them about the objectives of the group. There was a general need to address the health issues given the high prevalence of HIV/AIDS among the youth. Ignorance and lack of adequate information led to increased cases of infections hence the need to start campaigns geared towards the provision of appropriate information in regard to HIV/AIDS. Originally the format used to pass on information was stage acting and speech and this was later discovered to be boring to youth and other audiences. There have been efforts to earmark the creativity of youth towards making lively presentations to the audiences while facilitating a learning process. We have employed different forms of arts, i.e. songs, poems, skits and narrations.

All this was being done to a backdrop of inadequate skills in the format that can transform the community in the easiest way. The new era started when a volunteer from Winchester University showed interest in training us in Theatre for Development skills. The training lasted for three and half months opening another door in our theatre activities. The art of improvisation, understanding, accepting everyone's ideas, concentration while working in a team became a reality from the learning sessions we had. Team work now remains the key to all of our activities with facilitation in the community outreaches picking up well, resulting from self-confidence gained through the training. It was never too late for Ly to show up as she has impacted greatly on our acting skills as a group. There is need for support for us to scale this work up and reach a larger audience.

Commentary by Fredrick Ouko (KCYP director)

In one of the largest slums in sub-Saharan Africa, Kibera, where the majority live below the poverty datum line, everyone would expect to meet frowning faces with lots of despair, this is not the case. There is a ray of hope coming from a group of energetic and innovative youth who are ready to go an extra mile in serving their community needs. Early in 2002, a group of them joined hands to found what is now referred to as Kibera Community Youth Programme (KCYP) whose core function is to look into issues that relate to youth empowerment in Kibera and its environs through a multi-sectoral approach which is based on a self-help model.

Given the poor economic status of Kibera as a slum dwelling place, there exists a problem of unemployment with the majority of the unemployed being youth because they account for 60 per cent of the general population of Kibera, which is estimated to be one million. Kibera harbours a set of multi-ethnic groupings from various parts of the country who come to the capital city of Nairobi to look for employment opportunities and decide to stay in the slum due to the low-cost housing. KCYP is therefore trying to engage the youth whom it recruits as volunteers/ members in self-reliance activities that enable them to stay afloat and meet some of their essential basic needs.

There are five programmes that form the bulk of KCYP's work, these are: youth development and empowerment, reproductive health, arts for development and social change, environment and sanitation and special programmes. The fact that KCYP is not a funded initiative makes it necessary to find partners in implementing some of its programmes and projects and a greater need to undertake income-generating activities.

Community theatre outreach has been one such activity where skits, poems, songs are composed with a specific audience in mind and subject, mainly on social problems e.g. HIV/AIDS, drug abuse. These are taken to the community and they are allowed to ask questions to promote greater understanding and learning. Members are motivated to do this kind of work based on their personal interest in learning from the different encounters. KCYP also provides various opportunities as incentives to its members i.e. training, exchange visits, talent building support, assistance in times of problems and allowances when available.

KCYP looks forward to being a strong youth social initiative that imparts positive views into the lives of youth so that they can have a bright future. There is an urgency of working towards the reduction of HIV/AIDS among young people the youth and the community in general, and theatre has been identified as a viable and impactful entry point. After the training offered to KCYP on theatre for development by an MA student (Ly) from Winchester University, for about three and a half months, the group has now adapted Forum theatre in educating the community-based on its effectiveness. One typical example is during the international workshop organized by KCYP in partnership with Atlantic College from Wales, the performances were at Uthiru Girls High School with an audience of 400 people. The participants were touched by the problems presented and took active roles in suggesting solutions with others playing character roles in the skit. This form of theatre makes the audience participate in the problem-solving as opposed to listening and being lectured to.

KCYP is now forming an Arts agency that will deal with all aspects of arts-related work. The initiative will be known as Creative Art Promotions (CAPs). There is great enthusiasm amongst members to continue with this kind of work. We, however, face the challenge of securing resources towards the implementation of broad-based programmes in the community in order to make an impact. There is need to secure support to establish a well-coordinated arts agency that will be effective in the implementation of arts-related projects.

NOTE

KCYP's contact address:
Kibera Community Youth Programme
P. O Box 5837 – 00200
Nairobi
Kenya
Cell:+ (254.720) 786 218 / (254.720) 140 968
Fax:+ (254.020) 570088
E-mail: kcyp2000@yahoo.com
General comments and enquiries: info@kcyp.kabissa.org
Programme information and projects: admin@kcyp.kabissa.org

The Ghosts Return

Transcribed & with an introduction by DAVID KERR
Devised by students at the University of Botswana

The Ghosts Return was created between 1999 and 2000 by UBE423, the name given to a theatre group associated with a fourth year 'Theory and Practice of Drama' course within the English Department at the University of Botswana. At the time I was the tutor for the course. Most of the students undertaking E423 had no or little experience of practical drama, but many hoped to become patrons of drama clubs in Botswana's Secondary Schools. While I was the tutor, an annual, collectively devised play became the key element in the practical component of the course, by means of which the students picked up skills in acting, design, direction and script-writing.

Throughout the mid and late 1990s UBE423's plays developed a methodology, which suited the needs of the students and fitted in with a tradition of collective creativity that underpins Botswana's cultural praxis. The process was one in which the group decided on a topic (invariably a topical or controversial one) and used research, theatre games and improvisation to build a play about it. The development of negotiation and democratic decision-making became an important element in the success of the productions.

The research almost always involved seeking help from NGOs specializing in issues of human rights, particularly those of women and children. UBE423 always attracted more young women than young men, so not surprisingly women's issues were particularly attractive. Frequently the research used historical documents such as letters, court transcripts and newspaper interviews, so that the plays mixed fictional and 'real' texts. Among the issues which the plays presented over the years were: Botswana legislation discriminating against women, the marginalization of the Basarwa (San) people, inter-racial love relationships, corruption in the government-run land boards, and sexual abuse of children. A few of the plays were performed in South Africa and attracted favourable attention in newspaper reviews there; one 1993 play, *You Are Not Dead* was translated into Setswana (as *Thari ya Lelwapa*) and published by Longman Botswana (1997).

The 1999–2000 cohort faced particular problems. There were 39 students, with only 11 males and 28 females; this was far too big a group to comfortably devise a single play. In the early exercises and improvisations two play concepts emerged among the students. One group wanted to do a play that commemorated the 15th anniversary of the 1985 raid on Gaborone by South African commandos seeking to eliminate ANC cadres. The other wanted to do a play about issues of power, transparency and ethics concerning the soon-to-be-launched Botswana Television (BTV). It seemed sensible to split the cohort into two and allow them to work on two separate plays. After some initial work on these lines, the whole cohort decided that it would be better to combine both concepts, by creating a play about a producer for the new BTV making a documentary on the anniversary of the 1985 raids. This is what we proceeded to do.

The research on BTV proved not too difficult in that one of the first trainees for BTV, Doreen Moapare, was an enthusiastic graduate from a former UBE423 cohort (1997–8) and was able to give the group some indication of the issues facing the emergent station. These centred in particular on to what extent BTV would be independent of the government, as a public service broadcaster, or whether it would, like Radio Botswana, fall under the Government Department of Information and Broadcasting, and be subject to strict Government gate-keeping. The press in 1999 and early 2000 had many stories and editorials illustrating or debating these issues.

The research on the 1985 raids was somewhat more difficult. A few students were able to find witnesses who gave first-hand accounts. These were particularly useful for providing contextual information on life in Gaborone fifteen years earlier. For most of the factual information, however, the students had to rely on scouring newspaper reports of the time and journal articles or theses written about the events.

For quite a long time, the two groups (BTV and raid) worked separately on developing plot and characterization. Bringing the groups together entailed a process of debates, story-telling sessions, improvisations and continuing research. This allowed the BTV scenes to become a frame for the raid scenes. The frame was created as fairly realistic, while the raid episodes, despite the use of drama-doc techniques of verbatim speeches, were far more stylized.

In contrast to earlier plays by UBE423 the casting was done (democratically by the whole cohort) quite early, as soon as the scenario allowed the huge list of characters to be assembled. Despite the large cohort, the play had such epic scope, there was a need for doubling up. It was also necessary to use non-racial and non-gender casting, with some of the most macho roles (for example, South African commandos) being played by young women. All this contributed to the stylization of the raid scenes.

The cohort developed the scenario collectively. The script-writing was done by allowing the actors playing in each scene (most of which were very short) to write out the lines they had improvised. A small script committee (consisting of myself and two students) eventually assembled and edited all these scenes. The same committee revised the script after a dramatized reading of the whole play towards the end of the first semester. About 70 per cent of the text, however, came from the lines written up by the actors from their own improvisations. Much of the rest consisted of verbatim quotations from historical figures. The play was photocopied so that actors could learn their lines over the Christmas vacation.

The second semester was spent rehearsing the play, a process that sometimes entailed making yet more, but minor, changes to the script. The rehearsal process also included working out the design of the stagecraft. The stage in the echoing, concrete, multi-purpose hall usually employed for drama at the university, was too small for the crowd scenes and for the violent action of the play. The cohort, during improvisations and rehearsals had to use the auditorium for some of the action and this was incorporated into the stagecraft. The imaginary 'houses' (portrayed by chairs) of Eugena and Gladys, George Pahle's family, and Mike Hamlyn, hit by the South African commandos were established in zones carved out of the auditorium. Those of the Machobanes and of Thami Mnyele were on stage. The South African commandos also used the auditorium for most of its sphere of operations. During the performances at the university, a follow-spot chased the action of the raids from house to house within the audience and on stage. However, when UBE423 performed *The Ghosts Return* at the Maitisong Festival, it was possible to use the professional facilities at Maru a Pula School. Some of the victims' homes were still set in the auditorium, but there were enough lamps to have lights fixed on the different 'houses'.

Some explanation needs to be made about the language of the play. The early improvisations tended to be in a mixture of Setswana and English. Once the scenario had been fixed, the group gave much thought to appropriate language. For those actors playing characters for whom Setswana would be the natural language choice, the code-switching between Setswana and English, typical of young Batswana in Gaborone, was maintained. Lydia Machobane, a Mosotho woman, uses a mixture of English and Sesotho. The South African commandos use English, with a few words of Afrikaans thrown in. In this text the Setswana and Sesotho have been retained in italics, with the English translation following immediately in brackets. Owing to the use of code-switching, many sentences switch rapidly from one language to another. There are also notes to explain some of the historical and cultural references in the play, although historical figures whose historical role is explained in the text, are not provided with footnotes. The translation of Setswana and Sesotho into English was done by Selina Omphile, and the ixiZulu song during the demonstration in scene 2 was translated by Victor Mtubani. The occasional phrases in Portuguese, Afrikaans and Tsotsitaal are so common in Southern African English that no formal translator was needed.

A little postscript to this Introduction needs to examine to what extent the students' fantasy of the future of the new BTV measures up to reality. The prophecy that there would be a major conflict over Government control of the TV station (despite its mandate to be a public service station) proved accurate. The incident, which initiated the crisis, however, did not fall neatly into a clear paradigm of neo-colonial machinations. The real-life figure who contested Botswana Government's interference, Tony Bishop, the then BTV news director, was a British citizen, with a quite different attitude from the

Machiavellian Richard Williams of the play. Bishop made a documentary in 2001 about Marietta Bosch, a South African citizen, who was executed on 31 March 2001 for murdering her husband. When the Director of Information and Broadcasting, representing the Government (which had faced some criticism over the Bosch judgment), prevented the documentary from being shown, Bishop resigned from the station.[1] After this incident BTV began to toe the government line, and made little pretence at being a public service station. Up to the present time the Government has not provided the broadcasting guidelines which could allow the National Broadcasting Authority to issue a licence. BTV continues to function without a licence.

[1] For information on these events see www.cpj.org/attacks01/botswana

CAST IN ORDER OF APPEARANCE

Refilwe (a Botswana TV producer) — Phatsimo Kelobang
Dora (a BTV announcer) — Gorata Kabelo
Thata (a BTV camera operator) — Eyani Sesinyi
Tshepo (a BTV interviewer) — Daisy Samuel
Bernard (BTV station manager) — David Kerr
President Masire (video clip) — Aubrey Pale
Magnus Malan (video clip) — Kabelo Mmusi
Archie Mogwe (video clip) — Mothusi Kebadilwe
Boitshwanelo (eye witness) — Moratiwa Mangwegape
Duke Machobane (massacre victim) — Collen Mokalake
Lydia Machobane (Duke's wife) — Jane Senobe
Eugena Kolobi (massacre victim & ghost) — Masego Rammekwa
Gladys Kesupile (massacre victim) — Changu Kenosi-Batsami
Mpho (friend of Eugena & Gladys) — Portia Liphoko
Tebogo Kebitseng (eye witness) — Francinah Moses
1st **art student** — Mompati Moatlhodi
2nd **art student** — Ketshedile Mosarwa
3rd **art student** — Tshegofatso Kgope
4th **art student** — Boitumelo Harry
5th **art student** — Salamina Kgwefane
Thami Mnyele (massacre victim & ghost) — Nkiwane Ndaba
Matshidiso (eye witness) — Berlinah Motswakhumo
Wally Serote (MEDU activist) — Benjamin-John Kebadimetse
Impressario (theatre agent) — Tebogo Norman
Moitse Botsholo (injury victim) — Phomolo Rachaba
Prince Maopane (injury victim) — Aubrey Pale
Major (South African platoon commander) — Letlhogonolo Keepilwe
Captain (South African commando) — Mothusi Kebadilwe
3rd **commando** — Kabelo Mmusi
4th **commando** — Seonyatseng Motswagae
5th **commando** — Opelo Sebonego
6th **commando** — Percy Mopedi
7th **commando** — Bridget Nyoni

8th commando	Francinah Moses
9th commando	Christine Cassim
10th commando	Mompati Moatlhodi
Peter Mofoko (Lydia's nephew, massacre victim)	Lizzy Dineo
George Pahle (massacre victim)	Daisy Samuel
Lindi Pahle (George's wife, massacre victim)	Salamina Kgwefane
Livy Pahle (George's brother, massacre victim)	Tshegofatse Kgope
Joe Malate (George's cousin, massacre victim)	Shatani Chilume
Mike Hamlyn (UB student, massacre victim)	Dintle Kenosi
Ahmed Gehr (Mike's friend, massacre victim)	Boitumelo Harry
Mrs Ghehr (Ahmed's wife, massacre victim)	Gaogelwe Samson
Lynn (eye witness)	Olivia Tsumake
Dr Chiepe (video clip)	Watiwa Keistsiwe
President Botha (video clip)	Kabelo Mmusi
Sefawantsho (interviewee)	Ben-John Kebadimetse
ANC spokesperson (interviewee)	Salamina Kgwefane
General Merafhe (video clip)	Letlhogonolo Keepilwe
Mayor Paul Rantao (video clip)	Percy Mopedi
Mmegi reporter (interviewee)	Sebaga Sebele
Secretary (BTV worker)	Dintle Kenosi
Clerk (BTV worker)	Shathani Chilume
Photographer (BTV worker)	Gaoagelwe Samson
4th BTV worker	Shirley Nkarabang
5th BTV worker	Lizzy Dineo
Stage Manager	Watiwa Keisitswe
Assistant Stage Managers	Changu Kenosi-Batsani
	Shirley Nkarabang
Production team	David Kerr, Kabelo Mmusi,
	Daisy Samuel
Prompts	Gorata Kabelo, Shirley Nkarabang
Sound	Ketshedile Mosarwa
Lighting assistants	Eyani Sesinyi
	Aubrey Pale
Script Committee	Phatsimo Kelobang, David Kerr,
	Kabelo Mmusi

SCENE ONE: TV PROGRAMME DISPUTE

(The scene is set in a BTV studio. there is a camera on a tripod, a large desk with a telephone for the producer and a small desk for the anchor. Thata, the camera operator stands by one camera. there is also a table with a stylised monitor screen. Refilwe looks through the lens of thata's camera. Dora, sits at the anchor's desk. Refilwe indicates to Thata that she's happy with the shot, and goes to her desk and switches off the phone. She half-sits upon the desk so that she faces the action.)

Refilwe *(Raising her arm)* Cue camera. Cue talent. *(Dropping her arm suddenly)* Action!
(Thata looks through the viewfinder, begins filming and operates the zoom)

Dora Friday, June 15th 1985, 1.30 a.m. It's a cold winter's night in Gaborone. Some people are enjoying themselves at night spots, but most are keeping themselves warm, covered by blankets, and fast asleep. Little did they know that…
(*Bernard, holding a script, bursts into the studio in a very animated manner*)
Refilwe (*Noticing that Dora is distracted*) Cut! (*Angry*). Who on earth is disturbing us in the middle… (*Noticing Bernard*) Oh, Mr Williams, it's you. Why … I mean … Is there something urgent you need to see us about?
Bernard (*Waving the script*) I've just seen a copy of your script for this documentary.
Refilwe Is that a problem, sir?
Bernard I think it is.
Refilwe (*Turning to the other two*) Okay, Dora, Thata, *ke kopa gore le mphe metsotsonyana ke utlwe gore Mr Williams are o batlang. Dora o tswelele ka go lebelela dilaene tsa gago ka gore ke batla o supe gore o na le kgatlhego mo go se o buang ka sone, o a utlwa? Ke tla lo bitsa fa re feditse.* [Thata, Dora can you give me a few minutes to find out what Mr Williams wants. In the meantime Dora continue reading your lines because I want you to express your words through your voice. Is that clear? I will call you as soon as we are done.]
(*Thata switches off the camera. She and Dora go off stage*). Mr Williams, in my training in Mmabatho, they taught me that when the red studio light is on, nobody is to enter the studio.
Bernard I know perfectly well what the studio regulations are, but I don't think you know what BTV programming policy is.
Refilwe (*With studied politeness*) Then perhaps you'd like to take a seat, sir and explain.
Bernard (*Sitting down on Dora's chair*) It's very simple really. When you first brought me this concept for a documentary, I thought you had in mind a simple historical piece. But now I've looked at the script itself, I see it's far more than that.
Refilwe I'm sorry, Mr Williams, I can't just understand. I thought since June 2000 is the fifteenth anniversary of the Gaborone raids, *gore* [that] it was a good opportunity to remind the public.
Bernard Well, to start with, I never did see why you want to start digging into the past when we've got so many current issues to explore.
Refilwe What kind of issues, sir?
Bernard Like AIDS. Half of you people are going to be dead in another fifteen years, so why bother about what was happening fifteen years ago? Think about the future.
Refilwe Mr Williams, Joshua is doing a documentary on AIDS *ga ke re?* [Isn't that so?] And isn't it also there in the new soapie?
Bernard Our advisory board says we must bombard the public with the message.
Refilwe Fine, but if we bomb them so much that they get bored and switch to M Net, how will the message get through? We have to have some variety.
Bernard Obviously. That's why I gave you the green light last week. But now

I've seen the script...
Refilwe What's wrong with the script?
Bernard You're not just talking about the 1985 raids, there's a whole lot of current issues, the army and all kinds of other stuff.
Refilwe (*Passionately*) But, Mr Williams, just now you were complaining *gore* [that] we should be looking at current issues! I'm trying to show how the 1985 raids have affected us even now in the year 2000.
Bernard (*Containing himself with difficulty*) Refilwe, this is our first year of operation. We've only been on the air a few months. I can't afford to let these early broadcasts rub the government up the wrong way. Remember, the one who pays the piper calls the tune.
Refilwe But I thought this was a public broadcasting channel with obligations...
Bernard (*Very firmly*) I want you to look at your script again. Tone it down so we don't tread on anyone's toes, and then you can start shooting. Really, I've got more important problems than looking at every full stop and comma in every script.
(*Bernard stands up, drops the script on Refilwe's desk and goes off stage quickly. Refilwe goes over to her desk, puts both scripts together and looks at them dejectedly. Making a decision, she picks up the phone*)
Refilwe Lulu, can you call Dora and Thata to come back please?
(*Refilwe puts one of the scripts away and writes on the back page of the other. Dora, Thata and Tshepo come back in.*)
Dora Is everything alright?
Refilwe Yes.
Thata Are you sure?
Refilwe Yes.
Tshepo Mr Williams didn't sound alright. *O ne o kare o jele magala.* [He sounded angry]
Refilwe I said everything's alright. Now let's carry on with our jobs. Tshepo, you've got the list of interviewees.
Tshepo Yes.
Refilwe I've arranged transport for you to go and talk to the interviewees. Make them feel comfortable. Don't take any camera. This is just a preliminary recce. Background information.
Tshepo Okay. Shall I go now?
Refilwe Sure, the driver should be waiting in the car park.
(*Tshepo collects her note pad and leaves*)
Thata And what do you want me to do?
Refilwe Thata, I want you to go to the library and see what visual material you can dig up from 1985. Stills or video. Even newspapers. Concentrate on the raids, but other stuff might be useful. *Waitse* [You know] Botha threatening to blast the ANC into the Ocean.[2] Just make a list of anything you think might be relevant, and a brief description. Make a note of any film

---

[2] P.M. Botha, Prime Minister (later President) of South Africa, 1978–89.

clips with a strong visual content – bombs, explosions – all that sort of stuff. (*Thata exits*)
Dora And me?
Refilwe Let's have a go at the script. Your narrative.
(*Dora sits down and opens the script*)
Dora From the beginning?
Refilwe No miss out that first stuff that we already worked on about 'the day Batswana will never forget' etcetera etcetera.
Dora Okay. (*Finding her place in the script*). From here. (*Reading*) By the early 1980s the United Democratic Front, a thin disguise for the ANC, was beginning to make South Africa ungovernable. Botha and the South African government were desperate. They wanted to create a *cordon sanitaire* around South Africa. (*Breaking off*) Is that how you pronounce this 'cordon' business?
Refilwe No, sweetie. It's French – 'cordon sanitaire'
Dora (*Trying it*) 'Cordon sanitaire' (*Reading again*). They wanted to create a *cordon sanitaire* around South Africa. They wanted to intimidate neighbouring countries into expelling the liberation movements. The most intense pressure was on Mozambique. After a campaign of ruthless bombing…
Refilwe Try and make that phrase 'ruthless bombing' come out very strong, as if you hate Botha. Otherwise it's sounding good so far.
Dora After a campaign of ruthless bombing, the Mozambican government was in 1984, forced into signing the Nkomati Accord, by which it agreed to expel *Umkhonto we Sizwe* cadres.[3] Shortly after that the South African government put pressure on Botswana to sign its own non-aggression pact with South Africa. The Government of Botswana resisted this pressure. President Masire declared…
Refilwe Right, that's where we slot in some video footage of Masire. The one that Thata found yesterday.
(*Refilwe hits the remote control*)
President Masire (*On video monitor*) You cannot tell someone with whom you are not fighting to sign a non-aggression pact.
(*Refilwe hits the remote control, using this for switching on and off all the subsequent video clips*)
Dora The South African government, however, insisted that the South African refugees in Botswana provided cover for MK incursions into South Africa. The South African Defence Minister, Magnus Malan, warned Botswana.
Magnus Malan The ANC is allowed free rein to invade South Africa. If the communists continue to use Botswana as a launching pad, our Defence forces will have no choice but to take preventive action.
Dora The Botswana government reacted strongly to this. Archie Mogwe, Minister for Land and Water Affairs, remarked sarcastically:
Archie Mogwe The mere presence of refugees in a country qualifies that

---

[3] Umkhonto we Sizwe (Spear of the Nation), the military wing of the ANC, sometimes abbreviated to MK.

country for an invasion from South Africa these days.
Dora Phrasing similar sentiments rather more diplomatically, President Masire said.
President Masire If any person has succeeded in acting in violation of the non-aggression policy in the past it was not with the knowledge or approval of the Botswana authorities.
Dora Despite these protests, the South African government decided to make a serious cross-border raid into Botswana in order to liquidate South African refugees, which it claimed were MK operatives, or, to use its own vocabulary, 'terrorists'. The South Africans entered the country...
Refilwe We added a sentence there, remember.
Dora Okay. (*Marking the script*) The invasion was a slickly planned operation. A group of about fifty South African soldiers infiltrated the border disguised as businessmen or tourists. Others crossed illegally soon after midnight, using Datsun vans and *bakkies*, [pick-up trucks] fitted with Botswana Government number plates. Some of the soldiers were white, others black...
(*The telephone rings. Refilwe answers*)
Refilwe Hello, Refilwe here. Oh, Tshepo. How's it going? Okay... Good... Very good... In that case we can send Thata with you this afternoon and you can shoot some of the interviews...Yes, while they're still keen. (*She puts the phone down*). That's Tshepo. She's doing well with the interviewees. Let's carry on. So far so good.
Dora It is obvious that the South African military were using spies inside Botswana to get information about South African refugees. They knew precisely which houses to hit. For example, Thami Mnyele had just moved into a new house in Tlokweng, but the soldiers knew the house. Some of the information, however, was faulty, and this led to people losing their lives who had nothing to do with the South African struggle. The victims were a very mixed group of people.
Refilwe Let's stop it there, because that's where we slot the inserts from Tshepo and Thata. The interviews with eye witnesses and so on.
(*Lights fade*)

SCENE TWO: THE SLAUGHTERED CHILD

(*The lights come up. Refilwe is watching the filming. Thata has her camera on Dora. Tshepo and Boitshwanelo are on the monitor*)
Refilwe (*Bringing down her arm*) Action!
Dora Undoubtedly the most tragic of all the deaths was that of a little boy, six year-old Peter Mofoko, a citizen of Lesotho. We talked to Boitshwanelo Wasetso, who knew the family.
Tshepo How did this innocent little boy, Peter manage to be dragged into these slaughters?
Boitshwanelo I don't know why the racists killed him. But I did know the family. Duke Machobane and his wife, Lydia, were my neighbours in Broadhurst.

Tshepo And what kind of people were they?
Boitshwanelo They were very good people, hard working and leading a devoted family life. Lydia never had problems from Duke, he loved her too much. And they were always helpful to people in the neighbourhood.
Tshepo And how did Peter come into the picture?
Boitshwanelo As far as I remember, Peter was Lydia's sister's son. They were all from Lesotho. Duke was also a Mosotho but from South Africa. Peter came to stay with his aunt. He had only been in Gaborone a few days when the attack came. (*Almost in tears*) He was a cute little boy, we all loved him.
Tshepo I'm sorry *mme* [Mrs] Wasetso. But can you remember why Duke and Lydia came to Botswana in the first place?
Boitshwanelo I'm not sure. Duke was a teacher. I think it was some political thing. There was too much politics in those days.
(*Tshepo and Boitshwanelo leave the monitor. Flashback. Lydia is on stage peeling vegetables, stage left. Off stage there is a rousing liberation song. Duke comes on stage singing. The chorus finish the song but Duke carries on singing on his own, as if giving himself courage to face his wife. He enters the house*)
Duke My darling, there's a problem we must discuss. I've decided that we should leave this country.
Lydia (*Wiping her hands dry on a cloth*) You're saying we leave South Africa? *Che e bo ntate! Ha ke dumele, ha eba ntate ho tla etshalang ka metswalle le meloko ya bo rena. Nkeke ka etsa jwalo.* [No, sir! I don't agree, what will happen to our family members and friends? I will not do such a thing.]
Duke (*With quiet persuasion*) You don't understand. I'm saying this from deeper heart. I'm concerned about our security. I can no longer tolerate this apartheid regime. As an activist, my life is in danger. You too are in danger, because you are married to a political activist. So I can be killed at any time, and you will also be the victim. I don't want that to happen. Please, dear, let's run away to Botswana.
Lydia No, no, no, Duke! That cannot happen. You took me from my own country to South Africa. Let me die here. Move again? There in Botswana we will be living like strangers, refugees... and what about your job?
Duke My job is not a problem. Botswana has a shortage of teachers. So the very day we get to Botswana I will be hired.
Lydia Then, what about me? I will be bored at home, whilst you are at work. In a strange neighbourhood ... There will be no one to visit, no relatives, no friends. That is not the kind of life I want to live. I will rather suffer here! (*With all her heart*) Please, my husband.
Duke (*Reluctantly giving in*) Well, Lydia, I can't force you. If that's what you want, we'll stay.
Lydia I knew you will agree with me. *Kealeboha. Ke thabile ha holo, ntate!* [Thank you, I am so happy.]
(*They hug each other, then Lydia carries on peeling the vegetables. The lights fade. The liberation song starts again. Lydia goes off stage but the furniture indicating her house is left on stage. The lights come on and a crowd of protesters enter, singing, chanting*

slogans and toyi-toying stage right.[4] *Duke stands on a rostrum and addresses them)*
Duke Viva FRELIMO viva! Viva ANC viva!
Crowd Viva! Viva!
Duke Comrades, our brothers and sisters in Mozambique have now won their independence from the colonial aggressors, the Portuguese. Our comrades in Mozambique have shown us the way. When the bombs and grenades exploded amongst them, they did not give up the struggle. They fought with every drop of their blood. And now they are free. In Angola it is the same story. The South Africans are trembling in their fascist boots. They know that it is South Africa's turn next. It is time comrades that we get rid of these white bastards. It is time for democracy. It is time for us to elect our own leader, for Nelson Mandela to lead our country. It is up to us blacks to earn our respect by taking back what rightfully belongs to us, as our brothers and sisters did in Mozambique. Long live the struggle! *A lutta continhua!* [The struggle continues!] Viva people's power.
Crowd Viva! Viva!
Duke *Phanzi* [Down] with apartheid. *Phanzi!*
Crowd *Phanzi! Phanzi!*
Duke Do you want to be ruled for ever in this beautiful land by the Boers? Brothers and sisters let us unite. Our lives are worthless if we don't have freedom.
(He starts a song in which the others join energetically)
Crowd *Siyabesaba na?* [Are we afraid?]
Cha! Asibesabi! [No! We're not afraid!]
(As the song reaches a climax the policemen enter from different directions. They throw teargas and disperse the crowd. One policeman beats Duke with a baton. Duke falls but escapes from the police. Off stage. When the stage is clear Lydia comes back into her chair. Duke rushes back on stage, bleeding from a head wound.)
Lydia *Ntate ho etsa halang ha!* [Darling, what's happening here?]
Duke Pack up, pack up! No time to waste. We are leaving for Botswana now!
Lydia What!
Duke *(Pointing at the wound)* Maybe this will convince you.
Lydia *Ijo we-e-e. Maburu a kelemile. Ha re tlohe mona ntate.* [No! The Boers are too angry. Let's leave straight away!]
Duke Let's pack up and go!
(They both rush off stage. The lights fade)

SCENE THREE: TWO BATSWANA WOMEN

(The lights come up on the studio. Dora is in the chair, Refilwe watching. Tshepo and Tebogo are in the monitor.)
Dora The South African government insisted that the raid on Gaborone was aimed exclusively at South Africans, 'ANC terrorists' as they called them. This was certainly not what actually happened. Two of the most pitiful

---

4 Toyi Toyi – a high-kicking dance associated with demonstrations against the apartheid regime.

deaths that night were young Batswana women who had nothing to do with South Africa, Eugena Kolobi and Gladys Kesupile. Mrs Tebogo Kebitseng knew Eugena.

Tshepo Tebogo, what sort of woman was Eugena?

Tebogo *Ao*, [Oh!] Eugena, she was a lovely girl. I did night school with her – accounts. She was so hard-working, and never complained. *Gape* [And] she was just too religious. She and her friend, Gladys, they were members of this Watchtower thing…

Tshepo Jehova's Witness?

Tebogo Yes. They were always praying. The last words I heard from her was giving thanks to God for getting her a job at, where was it again… the company didn't last long. Zonza Insurance. She was so excited about getting the job.

Tshepo Why did the South Africans kill these two young women?

Tebogo I really don't know. It was a mystery to me. There was another lady staying with them. Someone said it was something to do with her. I think the whole thing must have been a mistake.

(Flashback to Eugena and Gladys at home having supper.)

Eugena Gladys, *ke ipotsa gore o a bo a le kae Mpho*. [I wonder where Mpho could be?] She stays out late nowadays. *Go setse go nna lefifi ko ntle* [It's getting dark outside.]

Gladys I'm also worried about her, Eugena. *Re tshwanetse go ya le ene ko kerekeng. O tlhoka thuso le tshireletso ya Morena*. [We have to go with her to church. She needs Gods help and protection.]

Eugena *Ke lekile go mo kopa gore re tsamae rotlhe ko kerekeng mme o a gana.* [I have tried to convince her to come with us to church but she is refusing.] This Joseph of hers *o mo itaa tsebe. Fa a mmone o kare o bone kgosi ya gagwe.* [She is distracted by this Joseph of hers. Once she sees him its like she has seen her king.]

Gladys *Se bue jalo* [Don't talk like that] sister. We can't give up on her, not now when she really needs our help. *Batho ba ba tshwanang le ene jaana, ke bone ba tlhokang thuso ya rona thata.* [It is people like her who really need our help.]

(They finish their meal and clear up their dishes, but leave some food for Mpho)

Eugena Okay, we will try talking to her again when she comes. That is *if* she comes.

Gladys *Ke itsile gore o tlaa dumelana le nna.* [I knew you would agree with me.] Jehova loves us all and *ga a latlhe o pe*. [He never rejects anybody.]

Eugena Now that we've finished eating, I can tell you my news.

Gladys *O a reng, Eugena?* [What are you saying Eugena?]

Eugena I've been offered a job at Zonza Botswana Insurance. *Tumelo yame le dithapelo di mpuseditse maduo a mantle. Ke leboga Morena go ba a utlwile dithapelo tsa me. A re mo leboge mme le wena o tlaa segofadiwa ka tiro. Ke tlaa tlhatswa dijana kgantele.* [My prayers and faith have paid off. I thank God for answering my prayers. Let's praise him and he will bless you too with a job. I will wash the dishes later.]

(*They kneel down and start praying. Mpho bursts into the house drunk*)
Mpho (*Laughing*) Heelang bo Marea le Magadalena, le a bo le ntse le rapela Modimo o wa lona. Ke lapisitswe ke go utlwa lefoko Jesu gongwe le gongwe fa ke gatang teng. [Hey, you Maria and Magdalene, you are praying to your God as usual. I am tired of hearing about Jesus in this house! You guys should get a life.] (*Nearly falling on the table*) Bo ausi [Sisters] what's for supper?
Eugena Mpho, why are you doing this to yourself. *Mosadi ga a tshwanela go nwa bojalwa.* [A woman is not supposed to drink beer.] As a child of Jehova…
Mpho (*Interrupting and pushing her away*) Hey, stop talking nonsense and let me have my supper in peace. *O intshwarele mma ka Modimo o o wa gagwe. Ke na le batsadi,* [If you will forgive me with your lectures on God, I have parents] so stop this mumbo-jumbo junk about me being a child of Jehova.
(*Mpho starts eating*)
Gladys *Morena o a go rata* [God loves you] Mpho and he wants you to give your life to him. We are not going to let you ruin your life *ka bojalwa le banna* [on beer and men].
Mpho (*Becoming angry*) *Banna!* [Men!]
Gladys *E bile ke bona gore o tshwanetse go tlogela Joseph yo wa gago. Ga ke mo tshephe. Matlho a gagwe* [And I suggest that you should leave this Joseph of yours, I don't trust him at all. His eyes] spell trouble with a capital T.
Mpho (*Giving up on her food*) *Heela, mosadi,* [Hey, woman] don't even go there. *Joe ene ke wame, ga se wa rona. Ke robala Joe, ke ja Joe e bile ke apara Joe.* [I sleep Joe, I eat Joe, I wear Joe.] What more could a girl want? *O bue ka di sele eseng ka Joe. Fo o gone o nkgata corns, mama.* [You can talk about all other things not Joe, or else you will step on my little toe, my dear.]
Eugena *Mpho, re batla gore o itlhaloganye gore o batlang mo botshelong.* [Mpho we want you to know what you want in life.] You need to find the right direction. Only God can lead you there.
Mpho Listen here, Miss high and mighty, the only direction I need will lead me to Joe. Ooh! I get it. You guys don't want me here. I interfere with your prayer meetings. Don't worry, *ke a tsamaela. Ke tlaa tla go tsaya dilwana tsame nako nngwe. Ke lapitsitswe ke modumo wa lona wa tsatsi le tsatsi.* [I am so sick and tired of your lectures. I am leaving now and for good and I hope you are happy. I will come to collect my things some other time.]
(*Mpho exits angrily*)
Gladys Sister, Eugena, *re lekile fa re lekileng, mme ga a batle go reetsa.* [I guess there is nothing more we could do, we have tried our best and she wouldn't listen so…] *Ke kopa gore re mo rapelele.* [I think we have to pray for her soul.]
(*They kneel down to pray for her as the lights fade*)

SCENE FOUR: THE ARTIST

(*The lights come up on the studio. Tshepo is interviewing Matshidiso, in the monitor. Dora and Refilwe are in their usual places.*)
Dora Probably Thami Mnyele was the most famous of the victims of the 1985 raid on Gaborone. We talked to Matshidiso Sirang, who remembers

meeting Thami when she was only fifteen.
Tshepo So how did you get to know Thami Mnyele?
Matshidiso It was at the Museum.
Tshepo In Gaborone?
Matshidso I was at school in GSS.[5] I was interested in art, and Thami was a wonderful artist. He used to give lessons at the museum. It was 1979 I think. I remember one occasion in particular. We were all excited because there was going to be a visit of a famous South African musical play. What was it now? Okay, *Ipi Tombi*.[6]
(*Flashback. Matshidiso goes off stage and changes into a teenager's clothes. A bunch of students come onto the stage chattering animatedly about Ipi Tombi. Some of them try to imitate one of the songs from the play. Matshidiso joins them. Dora, Thata and Tshepo withdraw.*)
Thami (*Entering, surprised at the noise*) What is wrong, if I may know? *Go rileng*? [What's happening?] Please tell me.
1st student *Ga o itse? Ipi Tombi e e tla.* [You don't know? Ipi Tombi is coming.] (*General shouts of agreement and excitement*)
2nd student Just imagine, *Ipi Tombi* here in Botswana! I can't wait!
Thami (*Clearly upset*) Where did you get all this stuff? (*More to himself than to the students*) No! I must confirm this. MEDU will have to do something about it. (*Back to the students*) Okay, let's start. As I know some of you don't know me, my name is Thami Mnyele. I am an artist, as you can see from all this stuff I am carrying here. *Ke Mozulu* [I am a Zulu] from South Africa. Now let me show you this picture. What can you say about it?
3rd Student *So o itse Ipi Tombi*. [So you know *Ipi Tombi*? Tell us more about it.] *O tlogele ka* art. [Forget about art.]
(*Other students shut him up*)
4th Student Mr Thami, that is a place where there is no grass. Look it is very dry!
5th Student No, Thembi is not telling the truth. This is a hill, suspended on something.
Thami Your answers are very identical and almost the same. This is actually what happens where I come from, RSA. People are suffering, *jaaka le bona. Thaba jaana.* [As you see. This mountain.] Some people are living as if they are holding some mountains *ba sotlega* [in poverty] etcetera. So in art you can do some things which mean a lot. You can say out your general feelings or what you think it's others' concern, just like here. (*The students crowd round to look at more paintings*) I hope you have understood me. While you're still looking, are there any more questions?
3rd Student I understand you are from RSA. Tell us more about *Ipi Tombi*, which will be here in Botswana soon!
(*Several students support the third student's request*)

---

[5] GSS – Gaborone Secondary School.
[6] Ipi Tombi – Simplified Zulu title (meaning 'Where are the girls'), a musical, assembled by Bertha Egnos in 1974 and supported by the apartheid regime for overseas tours.

Thami Actually, I do not have enough time to talk about *Ipi Tombi*. Soon you will see and hear advertisements from MEDU, the organization I work for.[7] They'll be calling for a meeting about *Ipi Tombi*. Make sure you come to that meeting. (*Shouts of support*). Right now I'm in the business of art. And it's about time I gave you papers and you show me how you can draw and paint.
(*More cries of support. Blackout. South African freedom song. When the lights come back on, Thami and Wally Serote*[8] *are on a table, leading the singing. An enthusiastic crowd stands around them, including some of the students from the class.*)

Wally Comrades, I think you all know Thami Mnyele, South Africa's greatest artist. (*Cheers from the crowd*) Many of you have heard about a musical which is supposed to come from South Africa, called *Ipi Tombi*. Thami is going to explain why it is not a good idea for *Ipi Tombi* to be shown in Botswana.
(*There is a reaction of shock and disappointment from the crowd*)

Thami I know many of you like the music from *Ipi Tombi*. (*Shouts of approval from some.*) Of course, there's some very good singing and drumming and dancing. But let me tell you something about this play. It portrays life in the rural bantustans. I don't have to tell you about life in the bantustans. You've seen Mangope's little empire.[9] Tin shacks. Dusty land. Villages with no water or proper toilets. Poverty. While in Zeerust the whites are jumping into their swimming pools and getting their gardener to put water sprinklers on the lawns. (*Shouts of anger against Mangope and the bantustans*) Do you know how *Ipi Tombi* shows the bantustans? Wonderful places where there is an abundance of food, and Africans have nice smiles with teeth as big as mealies (*Demonstrates*), and everyone spends all day going to weddings and doing gumboot dances, and being prosperous and happy. Is there an abundance of food in the bantustans?

Crowd No!

Wally Are people prosperous in the bantustans?

Crowd No!

Thami Are people happy in the bantustans?

Crowd No!

Thami In 1976 when the racist police were shooting Hector Peterson and all the other innocent children of Soweto, do you know what the South African government sent to Europe and America?
(*Shouts of 'Tell us'*) *Ipi Tombi*. They wanted to show the world that South Africa was really fine and everyone is happy. Is this the play you want to see in Botswana?

Crowd No! Never! Send it back to Pretoria!

Thami The democratic forces have called for a cultural boycott on South

---

[7] MEDU – an organization of anti-apartheid artists closely associated with the ANC, with headquarters in Gaborone.
[8] Wally Serote, well-known anti-apartheid poet, who was director of literature for MEDU.
[9] Bantustan – name for a nominally independent state, run as a puppet state by black rulers appointed by the apartheid regime. Bophuthatswana, a Bantustan close to the Botswana border, was run by Chief Lucas Mangope.

African cultural propaganda. Do you want to break that boycott?
Crowd No!
Thami Do you want to support the racists?
Crowd Never!
Impressario (*From the back of the crowd*) So what are we going to replace it with? Many people were looking forward to this play. And Batswana businessmen were going to make money.
(*Some people boo him*)
Thami If you want to bring a good play here, bring any play the racists have tried to ban or harass. Bring *Survival*. Bring *The Hungry Earth*. Bring *Egoli*.[10] Or don't bring anything. Support our own MEDU anti-apartheid play, *Shades of Change*. But whatever you do, don't bring *Ipi Tombi*. Don't let your minds get contaminated by apartheid. (*Crowd support*) Don't let yourselves be mentally colonised! (*More support*) Viva peoples' power!
Crowd Viva!
Thami Viva cultural struggle!
Crowd Viva!
(*Wally Serote starts a freedom song and the crowd joins in. Lights fade as the crowd go off. We come back to the interview with Matshidiso. Thata is behind the camera and Refilwe watching*)
Tshepo So do you think this was the reason the South African security forces wanted Thami killed?
Mtsidiso Maybe. I don't know really. But there could have been other things. His paintings were very good and attracted a lot of attention when he had an exhibition at the museum. And he was always doing posters which the ANC sent to their underground supporters in South Africa.
Dora It was probably this, more than anything else which got Thami Mnyele his death sentence. By the mid-1980s South Africa was desperate. It was completely losing the propaganda battle. Thami's posters made a powerful contribution to the cultural struggle against apartheid.
Refilwe: Thank you, Dora. That's fine.
(*Matshidiso goes off stage. Tshepo comes from the monitor to join the others*)
Tshepo *O a itse*, guys. [You know guys.] These interviews are stressing me. I didn't know people suffered like this.
Dora It makes you think.
Refilwe When you see how those guys like Duke and Thami were so committed to their cause. And look at us now, with our cell phones and MTV and our three-day parties… Anyway, we've got a documentary to make. Tshepo and Thata, you can take five. Dora let me just go over the next bit of the script with you.
(*Tshepo and Thata leave. Dora re-opens her script*)
Dora (*Reading*) One of the first things the South African soldiers did was to demobilize the Botswana Defence Force. One group cut the telephones to

---

[10] *Survival* (Workshop 71), *The Hungry Earth* (Maishe Maponya) and *Egoli* (Matsemela Manaka) were famous anti-apartheid protest plays of the 1970s.

BDF, while another went to the headquarters in Mogoditshane, where they scattered triangular nails on the road to puncture the tyres of any BDF trucks which might try to leave the camp. Some commentators later suggested that the South Africans had actually warned the BDF about the attack, so that the Botswana troupes should not intervene, thus reducing casualties. This, however, is only speculation. (*Breaking away from the text*). Refilwe, am I really going to say this?
Refilwe Why not?
Dora It sounds a bit touchy. Has Mr Williams approved?
Refilwe Hey, that's my headache. Not yours. Let's just carry on with the text.
Dora (*Reading*) One of the other targets of the South African troops, was an unlikely place, the Beat Street disco in Oasis Motel in Tlokweng. The South African troops made this their operational command post.
(*The lights fade*)

SCENE FIVE: OASIS MOTEL

(*Beat Street disco is in full swing at Oasis Motel. People are drinking and dancing. The singing stops but the revellers carry on dancing in mime form.*)
Moitse My man, we better leave. You know how people are at night, especially here in Tlokweng.
Prince *Mare wa phapa, o nagana gore* [But you always think] you are better. Let's enjoy ourselves man! The night is still very, very young. Virgin, *mfana!* [my boy!]
Moitse The problem is I'm very drunk. *E bile* [And] I might own a blackout now! Give me a cigarette. *Ke batla go fua, waitse.* [I want to smoke you know.]
Prince Let's go for a piss out there.
Moitse Good idea, man. Then we should think of leaving.
Prince What's your hurry, *monna*? [man]
(*Moitse and Prince go off stage to urinate. The dancing becomes loud again. The South African soldiers approach the stage through the audience. The dancing continues quietly again.*)
Major (*Addressing his men*) So we make this disco our operational command post. You all know your duties. But first we've got to occupy the disco.
3rd Soldier Do we shoot the *munts* [bush niggers] in the disco?
Major Of course not, stupid. Our orders are to shoot only South Africans. Batswana should be shot only if there's resistance. So after we've taken the disco, *maak sier* [make sure] there's no movement.
3rd Soldier And if they give us shit?
Major Then you can shoot the bastards. Right, let's go.
(*The major leads his men into the disco. There is pandemonium and screaming. The soldiers make everyone stand in a corner without talking. Some of the dancers talk, complaining*).
Major (*Shouting*) Shut up, you *kaffirs* (niggers). *Vas die* [What's the] matter

with you? I will kill all of you. *Jy verstan?* [Do you understand?]
(*Prince and Moitse start moving towards their car. Not understanding the situation*).
Prince *Waitse, nna ke rata* beer. [You know, I love beer.] Just look at me, now!
Moitse *Nna, ke tshaba di-trink.* [I fear them drinks]
Prince *Monna,* [Man] I am still strong, I can still drink a case.
Moitse You're crazy. Thin as you are.
Prince Now where are you going?
Moitse *Ao, bra* [Hey, brother] I told you, I'm going home.
Prince (*Trying to pull Moitse towards the bar*) Ah, just one for the ditch!
(*The South African soldiers notice Prince and Moitse*)
3rd Soldier (*Pointing a gun*) Hey you, over there! Stop! Don't move an inch!
Prince Ah, who do you think you are? A *tsotsi* [thief] or what?
Moitse Who are you to stop me going home? *Voetsek!* [Fuck off!] This is a free country.
(*Prince and Moitse start moving to their cars*)
3rd Soldier I said stop! (*Prince and Moitse take no notice*) Captain, they're refusing orders.
Captain The fools think they're clever.
(*The captain takes a hand-grenade, removes the pin and throws it. The two men scream. Moitse collapses on the floor. Prince drags himself away off stage.*)
Major (*Running to the scene*) What happened?
Captain Some local *kaffirs* tried to raid our command post. I hit them with a grenade. I think they may not be dead.
Major It's okay, leave them. But if any ambulance tries to come near to pick them up, shoot at it. We don't want any tricks.
(*The lights fade. Dora takes up her position*)
Dora Both Moitse and Prince survived the mortar and grenade attacks, but Moitse was critically injured. Word came to Princess Marina hospital that there had been shooting in Tlokweng. An ambulance team set off for the Oasis. Before they arrived, however, they were met by South African soldiers, manning a road block, who made the ambulance driver abandon his vehicle and walk back to the hospital.

SCENE SIX: THE MASSACRES

(*The five households to be attacked set themselves up, as if preparing for bed, in various parts of the stage and auditorium. At the back of the auditorium the South African soldiers sing a military song. The follow spotlight comes on Dora, as the song fades*)
Dora But for the majority of families in Gaborone on that cold winter night of June 14th, everything seemed normal. Most people did not know what was going on at the Oasis. (*Dora approaches Duke's house. Peter runs into the arms of Lydia while Duke watches. They freeze*) By 1985 Duke Machobane had been a teacher in Botswana for many years. A few days before the 14th his wife's sister's son, Peter, was brought to stay with them for some time in their house in Broadhurst. Duke and his wife went to bed. Peter slept in another room. (*The Machobanes unfreeze and go to bed. Dora walks to the Pahle's house,*

where George, Lindi, Livy and Joe are standing. The follow spot accompanies her) Not far away in Maru a Pula, another family settled down for the night. George Pahle, a South African refugee, was a taxi driver; he drove his own combi every day on the Lobatse route. After the raid the South Africans accused him of masterminding the Carlton Centre bombing, in order to justify the raid. Some months later an altogether different person was to be arrested and convicted of the bombing. George's wife Lindi had a degree in social work from the University of Botswana. She was a social welfare officer in Serowe, and was well-known for her work championing the youth of Botswana. That weekend she came to see her husband in Gaborone. (*George and Lindi hold hands*) Staying in the same house was George's brother, Livy who was a well-known jazz pianist who often jammed with Hugh Masekela and Tshepo Tshola at the Blue Note.[11] Their cousin, Joe Malate, was also visiting the household. (*They all go to bed. Dora walks to Eugena's house, where Eugena and Gladys are praying*) Eugena and Gladys, as always, prayed before they went to bed. They had a special place in their prayers for their friend, Mpho. (*Eugena and Gladys go to bed. Dora walks to Mike's house. Mike is standing there, with Ahmed and Mrs Gehr nearby*) Michael Hamlyn was a young white South African. During the late 1970s he had been called up to join the South African army to fight in Angola. His conscience would not allow him to fight in this immoral war. He ran away to Botswana, where he became involved in the cultural struggle against apartheid. He joined the University of Botswana where he studied Sociology. In June 1985 he had just finished his final year at UB. He had just set up a small company with a Somali friend, Ahmed, using a computer to start a data-base on Batswana social indicators. Michael, Ahmed and Ahmed's Dutch wife, all lived together in a small house in Extension 9. After Michael's death the University awarded Michael Hamlyn a posthumous first class degree in Social Science. (*Mike and Mr and Mrs Gehr go to bed. Dora walks to Thami's house. Thami is painting*) Thami Mnyele was staying on his own in a small house in Tlokweng. His room was mostly taken up with his painting materials, his easel, his brushes, his canvases, and his silk-screen printing equipment. (*Thami goes to bed. Dora goes to the side of the downstage right area*) From their operational headquarters at the Oasis Motel, several platoons of South African soldiers spread out across the city to begin their work of destruction.

(*First platoon approaches the house of Duke Machobane. They kick down the door and enter*)

1st Soldier Check all the rooms for those bastards.
2nd Soldier (*Entering bedroom*) He's here, sir.
1st Soldier Shoot him!
(*The Machobanes scream*)
Duke Kill me, you fascists! A thousand more will spring from my blood.

---

[11] Hugh Masekela, well known jazz trumpeter. Tshepo Tsola, leader of popular Lesotho jazz group, Sankomota.

1st soldier Shoot!
(*The 2nd soldier shoots Duke dead. Lydia screams even more*)
Lydia *Jona weeee. Ke tla etsa jwang, ba bolaile monna wa ka weeee!* [Oh! What am I going to do? They have killed my husband!]
2nd Soldier (*Surprised*) *E he, sesi o mosotho?* [So sister you are a Sotho?]
Lydia (*Sobbing*) *E ya ntate, ke ngwa na wa moshoeshoe.* [Yes, Sir, I am Moshoeshoe's daughter.][12]
1st soldier (*Furious*) What are you saying? Shoot her. Why are you wasting time?
2nd Soldier She's not a South African, sir. She's from Maseru.
1st Soldier Okay, leave her.
(*Disturbed by the noise Peter moves sleepily towards the bedroom*)
1st Soldier (*Hearing the noise*) Who's that?
(*The first soldier swings round and shoots Peter*)
Lydia (*Screaming*) You bastards! Brutes! Cowards!
2nd Soldier It's a child.
1st Soldier Tough. He got in the way. They never told us this terrorist had kids. Let's go.
(*The scene freezes. The 3rd and 4th soldiers approach George Pahle's house*)
3rd Soldier Remember, we shoot everything that moves. There should be no survivors.
(*They burst inside with guns blazing. They kill George and Lindi. Livy hides under the bed. Joe tries to get into a wardrobe*)
4th Soldier I think there's one hiding in the wardrobe.
3rd Soldier Just shoot.
(*They kill Joe and then retreat. Livy comes from under the bed, his face a mask of horror at the massacre. The scene freezes. The 5th and 6th soldiers approach Eugena's house*)
6th Soldier The neighbours have opened the door.
5th Soldier (*To neighbours*) Get back inside your houses. Keep your doors closed. If you do as you're told you won't be hurt. If you come out we'll kill you.
(*Eugena and Gladys wake up upon hearing the noise*)
Gladys What's that noise?
Eugena I heard voices telling us to stay inside.
Gladys Could it be crooks?
Eugena Maybe. Let's pray to Jehova to deliver us.
(*They kneel down to pray*)
6th Soldier They're all back inside now.
5th Soldier Let's finish off this ANC bastard
(*The soldiers hurl grenades through the window. The women scream and collapse. The two soldiers burst into the house*)
6th Soldier That bastard isn't even here. It's just women.
5th Soldier We've done our duty.

---

[12] Moshoeshoe – King of the Basotho, 1823–1870, commonly known as father of the Sotho nation.

(The scene freezes. The 7th and 8th soldiers approach Mike's house)
8th Soldier Is this the place?
7th Soldier *Ja* [Yes]. This *kaffirboetie* [nigger-lover] thinks he can run away from our army.
8th Soldier Fucking traitor!
7th Soldier He didn't want to shoot kaffirs.
8th Soldier Fucking *moffie!* [queer]
7th Soldier Let's show him what he's been missing.
(They burst into the house and find Ahmed and his wife)
8th Soldier Where's Hamlyn?
Mrs. Gehr We don't know.
7th Soldier Stupid!
(The soldiers shoot Ahmed and his wife. Mike wakes up and goes into the Gehrs' room)
Mike What do you want?
7th Soldier We want you, Hamlyn.
Mike *(Noticing the slaughtered Gehrs)* What have you done? You brutes. These are innocent people. They're not even South Africans. Ahmed's a Somali, and this woman is Dutch.
8th Soldier That's their fault for living with a *kaffirboetie*.
Mike You fools. You should be back in your *dorp* [small town] playing rugby.
7th Soldier Shut up you traitor.
(The 8th soldier kills Mike. The scene freezes. The 9th and 10th soldiers approach Thami's house. The 10th soldier throws in a teargas grenade. Thami starts coughing and runs out of the house. The 9th soldier shoots Thami in the back, and he drops down dead. The two soldiers enter the house)
10th Soldier There's nobody else here.
9th Soldier Shoot the paintings.
10th Soldier Shoot the paintings?
9th Soldier I said shoot the fucking painting!
10th Soldier Why?
9th Soldier Because these are the posters he was smuggling into the country to make people hate our government. So shoot the motherfuckers!
(The 10th soldier shoots the paintings and the print equipment)
9th Soldier Now let's go.
(All the scenes unfreeze. All the soldiers gather together and jog in step, singing a song of triumph through the auditorium till they are all off. The lights fade)

SCENE SEVEN: CONSEQUENCES OF THE RAID

(Dora, Refilwe, Thata and Tshepo continue working on the film)
Dora For ordinary Batswana who witnessed the raid, there was shock and disbelief. One of witnesses to the deaths of Gladys and Eugena, called Lynn Mmupi, saw innocent neighbours caught up in the violence.
(Refilwe flicks on the remote)

Lynn It was in the early hours of the morning. I heard men shouting loud, 'Open the door! Open the bloody door.' They were knocking the door of the house. Then again 'Switch off your lights and stay in your houses.' I think they had a loudhailer. Then there was shooting, a lot of shooting and screams and an explosion. When they had driven off I opened the door. I was going to run into my neighbour's place. Then I heard the little girl screaming to me because she knew me. 'Auntie, please help me, I'm here.' I thought, 'Oh, my god, I can't leave her!' But I couldn't go inside because of the flames. So I ran to my neighbours and they got her and took her to the hospital. We neighbours used our own hoses to put out the flames.
(Refilwe flicks off the remote)

Dora Some ordinary Batswana were angry at the lack of action by the security forces. However, as soon as the South African troops had re-crossed into South African territory, the Botswana security forces went into action. The wounded were taken to hospital, the dead to the mortuary. Both the badly injured Batswana survivors, Moitse Botsholo and Prince Maupane, eventually recovered from their injuries. Military intelligence examined the target buildings for forensic evidence. Altogether eight houses and two offices were attacked. Four houses were completely demolished and others damaged. At the Solidarity News Service the soldiers had sprayed equipment in a frenzy of shooting. They destroyed a typewriter, photocopier, plate-maker, telex-machine, computer and computer discs. They also stole another computer. Reaction from the international community was swift. A special meeting of the United Nations General Assembly was called. Botswana's Minister of External affairs, Dr Chiepe, addressed the assembly.

Dr Chiepe The South African raid of 14th June was an unprovoked act of aggression violating the territorial integrity of Botswana and the national sovereignty of Botswana and its people.

Dora The General Assembly agreed with Dr Chiepe, and issued a statement condemning South Africa for its aggression. The United States recalled its ambassador from Pretoria for a time as a protest. The South Africans were in no way repentant. They justified their actions as self-defence. President Botha said:

Botha I am not prepared to lead white South Africans and other minority groups on a road to abdication and suicide.

Dora Within Botswana there were considerable repercussions. Many people gathered outside police stations calling for spies and others plotting against Botswana to be punished. Many people used the media to express their outrage. T.J. Sefawantsho, for example, in a prophetic vein, said:

Sefawantsho South Africa should desist from barbarous acts of death, sorrow and apprehension to neighbouring countries. A day shall come when the white minority regime in South Africa shall crumble like a pack of cards. And the sorrow will be felt by the other side.

Dora One important action of the government was to identify some important South African refugees, which it considered at risk from renewed South African aggression, and to send those refugees to other countries like

Zambia or Tanzania for their own protection. The ANC was obviously worried about the possibility of Botswana turning against ANC cadres altogether, as happened in Swaziland. The ANC issued a statement to this effect.

ANC Spokesperson The Gaborone raids were an exercise in overkill, aimed at alienating the Botswana community from the South African exiled community.

Dora One of the most interesting debates arising from the raids was about the Botswana security forces. Major General Merafhe was clearly dismayed by the rumours circulating in Botswana that the BDF had collaborated with the South African defence forces.

Merafhe We are terribly upset and very frustrated.

Dora When people asked why the BDF was helpless in the face of the South African onslaught, firing not a single bullet in response, the Major General said:

Merafhe BDF cannot be on a constant alert basis.

Dora Several people called for enhanced security in Botswana. The mayor of Gaborone, Paul Rantao said:

Paul Rantao The nation of Botswana, all political parties, churches and the people of Botswana must take practical steps to ensure that Botswana is safe for Batswana and all members of the international community who live in Botswana.

Dora Several people expressed concern that the mood of hysteria in the country might lead to the unnecessary expansion of the army and the introduction of harsh security measures. An editorial in *Mmegi* on 20th June 1985, expressed these concerns.

Mmegi The solution does not lie in spending more money on an expanded army and expanded police and the special branch. We do not need more and more secret agents or any other kind of solution that threatens our democracy… We need a citizen's volunteer army and all party security conferences.

Dora The embarrassment felt by the BDF owing to their inaction over the raids had important consequences. Many people see it as the decisive factor in the controversial expansion of the army during the subsequent decade and a half. (*Breaking off*). *Bona, mma,* [You see madam] this is where the script gets very touchy, *ga ke re.* [in my opinion]

Refilwe In what way?

Dora All this stuff about the BDF chewing an ever increasing chunk of the national budget, the lack of transparency, the power of the military intelligence. Some of the workers in the station are getting worried in case this all gets out of hand.

Refilwe You'd better let me do the worrying. In fact, Mr Williams wants to see me about all this. I've got an appointment to see him on Monday.

Dora I think some of the others who are involved in the film want to talk to you before then.

(*Lights fade*)

SCENE EIGHT: REFILWE TALKS TO WORKERS

(*The workers gather together in the studio to confront Refilwe*)
Thata Hey, Refilwe, *lekgoa la re mathata ke eng? Fa a ne a shibitse jaana.* (Refilwe what's up with the white man? He was looking even more red) Are we in trouble or what?
Refilwe Okay, ladies, there is a problem yes, but do not get discouraged. Mr Williams wants us to tone down our documentary. *A re* [He says] we shouldn't say anything about this army thing. *O bua bo hee* [He says] it's a sensitive issue, what not and…
Thata What if he is right? *Le nna* [As for me] I don't see how the army should be included in the documentary. BDF *kante yone e amana jang le the 1985 raids.* [I don't see how BDF was connected to the raid.] *Ga gona mathatha for you ka gore* [You may not have a problem because] you've got a degree, but some of us sweated for these jobs.
Refilwe *Kana* [But] I also want this job, just as much as you want yours.
Tshepo *Gape* [And] Mr Williams being the station manager, must have a reason for saying it's a sensitive issuue.
Refilwe Exactly, he is the station manager and is only concerned with his own welfare. Don't you think the public need to be informed about these things? Remember this, *ka* [in] 1985, we had only a handful of soldiers and the numbers were kept constant even after the raids. This was the time that we needed a huge army to alleviate the problem. And what is happening right now? Every month *go nna le diadvert, re batla bo private, re batla dipilot* [BDF advertises for the recruitment of more privates, pilots] and what not. What are all these people doing? Every year the BDF is investing in more expensive vehicles, posh houses and messes. There's fantastic sports facilities for the soldiers, squash courts, tennis courts and immaculate football pitches. But no recreational facilities for ordinary youths. No wonder they're turning to crime. There are three swimming pools at the BDF camp, but not a single public swimming pool in Gaborone for the people.
Thata *Utlwa fela gore o bua dilo tse di sa amaneng gope le documentary ya rona.* [Just listen to yourself. You are talking about things that have nothing to do with our documentary.] What if the board gets upset. We might get fired for insubordination. This public that we say we want to inform won't be anywhere near to help us get other jobs. We don't want this to happen to us, or do we? We all have families to feed and care for. Just think of that.
Dora I agree. This army thing is very sensitive.
Refilwe Ladies, listen here. *Kana* (But) if we avoid sensitive issues, we are going to have nothing to report. Everything that affects lives of people is sensitive. So *a re tsweleleng, yoo* Mr Williams *o tlaa ithomiwa ke nna ka sebele.* [So let us proceed, I will personally talk to Mr Williams.]
Tshepo *Ga ke gane,* [I agree] but I feel that we have enough information on the lives of the people who were affected by the raids. We can still come up with a good documentary without including the army expansion.

Refilwe (*Becoming animated*) I know what I'm trying to do. *Ka re re a tswelela ka kgang ya sesole sa rona.* [We are continuing with the issue of our army.] BDF is just a big white elephant *e e sa direng le fa e le sepe* [which is absolutely doing nothing]. We are the tax payers. Our money goes to BDF for nothing. They never go to war 'cause there is no war. Or are anticipating war. It's only when there are floods *ko bo* [in places like] Mahalapye that less than a hundred go to help. The rest *ba dira eng kana?* [what are they doing?] Everyone *yo o yang ko.* BDF *o reka koloi ka madi a rona* [They own cars bought with our tax money] within two months. We are including the BDF issue and that's final.

Dora *Jaanong o intsha Hitilara.* [Now you are becoming Hitler.] You are forgetting we are a team. All our ideas matter.

Refilwe Sorry. The thing is you guys do no want to understand. *Re tshwanetse re ikakanyetse. Fa re nna ra reetsa se makgoa a se buang ga rena go tswelela. Puso ya ga mmamosadinyana e fedile.* [We have to start making our decisions. If we keep on listening to these whites we won't progress. British colonialism is over.]

Tshepo Okay, let us just do it. *Re tla bona gore re tlaa felela kae.* [And see how far this will take us.]

Thata *Ee o a bua le fa gone...* [I agree with what you are saying even though...]

Dora *Nyaa a re se ngoseleng.* [No let us not be fearful] We will do it.

Refilwe Bravo, ladies. This is the spirit that I want. *Le tlaa bona,* [You will see] everything is going to be okay.

(*Refilwe goes off stage as the lights fade*)

SCENE NINE: BERNARD & REFILWE

(*Bernard is on the phone in his office when Refilwe enters*)

Bernard It's unbearably hot here. (*To Refilwe*) Come in. (*Waving her to a seat*) Listen Mike. I'm going to have to cut you short ... I don't know yet. I have to see the project off its feet first ... I might fly over next month for a week ... Bye and take care.

Refilwe You wanted to see me Mr Williams.

Bernard Yes. I thought I told you to tone down your script?

Refilwe I did change it, Mr Williams.

(*Bernard pulls out a copy of the documentary 'rushes' from his drawer*)

Bernard Yes. You changed it to make it even more confrontational.

Refilwe Confrontational?

Bernard All those sensitive issues about the military are still there. Even more blatant than before!

Refilwe If I have to tone down the script too much, it will lose its impact, and won't portray the message I want...

Bernard Listen here, my girl. This documentary as it stands will cause havoc. How many times do I have to remind you that this is a government TV station?

Refilwe Correction. It's a public TV station.

Bernard A public TV station almost fully funded by government.
Refilwe There's a difference.
Bernard You cannot criticise the government and its departments on its own TV station. That's a simple fact of life.
Refilwe Why not, if it's in the public interest?
Bernard Because I run this TV station, not you.
Refilwe But, sir…
Bernard No 'buts'. I'm sick of having to call you over trivial issues, inappropriate to this station.
Refilwe Mr Williams, if you censor this programme…
Bernard I never said 'censor'…
Refilwe We will be denying the people their right to know.
Bernard Their right to know, my foot. Listen to yourself. You talk like a primary school kid…
Refilwe But what you are asking me to do is unethical. At least let me finish the documentary and then we can look at how to edit any passages that might strike a raw nerve.
Bernard No! I cannot take that chance. If the board hears about this there might be hell to pay. Just do as I say, period.
Refilwe Can we at least talk about this in a rational manner?
Bernard Rational? I tell you to suspend filming and you go ahead anyway! You call that rational?
Refilwe Mr Williams, please calm down.
Bernard Calm down! My job is on the line and you tell me to calm down! Hell, no! I did not come here to be told what to do by my employees who don't have a clue about TV production.
Refilwe You should not talk like that Mr Williams. In our culture, respect for other people is vital. How do you expect me to respect you if you behave like that?
Bernard I'm not here to be respected. I came to do a job. Right now my job is to tell you to stop filming.
Refilwe I've already shot so much and done so much recce work. It'll be a waste of government money.
Bernard It'll be an even bigger waste later on when the whole project is scrapped.
Refilwe I can't believe I'm hearing this. What you're saying is the opposite of what I was taught about media responsibility.
Bernard Well, blame your government, not me. Now, please go and do something useful, not digging up ghost stories which are bound to cause chaos in your peaceful country.
Refilwe Mr Williams…
Bernard (*Banging on the table*) Refilwe, the meeting is over. There's nothing further to discuss. Consider this an official warning. Now please, leave my office.
(*Refilwe, seething with anger, leaves. Bernard puts the tape back in the drawer. The lights fade*)

SCENE TEN: THE WORKERS CONFRONT REFILWE

(*The workers are waiting anxiously for Refilwe to report back about her meeting with Bernard*)

Secretary *Bathong* [People], can somebody tell me what is all going to happen, or what is the meeting all about? *Kana* [Since] I haven't been around. *O aitse leave e, e ncostile.* [I have lost a lot because of this leave.]

Clerk *Nna tota,* [As for me] I'm getting bored. I don't like meetings which are directionless. The writings are on the wall. Why can't she stop all this. I've got a lot to do. *Tiro yame ya sufferer waitse!* [My work is suffering!] Productivity, my dear.

Tshepo I knew it was you. (*Pointing*) You think you are the only one working. What did you take us for? You think we are happy to be here? This is our TV station, not just for you and Bernard.

Secretary *Jaanong, go rileng neh, Tshepho?* [So what's matter Tshepho?]

Tshepo *Waitse mmantseanenyane yo wa phapha!* [This young woman is too sure of herself you know.] We are waiting for Refilwe. This one is busy misleading others, telling them how her work is pending. *Gongwe e bile ke* [Maybe you are even a] 'dead wood'.[13] Who is not working here? Just tell me one of them!

Photographer Ah! This one (*Pointing to the clerk*) will and can never be a 'dead wood' she is a dead seedling. *Rona mma re lekanya madi le tiro.* (*We work for what we get*). Understand baby?

(*As people are laughing at this Refilwe arrives in a hurry looking exhausted and frustrated with her handbag tightly clutched under her arm*)

Refilwe Ladies and gentlemen, I would like to apologise for keeping you.

Heckler 1 *Mosadi a o tlaa bua gore o re phuthetseng? Kana re itlhoboge.* [Lady are you going to say why you have assembled us here or not?]

Tshepo Please give her a chance. *Ke a kopa.* [Please.]

Refilwe As you all know that we have been working hard for our documentary.

Photographer *Moo! Re a itse* [That we know], Refilwe. Stop wasting time and tell us about Bernard, *kana gatwe mang? Ene yoo!* [Or whatever his name is!]

Secretary *Ijoo* [Hey], don't say that in front of some of us. (*Looking at the clerk*) *Bompimpi cheri ya gagwe* [His girlfriend] is right here and will tell him.

Refilwe Thank you, can we continue, please. Like I was saying our big boss, Bernard, is refusing to grant us permission to continue with the documentary film, so I have decided to give up.

Heckler 1 *Le wena, monna, Refilwe.* [I think he served you right.] What do you think?

Photographer Myself I've got some twins, where do you think I could possibly go to work after being sacked by TV Bots? *Kana* [But] there is only one TV station, and my qualifications are only the TV and nothing else.

---

[13] Refers to a campaign run by the Productivity Centre in Botswana to weed out unproductive civil servants.

Refilwe *Jaanong* [So] I would like to hear from you what is the way forward.
Tshepo All our efforts. This man is frustrating all our efforts. Anyway, Refilwe, *se nkganang se nthula morwalo. Wena? GBC e teng* [our Setswana proverb says if you try to do something and circumstances doesn't allow you, the best thing to do is to abandon it as that may be a blessing. Anyway GBC is available.]
Dora Hard luck, Refilwe.
Thata Next time!
Refilwe Thanks comrades, let the spirit of cooperation be lifted up. (*With disgust*) Bernard *Ene*! [him!]
Clerk (*Sighing with relief*) That was a relief. I wonder how many calls I have missed! This work is many.
Tshepo *Heela, motho ke wena* [Hei you!], rather say 'challenging' to reach our standard. You talk as if you never went to school. Anyway, *tsamaya,* [go] and tell him all what we have said.
Secretary *Ijoo*! [oops!] I nearly forgot *gatwe o nwa lethe le* Bernard [that you are supposed to be having an affair with Bernard].
(*Tshepo and the secretary kiss each other, in a parody of the relationship*)
Tshepo *Batho, tlhe ga ba tshabe* AIDS! [Some people don't even fear AIDS!]
Photographer Jealous, *bafana* [guys], jealous!
(*The meeting breaks up, leaving Refilwe, Dora and Tshepo*)
Refilwe *Waitse* [You know], I don't know what is wrong with me.
Dora *Nnyaa* [No], sweetie, take things as they come.
Refilwe You know I haven't given up on this documentary yet. It's just that time wasn't ripe to push things today. *Ke tlaa bona kwa pele.* [I will see in future]
Tshepo Good luck, call me, whenever you need help.
(*Dora and Tshepo leave. Refilwe sits down in the chair exhausted, facing the monitor. There is no break between this and the next scene*)

SCENE ELEVEN: GHOSTS

(*Refilwe, still staring blankly at the empty TV monitor, turns away lost in thought. When she looks back, the ghost of Eugena is there*)
Refilwe (*Stunned*) Who are you?
Eugena I'm Eugena Kolobi.
Refilwe Don't be crazy. Eugena Kolobi died 15 years ago.
Eugena That's right.
Refilwe Where's that remote? (*She finds the remote and tries to switch off the monitor*) Hey, you're supposed to switch off. Go away! (*She looks away and then back again*) Still there? (*Talking to herself*) I must be tired. I'm seeing things that aren't there. This documentary's stressing me out. (*Talking to the screen again*) What do you want?
Eugena I want to help you.
Refilwe With what?
Eugena Your decision about the film.

Refilwe How can you help?

Eugena This resistance to Mr Williams, do you think you can achieve anything?

Refilwe Why not?

Eugena Innocent people might get hurt.

Refilwe People always get hurt in a struggle.

Eugena There's no problem if *you* get hurt. That's your decision. But what about Dora and Tshepo and Thata and the others?

Refilwe I've consulted them.

Eugena They don't really understand. They could get the sack too.

Refilwe What's it got to do with you?

Eugena Because I was also an innocent bystander in 1985. I didn't know anything about the ANC or AK45s or grenades. I was simply dedicated to Yehova. And just because of Mpho's boyfriend, Gladys and I were killed.

Refilwe That goes to show no one can be a bystander.

Eugena No. It goes to show that those who struggle for human things instead of Yehova's are selfish. They don't care who gets hurt in the process.

Refilwe (*Worried by this idea and turning from the screen*) Don't say that. (*Eugena disappears from the screen, as Refilwe talks to herself*) What if Eugena is right? (*Looking back at the blank screen*) Hey, Eugena. Where have you gone? I want to ask… (*to herself*) I'm going mad. Seeing ghosts now. (*She looks away again. Thami Mnyele comes on to the screen. Refilwe notices him*) Oh no, not another! Who are you?

Thami I'm Thami Mnyele.

Refilwe The artist? Another ghost! And what do *you* want?

Thami I want to encourage you, Refilwe. You're doing the right thing. Why do you think the South African racists killed me?

Refilwe Because of your art. You should see my documentary. It's all there.

Thami And after they killed me?

Refilwe They shot your paintings.

Thami My little posters. They were my children. They fired round after round of bullets into canvas and paint. Why do you think they did that?

Refilwe Because your art was dangerous to the regime.

Thami More dangerous than bombs and bullets. Art can cross borders so easily, it can be reproduced, it can lay seeds in people's minds and grow like a forest.

Refilwe And why are you telling me all this?

Thami Because you're also an artist.

Refilwe No I'm not. I'm a TV producer.

Thami A TV documentary is just like a painting. It's art.

Refilwe Maybe. But things are different now. You were struggling against apartheid. And after your death the ANC won. For your information, in case they didn't tell you up in heaven, since 1994 the ANC have been in power. Mission accomplished.

Thami Things are different, but also the same.

Refilwe What do you mean?

Thami Apartheid has gone, but imperialism hasn't gone.
Refilwe How?
Thami The economic power is still in the hands of the northern metropoles, mostly the same Western nations that gave secret support to apartheid.
Refilwe What's that got to do with me? That's Thabo Mbeki's problem.
Thami Your struggle with Mr Williams. It's an extension of my struggle.
Refilwe How?
Thami Imperialism is so strong because it keeps changing its face. In 1985 it was easy to see imperialism – you could aim your gun or your paint brush at the Bothas and the General Malans.
Refilwe And now?
Thami The imperialists have become even more clever. They talk about 'grass-roots development'. They sing the praises of 'accountability' 'participation', 'African Renaissance'. While all the while they're sucking African wealth and labour, and finding ways to control our minds. Your struggle is just as important as mine. You must help Batswana to decolonize their minds and souls. You can't give up now.
Refilwe (*Turning away*) But it's so hard. (*Noticing the empty screen*) Thami, where have you gone? I haven't finished with you yet. Come back! I'm so confused!
(*Lights fade, but not to black out. Refilwe stretches back, exhausted, closing her eyes. When she opens her eyes, Eugena is back in the monitor*)
Eugena Refilwe, I'm going to show you how all these problems might end.
(*Eugena leaves, the lights come up to full and Refilwe wakes up from her 'trance'. There is no break before the next scene*)

SCENE TWELVE: ENDING (A)

(*Thata enters the studio with the master tape of the documentary*)
Refilwe *O a reng*, Thata? [What are you saying Thata?] You've brought the master tape?
Thata Yes, it's here. I was just about to take it to Mr Ferguson.
Refilwe No, I'll keep it.
Thata But, Refilwe, the procedure is…
Refilwe Procedure?
Thata You know… Mr Fergson's supposed to check all the master tapes to ensure that they're broadcast quality, before we can make any copies.
Refilwe I know, Thata, but for the time being this is how I want things. I'll keep it myself.
Thata But you're not trained to check it for quality. It's an engineering job.
Refilwe I know all that, Thata. You'll just have to trust me. I'll make sure the quality is checked.
Thata (*Handing over the tape*) I hope you know what you're doing.
(*Bernard enters, unobtrusively*)
Refilwe I know. It's just that this tape … it's becoming a bit of a hot potato.
Bernard 'Hot potato'? That's a good way of putting it.

(*Refilwe and Thata are shocked by his entry*)
Bernard (*To Thata*) Okay you can leave. Refilwe and I need to discuss this. (*As Thata begins to leave*) By the way, what's your name?
Thata Thatayaone Modiri, sir.
Bernard Okay, you can go now. (*Thata leaves*) So, Refilwe, what do you intend to do with this hot potato of yours?
(*He approaches Refilwe as if to snatch the tape from her. Refilwe places it behind her back. Bernard hesitates and retreats. Refilwe brings the tape into sight again*)
Refilwe I intend to persuade you to let us broadcast it.
Bernard After all that I've said? You're very optimistic.
Refilwe Not really, Mr Williams, just very determined.
Bernard You know, Refilwe, I feel sorry for you in a way. I admire this stupid determination of yours. It's unusual. Of course, it's already ruined your TV career. I'll make sure, somehow or other, you are kicked out of Botswana Television. And don't think the others will protest. Once they see their jobs are threatened, they'll toe the line.
Refilwe We'll see about that.
Bernard But this determination of yours, it's going to make it difficult for you to fit in anywhere.
Refilwe What do you mean?
Bernard All this idealism of yours. (*Imitating Refilwe*) 'The people's right to know'.
Refilwe Is there anything wrong with that?
Bernard It's all crap.
Refilwe You disgusting old cynic. Don't you realize it's a fundamental human right enshrined in the United Nations Charter?
Bernard Of course it is, and it's a wonderful ideal. But...in modern Botswana...in real life...
Refilwe It's crap.
Bernard Absolutely.
Refilwe It's fine for you to come here and say these rights are too much altruistic. But when you get back to UK – the people's right to information is guaranteed. But we natives are too primitive to appreciate such rights, is it?
Bernard That's not the point. The British people have no more access to accurate media information than the people here have. Perhaps even less. They spend all their time watching rubbish about the Royal Family.
Refilwe But at least...
Bernard Let me tell you how I found out about media so-called transparency. Just a few years ago, when I was already an experienced producer, I was still very idealistic. Not much different from you. I was doing a documentary on Bosnia for BBC Channel 4. We'd managed to get some incredible shots of Bosnian civilians massacred by Serbs in Sebrenica – more than twenty bodies laid out in a row. I got the camera to track along the line of bodies. (*Demonstrating*) When we finished editing in London, I showed the documentary to my boss at the Beeb. Do you know what he did? He freeze-framed the shot of the massacre. 'You can't show that', he said. 'Why not?' I

asked. He hummed and hahed a bit. 'It's a sort of policy. If it's Liberia or Ruanda or Sri Lanka, you can show as many bodies as you want. But if it's Northern Ireland or Bosnia, it's twelve bodies max.' I couldn't believe what I was hearing. We looked at each other in silence. He didn't need to spell it out. British viewers could see hundreds of black bodies, but for white bodies, there's a rationing system – no more than twelve.

Refilwe Why didn't you protest?

Bernard To whom?

Refilwe To whoever wrote the policy, the rule-book or whatever it is.

Bernard No-one wrote the rule-book. That's the cleverness of the system. It's an unwritten rule. An understanding between so-called gentlemen.

Refilwe A pack of lies. So you changed your film?

Bernard I squealed at first, but in the end I had to change to get the thing screened. I cut the shot when I reached the twelfth body. And I'm afraid that, Refilwe, is how the global media operate, a complex network of unwritten rules. There are some things you do, and some things you don't do.

Refilwe And I've just done something you don't do.

Bernard Exactly.

Refilwe And principles can go hang.

Bernard You're learning fast.

Refilwe (*Disgusted*) If you can't beat them, join them.

Bernard Very fast. You see, Refilwe, thirty or forty years ago, your kind of principles might have made some sense – the time of Lumumba and Nyerere and the first flush of African emancipation. But now? In the global village? Botswana's just a tiny part of a big media empire. Ted Turner's CNN and Murdoch's CBS. These are the people who tell us how to think. If you try to run away from Botswana government control, who will you run to? Private enterprise? That's worse.

Refilwe How?

Bernard The political and commercial lobbies, the advertisers, the invisible strings. This is the new imperialism. Indirectly the Turners and Murdochs will tell you what to think. At least your government claims to have the interests of the Batswana people at heart. Do you think private enterprise has any interest? It's just the bottom line and don't rock the boat for them. Better the devil you know.

(*Refilwe looks depressed and subdued. Bernard takes the tape from her without any resistance. He starts to leave*)

Bernard Oh, by the way, Refilwe, I think I've changed my mind about sacking you. You might turn out to be a very useful member of the team.

(*He continues his journey off stage and the lights fade almost, but not completely to blackout*)

SCENE THIRTEEN: ENDING (B)

(*Thami appears on the monitor and talks to Refilwe*)

Thami It doesn't have to end like that. Listen to me, Refilwe. I'm going to

show you a different possible ending to your problems.
(Thami fades from the screen. The staff enter excitedly. Refilwe stands on the table to address a general meeting of staff)

Refilwe I think all of you are aware that in the last two weeks I have been involved in a difference of opinion with Mr Williams. I don't need to bore you by telling the whole story again. The basic issues are simple. Mr Williams thinks that the recently completed documentary that I directed, the one about the 1985 raids by South African troops upon Gaborone should not be screened. He says that remarks, which we make in the film about the expansion of the BDF after the raids are, to use his words, 'inflammatory'.

Heckler 1 O a reng? [What do you mean?]

Refilwe Meaning that the government, or the BDF commanders, or ex BDF commanders, I'm not quite sure who, might not like what we have said, especially as Botswana Television is just starting, and there's a lot of people on our case.

Heckler 2 Is it the government's business?

Refilwe Mr Williams says it is, because the government pays for Botswana Television.

Thata What about the adverts?

Refilwe Yes, there's some sponsorship, but the bulk of the money comes from government.

Heckler 1 And what do you say?

(Refilwe hesitates)

Heckler 2 What's wrong?

Heckler 1 What's she looking at?

Thata Come on, Refilwe, what do you say?

(On the TV monitor Thami appears again. He gives Refilwe an encouraging gesture, she smiles, responds and then focuses on the crowd. Thami disappears)

Refilwe I say, this difference between Mr Williams and me is the first test-case about what kind of Botswana TV station is going to have. My vision is that the station is a public service – it is independent of government. It is free to give the people information. According to the United Nations charter of Human Rights, people have a basic, fundamental right to information. If Mr Williams has his way, this station will become a mere propaganda tool of the government. Before long we'll be another banana republic, where the journalists, writers and film-makers are thrown into prison if they even cough out of tune with the government. Is that really what we want?

Crowd No!

Refilwe Mr Williams doesn't mind if we turn this station into a megaphone for the government.

Heckler 2 Why not?

Refilwe Because he's only concerned with his contract. He doesn't want to rock the boat. As long as he gets his gratuity at the end of three years, he can go home and tell his friends he helped to develop the media in Botswana. This is the essence of neocolonialism. When the British were here they used

the media to tell us what to think. Then our government took over and saw that the British system was handy. The media could tell us what to think. Mr Williams has no reason to change that system. He's part of it.
Various Hecklers William's out!
Refilwe If we give in to Williams now, we may lose our opportunity for a long time to come.
Thata So what shall we do?
Refilwe I say we must unite to oppose this rape of our freedom of speech. I have drawn up a brief petition. It reads: 'We the undersigned citizen employees of Botswana Television, demand that management should cease to operate as an internal Censorship Board. We, citizen workers, demand the right to be consulted about issues of programming, programme content and editorial decision-making. (*Shouts of agreement*) I say, let us all sign this petition to let Mr Williams know that we mean business. We will not allow the people of Botswana to remain in ignorance about issues that vitally affect them. I say, let us all show our solidarity in the face of neocolonialism and creeping censorship!

(*Acclamation for Refilwe's ideas. The paper goes from hand to hand, being signed. Thami appears on the TV monitor, looking very happy. Someone starts a song of solidarity and everyone joins in. Thami comes down from the screen to join the 'living'. After the song, the curtain call. After the curtain call the audience can choose the ending, either at the explicit invitation of the MC or in informal discussion*)

Book Reviews

Every attempt has been made to provide full bibliographic details. UK prices have been provided where available. All editions are paperback except where otherwise stated.

Richard Boon and Jane Plastow (eds), *Theatre and Empowerment: Community Drama on the World Stage*
Cambridge: Cambridge University Press, 2004, xi + 267 pp.
ISBN 0-521-81729-3, £60

The editors of *Theatre and Empowerment* have brought together eight case studies of Theatre for Development (TfD) projects that are diverse in their geographical locations, research and performance methods, and positions of the authors. The collection marks how far the field has itself developed, because whereas at its inception, 'development' was often conceptualized in terms of limited goals such as teaching the need for child vaccinations, the objective is now empowerment. The projects discussed here aim at 'enabling people to discover and value their own humanity, both individually and in relation to others' (p.8). Obviously, this is a much more difficult objective to define and to achieve. Seemingly, it would demand documentation in a multi-vocal writing style that empowers readers to gain insight into the various ways participants understand the term. Unfortunately, while authors report on fascinating, socially significant projects, on balance, they allow little opportunity for participants to speak.

Yet, many of these essays, written by project leaders from 'the ground up', are forthcoming in expressing ambivalence about the efficacy of their practices, recording differences in perspective and agenda between the theatre group and the sponsoring NGO, acknowledging tensions within the groups themselves, and noting a range of participant and spectator responses such that what qualifies as important, liberatory gestures for some individuals are seen as also potentially authorizing for others' maintenance of an oppressive status quo. Significant also is the fact that this anthology includes essays concerning TfD projects in the 'developed' world, thereby making yet again the point that 'development' encompasses more than material acquisition. While members of marginalized communities in the 'developed' world need no reminders of the impoverished, inhumane values of their societies, the point is still worth making in academic venues. Thus, the volume includes essays on projects with Protestants and Catholics in Belfast, black male prisoners in England, and a Native American-inspired parade contesting the American national myth of Thanksgiving.

As Boon and Plastow note, this collection espouses no one critical or methodological approach. But the essays can be grouped according to the authorial position from which participants' views are mediated. Writers are distanced observers, visiting practitioners, or community practitioners. Each position has its own strengths and weaknesses.

Contrary to the editors' promises of insider perspectives, Richard Villaneuva adopts the most distanced scholarly stance in his analysis of competing Pilgrim Progress and Day of Mourning thanksgiving parades, organized by those who see themselves as religious descendants of early European settlers and those who use the national holiday as an occasion to bring visibility to Native American and environmental concerns. For Villaneuva, empowerment seems to reside mainly in the fact that the resistant Day of Mourning activities have been sustained for over thirty years. While clearly there is much at stake for all participants, a sense of the deep engagement of performance in exacerbating, clarifying, or working through the conflict is missing from the essay.

Writing seemingly from the position of a repeat spectator, Richard Andrews reports on the *autodrammi* or community plays that the Tuscan village of Monticchiello has annually created since the late 1960s in order to honour its peasant background and reflect upon present circumstances. Most residents in this relatively small community participate in the year-long process of debating content, securing funding, rehearsing and performing for itself and, as their fame increased, for outsiders. More recently, cultural activity has been organized into the non-profit cooperative *Teatro Povo* (Poor Theatre) and broadened to encompass exhibitions, concerts and conferences; residents are now more likely to argue about representations of a vanished peasantry or the predicament of small rural communities within Italy as a whole. Empowerment has meant that villagers – particularly women – have successfully seized upon performance as a public sphere and in so doing, have also attracted a better physical infrastructure and tourist revenues. Unfortunately, Andrews' style is monologic, so the reader must accept his narrative as an accurate representation of the villagers' perspectives.

Though Stephanie Marlin-Curiel is also a researcher, rather than a practitioner, her essay on the Victory Sonqoba Theatre Company (VSTC), located in Soweto, Alexandra, and KwaZulu-Natal, South Africa captures more of the polyphony of meanings and contradictions inherent in facilitating formerly silenced communities to regain their voices. In 1991 Bongani Linda, a former ANC soldier of Zulu background, brought together members of the warring Inkatha Freedom Party and the African National Congress to create a theatre of peer education and 'conflict transformation'. Pursuing the principle of 'each one teach one', Linda selects casts, with stories to tell, who are the peers of the target audiences. Noteworthy is the theatre's work around ethnic conflict, sexual violence and HIV/AIDS, because it raises issues about safety: the physical safety of actors who have occasionally been attacked by angry spectators, their psychological safety in revealing their health status or past anti-social behavior, and the safety of spectators, some of whom are known perpetrators of rape and thus potential targets of vigilante justice, or others who may feel further victimized by fellow audience members' laughter at images of sexual violence. Marlin-Curiel also takes up the important topics of funding and venue, noting that the largely white, middle-class audience capable of financially supporting VSTC prefers to sympathize with the poor at a safe, aesthetic distance far from the townships. While Marlin-Curiel is attentive to nuance, she allows Linda's voice to be heard only once; one wonders what additional complications or ambivalence Bongani Linda, like practitioner Gerri Moriarty (discussed below), might reveal, if allowed more space for reflection.

Occupying the second category of visiting practitioner are Jane Plastow writing on a dance theatre in Ethiopia and Michael Etherton, on the children's rights movement in South Asia. Plastow focuses on dance because as a non-verbal medium, it poses particular challenges to development officers invested in delivering specific messages directed towards quantifiable outcomes. What, she asks, is the value of offering a dance class to 'a group of economically useless, illiterate, old slum dwellers?' and – of relevance to both 'developed' and 'developing' societies: 'How do you value *fun*?' (p. 127). Evolving from providing dance classes to offering video training for a small cadre of Addis Ababa slum youth, the Adugna Community Dance Theatre's later decision to fuse the verbal medium of theatre with dance raises resource issues, for according to Plastow, few Ethiopians are skilled in merging traditional and modern dance or in teaching the history undergirding traditional performances. To meet the first need, Europeans are invited to teach, but their short stays do not allow the group to develop a style equally strong in both idioms. Though Plastow worries about undue European influences, she gives readers no information as to whether the skills of an Ethiopian diaspora community might be deployed. She points to tensions between middle-aged Ethiopian administrators and youth, now empowered with the skills to criticize their elders, but she does not allow any direct commentary on this point. This silence ironically implicates her own project, for her articulation of future policy issues implies the need for an indigenous infrastructure, not only expert in the art forms themselves, but also intellectually predisposed to fostering a nurturing cultural environment.

Working in Bangladesh, Pakistan, and Nepal between 1998 and 2001, Michael Etherton enthusiastically reports on theatre projects in which children, as young as eight, learn to create their own dramas through collective improvisation and perform before audiences of their choosing. Whereas earlier TfD projects involved adults directing the activities of youth, Etherton and other activists in what has become the Global Movement for Children now proceed from the principle that adults are facilitators servicing a children-determined agenda. Occasionally, this policy poses problems, as when in three Karachi slums, children identify drug usage as their dominant concern, and the local NGO initially objects because, 'We don't tackle drugs. Our funding doesn't allow us to do that' (p. 200). Honouring the children's perspective, Etherton and the other facilitators are impressed by participants' acute observations and vibrant performances. Further, audience members' responses result in a fiction film aired on community television; children acquire some video training, and additional workshops are offered for adult facilitators. But Etherton is honest in acknowledging that not all these projects result in clear-cut successes: in one instance, teenagers develop a performance piece on violence in Indian schools but decline to perform and opt instead to build a wider coalition amongst school-going children, when they determine that the adults facilitators cannot protect them from possible retaliation by education officials. Tensions sometimes flare between theatre activists chafing at NGO controls and local or international donors who want significant social change rather than better political theatre. Admitting to having taken each side at various points in his long career as a theatre activist, Etherton concludes by emphasizing TfD's potential for empowerment, because it offers a 'method and process that young people say enables them to deal with those in authority' (p. 215).

Michael Macmillan, Gerri Moriarty and Sanjoy Ganguly write from the position of practitioners who are either long-term residents in the community under discussion or in the case of Macmillan, share some of the predicaments of their target practitioners. Macmillan works in Britain with black male prisoners, youth and other artists on a variety of projects around the recurring theme of black men's emotional 'constipation' or inaccessiblity, developed in response to racist constructions of black males as hypersexual (heterosexual) deviants. While he has not been incarcerated, as a male son of immigrants, he has experienced the social stigmatization of the black body and the puritanical familial environment and stunted dreams that all too often characterize migrants' survival in Britain. Drawing from a variety of sources including Boal's Forum Theatre, cutting-edge African-American performances by The Hittite Empire and Pomo Afro Homos (Post-Modern African-American Homosexuals), contemporary critical theory, and collaborations with Asian and Turkish artists, Macmillan has sought to clear a space in which black men can safely explore their sexuality and perform an identity other than what has been imposed on them.

Stating her position as a participant and necessarily partisan commentator, given the historic 'Troubles' in the North of Ireland, Gerri Moriarty analyses a 1999 promenade theatre project that required some 150 Belfast community actors, professional arts workers, 700 spectators and an even larger newspaper readership to move through actual homes, a church and pub in celebration of a fictive marriage between a Protestant and a Catholic. She identifies two different models of community theatre. One proceeds from a collaborative, non-hierarchical creative process that is significantly time-consuming and difficult to sustain, given Western theatre practices privileging the writer and director; the second creates theatres about communities, using their testimony as raw materials for expert refashioning. Under the pressure of a performance date, the second model overtook the first, resulting in a powerful performance that both critics and the public received positively. Yet, Moriarty worries that *The Wedding* Community Project achieved less than what was possible, because there wasn't enough time to create a sufficiently safe space for performers to work through some of their deep-seated hostilities; thus, the performance became an end-product rather than the beginning of a longer process of conflict resolution, and no infrastructure was established to enable arts workers to facilitate other projects. Moriarty concludes on a soberingly honest note about personal costs that the reader suspects is shared by other activists, for she has turned her attention to the important policy area of long-term arts sustainability and reserves 'creative activity' for distant conflicts – Plastow's Ethiopian project, in fact.

Ending the collection is Sanjoy Ganguly's moving account of his twenty-year journey from naive but committed Communist political activist to founder of Jana Sanskriti, an organization of some thirty Indian theatre groups. Ganguly discovers in a rural Bengali village what his political study had not taught: the intelligence and humanity of desperately poor people. But nearly six years elapse from the beginnings of Jana Sanskriti to his devising techniques that decentre the artist-intellectual and honour poor people's abilities to articulate their own analysis of the world. Later in 1990–91 he becomes familiar with Augusto Boal's theatre and adapts it to Indian conditions. With excerpts from scripts, performance anecdotes and letters to a friend, Ganguly traces the theatre's trajectory away from an emphasis on material survival to a definition of empowerment as a 'fundamental change within the human being' (p. 255) or a process that allows people to discover hidden talents, humanize the oppressor harbored within and search for alternatives that uplift themselves as well as others. What makes the essay particularly powerful is Ganguly's willingness to name and learn from instances in which participants destabilize his perspectives and his lifetime commitment to a process in which art and social consciousness are continuous.

In summary, the strength of *Theatre and Empowerment* resides in its diversity and insights into the ways theatre can make a difference in people's lives. TfD practitioners will find ideas to adapt to their own situations; we scholars will be challenged to explore styles of documentation that share authority with those whom we study.

Sandra Richards
Northwestern University, USA

Louise M. Bourgault, *Playing for Life: Performance in Africa in the Age of AIDS*, Durham, USA: Carolina Academic Press, 2003, pp 315 + CD.
ISBN 0 89089 125 7, US$48

I came to this book with considerable optimism. It sometimes seems that every theatre company across Africa is making plays about HIV/AIDS in an effort to contribute to combating spiralling infection rates, and though many articles have been written about various of these productions, Louise Bourgault's is the first book-length study of AIDS-related performance practice in Africa since Marion Frank's examination of early AIDS-awareness theatre in Uganda in 1995. It is surely time for a new and more comprehensive study.

Playing for Life is divided into two sections. Part I, 'The African Continent and the AIDS Epidemic in Context', provides a background to enable anyone to approach an understanding of basic African history (Chapter 1); HIV/AIDS in Africa (Chapter 2); country profiles of South Africa and Mali (Chapter 3); and African performance forms (Chapter 4). Bourgault writes with a lucidity I found particularly useful in the HIV/AIDS chapter, which is packed with information and statistics whilst remaining accessible to the non-specialist.

Bourgault is evidently writing her book for American college students to introduce them to Africa, its AIDS epidemic and its art forms. At the end of each chapter the teaching agenda is emphasized with the inclusion of a number of 'Review Questions', obviously for use with student groups. A resulting problem: the flip side of her so-desirable clarity is that Louise Bourgault, in covering such a huge canvas, is at times necessarily perfunctory in her analysis and can seem rather reductionist and simplistic to a more informed reader.

The country profiles on South Africa and Mali provided in Chapter 3 are there because in Part II these are the countries Bourgault uses for her field studies to examine how AIDS performances can be used within the framework of a number of African performance forms. Part II is entitled 'Performance in Africa' and covers: Chapter 5, 'Oral Narratives'; Chapter 6, 'Chants and Songs'; Chapter 7, 'Dance' and Chapter 8, 'Drama'. A central aspect of the argument behind this book is that those working to convey information about HIV/AIDS and promote beneficial behaviour change must work through popular indigenous performance forms. This is not by any means a new argument, but *Playing for Life* includes analysis of a range of performance forms that challenges arts for development practitioners to be more wide-ranging in looking for ways to access target audiences.

Two examples given by Bourgault struck me as particularly powerful. The enormously influential work of Soul City in South Africa has been documented in a number of publications, but that does not make it any less pertinent. Soul City makes a hugely popular edutainment soap opera for television focusing on a range of health and social issues. This is the flagship operation, but there are also a range of radio programmes, magazines and cartoons aimed at both adult and youth audiences, plus education and information resource packs, all with high production values. Such a multi-media approach is feasible in industrialized South Africa. Impoverished, less-developed Mali is a very different nation. Here I was struck by the story of how the *griot* couple, Djeli Daouda Dembele and his wife Hawa Dembele, were commissioned to research, prepare and record on cassette tape a story, using traditional format, warning against practices leading to AIDS and other sexually transmitted diseases. The cassette was made for distribution amongst the long-distance truck drivers who are recognized as vulnerable to being infected and passing on infection along the network of roads they travel. It is also interesting that the initiative came out of partnership between a local NGO, the Association for the Development of Zegoue and the international CIDA (the Canadian Agency for International Development). The entire, delightful and detailed text of the resulting story, *Yiriba*, is given in translation in the chapter on oral narratives, and excerpts of the original are included on the CD that comes with the book. (There is also a twenty-minute video to accompany *Playing for Life*. This has to be bought separately and I have not seen it.)

In each chapter on a specific performance form Bourgault takes us through a variety of sub-forms and uses of the specific art in question. Her book is packed with interesting photographs and contains the texts of a plethora of songs, chants and stories, some of which also feature on the CD. Although these seem to be intended to help the reader understand African performance forms before seeing how they can be applied to AIDS-related productions, the sheer quantity of this material sometimes takes focus away from the central issues, and means that discussion of each individual form or case study is at times frustratingly brief and more descriptive than analytic. I really didn't think I needed three creation myths and four other stories to understand what are labelled 'Explanatory Tales', followed by four 'Fables', before understanding the two examples given of AIDS stories.

Although I was at times irritated by Bourgault's authoritarian tone and lack of in-depth analysis of the potential impact of various strategies in relation to AIDS performances – as well as a lack of discussion of the poor analytic and dramatic values of far too many HIV/AIDS performances produced across the continent that only serve to reinforce stereotypes about such stock figures as evil prostitutes and ignorant traditional healers – I was interested in the HIV/AIDS information and the insistence on the value of using people's own performance forms. However, in her last chapter Louise Bourgualt turns prescriptive, and it is a most extraordinary prescription that she offers. She begins Chapter 9, entitled 'AIDS and Performance for the 21st Century: Toward a Theory of Ritual and Performance', with a discussion of the work of Victor Turner and Richard Schechner. Specifically she focuses on ideas of the potential transformatory powers of ritual theatre on its participants. She then tries to make a case for participatory edutainment and development-based theatre having the potential, in some ritualistic manner, to transform those involved in performances – though whether this is supposed to work by magically removing infection or to miraculously transform people so that they no longer engage in unsafe sexual practices is unclear. Finally, and most bizarrely, Bourgault advocates a pan-African creation of an epic performance to in some way 'express the multiple issues that surround the AIDS epidemic' (p. 264). This piece is to be both secular and spiritual, to be scripted by Wole Soyinka and involve both Archbishop Desmond Tutu and the Dalai Lama (since when did he come from Africa?) Bourgault seems to argue that the resulting performance should be touted around the world and that when this happens – and this is the last line of the book, 'the ancestors will surely join them [African performers] on the world stage and usher in a transformation' (p. 266).

This pseudo-theoretical claptrap deserves nothing but contempt. The reduction of AIDS infections and understanding of AIDS-related issues has nothing whatsoever to do with ritual transformation, and the last thing Africa needs is a mega-touring show where Live Aid meets Ipi Tombi via a religious revival meeting. This final chapter shows only too clearly that Bourgault, despite her book's dedication to 'the memory of the 19 million Africans who have died of AIDS', writes ultimately for and from a purely American perspective and only insults the struggle of so many Africans to deal with the pandemic devastating their continent with her patronizing and sentimental invocation of the ancestors when what is needed is understanding, improved condom use and access to therapeutic medicines.

Jane Plastow
University of Leeds

Effiok Bassey Uwatt (ed.), *Playwriting and Directing in Nigeria: Interviews with Ola Rotimi*
Lagos: Apex Books Limited, 2002, 206 pp.
PB ISBN 9782126802, £20.95, US$33.95

Ola Rotimi (ed.), *Issues in African Theatre*
Ibadan: Humanities Publishers, 2001, 132 pp.
PB ISBN 9783626655, £20.95, US$29.95

Both books distributed by African Books Collective, Unit 13, King's Meadow, Ferry Hinksey Rd, Oxford OX2 0DP (www.africanbookscollective.com)

Both of these books celebrate the life of the Nigerian playwright and director Ola Rotimi, who died in 2000. Effiok Bassey Uwatt enterprisingly brings together interviews with Rotimi by various hands, some published, others previously unpublished, from 1973 to 1997. Although there is inevitably some repetition of matters raised and answers given, the interviews fascinatingly record the progress and preoccupations of Rotimi's work for the theatre and as a teacher and director, and are a fitting tribute to a major talent. Among the interviewers are leading scholars and practitioners of contemporary Nigerian theatre, including Bernth Lindfors (who offers a master-class in conducting an interview, i.e. let the subject do the talking), Dapo Adelugba and Onuora Ossie Enekwe, and other scholars and students who had met and worked with Rotimi in Ife, Port Harcourt and the United States. There is also a charming and helpfully informative interview, 'The Art of Adaptation: Understanding *The Gods Are Not To Blame*', originally given by Rotimi to his 13-year-old cousin Oluwale ('why should the gods not be blamed?' he pertinently asks) and later used by Rotimi in a lecture he was invited to give at Rivers State College of Education in Port Harcourt. Collectively these interviews locate Rotimi's creative imperatives – social, historical and political – his developing stagecraft, his very individualistic approach to directing (in equal measure supportive and demanding), his passions and great humanity. The editor's own interview with Rotimi, 'Indices of Authentic Nigerian Drama and Theatre', shows the playwright's enthusiasm for the potential of theatre in Nigeria, a country where he speculates there are four hundred languages, and argues for a drama that, whilst necessarily speaking the language of those in power, reaches out to the widest possible public often on an epic scale of both resources and imagination. This is a political and social commitment so evident in, for instance, *If...* and *Hopes of the Living Dead*, and in plays that revisit incidents of Nigerian history and present them from a Nigerian perspective. Dr Uwatt has done a service to the memory of Ola Rotimi in this affectionate and important collection.

Although *Issues in African Theatre* proclaims Rotimi as its editor, it is explained that the project (to give a voice on theatrical matters to Rotimi and his colleagues at Obafemi Awolowo University, Ile-Ife) was commenced under his guest editorship but substantially completed by others after his death. Rotimi himself contributes a short essay on the Ghanaian playwright Efua Sutherland, a playwright he admires for her use and development of the 'appropriate traditional image, expressive idioms and structural devices' and her commitment, as a director, to the practice of theatre. It is no wonder Rotimi admired Sutherland, for these are qualities he brought to his own work. The other seven essays in the collection are quite eclectic. They consider, amongst other themes, radical poetics in Nigerian theatre, the use of language by Rotimi and Ngugi wa Thiong'o, the work of Rotimi's important contemporary as a playwright, Bode Sowande, and issues concerning television drama, copyright and community theatre. There is also a short essay on an 'African Operetta', *Edi Ke Marina* by Adam Fiberesima. Although there is no single theme uniting these essays they serve to represent the vitality and productivity of work in a department to which Rotimi returned to carry out what is described as 'the final thrust of his life's creative and academic work'. The persistence of his colleagues in completing this collection is another measure of the respect and affection in which he was held.

A postscript. Of Ola Rotimi's stature as a playwright there can be no argument. Individual plays have been published by a variety of university presses, from Oxford University Press, *The Gods Are Not To Blame* (1971) to *Akassa You Mi* (Port Harcourt: Onyoma Research Publications, University of Port Harcourt Press, 2001). Oxford also published *Kurunmi* (1971), *Our Husband Has Gone Mad Again* (1977), and in conjunction with other Nigerian publishers, *Ovonramwen Nogbaisi* (1974) and *Holding Talks* (1979). Other plays have come from a variety of publishers, mostly Nigerian, including the extraordinary *If...a tragedy of the ruled* (Heinemann, 1983) and *Hopes of the Living Dead* (Ibadan: Spectrum, 1991). In addition *When Criminals Turn Judges* appears in ed. Dele Layiwola's *African Theatre in Performance* (Amsterdam: Harwood, 2000). The works of Rotimi's contemporaries Wole Soyinka and J.P. Clark-Bekederemo, the latter in Abiola Irele's splendid collection for Howard University Press (1991), are properly celebrated in collected form. One must hope that a significant publisher and a dedicated editor may bring Rotimi's work together for an international audience that is sadly unaware of the range and quality of his plays. His was an enormous theatrical talent.

Martin Banham

John Conteh-Morgan and Tejumola Olaniyan (eds), *African Drama and Performance*
Bloomington: Indiana University Press, 2004
ISBN 1-800-842-6796, US$49.95

While certainly no expert on theories of reincarnation, the rebirth in book form of a sold-out drama and performance issue of *Research in African Literatures* (30.4, Winter 1999) promises a textual (perhaps even theatrical) metempsychosis onto a higher, not lower, plane. This collection indeed exceeds its original scale, with eighteen instead of the previous thirteen essays, thus not only adding to quantity, but also making available an even richer variety of theatre scholarship on sub-Saharan Africa. Contributions on North and North-East Africa have not been included, but their habitual absence in works on African theatre has at least been noted of late, and a first (re-)integration been attempted (see Banham 2004). The publication of *African Drama and Performance* thus confirms 'the growth of critical interest' (p. 1) in the field, which the editors recognize as 'one of the exciting developments in African cultural criticism over the past decade' (p. 1). Whilst I cannot but wholeheartedly agree, we still need to ask what an expanded 'reprint' brings to the study of African theatre, apart from bringing the well-established out of the 'specialist closet' of an African studies journal into a, hopefully wider, academic arena.

Taking stock of the 'new' version as against the 'old', it becomes immediately apparent that the once ostensibly unrelated compilation is now grouped into five thematic sections; 'General Contexts', 'Intercultural Negotiations', 'Radical Politics and Aesthetics', 'Popular Expressive Genres and the Performance of Culture', and 'The Social as Drama'. Affiliations are said to be explicitly thematic to discourage any kind of performative pecking order, particularly the privileging of 'literary drama'; and no 'single sub-class of performance [is to be] held up as a model in relation to which all others are judged' (p. 2). This argument co-editor Conteh-Morgan has also made elsewhere (in Banham 2004: 87), and he is right in doing so, especially if we want to avoid a narrow understanding of 'African theatre' as the stage drama of Western-educated elites. Thus it is somewhat surprising that in the 'purely' thematic sections – 'Intercultural Negotations' and 'Radical Politics' – literary drama is entirely dominant, while Sections Four and Five – whose titles are already indicative of *genres* rather than *topics* – deal only with 'other' performances; the 'non-literary' long-established performing arts, social 'enactments', and 'popular' media. Whether this 'segregation' ultimately suggests that there is still a divide between scholars researching literary drama and those studying performance forms which are *not* primarily text-based is difficult to determine, and perhaps not even the most productive exercise to engage in. The split is, however, noticeable, particularly in view of the obvious thematic overlaps of the various parts. These intersections are one of the collection's strengths and also one of its pleasures; the sense that chapters relate to each other, no matter how different their subject matter, and the discovery of issues previously raised, but now discussed from another, at times contrasting, angle.

Johannes Fabian's personal vignette 'Theater and Anthropology, Theatricality and Culture' in Part One, for example, in which he cautions against an indiscriminate usage of 'drama as a root metaphor for society and history' (p. 40), thus sets the stage for the final section, 'The Social as Drama'; as does Joachim Fiebach's 'Dimensions of Theatricality in Africa'. Taking us from the Middle Ages to modern *egungun* masks with calling cards, Fiebach demonstrates how various spheres of African societies are performatively constructed. Ato Quayson's take on the question of history (an update of his contribution to the Africa volume of Rubin, Diakhaté and Eyoh's 1997 *The World Encyclopedia of Contemporary Theatre*) also reverberates in various chapters, such as Nicholas Brown's on Ngugi's dramatic oeuvre and the problems of Kenyan history. Sandra L. Richard's spellbinding reading of Yoruba cosmology in the work of the African-American Angus Wilson thematically relates to Tejumola Olaniyan on 'uncommon sense' as the dramaturgical leitmotif of Femi Osofisan, which, in turn, loosely connects with the chapter on Sylvain Bemba's adaption of *Antigone* by Conteh-Morgan. Bemba's *Noces posthumes de Santigone* brings to mind Osofisan's drama *Morountodun*, because both are about the staging of a play, and in both the female protagonist no longer acts, but eventually *becomes*, the historical rebel activist she was asked to embody. And, as a final example, Karin Barber's 'Literacy, Improvisation, and the Virtual Script in Yoruba Popular Theatre' – the revised and abridged version of a previous text which has lost none of its freshness – links up with Akin Adesokan on Nigerian video film. The individual chapters thus engage in a critical dialogue, verifying, complementing or contesting each other in the form of textual readings, performative context analyses or theoretical debates.

Of the original thirteen essays, two have not been included: Sidibé Valy's 'Bin Kadi-So and Dramatic Innovation' (whose loss remains unaccounted for, but which could have added context to Marie-José Hourantier's description of gestures in the production of Bin Kadi-So's *Macbet*); and Soyinka's wonderful autobiographical piece on *Orisunitis* (roughly, 'theatre fever'), which has since been committed elsewhere. His new keynote, 'King Baabu and the Renaissance Vision', however, is an appropriate replacement. While lacking the personal touch of his earlier piece, but none of its conviction, it sets the tone for this volume in that it links African theatre 'as a site of cultural self-definition, political and social critique' (Introduction, p. 1) with the theatricality of socio-political existence. Actually, this piece is all about the theatrics of politics, and an indictment against the present-day King Baabus and their 'Lady MacZim[s]' (p. 17) whose leadership has been corrupt and debilitating, and thus ultimately betrayed 'the primary wealth of a nation [–] its people' (p. 12). While it seems unusual for Soyinka to resort to populist appeals – 'Let the trampled will of the people triumph' (p. 23; projected, admittedly, onto imaginary banners) – it is these very 'people' for whom 'renaissance is a genuine yearning' for 'social transformation' (p. 11), not just another inflationary metaphor. Indeed, Soyinka mentions the term 'rebirth' (p. 11) as the true meaning of 'renaissance'; and it is the topoi of 'rebirth', 'transformation' and 'resistance' that reverberate most strongly in the book. Part Two, for example, addresses the 'rebirth' and intercultural transformation of European classics and African belief systems into other African contexts and the diaspora; in the 'Radical Politics' of Part Three we encounter forms of theatrical 'resistance'. 'Rebirth' is also the underlying theme of Catherine M. Cole's noteworthy chapter on the Truth and Reconciliation Commission in South Africa. Cole reads the TRC as a form of theatre, but cautiously interrogates her approach, though she is by no means the only one to respond to the 'inherent theatricality' (Davis 2000: 60) of the Commission. Theatricality has been a feature of much South African political culture; just recall the performance of rallies or mass public funerals during the days of apartheid (cf. Bozzoli 2004). There is no doubt that a lot can be gained from a performance studies approach to the public staging of a nation's traumatic memories and, in the second instance, its meta-performative reincarnations, such as *Ubu and the Truth Commission* by the Handspring Puppet Company.

Finally, a word or two on some of my favourites in this book, all 'reincarnations' from the original special issue. Richards I have already mentioned above, who excels in linking African and African-American belief systems in theatrical representations, and who offers an important critique of one-dimensional Afrocentricity. Noting that Wilson's play refuses to bow to the 'nostalgic desire for a fixed center' (p. 99), she argues that the text 'implies an Africa that is always-already hybrid' (p. 95), and in which migratory movement, not static permanence, is projected as the norm. Loren Kruger's chapter on *Soul City*, a hospital serial and South Africa's most prominent TV edutainment, not only provides an analysis of how theatre-for-development and soap opera glamour have been successfully merged, but also offers rich insights into the context in which the serial was produced, including a close reading of selected episodes. Last but not least, Bob W. White's deft and immensely readable piece on Congolese popular dance music must be brought to attention here, a beautiful 'thick' description which captures the joy and excitement of the performance event while giving a thorough analysis of the *atalaku*, the 'trickster' figure on stage. A crucial, but critically still neglected player, an animateur-cum-praise-singer before a live audience, the *atalaku* utilizes the 'traditional' art of shouting in a 'modern' context to 'warm up' the dance floor and exalt the sponsors and supporters of the band.

All in all, much good can be said about this 'reborn' collection which should not be missing from any African studies or theatre library. It has something to offer to practically everyone, so diverse are its approaches, so varied its subject matter. We should, however, be aware that a number of performance forms discussed – such as Yoruba travelling theatre, Anlo-Ewe *Halò*, Ngugi's Kamiriithu experience or the staging of Nigerian literary drama in the country itself – are either things of the past or have been reduced to such an extent that those involved have already begun to compose dirges for their funeral. At the Leeds *Performing Africa* Conference in May 2004, for example, Femi Osofisan bemoaned the dearth (or virtual death) of live theatre in Nigeria while jealously eyeing the opulent theatricality of the growing number of local revivalist churches. But perhaps we should just see them as yet another reincarnation of theatre and social drama in Africa, instead of praying for the rebirth of forms long past. Or we can hold with Soyinka and read the transformations of African performance forms as part of a greater renaissance.

Christine Matzke
Humboldt-University at Berlin

WORKS CITED

Martin Banham (ed.) (2004), *A History of Theatre in Africa*, Cambridge: Cambridge University Press.
Belinda Bozzoli (2004), *Theatres of Struggle and the End of Apartheid*, Edinburgh: Edinburgh University Press.
Geoffrey V. Davis (2000), 'Addressing the Silences of the Past: Truth and Reconciliation in Post-Apartheid Theatre', in Yvette Hutchison and Eckhard Breitinger (eds) *History and Theatre in Africa*, Bayreuth: Eckhard Breitinger, pp. 59–72.
Don Rubin, Ousmane Diakhaté and Hansel Ndumbe Eyoh (eds), *The World Encyclopedia of Contemporary Theatre*, Vol. 3: Africa, London: Routledge (1997).

Martin Banham (ed.), *A History of Theatre in Africa*
Cambridge: Cambridge University Press, 2004.
ISBN 0521808138, £80

The first time I came across Martin Banham's name he was the co-author (with Clive Wake) of an oddly-shaped little black book entitled *African Theatre Today* (Pitman, 1976). In it, Banham began by pointing out that the critic familiar with the form and nature of British or American drama 'may have to accept a different set of critical criteria if he or she is to come to terms with much African drama'; by which he meant accepting that African theatre was 'functional', that is, directly related to the ritual, communal roots of all theatre, but which in its European development has left those roots far behind, becoming a more fixed and rule-bound phenomenon, created for entertainment and diversion rather than – as was the case in Africa – for chronicling a people's history or voicing its conscience.

This change of perspective may no longer sound as challenging as it once did; indeed, it is almost a truism. But that is in large part due to Professor Banham's own influence as a prolific commentator upon African theatre over the intervening decades, until now he enjoys unquestioned authority in the field. His approach has not altered: in the Preface to the present volume, he asserts that the 'defining and uniting quality' of African theatre lies in 'a sense of function', its roots in 'ritual, seasonal rhythms, religion and communal communication' with which – unlike, say, European theatre – it is in closer and more direct relation 'even at the beginning of the twenty-first century'.

Hence the overall emphasis of this collection of eighteen new essays, upon performance broadly interpreted: an emphasis that allows contributors to range far back into the past – to the pharaonic period in Egypt, for example, or the San rock art of prehistoric South Africa – as well as to confront the issues of the present, such as the relevance of 'theatre for development' in rural areas, or the influence of Islamic and other, Western cultures upon African urban theatrical traditions. As Banham points out, 'A continent that has been invaded and colonized, and subject to the imposition of alien languages and governments, cannot have a convenient linear history.' Indeed not. Yet asking contributors to adopt an historical perspective has the signal advantage of properly contextualizing the wide range of cultural activities that may be considered theatrical in the broadest sense. On the other hand, perhaps inevitably, this historicist approach also leads to some rather foreshortened and over-generalized accounts of the development of different societies. Nobody can deny the long histories of the various cultures, regions, countries of the continent; but to try and survey them before there were accounts of specific events leads to an occasional sameness that works against the sense of variety and complexity this book sets out to celebrate. Perhaps this is why the editor himself abjures any but the most general remarks at the outset (although he has allowed Nigerian writer Kole Omotoso space for some rather rambling thoughts on the general concepts of 'history and theatre' in Africa as a kind of introduction). And perhaps this is why the editor has ensured that many of his contributors concentrate on more recent history, after due genuflection towards the ancient ancestry of the African performing arts.

Thus, for example, the essay on Nigeria (by Dapo Adelugba and Olu Obafemi, with Sola Adeyemi) in the section on Anglophone West Africa, devotes only a page and a half to the pre-nineteenth century scene, before taking us through the 'traditional theatre' of dance dramas and masquerades, the 'cultural nationalist phase' of reaction to mission-influenced concerts and musicals, and the 'modern' or post World War Two phase including 'travelling theatre' (Herbert Ogunde and his successors), the 'literary theatre' of Onitsha and Ibadan (Wole Soyinka and Femi Osofisan) and, finally, the theatre work developed around Ahmadu Bello University, which has addressed such issues as the problems of land usurpation and health. The remarkable theatrical productivity of the continent's most populous country over the last half-century, despite its tremendous social and economic upheavals, is well documented, the main trends effectively defined; although without providing more than the briefest mention of plays and their creators, influential figures such as Soyinka, Rotimi or Osofisan almost disappear from sight, their achievement seemingly taken for granted. By contrast, the essay on Kenya (Ciarunji Chesaina and Evan Mwangi) in the 'East Africa' section, while devoting appropriate space to indigenous and traditional roots (with telling examples of community courtship and wedding songs), devotes two pages to Ngugi wa Thiong'o's formative influence upon his country's theatrical practice, which he helped to move towards a more participatory and democratic form, freely admitting he is no major playwright. Surveys, especially where they are (as almost all the contributions in this volume are) really well-sourced with references and further reading, are helpful to newcomers and old hands alike; but there could well have been more selectivity in outlining the shape of theatrical history than is shown by some of the contributors, and a greater sense of the significance of particular works and/or practitioners.

The overall structure of the volume seems rather haphazard, while broadly working down the continent from north to south, but it is appropriately inclusive. North Africa opens the volume, with sub-sections on Egypt (Ahmed Zaki), Morocco, Algeria and Tunisia (Kamal Salhi) and Sudan (Khalid AlMubarak Mustafa); John Conteh-Morgan provides a judicious and thoughtful essay on 'Francophone Africa south of the Sahara' (which, he depressingly concludes, will become an 'extraverted' activity, entirely oriented towards the outside); this is followed by the aforementioned sections on West and East Africa, Nigeria succeeded by James Gibbs's succinct account of Ghanaian theatre, with Mohamed Sheriff on Sierra Leone, and an interesting note on 'recent Anglophone Cameroonian theatre' (Asheri Kilo), before we come to Jane Plastow's informed essay on Ethiopia and Eritrea (particularly interesting on the performers known as *azmaris*), Amandina Lihamba on Tanzania (including some enlightening remarks on radio theatre), and Eckhard Breitinger on Uganda.

As these names suggest, the contributors – predominantly but not exclusively African – are people with an intimate as well as expert knowledge of the regions and countries they are dealing with, wherever they are now based. This seems to have led to disproportionate space going to certain regions. David Kerr and Yvette Hutchison are both well-known for their writings upon Southern African theatre – here divided into South and Southern, which leads to some overlap (both tell us about the San forebears of modern day storytelling, and Zakes Mda appears as an expatriate writer in Kerr's Lesotho as well as a representative of the Black Consciousness theatre in Hutchison's South Africa), but also to much lengthier treatment than any other area of the continent: together, Southern and South Africa take up over a hundred pages, while the theatre of Nigeria, say, is allowed just over twenty. Does this simply reflect the dominance of Southern Africa in economic and political terms? Or the relative richness of the historical development and present achievement of the South? Editorial guidance would have been useful here. In any case, the detail in Kerr and Hutchison's essays is accurate and revealing: of the recent proliferation of plays about HIV/AIDS, on stage and in the electronic media (on radio Malawi and Television Zambia, for example); of the new concern for ecological issues among artists in Zimbabwe and Botswana; and of the quite extraordinary flowering of everything theatrical in South Africa before, during and even (to a lesser extent) after the apartheid era.

Effectively a coda to the volume, the last three brief sections – on theatre in the Lusophone territories (Luis Mitra), Mauritius and Réunion (Roshni Mooneeram) and the African diaspora of the Caribbean and South America (Osita Okagbue) – demonstrate the continuing creative power of African theatre, despite slavery, colonialism and post-colonial tyrannies. The famous San lament tells us that 'the string' has been 'broken', the shaman is dead; if so, as this attractive and wide-ranging book proves, the magic of theatre remains.

Dennis Walder
Open University

Dennis Walder, *Athol Fugard*
Horndon: Northcote House Publishers Ltd in association with the British Council, 2003.
ISBN 0-7463-0948-1 PB, £10.99; 0-7463-1021-8 HB, £25.00.

There is little doubt that Athol Fugard is South Africa's best known and most prolific playwright, though doubts have been expressed by critics and by Fugard himself, particularly concerning his continued relevance in a post-apartheid world. Happily, Fugard has continued to produce meaningful work, and in this study Dennis Walder offers a highly readable book that argues convincingly for the value of Fugard's plays, both those written during the apartheid era, and those written after. *Athol Fugard* is written in a style that will be immensely useful for students and academics, but also very accessible for the lay reader with an interest in Fugard's work.

Dennis Walder is well known as an authority on Fugard's work, having written critically about it for many years, and edited and introduced collections of his plays. This latest book, however, is not a rehashing of previous material; it is fresh and up to date, offering new insights into Fugard's more recent works as well as his much studied, performed and discussed earlier plays. The book is divided into five sections: 'Protest and Survival', 'Plays of Place', 'Township Witnessing', 'Carnal Realities' and 'Memory Plays'. Whilst the book has a broadly chronological logic to it, it is by no means simply a chronological survey; rather, Walder artfully weaves his discussion across all the plays, from the earliest to the latest, in each chapter. From the outset, Walder contextualizes Fugard's contribution within the broader South African theatre, and within the politics and society from which it emerges. He also draws astutely from diverse scholarship on Fugard's work and media critiques of his plays.

In his introduction, Walder sets out two key themes of the book: the 'tightrope' that Fugard has had to walk between the personal and the political, and the significance of Fugard's work in 'bearing witness'. Arguably, one of the reasons that Fugard's continuing relevance is questioned is because of a fundamental tension between personal introspection and social examination in his work. Walder refers to Fugard's description of this as 'a very precarious balancing act' between 'the two safe platforms' of 'the private and the public, the personal and the political' (p. 3). At the heart of Fugard's work, however, has been what Walder describes as the 'urge to tell a story; and not just to tell a story, but to bear witness' (p. 1).

Focusing predominantly on the earlier plays, the first chapter, 'Protest and Survival', offers insights into what has motivated and inspired Fugard personally, intellectually, politically and experientially. The interconnecting sense of the local and the global is striking – from his family stories and histories, to the landscape and language of his home city, Port Elizabeth, to the works and ideas of Synge, Faulkner, Williams, Camus, Beckett, Sophocles and Grotowski. Succinctly discussing Fugard's childhood, family, travels, studies, non-theatre work and early theatre collaborations, Walder offers a strong sense of how these biographical details resonate in the plays, sometimes implicitly, sometimes quite explicitly.

A key theme of this early chapter is the significance of collaboration, particularly within the context that Fugard was working in. Collaborations with the likes of Zakes Mokae and Barney Simon, and later the Serpent Players, not only resulted in plays such as *No Good Friday, Nongogo, The Blood Knot*, and later, *Sizwe Bansi is Dead* and *The Island*, but was in itself a direct challenge to the apartheid system. Furthermore, as a way of working within South African theatre, these plays and processes of playmaking would influence South African theatre for decades to come. What becomes clear from Walder's discussion is the range of work that Fugard and his collaborators were experimenting with, and so his discussion of *Orestes*, for example, a play which radically used image and gesture to portray its story, offers an excellent juxtaposition to the more text-based works discussed.

The rootedness of Fugard's work in specific locales and the inseparability of people from their time and place is the key focus of the second chapter, 'Plays of Place'. Critically highlighting the importance of 'place' within colonial and post-colonial discourses, Walder argues that in plays such as *The Blood Knot, Hello and Goodbye, Master Harold... and the Boys, Boesman and Lena* and *People Are Living There*, the 'impulse or compulsion' to represent the marginalized and to bear witness is realized on two levels: 'by representing others, and by representing himself and his family' (p. 27). The city of Port Elizabeth, where Fugard grew up and has lived much of his life, is the setting for the stories of the range of diverse characters that we encounter in these plays. But as Walder points out, it is not only a fixation with place, but also with his family as 'a site of powerlessness and ambivalence' (p. 28) that is so striking. Walder's discussion of *The Blood Knot* (later revised as *Blood Knot*) is central to this chapter, and he offers an insightful analysis that gives a clear sense of its significance within South African theatre more broadly, and highlights the survival value of a play that might otherwise be dated in its witnessing of 'the secret yearnings for recognition, and for the freedom to escape from the internalised boundaries within and between people, in our various but historically specific situations' (p. 34).

It is some of Fugard's best known plays such as *The Island* and *Sizwe Bansi is Dead* that come into focus in the third chapter, appropriately titled, 'Township Witnessing'. Fugard's collaboration with the Serpent Players, including John Kani and Winston Ntshona, led to a series of plays that sought to challenge the political system, especially the rigid racial divide. Discussing *Sizwe Bansi*, Walder highlights Fugard's radical and democratic conception of theatre's role, represented strikingly in the image of the character, Styles, talking about his little photographic studio which he calls his 'Strongroom of Dreams', the dreamers being his people; those never found mentioned in the history books, or whose deeds never get commemorated (p. 54).

The contextualizing of these plays is well handled, and is particularly useful to those encountering these plays for the first time in a post-apartheid world. A clear sense of time and socio-political experience is offered. This is not only useful for an international audience, but, I would argue, is crucial for South Africans ourselves, especially given that fact that most school and university students now will have had little or no direct experience of the apartheid system (although the legacy is of course still being lived through). Walder rightly argues for the need to consider the changing impact of plays on different audiences in changing circumstances when considering their lasting qualities. Such qualities in these plays, he suggests, are borne out of the fact that they 'strove to bear witness to what [Fugard] described as 'the nameless and destitute' of his 'little corner of the world', which must mean *all* those excluded from the structures of his society' (p. 60).

It is in the next chapter, 'Carnal Realities', that the tensions between the public and the private become clear, as exemplified in Walder's discussion of *Dimetos* and *The Road to Mecca*, and as Walder rightly asserts, given the changing social and political circumstances in South Africa, 'Fugard's more interior dramas beg to be reconsidered and evaluated' (p. 63). However, it is not only the more 'interior dramas' that are of concern here, and Walder's discussion of *Statements after an Arrest under the Immorality Act* brings the notion of bodily presence to the fore.

Walder identifies a key element of Fugard's drama as being 'the struggle to express "carnal reality"' (p. 67), referring to the playwright's own earlier comment on his faith in the carnal reality of the actor in space and time. What this raises is the importance of considering these plays *as performance*, because it is the physical specifics, the actors' bodies, and the detailed actions that are so fundamental to the power of this work. It is also *physically*, in action, that the transgressive nature of these plays can be clearly understood. Without ever abandoning the importance of 'carnal reality', it is clear, as Walder points out, that a new phase of playwriting and performance was ushered in with *The Road to Mecca*, turning inward, focusing on the psychology of characters, and in particular the psychology of isolation, as well as exploring the nature of the artist and artistic expression. Walder's discussion of this play offers excellent insight into understanding a shift in Fugard's work.

In the final chapter, 'Memory Plays', Walder suggests that in the context of contemporary South Africa, plays about memory such as Fugard's later plays, *Valley Song*, *The Captain's Tiger* and *Sorrows and Rejoicings* have a particular value and significance. These works not only draw on memory, but interrogate the very idea of it. Yet, the concern with memory goes right back to Fugard's earlier work, most notably *Master Harold... and the Boys*. Walder's discussion of this play is well placed within this chapter, and offers fresh perspectives on this much documented and studied work.

Memory in terms of a personal past, and a continued interest in the power of the imagination are fundamental to Fugard's work. *A Place with the Pigs* is set 'in a pigsty, in a village, somewhere in the author's imagination'; *The Captain's Tiger*, dedicated to his mother, is subtitled 'A Memoir for the Stage' (p. 91). In discussing Fugard's later plays, Walder writes: 'Bearing witness as a function of social responsibility seems to have been replaced by a kind of personal witnessing as a function of individual moral responsibility. But have these aspects of his work ever been entirely absent or separate? I do not think so' (p. 97). As Walder points out, *Valley Song* is one of the plays that perhaps most clearly signals Fugard's own shifting identity. Fugard is not only the writer and director, but also an actor playing two characters of different racial origins, which for Walder suggests 'a connection between his changing sense of personal identity and the nation's developing sense of itself as increasingly aware of its mixed origins' (p. 88).

Overall, the book is characterized by a richness of source material and a wonderfully broad range of differing perspectives on Fugard's work. While such a diverse range of source material could lead to a very dense work, Walder manages to integrate it fluidly into a well-written and highly readable book. Whilst Walder argues passionately for Fugard's continued relevance, this does not mean he feels that the work is beyond criticism, and so while celebrating the playwright's work, this book also offers astute critique.

Michael Carklin
University of Glamorgan

Index

Abah, Oga 42, 44
Abdulkadir, Hamsa 141
Abdullah, Miatta 99
Aberen, Yeergalem 141
Abidjan 110, 112
abuse, child/sexual 25-7, 92, 109, 117, 132, 142, 169, 183, 192, 202
Adem, Kedija 143
adolescence xi, 4, 11, 19, 38, 42-6, 50-1, 57, 97-103, 105, 110, 112, 115, 125, 143, 181
Ahmadu Bello University 42
Ainom, Meseret 142-3, 145
Akan, concept of *Sankofa* 22n
Alfred, Derik Uya 78
Alhassan, Saint Abdulai 19-20
Ananse 5-7, 20
Angola 105, 117, 121
Artaud, Antonin 35
Asmara 144
Avenir de l'Enfant 86-7, 89-90, 95

Banda, Hastings Kamazu 23-4
Batwa community performances 39-40
Bell, Bill 1
Ben Boy International 86, 94
Ben Hirsch Women in Development and Child Care 122-3, 129, 131
Bereket, Yohannes 141
Blair, Tony 33
Blaise Senghor Cultural Centre 86, 89, 94; *Batt Maam* 95
Boa Amposem Secondary School (Ghana) 20-1
Boal, Augusto vii, xi, 45, 47, 64, 66, 91, 100, 103, 106, 112, 178-9, 187n; stroboscope technique 67-68
Bono 33
Booker, Salih 40-1
Botswana, xi, 25-6, 113, 152, 154, 161, 165, 187n; University of 25
Bourgault, Louise 32, 41; *Playing for Life: Performance in Africa in the Age of AIDS* 32. 38
Brecht, Berthold 35, 83
Britain 139
British Council 62, 65, 73, 76, 142
Broadway (New York) 34, 37
Buhoma Community 39
Burkina Faso 109, 110, 112
Bush, George 33

Cameroun 34, 36-7
Campbell, Joseph 126
Catholic Church 27, 82
Centre for National Culture, Accra 17
Chaka Chaka, Yvonne 33
Charley, Mike 119, 123, 130, 133
Child Rights Theatre for Development (CR-TfD) 97-114
child soldiers xi, 100
Children's Drama Development Programme 2
Children of Uganda 39
CHIPAWO xii, 166-82
choric storytelling 5, 8, 10

269

Clark, Daniel 17-18, 21
Cockerel and the King's Ear, The 64-74
colonialism 24, 36, 138-9
comedia dell'arte 86
Côte d'Ivoire 112
Cottage, Lynn 39
Crow, Brian 100

Dakar 87, 89-90
dance xi-iii, 5, 18, 20, 24-5, **28**, 34, 38-40, 75, 78-9, **80**, 82-3, 87-8, 117, 127, 140-1, 144, 146, 164, 166-7, 169-70, 177, 179, 181-2, 184, 190
Darfur 62, 85
Daru 122-5, 127
de Graft, Joe 18-21
de Rivero, Oswaldo 106
Derg, The 142
DFID (Department for International Development) 112
Diallo, Ibrahima 88
Dinka 82
disability 145, 150
Dorbgadzi, Sarah 17
Dori workshop 109
dramAIDE 38
drug abuse, 45, **48**, 50-2, 55, 58, 72, 202, 216

Eager Artists 38
Empire des Enfants 86
Eritrea 138-47; Ministry of Labour and Welfare 145
Eritrean Liberation Front (ELF) 139
Eritrean People's Liberation Front (ELPF) 139
Ethiopia 138, 139

facilitation (in development theatre) 61-73, 100
Fesehatsion, Nechi 143
Feshaye Yohannes 'Joshua' 140
Fest'Art International Theatre Festival for Peace 86, 89, 95
Fitwi, Senait 143
'*For Tomorrow…*' Project 42-60
Forum Theatre 44-5, 47, 51-2, 73, 100, 103, 112-13, 132

Foyer d'Observation 90-1
Foyer Familiale 90-1
Freetown Workshop 109
Freire, Paulo 62
Freud, Sigmund 126
Fry, Juliet 45
Fulfulde language workshop 111-12

games xiii, 5, 10-11, 34, 64, 88, 91-2, 116, 123, 131, 197, 210
Geldof, Bob 33
General Union of Eritrean Students (GUES) 139
Gesa Gesa 147
Ghana x, xiii, 1-22, 91, 119, 121; Ministry of Education 17-18; Centre for National Culture 19, 21
Ghana Broadcasting Corporation 18
Ghana Drama Studio 2, 14n
Ghana International School 16
Ghana, University of 17
Global Movement for Children 98, 103, 114, 119n
GOAL (INGO) 123, 136
Gold Diggers, The 110
Governing Instrument 130
group dynamics 8, 10-11, 17, 27, 38, 44-6, 53, 59, 61-2, 65-9, 76, 82, 83, 85, 87-90, 93, 94, 98, 102-3, 107-11, 115-17, 139-40, 156-7, 174, 179, 189-94 *passim*, 195, 200-1, **203**, 204, 205, 208-9, 215-16

Hansille, Peter 128
HIV/AIDS xi, xii, 23, 31-41, 43, 51, 62, 67, 73, 82, 101, 112, 119n, 145, 150; and globalization 32-5
Hull, Deborah 45

Ibrahima Beye Primary School 88
Image Theatre 65
improvisation xii-xiii, 49, 87-8, 92, 95, 104, 106-8, 115-16, 118, 119n, 123, 132, 171, 195, 207, 209, 215
India 117
Institute of African Studies 1
Internally Displaced Peoples' Camps 78
Ireland, Northern 135

Isaac, David 141
It's All About Dialogue 27

Jana Sanskriti's Festival of the Theatre of the Oppressed 63
Jirieff Children's Reformatory 62, 73, 74-6
Jos 52
Juba 82

Kasozi, Fred 99, 104, 119n
Kebede, Simret 143
Kenema 123
Kenya, 38
Kerr, David 23, 24, 26
Keyahti Embaba (The Red Flowers) 139
Khartoum 62, 78-9
Ki Yi M'bock Theatre collective 35-6; *The Marriage of a Pygmy and a Tuareg* 35
Ki Yi Pan-African Centre for Training and Creation 35
Kidd, Ross 113
Killion, Tom 139
Kwoto Cultural Centre 78-85

language, creole 108, 112, 119n; colonial 2; indigenous xiii, 12, 24, 27, 53, 79, 82, 111-12, 119n, 141, 155, 166; multilingualism 12, 66, 91, 119n; sign 179
Lesotho 100, 117, 121
Liberia 98-104, 105, 117, 131, 135
Liking, Werewere 34-6
Lirondo, Jean Ngo 19-20
Luanda 117
Lumière (Senegalese NGO) 96

McCreery, Kathleen 91-2
Magalasi, Mufunanji 23
Mahber Theatre Asmara (Asamara Theatre Association) 144
Maimane, Arthur 19-20
Malawi, University of 23-4
Mali 38, 109, 112
Mandela, Nelson 33-4
Mende 133
Mensah, Atta 24

mime 5, 6, 20, 24-7, 34, 38, 77, 147, 177, 179-80, 188
Mine Action Education (MAE) 145
Minter, William 40-1
Mistir Nayta Kofo (The Secret of the Grain Basket) 145
Mnouchkine, Ariane 35
Monrovia 100, 103
Monster Within, The 23-5
Mozambique 105, 117, 121
Muluzi, Bakili 25
Murdering the Soul 25-7
Musa Wo 133
music 143
Mussolini, Benito 139
M'vet orature 37

National Union of Eritrean Youths and Students (NUEYS) 144
Nepal 117
Niger 95
Nigeria x, 117, 121
Nigerian Popular Theatre Alliance (NPTA) 42-4
Non-government Organisations (NGOs) 17, 23, 43, 61, 76, 86, 89, 96, 98-100, 106, 107, 109, 114, 116, 118, 122, 124, 128, 132-4, 141, 143, 191-5, 197

Ochalla, Stephen Affear 78, 82
Omdurman 79
orature, epic 37; oral tradition 95, 133
Osofisan, Femi 18

People's Front for Democracy and Justice (PFDJ) 140-1
Phakama, Project xii, 151-65
Plastow, Jane xii, 62
play, right to xiii, as dramatic process 2, 3, 6, 12; language of 12; 'play power' 13-14; *see also* games
Play House, The (Birmingham) 43
Presbyterian Boys' Secondary School (Ghana) 21
Promenade Theatre, Sudan xii, 61-77

Revolutionary United Front (RUF)

(Sierra Leone) 122, 130, 137n
Richards, Paul 133
Rwanda 39-40

Save the Children (UK) xii, 97, 104, 114-15, 119n, 123, 124, 127, 131, 135, 143
Sankofa 17
Schechner, Richard 32
Second Chance Organization of Nigeria (SECON) 43-5; *Onya's Passage* 43; *Jummai* 49-51
Segbwema 124, 127
Senegal 86, 87-8
Sewit Children's Theatre 138-47
sex/sex health/sex education xii, 43-6, 49-51, 53, 101-2, 143
Shakespeare, William 139
Shangri-La Kids Theatre Club 18
SIDA (Swedish International Development Agency) 112
Sierra Leone xi, 100, 104-7, 117, 119n, 121, 122-37; Ministry of Social Welfare 123
Sinje 100-3, 119n
song 5-6, 34, 37, 79, 82-3, 92, 105, 109, 131, 140-1, 143, 145, 148n, 177-9, 190, 207, 215-16
Soul City TV drama 38
South Africa xii, 31, 33, 38, 41n, 100, 117, 121, 151-9, 161, 163-5, 169, 187n
Sow, Moussa 89
Sowra SchoolStage Motion 16-19, 21
Soyinka, Wole 31
storytelling 34, 126, 133-4
Story Workshop, The 23
Street Children Task Force 128
street theatre xii, 38
Studrafest x, 16-21
Sudan xi, 78-85
Suleman, Mohad 143
Sutherland, Efua xiii, 1-14, 19; *Ananse and the Dwarf Brigade* 1, 5-7, 14; *Children of the Man-Made Lake*, 1, 4, 7, 11, 12-13; *Playtime in Africa* 1; *Tahinta* xiii, 1, 4, 7, 11, 14; *Tweedledum and Tweedledee* 1; *Vulture! Vulture!* xiii, 1, 4, 5-6, 12, 14

Tanzania 121
Teckle, Aaron 141
Tesfagergish 'Maabel', Mesfin 143
Tesfai, Alemseged 140
The Aids Support Organization (TASO) 37
The Meeting Point 38
Theatre for Development (TfD) xi, 44, 122-3, 131-2, 134-6; *see also* Child Rights Theatre for Development
Theatre in Education (TED) x, 45
Theatre of Necessity xi, 34-9
tradition, festival and ritual x, 2, 34-6; orature 37, 144
Training for Trainers workshop 62
Tsebah cultural group 139
Tseggai, Esaias, 140-1, 143, 146; *Gesa Gesa* 145-6

United Nations Children's Fund (UNICEF) 123
United Nations Convention on the Rights of the Child (CRC) 97
Uzo, Blessing 42

Valco Trust Fund 2, 14n

Walcott, Derek 32
Wartenberg, Joris 18
West End (London) 34, 37

Yirenkyi, Asiedu 18

Zambia x, xi, 189-200
Zaria xii, 42-6, 48-9, 52-3, 56